The
Oxford Book
Of Light Verse

Oxford University Press, Amen House, London E.C. 4

GLASGOW NEW YORK TORONTO MELBOURNE WELLINGTON
BOMBAY CALCUTTA MADRAS KARACHI LAHORE DACCA
CAPE TOWN SALISBURY NAIROBI IBADAN ACCRA
KUALA LUMPUR HONG KONG

FIRST EDITION 1938

SECOND IMPRESSION (WITH CORRECTIONS) 1939
REPRINTED PHOTOGRAPHICALLY IN GREAT BRITAIN BY
LOWE & BRYDONE, PRINTERS, LTD.
FROM SHEETS OF THE SECOND IMPRESSION
1941, 1942, 1945, 1949, 1952, 1962

The
Oxford Book
Of Light Verse

Chosen by

W. H. Auden

Oxford University Press

A *

PRINTED IN GREAT BRITAIN

To
Professor E. R. Dodds

INTRODUCTION

I

BEHIND the work of any creative artist
there are three principal wishes: the wish
to make something; the wish to perceive something, either in the external world of sense
or the internal world of feeling; and the wish
to communicate these perceptions to others.
Those who have no interest in or talent for
making something, i.e. no skill in a particular
artistic medium, do not become artists; they
dine out, they gossip at street corners, they
hold forth in cafés. Those who have no interest in communication do not become artists
either; they become mystics or madmen.

There is no biological or mathematical law
which would lead us to suppose that the quantity of innate artistic talent varies very greatly
from generation to generation. The major
genius may be a rare phenomenon, but no
art is the creation solely of geniuses, rising
in sudden isolation like craters from a level
plain; least of all literature, whose medium
is language—the medium of ordinary social
intercourse.

If, then, we are to understand the changes
that do in fact take place, why in the history
of poetry there should be periods of great

fertility, and others comparatively barren, why both the subject-matter and the manner should vary so widely, why poetry should sometimes be easy to understand, and sometimes very obscure, we must look elsewhere than to the idiosyncrasies of the individual poets themselves.

The wish to make something, always perhaps the greatest conscious preoccupation of the artist himself, is a constant, independent of time. The things that do change are his medium, his attitude to the spoken and written word, the kind of things he is interested in or capable of perceiving, and the kind of audience with whom he wants to communicate. He wants to tell the truth, and he wants to amuse his friends, and what kind of truth he tells and what kind of friends he has depend partly on the state of society as a whole and partly on the kind of life which he, as an artist, leads.

When the things in which the poet is interested, the things which he sees about him, are much the same as those of his audience, and that audience is a fairly general one, he will not be conscious of himself as an unusual person, and his language will be straightforward and close to ordinary speech. When, on the other hand, his interests and perceptions are not readily acceptable to society, or his audience is a highly specialized one, perhaps of fellow poets, he will be acutely aware of himself as the poet, and his method of expression may depart very widely from the normal social language.

In the first case his poetry will be 'light' in the sense in which it is used in this anthology. Three kinds of poetry have been included:

(1) Poetry written for performance, to be spoken or sung before an audience [e.g. Folk-songs, the poems of Tom Moore].

(2) Poetry intended to be read, but having for its subject-matter the everyday social life of its period or the experiences of the poet as an ordinary human being [e.g. the poems of Chaucer, Pope, Byron].

(3) Such nonsense poetry as, through its properties and technique, has a general appeal [Nursery rhymes, the poems of Edward Lear].[1]

Light verse can be serious. It has only come to mean *vers de société*, triolets, smoke-room

---

[1] A few pieces, e.g. Blake's *Auguries of Innocence* and Melville's *Billy in the Darbies*, do not really fall into any of these categories, but their technique is derived so directly from the popular style that it seemed proper to include them. When Blake, for instance, deserts the proverbial manner of the *Auguries* for the eccentric manner of the Prophetic Books, he ceases to write 'light verse'.

limericks, because, under the social conditions which produced the Romantic Revival, and which have persisted, more or less, ever since, it has been only in trivial matters that poets have felt in sufficient intimacy with their audience to be able to forget themselves and their singing-robes.

II

But this has not always been so. Till the Elizabethans, all poetry was light in this sense. It might be very dull at times, but it was light.

As long as society was united in its religious faith and its view of the universe, as long as the way in which people lived changed slowly, audience and artists alike tended to have much the same interests and to see much the same things.

It is not until the great social and ideological upheavals of the sixteenth and seventeenth centuries that difficult poetry appears, some of Shakespeare, Donne, Milton, and others. The example of these poets should warn us against condemning poetry because it is difficult. Lightness is a great virtue, but light verse tends to be conventional, to accept the attitudes of the society in which it is written. The more homogeneous a society, the closer the artist is to the everyday life of his time, the easier it is for him to communicate what he perceives, but the harder for him to see honestly and truthfully, unbiased by the conventional responses of his time. The more unstable a society, and the more detached from it the artist, the clearer he can see, but the harder it is for him to convey it to others. In the greatest periods of English Literature, as in the Elizabethan period, the tension was at its strongest. The artist was still sufficiently rooted in the life of his age to feel in common with his audience, and at the same time society was in a sufficient state of flux for the age-long beliefs and attitudes to be no longer compulsive on the artist's vision.

In the seventeenth century poetry, like religion, had its eccentric sports. Milton, with the possible exception of Spenser, is the first eccentric English poet, the first to make a myth out of his personal experience, and to invent a language of his own remote from the spoken word. Poets like Herbert and Crashaw and prose-writers like Sir Thomas Browne are minor examples of the same tendency. Marvell and Herrick are 'traditional' in a way that these others are not, even though the former often use the same kind of tricks.

The Restoration marks a return both to a more settled society and to a more secure position for the artist under aristocratic patronage. His social status rose. When Dryden in his 'Essay on the Dramatic Poetry of the Last Age' ascribes the superiority in correctness of language of the new dramatists to their greater opportunities of contact with genteel society, he is stating something which had great consequences for English poetry. With a settled and valued place in society, not only minor poets, but the greatest, like Dryden and Pope, were able to express themselves in an easy manner, to use the speaking-voice, and to use as their properties the images of their everyday, i.e. social, life.

Their poetry has its limits, because the society of which they were a part was a limited part of the community, the leisured class, but within these limits, certain that the aim of poetry was to please, and certain of whom they had to please, they moved with freedom and intelligence.

This ease continued until the Romantic Revival which coincided with the beginning of the Industrial Revolution. From a predominantly agricultural country, where the towns were small and more important as places for social intercourse than as wealth-producing centres, England became a country of large manufacturing towns, too big for the indivi-

dual to know anybody else except those employed in the same occupation. The divisions
between classes became sharper and more
numerous. At the same time there was a great
increase in national wealth, and an increase
in the reading public. With the increase in
wealth appeared a new class who had independent incomes from dividends, and whose lives
felt neither the economic pressure of the wage-
earner ncr the burden of responsibility of the
landlord. The patronage system broke down,
and the artist had either to write for the general
public, whose condition was well described
by Wordsworth in his preface to the *Lyrical
Ballads*,

'A multitude of causes, unknown to former times,
are now acting with a combined force to blunt the
discriminating powers of the mind, and, unfitting
it for all voluntary exertion, to reduce it to a state
of almost savage torpor. The most effective of these
causes are the great national events which are daily
taking place, and the increasing accumulation of
men in cities, where the uniformity of their occupa-
tions produces a craving for extraordinary incident,
which the rapid communication of intelligence hourly
gratifies';

or if he had an artistic conscience he could
starve, unless he was lucky enough to have
independent means.

As the old social community broke up, artists were driven to the examination of their own feelings and to the company of other artists. They became introspective, obscure, and highbrow.

The case of Wordsworth, the greatest of the Romantic poets, is instructive. While stating that he intended to write in the language really used by men, in particular by Westmorland farmers, whenever he tries to do so he is not completely successful, while in his best work, the *Odes* and *The Prelude*, his diction is poetic, and far removed from the spoken word. The sub-title of *The Prelude*, *The Growth of a Poet's Mind*, is illuminating. Wordsworth was a person who early in life had an intense experience or series of experiences about inanimate nature, which he spent the rest of his poetical life trying to describe. He was not really interested in farm-labourers or any one else for themselves, but only in so far as they helped to explain this vision, and his own relation to it. When he objects to eighteenth-century diction as 'artificial', what he really means is artificial for his particular purpose. The diction of the Immortality Ode would be as artificial for Pope's purposes as Pope's was for Wordsworth's.

Wordsworth's case is paralleled by the

history of most of the Romantic poets, both of his day and of the century following. Isolated in an amorphous society with no real communal ties, bewildered by its complexity, horrified by its ugliness and power, and uncertain of an audience, they turned away from the life of their time to the contemplation of their own emotions and the creation of imaginary worlds. Wordsworth to Nature, Keats and Mallarmé to a world of pure poetry, Shelley to a future Golden Age, Baudelaire and Hölderlin to a past,

> . . . ces époques nues
> Dont Phoebus se plaisait à dorer les statues.[1]

Instead of the poet regarding himself as an entertainer, he becomes the prophet, 'the unacknowledged legislator of the world', or the Dandy who sits in the café, 'proud that he is

---

[1] Mr. Stephen Spender, in his essay on Keats in *From Anne to Victoria*, has analysed the gulf between the world of the poems and the world of the letters. Keats's abandonment of 'Hyperion' with the remark that there were too many Miltonic inversions in it, is a sign that he was becoming aware of this gulf. When the subject-matter of poetry ceases to be the social life of man, it tends to dispense with the social uses of language, grammar, and word-order, a tendency which Mallarmé carried to its logical conclusion.

Browning is an interesting case of a poet who was intensely interested in the world about him and in a less socially specialized period might well have been the 'easiest' poet of his generation, instead of the most 'difficult'.

less base than the passers-by, saying to himself as he contemplates the smoke of his cigar: "What does it matter to me what becomes of my perceptions?" '

This is not, of course, to condemn the Romantic poets, but to explain why they wrote the kind of poetry they did, why their best work is personal, intense, often difficult, and generally rather gloomy.

The release from social pressure was, at first, extremely stimulating. The private world was a relatively unexplored field, and the technical discoveries made were as great as those being made in industry. But the feeling of excitement was followed by a feeling of loss. For if it is true that the closer bound the artist is to his community the harder it is for him to see with a detached vision, it is also true that when he is too isolated, though he may see clearly enough what he does see, that dwindles in quantity and importance. He 'knows more and more about less and less'. It is significant that so many of these poets either died young like Keats, or went mad like Hölderlin, or ceased producing good work like Wordsworth, or gave up writing altogether like Rimbaud. . . . 'I must ask forgiveness for having fed myself on lies, and let us go. . . . One must be absolutely modern.' For the private world is fascinating, but it is exhaustible. Without a secure place in society, without an intimate relation between himself and his audience, without, in fact, those conditions which make for Light Verse, the poet finds it difficult to grow beyond a certain point.

III

But Light Verse has never entirely disappeared. At the beginning of the Romantic age stand two writers of Light Verse who were also major poets, Burns and Byron, one a peasant, the other an aristocrat. The former came from a Scottish parish which, whatever its faults of hypocrisy and petty religious tyranny, was a genuine community where the popular tradition in poetry had never been lost. In consequence Burns was able to write directly and easily about all aspects of life, the most serious as well as the most trivial. He is the last poet of whom this can be said. Byron, on the other hand, is the first writer of Light Verse in the modern sense. His success lasts as long as he takes nothing very seriously; the moment he tries to be profound and 'poetic' he fails. However much they tried to reject each other, he was a member of 'Society', and his poetry is the result of his membership. If he cannot be poetic, it is because smart society is not poetic. And the same is true, in a minor way, of Praed, whose serious poems are as trivial as his *vers de société* are profound.

IV

The nineteenth century saw the development of a new kind of light poetry, poetry for children and nonsense poetry. The breakdown of the old village or small-town community left the family as the only real social unit, and the parent–child relationship as the only real social bond. The writing of nonsense poetry which appeals to the Unconscious, and of poetry for children who live in a world before self-consciousness, was an attempt to find a world where the divisions of class, sex, occupation did not operate, and the great Victorian masters of this kind of poetry, Lewis Carroll and Edward Lear, were as successful in their day as Mr. Walt Disney has been in ours. The conditions under which folk-poetry is made ensure that it shall keep its lightness or disappear, but the changing social conditions are reflected in its history by a degeneration both in technique and in treatment. The Border ballad could be tragic; the music-hall song cannot.[1] Directness and

[1] Kipling, who identified himself with British middle-class

ease of expression has been kept, but at the cost of excluding both emotional subtlety and beauty of diction. Only in America, under the conditions of frontier expansion and prospecting and railway development, have the last hundred years been able to produce a folk-poetry which can equal similar productions of pre-industrial Europe, and in America, too, this period is ending.

The problem for the modern poet, as for every one else to-day, is how to find or form a genuine community, in which each has his valued place and can feel at home. The old pre-industrial community and culture are gone and cannot be brought back. Nor is it desirable that they should be. They were too unjust, too squalid, and too custom-bound. Virtues which were once nursed unconsciously by the forces of nature must now be recovered and fostered by a deliberate effort of the will and the intelligence. In the future, societies will not grow of themselves. They will either be made consciously or decay. A democracy in which each citizen is as fully conscious and capable of making a rational choice, as in the

imperialism, as Pope identified himself with the 18th-century landed gentry, wrote serious light verse; and it is, perhaps, no accident that the two best light-verse writers of our time, Belloc and Chesterton, are both Catholics.

past has been possible only for the wealthier few, is the only kind of society which in the future is likely to survive for long.

In such a society, and in such alone, will it be possible for the poet, without sacrificing any of his subtleties of sensibility or his integrity, to write poetry which is simple, clear, and gay.

For poetry which is at the same time light and adult can only be written in a society which is both integrated and free.

W. H. A.

EDITORIAL NOTE AND ACKNOWLEDGEMENTS

CERTAIN notes should be added on the editorial methods and arrangement which have been followed. To avoid overlapping, no poem which appears in *The Oxford Book of English Verse* is included (with the exception of a poem by Thomas Jordan which appears here in a fuller version). Many of the poems in that anthology, particularly in the earlier sections, are, of course, 'light' in the sense in which the word is used here.

The order of the poems is chronological. Poems of known authorship are arranged by the dates of their authors' births, but more varied criteria have been used to determine the position of the large number of anonymous poems, ballads, and songs which the volume contains. The earliest versions of the ballads and nursery rhymes have been used, except where later versions were more complete, or of greater literary merit. The nursery rhymes have generally been placed at the date of the earliest extant version, but when there is evidence that a rhyme existed earlier, it has been placed at the earlier date. The vexed question of ballads has been settled, in some cases perhaps rather arbitrarily, by dividing them

B

according to the general evidence of their antiquity between the sixteenth and seventeenth centuries. Folk-songs have been grouped mainly in the late eighteenth and early nineteenth centuries: many of them could undoubtedly claim a much earlier position, but the forms in which we know them, and in which they were first collected, belong as a rule to this later period.

Details of the sources of poems not easily accessible, and some of the evidence of date, are given in an index at the end of the volume; but there are some poems, particularly in the modern period, for which the editor has had to rely on an oral tradition, often still changing, for his text.

The impossibility of adequately modernizing poems of the Middle English period has made it necessary to reproduce in their original forms all poems up to the early sixteenth century. From that point onwards poems have been modernized in spelling and punctuation, and the editions from which they are taken have been given in the index only when they are not to be found in the authors' collected works.

The editor's thanks are due to Madame Olive Mangeot, Miss Hedli Anderson, and Mr. John Betjeman for many valuable sug-

gestions, to Mr. J. A. W. Bennett of Merton
College for checking the early texts, and to
Mrs. A. E. Dodds, to whose industry, scholarship, and taste he owes more than he finds it
comfortable to admit.

My thanks are also due to those who have so kindly given
me permission to include certain copyright poems: to
Messrs. Gerald Duckworth & Co., Ltd. (for poems by
Hilaire Belloc); The Executors of the late Arnold Bennett
(for 'There was a young man of Montrose'); Messrs.
T. Werner Laurie, Ltd., and Mr. E. C. Bentley (for 'J. S.
Mill' and 'Lord Clive', from *Biography for Beginners*);
Messrs. Methuen & Co., Ltd., and Mr. E. C. Bentley
(for 'George III' and 'Savonarola', from *More Biography
for Beginners*); Messrs. John Murray and Mr. John
Betjeman (for two poems from *Continual Dew*); The
Delegates of the Clarendon Press (for 'Poor Poll', from
New Verse, by Robert Bridges); Jonathan Cape, Ltd. (for
'O God! O Montreal!', by Samuel Butler); Major
C. H. W. Dodgson and Messrs. Macmillan & Co., Ltd.
(for 'The Birds' Song', from *Sylvie and Bruno Concluded*,
and 'Humpty Dumpty's Song', from *Through the Looking-
Glass*, both by Lewis Carroll); The Executors of the late
G. K. Chesterton, Messrs. Burns, Oates & Washbourne,
Ltd., and Messrs. Dodd, Mead & Co., Inc. (for 'Ballade
d'une Grande Dame'); Messrs. Macmillan & Co., Ltd.,
and The Macmillan Co., New York (for 'The Nightmare
Song' from *Iolanthe*, by W. S. Gilbert); The Executors
of the late Thomas Hardy and Messrs. Macmillan & Co.,
Ltd. (for 'Liddell and Scott'); The Executors of the late
Thomas Hardy, Messrs. Macmillan & Co., Ltd., and The
Macmillan Co., New York (for 'Waiting Both'); Mr.
Maurice E. Hare (for 'There once was a man who

ACKNOWLEDGEMENTS

said: "Damn!""); The Trustees of the estate of the late A. E. Housman (for three poems); Mrs. Kipling, Messrs. Methuen & Co., Ltd., Messrs. Doubleday, Doran & Co., Inc., and The Macmillan Co. of Canada, Ltd. (for 'Danny Deever', from *Barrack Room Ballads*); Monsignor Ronald Knox (for two limericks); Messrs. Frederick Warne & Co., Ltd. (for poems by Edward Lear); Messrs. Pearn, Pollinger and Higham, Ltd., and Messrs. Alfred Knopf, New York (for two poems by D. H. Lawrence); The representatives of the late Vachel Lindsay, Messrs. Macmillan & Co., Ltd., and The Macmillan Co., New York (for 'Bryan, Bryan', from *The Collected Poems of Vachel Lindsay*); Messrs. Chatto & Windus and Mr. Norman Douglas (for pieces from *London Street Games*); Miss Rose Macaulay and Messrs. Victor Gollancz, Ltd. (for extracts from *The Minor Pleasures of Life*); Messrs. Methuen & Co., Ltd. (for three pieces from *The Sailor's Garland*, by John Masefield); Mr. Carl Sandburg and Messrs. Harcourt, Brace & Co. (for extracts from *The American Songbag*, by Carl Sandburg); Mr. Siegfried Sassoon and Messrs. William Heinemann, Ltd. (for 'The General'); Miss Maud Karpeles, Messrs. Novello & Co., Ltd., and Messrs. J. Curwen & Sons, Ltd. (for pieces from various volumes collected by the late Cecil Sharp); Country Life (for poems from *Victorian Street Ballads*); Nonesuch Press, Ltd. (for pieces from *The Week-End Book*); the late Mr. W. B. Yeats and Messrs. Macmillan & Co., Ltd. (for 'The Renowned Generations'); the late Mr. W. B. Yeats, Messrs. Macmillan & Co., Ltd., and The Macmillan Co., New York (for 'Running to Paradise'); Messrs. Francis, Day & Hunter, Ltd. (for 'Charlie Piecan').

W. H. A.

The Song of Lewes

SITTETH alle stille and herkneth to me!
the kyng of Alemaigne, bi mi leaute,
thritti thousent pound askede he
fforte make the pees in the countre,
     ant so he dude more.
    Richard, thah thou be euer trichard,
    tricchen shalt thou neuermore.

Richard of Alemaigne whil that he was kyng,
he spende al is tresour opon swyuyng,
haueth he nout of Walingford o ferlyng;
let him habbe ase he brew, bale to dryng,
     maugre Wyndesore.
    Richard, thah thou be euer trichard,
    tricchen shalt thou neuermore.

The kyng of Alemaigne wende do ful wel;
he saisede the mulne for a castel.
with hare sharpe swerdes he grounde the stel;
he wende that the sayles were mangonel,
     to helpe Windesore.
    Richard, thah thou be euer trichard,
    tricchen shalt thou neuermore.

The kyng of Alemaigne gederede ys host,
makede him a castel of a mulne post,
wende with is pride ant is muchele bost,
brohte from Alemayne mony sori gost
     to store Wyndesore.
    Richard, thah thou be euer trichard,
    tricchen shalt thou neuermore.

leaute] loyalty.   trichard] traitor.   swyuyng] lechery.
o ferlyng] one farthing.   dryng] drink.   maugre] in spite of.
Wyndesore] Henry III.   mulne] mill.   wende] supposed.
mangonel] catapult.

By God that is abouen ous he dude muche synne
that lette passen ouer see the erl of Warynne;
he hath robbed Engelond, the mores ant the fenne,
the gold ant the seluer, and yboren henne,
   for loue of Wyndesore.
  Richard, thah thou be euer trichard,
   tricchen shalt thou neuermore.

Sire Simond de Mountfort hath suore bi ys chyn
heuede he nou here the erl of Waryn
shulde he neuer more come to is yn,
ne with sheld ne with spere ne with other gyn,
   to help of Wyndesore.
  Richard, thah thou be euer trichard,
   tricchen shalt thou neuermore.

Sire Simond de Montfort hath suore bi ys top
heuede he nou here sire Hue de Bigot
al he shulde quite here tuelfmoneth scot,
shulde he neuer more with his fot pot
   to helpe Wyndesore.
  Richard, thah thou be euer trichard,
   tricchen shalt thou neuermore.

Be the luef, be the loht, sire Edward,
thou shalt ride sporeles o thy lyard
al the ryhte way to Douere ward;
shalt thou neuermore breke foreward,
   and that reweth sore.

henne] hence. yn] dwelling. gyn] device. top]
crown of head. scot] payment. pot] thrust. Be the
luef, be the loht] Whether it please thee or not. sporeles]
without spurs. lyard] horse. foreward] agreement.

2

Edward thou dudest ase a shreward,
    forsake thyn emes lore.
Richard, thah thou be euer trichard,
    tricchen shalt thou neuermore.

ANON.

2   *The Milleres Tale*

WHYLOM ther was dwellinge at Oxenford
    A riche gnof, that gestes heeld to bord,
And of his craft he was a Carpenter.
With him ther was dwellinge a povre scoler,
Had lerned art, but al his fantasye
Was turned for to lerne astrologye,
And coude a certeyn of conclusiouns
To demen by interrogaciouns,
If that men axed him in certein houres,
Whan that men sholde have droghte or elles shoures,
Or if men axed him what sholde bifalle
Of every thing, I may nat rekene hem alle.

    This clerk was cleped hende Nicholas;
Of derne love he coude and of solas;
And ther-to he was sleigh and ful privee,
And lyk a mayden meke for to see.
A chambre hadde he in that hostelrye
Allone, with-outen any companye,
Ful fetisly y-dight with herbes swote;
And he him-self as swete as is the rote

shreward] villain.   thyn emes lore] thy uncle's counsel.
gnof] churl.   coude a certeyn of conclusions] knew a certain number of operations   hende] clever, courteous.
derne] secret.   coude] knew, had experience of.   solas] pleasure.   ther-to] moreover.   fetisly] pleasantly.

Of licorys, or any cetewale.
His Almageste and bokes grete and smale,
His astrelabie, longinge for his art,
His augrim-stones layen faire a-part
On shelves couched at his beddes heed:
His presse y-covered with a falding reed.
And al above ther lay a gay sautrye,
On which he made, a nightes, melodye
So swetely, that al the chambre rong;
And *Angelus ad virginem* he song;
And after that he song the kinges note;
Ful often blessed was his mery throte.
And thus this swete clerk his tyme spente
After his freendes finding and his rente.

This Carpenter had wedded newe a wyf
Which that he lovede more than his lyf;
Of eightetene yeer she was of age.
Jalous he was, and heeld hir narwe in cage,
For she was wilde and yong, and he was old,
And demed him-self ben lyk a cokewold.
He knew nat Catoun, for his wit was rude,
That bad man sholde wedde his similitude.
Men sholde wedden after hir estaat,
For youthe and elde is often at debaat.
But sith that he was fallen in the snare,
He moste endure, as other folk, his care.

cetewale] a plant resembling ginger.   Almageste] treatise
by Ptolemy.   longinge for] belonging to.   augrim-stones]
counters.   falding reed] red cloth.   sautrye] psaltery.
After his freendes finding] So far as his friends provided for
him.   rente] income.

4

THE MILLERES TALE

Fair was this yonge wyf, and ther-with-al
As any wesele hir body gent and smal.
A ceynt she werede barred al of silk,
A barmclooth eek as whyt as morne milk
Up-on hir lendes, ful of many a gore.
Whyt was hir smok and brouded al bifore
And eek bihinde, on hir coler aboute,
Of col-blak silk, with-inne and eek with-oute.
The tapes of hir whyte voluper
Were of the same suyte of hir coler;
Hir filet brood of silk, and set ful hye:
And sikerly she hadde a likerous yë.
Ful smale y-pulled were hir browes two,
And tho were bent, and blake as any sloo.
She was ful more blisful on to see
Than is the newe pere-jonette tree;
And softer than the wolle is of a wether.
And by hir girdel heeng a purs of lether
Tasseld with silk, and perled with latoun.
In al this world, to seken up and doun,
There nis no man so wys, that coude thenche
So gay a popelote, or swich a wenche.
Ful brighter was the shyning of hir hewe
Than in the tour the noble y-forged newe.
But of hir song, it was as loude and yerne
As any swalwe sittinge on a berne.

ceynt] girdle.   barmclooth] apron.   lendes] loins.
voluper] cap.   suyte] kind.   filet] headband.   likerous]
wanton.   newe pere-jonette tree] pear tree in spring.   perled
with latoun] studded with brass.   thenche] imagine.
popelote] darling.   tour] the royal mint in the Tower.
yerne] eager.   berne] barn.

Ther-to she coude skippe and make game,
As any kide or calf folwinge his dame.
Hir mouth was swete as bragot or the meeth,
Or hord of apples leyd in hey or heeth.
Winsinge she was, as is a joly colt,
Long as a mast, and upright as a bolt.
A brooch she baar up-on hir lowe coler,
As brood as is the bos of a bocler.
Hir shoes were laced on hir legges hye;
She was a prymerole, a pigges-nye
For any lord to leggen in his bedde,
Or yet for any good yeman to wedde.

Now sire, and eft sire, so bifel the cas,
That on a day this hende Nicholas
Fil with this yonge wyf to rage and pleye,
Whyl that hir housbond was at Oseneye,
As clerkes ben ful subtile and ful queynte;
And prively he caughte hir by the queynte,
And seyde, 'y-wis, but if ich have my wille,
For derne love of thee, lemman, I spille.'
And heeld hir harde by the haunche-bones,
And seyde, 'lemman, love me al at-ones,
Or I wol dyen, also god me save!'
And she sprong as a colt doth in the trave,
And with hir heed she wryed faste awey,
And seyde, 'I wol nat kisse thee, by my fey,

---

bragot] a drink of honey and ale.   meeth] meed.
heeth] heather.   bolt] bolt of a cross-bow.   prymerole]
primrose.   pigges-nye] name of a flower used as term of
endearment.   rage] sport.   queynte] (1) artful (2)
pudendum.   spille] perish.   trave] frame for unruly
horses.

Why, lat be,' quod she, 'lat be, Nicholas,
Or I wol crye out "harrow" and "allas".
Do wey your handes for your curteisye!'

This Nicholas gan mercy for to crye,
And spak so faire, and profred hir so faste,
That she hir love him graunted atte laste,
And swoor hir ooth, by seint Thomas of Kent,
That she wol been at his comandement,
Whan that she may hir leyser wel espye.
'Myn housbond is so ful of jalousye,
That but ye wayte wel and been privee,
I woot right wel I nam but deed,' quod she.
'Ye moste been ful derne, as in this cas.'

'Nay ther-of care thee noght,' quod Nicholas,
'A clerk had litherly biset his whyle,
But-if he coude a carpenter bigyle.'
And thus they been acorded and y-sworn
To wayte a tyme, as I have told biforn.
Whan Nicholas had doon thus everydeel,
And thakked hir aboute the lendes weel,
He kist hir swete, and taketh his sautrye,
And pleyeth faste, and maketh melodye.

Than fil it thus, that to the parish-chirche,
Cristes owne werkes for to wirche,
This gode wyf wente on an haliday;
Hir forheed shoon as bright as any day,
So was it wasshen whan she leet hir werk.

Now was ther of that chirche a parish-clerk,
The which that was y-cleped Absolon.
Crul was his heer, and as the gold it shoon,

litherly biset his whyle] employed his time ill.   thakked]
stroked.   leet] left.   crul] curled.

7

And strouted as a fanne large and brode;
Ful streight and even lay his joly shode.
His rode was reed, his eyen greye as goos;
With Powles window corven on his shoos,
In hoses rede he wente fetisly.
Y-clad he was ful smal and proprely,
Al in a kirtel of a light wachet;
Ful faire and thikke been the poyntes set.
And ther-up-on he hadde a gay surplys
As whyt as is the blosme up-on the rys.
A mery child he was, so god me save,
Wel coude he laten blood and clippe and shave,
And make a chartre of lond or acquitaunce.
In twenty manere coude he trippe and daunce
After the scole of Oxenforde tho,
And with his legges casten to and fro,
And pleyen songes on a small rubible;
Ther-to he song som-tyme a loud quinible;
And as wel coude he pleye on his giterne.
In al the toun nas brewhous ne taverne
That he ne visited with his solas,
Ther any gaylard tappestere was.
But sooth to seyn, he was somdel squaymous
Of farting, and of speche daungerous.

This Absolon, that jolif was and gay,
Gooth with a sencer on the haliday,
Sensinge the wyves of the parish faste;
And many a lovely look on hem he caste,

strouted] spread out.　shode] parting.　rode] complexion.
wachet] light blue cloth.　rys] branch.　child] young man.
rubible] fiddle.　quinible] falsetto.　gaylard tappestere] merry
barmaid.　squaymous] squeamish.　daungerous] sparing

And namely on this carpenteres wyf.
To loke on hir him thoughte a mery lyf,
She was so propre and swete and likerous.
I dar wel seyn, if she had been a mous,
And he a cat, he wolde hir hente anon.

This parish-clerk, this joly Absolon,
Hath in his herte swich a love-longinge,
That of no wyf ne took he noon offringe;
For curteisye, he seyde, he wolde noon.
The mone, whan it was night, ful brighte shoon,
And Absolon his giterne hath y-take,
For paramours he thoghte for to wake.
And forth he gooth, jolif and amorous,
Til he cam to the carpenteres hous
A litel after cokkes hadde y-crowe;
And dressed him up by a shot-windowe
That was up-on the carpenteres wal.
He singeth in his vois gentil and smal,
Now, dere lady, if thy wille be,
I preye yow that ye wol rewe on me,'
Ful wel acordaunt to his giterninge.
This carpenter awook, and herde him singe,
And spak un-to his wyf, and seyde anon,
'What! Alison! herestow nat Absolon
That chaunteth thus under our boures wal?'
And she answerde hir housbond ther-with-al,
'Yis, god wot, John, I here it every-del.'

This passeth forth; what wol ye bet than wel?
Fro day to day this joly Absolon
So woweth hir, that him is wo bigon.

namely] especially.   hente] have caught.
shot-windowe] casement.

9

He waketh al the night and al the day;
He kempte hise lokkes brode, and made him gay;
He woweth hir by menes and brocage,
And swoor he wolde been hir owne page;
He singeth, brokkinge as a nightingale;
He sente hir piment, meeth, and spyced ale,
And wafres, pyping hote out of the glede;
And for she was of toune, he profred mede.
For som folk wol ben wonnen for richesse,
And som for strokes, and som for gentillesse.

Somtyme, to shewe his lightnesse and maistrye,
He pleyeth Herodes on a scaffold hye.
But what availleth him as in this cas?
She loveth so this hende Nicholas,
That Absolon may blowe the bukkes horn;
He ne hadde for his labour but a scorn:
And thus she maketh Absolon hir ape,
And al his ernest turneth til a jape.
Ful sooth is this proverbe, it is no lye,
Men seyn right thus, 'alwey the nye slye
Maketh the ferre leve to be looth.'
For though that Absolon be wood or wrooth,
By-cause that he fer was from hir sighte,
This nye Nicholas stood in his lighte.

Now bere thee wel, thou hende Nicholas!
For Absolon may waille and singe 'allas.'
And so bifel it on a Saterday,
This carpenter was goon til Osenay;

menes] go-betweens.   brocage] traffic in match-making.
brokkinge] quavering.   piment] sweetened wine.   glede]
glowing coal.   maistrye] skill.   the nye slye] the cunning
one near at hand.   ferre leve] distant love.

And hende Nicholas and Alisoun
Acorded been to this conclusioun,
That Nicholas shal shapen him a wyle
This sely jalous housbond to bigyle;
And if so be the game wente aright,
She sholde slepen in his arm al night,
For this was his desyr and hir also.
And right anon, with-outen wordes mo,
This Nicholas no lenger wolde tarie,
But doth ful softe un-to his chambre carie
Bothe mete and drinke for a day or tweye,
And to hir housbonde bad hir for to seye,
If that he axed after Nicholas,
She sholde seye she niste where he was,
Of al that day she saugh him nat with yë;
She trowed that he was in maladye,
For, for no cry, hir mayde coude him calle;
He nolde answere, for no-thing that mighte falle.

This passeth forth al thilke Saterday,
That Nicholas stille in his chambre lay,
And eet and sleep, or dide what him leste,
Til Sonday, that the sonne gooth to reste.

This sely carpenter hath greet merveyle
Of Nicholas, or what thing mighte him eyle,
And seyde, 'I am adrad, by seint Thomas,
It stondeth nat aright with Nicholas.
God shilde that he deyde sodeynly!
This world is now ful tikel, sikerly;
I saugh to-day a cors y-born to chirche
That now, on Monday last, I saugh him wirche.

sely] simple.   shilde] forbid.
deyde] should die.   tikel] unstable.

Go up,' quod he un-to his knave anoon,
'Clepe at his dore, or knokke with a stoon,
Loke how it is, and tel me boldely.'

This knave gooth him up ful sturdily,
And at the chambre-dore, whyl that he stood,
He cryde and knokked as that he were wood:—
'What! how! what do ye, maister Nicholay?
How may ye slepen al the longe day?'

But al for noght, he herde nat a word;
An hole he fond, ful lowe up-on a bord,
Ther as the cat was wont in for to crepe;
And at that hole he looked in ful depe,
And at the laste he hadde of him a sighte.
This Nicholas sat gaping ever up-righte,
As he had kyked on the newe mone.
Adoun he gooth, and tolde his maister sone
In what array he saugh this ilke man.

This carpenter to blessen him bigan,
And seyde, 'help us, seinte Frideswyde!
A man woot litel what him shal bityde.
This man is falle, with his astromye,
In som woodnesse or in some agonye;
I thoghte ay wel how that it sholde be!
Men sholde nat knowe of goddes privetee.
Ye, blessed be alwey a lewed man,
That noght but only his bileve can!
So ferde another clerk with astromye;
He walked in the feeldes for to prye
Up-on the sterres, what ther sholde bifalle,
Til he was in a marle-pit y-falle;

wood] mad.   kyked] gazed.   blessen] cross himself.
his bileve can] knows his creed.

He saugh nat that. But yet, by seint Thomas,
Me reweth sore of hende Nicholas.
He shal be rated of his studying,
If that I may, by Jesus, hevene king!

Get me a staf, that I may underspore,
Whyl that thou, Robin, hevest up the dore.
He shal out of his studying, as I gesse'—
And to the chambre-dore he gan him dresse.
His knave was a strong carl for the nones,
And by the haspe he haf it up atones;
In-to the floor the dore fil anon.
This Nicholas sat ay as stille as stoon,
And ever gaped upward in-to the eir.
This carpenter wende he were in despeir,
And hente him by the sholdres mightily,
And shook him harde, and cryde spitously,
'What! Nicholay! what, how! what! loke adoun!
Awake, and thenk on Cristes passioun;
I crouche thee from elves and fro wightes!'
Ther-with the night-spel seyde he anon-rightes
On foure halves of the hous aboute,
And on the threshfold of the dore with-oute:—

'Jesu Crist, and sëynt Benedight,
Blesse this hous from every wikked wight,
For nightes verye, the white *pater-noster!*—
Where wentestow, seynt Petres soster?'
And atte laste this hende Nicholas
Gan for to syke sore, and seyde, 'allas!

rated] scolded.   underspore] thrust under.   crouche]
mark with the cross.   night-spel] night-charm.   verye]
evil spirits.   syke] sigh.

13

C

Shal al the world be lost eftsones now?'
  This carpenter answerde, 'what seystow?
What! thenk on god, as we don, men that swinke.'
  This Nicholas answerde, 'fecche me drinke;
And after wol I speke in privetee
Of certeyn thing that toucheth me and thee;
I wol telle it non other man, certeyn.'
  This carpenter goth doun, and comth ageyn,
And broghte of mighty ale a large quart;
And whan that ech of hem had dronke his part,
This Nicholas his dore faste shette,
And doun the carpenter by him he sette.
  He seyde, 'John, myn hoste lief and dere,
Thou shalt up-on thy trouthe swere me here,
That to no wight thou shalt this conseil wreye;
For it is Cristes conseil that I seye,
And if thou telle it man, thou are forlore;
For this vengaunce thou shalt han ther-fore,
That if thou wreye me, thou shalt be wood!'
'Nay, Crist forbede it, for his holy blood!'
Quod tho this sely man, 'I nam no labbe,
Ne, though I seye, I nam nat lief to gabbe.
Sey what thou wolt, I shal it never telle
To child ne wyf, by him that harwed helle!'
  'Now John,' quod Nicholas, 'I wol nat lye;
I have y-founde in myn astrologye,
As I have loked in the mone bright,
That now, a Monday next, at quarter-night,
Shal falle a reyn and that so wilde and wood,
That half so greet was never Noës flood.

swinke] labour.   labbe] blab.

This world,' he seyde, 'in lasse than in an hour
Shal al be dreynt, so hidous is the shour;
Thus shal mankynde drenche and lese hir lyf.'

This carpenter answerde, 'allas, my wyf!
And shal she drenche? allas! myn Alisoun!'
For sorwe of this he fil almost adoun,
And seyde, 'is ther no remedie in this cas?'

'Why, yis, for gode,' quod hende Nicholas,
'If thou wolt werken after lore and reed;
Thou mayst nat werken after thyn owene heed.
For thus seith Salomon, that was ful trewe,
"Werk al by conseil, and thou shalt nat rewe."
And if thou werken wolt by good conseil,
I undertake, with-outen mast and seyl,
Yet shal I saven hir and thee and me.
Hastow nat herd how saved was Noë,
Whan that our lord had warned him biforn
That al the world with water sholde be lorn?'

'Yis,' quod this carpenter, 'ful yore ago.'

'Hastow nat herd,' quod Nicholas, 'also
The sorwe of Noë with his felawshipe,
Er that he mighte gete his wyf to shipe?
Him had be lever, I dar wel undertake,
At thilke tyme, than alle hise wetheres blake,
That she hadde had a ship hir-self allone.
And ther-fore, wostou what is best to done?
This asketh haste, and of an hastif thing
Men may nat preche or maken tarying.

Anon go gete us faste in-to this in
A kneding-trogh, or elles a kimelin,

dreynt] drowned.   this in] this house.
kimelin] brewing tub.

For ech of us, but loke that they be large,
In whiche we mowe swimme as in a barge,
And han ther-inne vitaille suffisant
But for a day; fy on the remenant!
The water shal aslake and goon away
Aboute pryme up-on the nexte day.
But Robin may nat wite of this, thy knave,
Ne eek thy mayde Gille I may nat save;
Axe nat why, for though thou aske me,
I wol nat tellen goddes privetee.
Suffiseth thee, but if thy wittes madde,
To han as greet a grace as Noë hadde.
Thy wyf shal I wel saven, out of doute,
Go now thy wey, and speed thee heer-aboute.

But whan thou hast, for hir and thee and me,
Y-geten us thise kneding-tubbes three,
Than shaltow hange hem in the roof ful hye,
That no man of our purveyaunce spye.
And whan thou thus hast doon as I have seyd,
And hast our vitaille faire in hem y-leyd,
And eek an ax, to smyte the corde atwo
When that the water comth, that we may go,
And broke an hole an heigh, up-on the gable,
Unto the gardin-ward, over the stable,
That we may frely passen forth our way
Whan that the grete shour is goon away—
Than shaltow swimme as myrie, I undertake,
As doth the whyte doke after hir drake.
Than wol I clepe, "how! Alison! how! John!
Be myrie, for the flood wol passe anon."

madde] go astray.

And thou wolt seyn, "hayl, maister Nicholay!
Good morwe, I se thee wel, for it is day."
And than shul we be lordes al our lyf
Of al the world, as Noë and his wyf.

But of o thyng I warne thee ful right,
Be wel avysed, on that ilke night
That we ben entred in-to shippes bord,
That noon of us ne speke nat a word,
Ne clepe, ne crye, but been in his preyere;
For it is goddes owne heste dere.

Thy wyf and thou mote hange fer a-twinne,
For that bitwixe yow shal be no sinne
No more in looking than ther shal in dede;
This ordinance is seyd, go, god thee spede!
Tomorwe at night, whan men ben alle aslepe,
In-to our kneding-tubbes wol we crepe,
And sitten ther, abyding goddes grace.
Go now thy wey, I have no lenger space
To make of this no lenger sermoning.
Men seyn thus, "send the wyse, and sey no-thing"
Thou art so wys, it nedeth thee nat teche;
Go, save our lyf, and that I thee biseche.'

This sely carpenter goth forth his wey.
Ful ofte he seith 'allas' and 'weylawey,'
And to his wyf he tolde his privetee;
And she was war, and knew it bet than he,
What al this queynte cast was for to seye.
But natheles she ferde as she wolde deye,
And seyde, 'allas! go forth thy wey anon,
Help us to scape, or we ben lost echon;

queynte cast] strange contrivance.

I am thy trewe verray wedded wyf;
Go, dere spouse, and help to save our lyf.'
    Lo! which a greet thyng is affeccioun!
Men may dye of imaginacioun,
So depe may impressioun be take.
This sely carpenter biginneth quake;
Him thinketh verraily that he may see
Noës flood come walwing as the see
To drenchen Alisoun, his hony dere.
He wepeth, weyleth, maketh sory chere,
He syketh with ful many a sory swogh.
He gooth and geteth him a kneding-trogh,
And after that a tubbe and a kimelin,
And prively he sente hem to his in,
And heng hem in the roof in privetee.
His owne hand he made laddres three,
To climben by the ronges and the stalkes
Un-to the tubbes hanginge in the balkes,
And hem vitailled, bothe trogh and tubbe,
With breed and chese, and good ale in a jubbe,
Suffysinge right y-nogh as for a day.
But er that he had maad al this array,
He sente his knave, and eek his wenche also,
Up-on his nede to London for to go.
And on the Monday, whan it drow to night,
He shette his dore with-oute candel-light,
And dressed al thing as it sholde be.
And shortly, up they clomben alle three;
They sitten stille wel a furlong-way.
    'Now, *Pater-noster*, clom!' seyde Nicholay,

swogh] groan.   balkes] beams.   jubbe] pitcher.   a furlong-way] a little time.   clom] mum.

And 'clom,' quod John, and 'clom,' seyde Alisoun.
This carpenter seyde his devocioun,
And stille he sit, and biddeth his preyere,
Awaytinge on the reyn, if he it here.

   The dede sleep, for wery bisinesse,
Fil on this carpenter right, as I gesse,
Aboute corfew-tyme, or litel more;
For travail of his goost he groneth sore,
And eft he routeth, for his heed mislay.
Doun of the laddre stalketh Nicholay,
And Alisoun, ful softe adoun she spedde;
With-outen wordes mo, they goon to bedde
Ther-as the carpenter is wont to lye.
Ther was the revel and the melodye;
And thus lyth Alison and Nicholas,
In bisinesse of mirthe and of solas,
Til that the belle of laudes gan to ringe,
And freres in the chauncel gonne singe.

   This parish-clerk, this amorous Absolon,
That is for love alwey so wo bigon,
Up-on the Monday was at Oseneye
With companye, him to disporte and pleye,
And axed up-on cas a cloisterer
Ful prively after John the carpenter;
And he drough him a-part out of the chirche,
And seyde, 'I noot, I saugh him here nat wirche
Sin Saterday; I trow that he be went
For timber, ther our abbot hath him sent;
For he is wont for timber for to go,
And dwellen at the grange a day or two;

   routeth] snores.   up-on cas] by chance.
        grange] abbey farm.

Or elles he is at his hous, certeyn;
Wher that he be, I can nat sothly seyn.'
  This Absolon ful joly was and light,
And thoghte, 'now is tyme wake al night;
For sikirly I saugh him nat stiringe
Aboute his dore sin day bigan to springe.
So moot I thryve, I shal, at cokkes crowe,
Ful prively knokken at his windowe
That stant ful lowe up-on his boures wal.
To Alison now wol I tellen al
My love-longing, for yet I shal nat misse
That at the leste wey I shal hir kisse.
Som maner confort shal I have, parfay,
My mouth hath icched al this longe day;
That is a signe of kissing atte leste.
Al night me mette eek, I was at a feste.
Therfor I wol gon slepe an houre or tweye,
And al the night than wol I wake and pleye.'
Whan that the firste cok hath crowe, anon
Up rist this joly lover Absolon,
And him arrayeth gay, at point-devys.
But first he cheweth greyn and lycorys,
To smellen swete, er he had kembd his heer.
Under his tonge a trewe love he beer,
For ther-by wende he to ben gracious.
He rometh to the carpenteres hous,
And stille he stant under the shot-windowe;
Un-to his brest it raughte, it was so lowe;
And softe he cogheth with a semi-soun—
'What do ye, hony-comb, swete Alisoun?

me mette] I dreamt.   trewe love] scented lozenge leaf of
herb-paris.   a semi-soun] a low noise.

My faire brid, my swete cinamome,
Awaketh, lemman myn, and speketh to me!
Wei litel thenken ye up-on my wo,
That for your love I swete ther I go.
No wonder is thogh that I swelte and swete;
I moorne as doth a lamb after the tete.
Y-wis, lemman, I have swich love-longinge,
That lyk a turtel trewe is my moorninge;
I may nat ete na more than a mayde.'

'Go fro the window, Jakke fool,' she sayde,
'As help me god, it wol nat be "com ba me."
I love another, and elles I were to blame,
Wel bet than thee, by Jesu, Absolon!
Go forth thy wey, or I wol caste a ston,
And lat me slepe, a twenty devel wey!'

'Allas,' quod Absolon, 'and weylawey!
That trewe love was ever so yvel biset!
Than kisse me, sin it may be no bet,
For Jesus love and for the love of me.'

'Wiltow than go thy wey ther-with?' quod she.

'Ye, certes, lemman,' quod this Absolon.

'Thanne make thee redy,' quod she, 'I come anon;'
And un-to Nicholas she seyde stille,
'Now hust, and thou shalt laughen al thy fille.'

This Absolon doun sette him on his knees,
And seyde, 'I am a lord at alle degrees;
For after this I hope ther cometh more!
Lemman, thy grace, and swete brid, thyn ore!'

The window she undoth, and that in haste,
'Have do,' quod she, 'com of, and speed thee faste,

swelte] faint.   turtel] turtle-dove.   ba] kiss.   hust]
hush.   ore] mercy.

21

Lest that our neighebores thee espye.'

This Absolon gan wype his mouth ful drye;
Derk was the night as pich, or as the cole,
And at the window out she putte hir hole,
And Absolon, him fil no bet ne wers,
But with his mouth he kiste hir naked ers
Ful savourly, er he was war of this.

Abak he sterte, and thoghte it was amis,
For wel he wiste a womman hath no berd;
He felte a thing al rough and long y-herd,
And seyde, 'fy! allas! what have I do?'

'Tehee!' quod she, and clapte the window to;
And Absolon goth forth a sory pas.

'A berd, a berd!' quod hende Nicholas,
'By goddes *corpus*, this goth faire and weel!'

This sely Absolon herde every deel,
And on his lippe he gan for anger byte;
And to him-self he seyde, 'I shal thee quyte!'

Who rubbeth now, who froteth now his lippes
With dust, with sond, with straw, with clooth, with
        chippes,
But Absolon, that seith ful ofte, 'allas!
My soule bitake I un-to Sathanas,
But me wer lever than al this toun,' quod he,
'Of this despyt awroken for to be!
Allas!' quod he, 'allas! I ne hadde y-bleynt!'
His hote love was cold and al y-queynt;
For fro that tyme that he had kiste hir ers,
Of paramours he sette nat a kers,
For he was heled of his maladye;
Ful ofte paramours he gan deffye,

        y-bleynt] started aside.   kers] cress.

22

And weep as dooth a child that is y-bete.
A softe paas he wente over the strete
Un-til a smith men cleped daun Gerveys,
That in his forge smithed plough-harneys;
He sharpeth shaar and culter bisily.
This Absolon knokketh al esily,
And seyde, 'undo, Gerveys, and that anon.'

'What, who artow?' 'It am I, Absolon.'
'What, Absolon! for Cristes swete tree,
Why ryse ye so rathe, ey, *ben'cite!*
What eyleth yow? som gay gerl, god it woot,
Hath broght yow thus up-on the viritoot;
By sëynt Note, ye woot wel what I mene.'

This Absolon ne roghte nat a bene
Of al his pley, no word agayn he yaf;
He hadde more tow on his distaf
Than Gerveys knew, and seyde, 'freend so dere,
That hote culter in the chimenee here,
As lene it me, I have ther-with to done,
And I wol bringe it thee agayn ful sone.'

Gerveys answerde, 'certes, were it gold,
Or in a poke nobles alle untold,
Thou sholdest have, as I am trewe smith;
Ey, Cristes foo! what wol ye do ther-with?'

'Ther-of,' quod Absolon, 'be as be may;
I shal wel telle it thee to-morwe day'—
And caughte the culter by the colde stele.
Ful softe out at the dore he gan to stele,
And wente un-to the carpenteres wal.
He cogheth first, and knokketh ther-with-al

viritoot] quick trot. roghte] cared.
As lene it me] lend it me. stele] handle.

23

Upon the windowe, right as he dide er.
    This Alison answerde, 'Who is ther
That knokketh so? I warante it a theef.'
    'Why, nay,' quod he, 'god woot, my swete leef,
I am thyn Absolon, my dereling!
Of gold,' quod he, 'I have thee broght a ring;
My moder yaf it me, so god me save,
Ful fyn it is, and ther-to wel y-grave;
This wol I yeve thee, if thou me kisse!'
    This Nicholas was risen for to pisse,
And thoghte he wolde amenden al the jape,
He sholde kisse his ers er that he scape.
And up the windowe dide he hastily,
And out his ers he putteth prively
Over the buttok, to the haunche-bon;
And ther-with spak this clerk, this Absolon,
'Spek, swete brid, I noot nat wher thou art.'
    This Nicholas anon leet flee a fart,
As greet as it had been a thonder-dent,
That with the strook he was almost y-blent;
And he was redy with his iron hoot,
And Nicholas amidde the ers he smoot.
    Of gooth the skin an hande-brede aboute,
The hote culter brende so his toute,
And for the smert he wende for to dye.
As he were wood, for wo he gan to crye—
'Help! water! water! help, for goddes herte!'
    This carpenter out of his slomber sterte,
And herde oon cryen 'water' as he were wood,
And thoghte, 'Allas! now comth Nowélis flood!'

        ther-to] besides.   **y-blent**] blinded.
                 toute] buttocks.

He sit him up with-outen wordes mo,
And with his ax he smoot the corde a-two,
And doun goth al; he fond neither to selle,
Ne breed ne ale, til he cam to the selle
Up-on the floor; and ther aswowne he lay.

Up sterte hir Alison, and Nicholay,
And cryden 'out' and 'harrow' in the strete.
The neighebores, bothe smale and grete,
In ronnen, for to gauren on this man,
That yet aswowne he lay, bothe pale and wan;
For with the fal he brosten hadde his arm;
But stonde he moste un-to his owne harm.
For whan he spak, he was anon bore doun
With hende Nicholas and Alisoun.
They tolden every man that he was wood,
He was agast so of 'Nowélis flood'
Thurgh fantasye, that of his vanitee
He hadde y-boght him kneding-tubbes three,
And hadde hem hanged in the roof above;
And that he preyed hem, for goddes love,
To sitten in the roof, *par companye.*

The folk gan laughen at his fantasye;
In-to the roof they kyken and they gape,
And turned al his harm un-to a jape.
For what so that this carpenter answerde,
It was for noght, no man his reson herde;
With othes grete he was so sworn adoun,
That he was holden wood in al the toun;
For every clerk anon-right heeld with other.
They seyde, 'the man is wood, my leve brother;'

selle] flooring.   floor] ground.
gauren] stare.

25

And every wight gan laughen of this stryf.
Thus swyved was the carpenteres wyf,
For al his keping and his jalousye;
And Absolon hath kist hir nether yë;
And Nicholas is scalded in the toute.
This tale is doon, and god save al the route!

GEOFFREY CHAUCER.

3   *The Wife of Bath's Prologue*

'EXPERIENCE, though noon auctoritee
    Were in this world, were right y-nough to me
To speke of wo that is in mariage;
For, lordinges, sith I twelf yeer was of age,
Thonked be god that is eterne on lyve,
Housbondes at chirche-dore I have had fyve;
For I so ofte have y-wedded be;
And alle were worthy men in hir degree.
But me was told certeyn, nat longe agon is,
That sith that Crist ne wente never but onis
To wedding in the Cane of Galilee,
That by the same ensample taughte he me
That I ne sholde wedded be but ones.
Herke eek, lo! which a sharp word for the nones
Besyde a welle Jesus, god and man,
Spak in repreve of the Samaritan:
"Thou hast y-had fyve housbondes," quod he,
"And thilke man, the which that hath now thee,
Is noght thyn housbond;" thus seyde he certeyn;
What that he mente ther-by, I can nat seyn;

swyved] lain with.

But that I axe, why that the fifthe man
Was noon housbond to the Samaritan?
How manye mighte she have in mariage?
Yet herde I never tellen in myn age
Upon this nombre diffinicioun;
Men may devyne and glosen up and doun.
But wel I woot expres, with-oute lye,
God bad us for to wexe and multiplye;
That gentil text can I wel understonde.
Eek wel I woot he seyde, myn housbonde
Sholde lete fader and moder, and take me;
But of no nombre mencioun made he,
Of bigamye or of octogamye;
Why sholde men speke of it vileinye?

  Lo, here the wyse king, dan Salomon;
I trowe he hadde wyves mo than oon;
As, wolde god, it leveful were to me
To be refresshed half so ofte as he!
Which yifte of god hadde he for alle his wyvis!
No man hath swich, that in this world alyve is.
God woot, this noble king, as to my wit,
The firste night had many a mery fit
With ech of hem, so wel was him on lyve!
Blessed be god that I have wedded fyve!
Welcome the sixte, whan that ever he shal.
For sothe, I wol nat kepe me chast in al;
Whan myn housbond is fro the world y-gon,
Som Cristen man shal wedde me anon;
For thanne th'apostle seith, that I am free
To wedde, a godd's half, wher it lyketh me.

gentil] excellent.　　　lete] leave.
leveful] allowable.

He seith that to be wedded is no sinne;
Bet is to be wedded than to brinne.
What rekketh me, thogh folk seye vileinye
Of shrewed Lameth and his bigamye?
I woot wel Abraham was an holy man,
And Jacob eek, as ferforth as I can;
And ech of hem hadde wyves mo than two;
And many another holy man also.
Whan saugh ye ever, in any maner age,
That hye god defended mariage
By expres word? I pray you, telleth me;
Or wher comanded he virginitee?
I woot as wel as ye, it is no drede,
Th'apostel, whan he speketh of maydenhede;
He seyde, that precept ther-of hadde he noon.
Men may conseille a womman to been oon,
But conseilling is no comandement;
He putte it in our owene jugement
For hadde god comanded maydenhede,
Thanne hadde he dampned wedding with the dede;
And certes, if ther were no seed y-sowe,
Virginitee, wher-of than sholde it growe?
Poul dorste nat comanden atte leste
A thing of which his maister yaf noon heste.
The dart is set up for virginitee;
Cacche who so may, who renneth best lat see.

But this word is nat take of every wight,
But ther as god list give it of his might.
I woot wel, that th'apostel was a mayde;
But natheless, thogh that he wroot and sayde,

brinne] burn.   shrewed] wicked.   defended] forbad.
drede] doubt.   dart] prize.   a mayde] unmarried.

28

He wolde that every wight were swich as he,
Al nis but conseil to virginitee;
And for to been a wyf, he yaf me leve
Of indulgence; so it is no repreve
To wedde me, if that my make dye,
With-oute excepcioun of bigamye.
Al were it good no womman for to touche,
He mente as in his bed or in his couche;
For peril is bothe fyr and tow t'assemble;
Ye knowe what this ensample may resemble.
This is al and som, he heeld virginitee
More parfit than wedding in freletee.
Freeltee clepe I, but-if that he and she
Wolde leden al hir lyf in chastitee.

I graunte it wel, I have noon envye,
Thogh maydenhede preferre bigamye;
Hem lyketh to be clene, body and goost,
Of myn estaat I nil nat make no boost.
For wel ye knowe, a lord in his houshold,
He hath nat every vessel al of gold;
Somme been of tree, and doon hir lord servyse.
God clepeth folk to him in sondry wyse,
And everich hath of god a propre yifte,
Som this, som that,—as him lyketh shifte.

Virginitee is greet perfeccioun,
And continence eek with devocioun.
But Crist, that of perfeccioun is welle,
Bad nat every wight he sholde go selle
All that he hadde, and give it to the pore,
And in swich wyse folwe him and his fore.

repreve] reproach.   make] husband.   al] although.
preferre] surpass.   shifte] ordained.   fore] path.

D

He spak to hem that wolde live parfitly;
And lordinges, by your leve, that am nat I.
I wol bistowe the flour of al myn age
In th' actes and in fruit of mariage.

Telle me also, to what conclusioun
Were membres maad of generacioun,
And for what profit was a wight y-wroght?
Trusteth right wel, they were nat maad for noght.
Glose who-so wole, and seye bothe up and doun,
That they were maked for purgacioun
Of urine, and our bothe thinges smale
Were eek to knowe a femele from a male,
And for noon other cause: sey ye no?
The experience woot wel it is noght so;
So that the clerkes be nat with me wrothe,
I sey this, that they maked been for bothe,
This is to seye, for office, and for ese
Of engendrure, ther we nat god displese.
Why sholde men elles in his bokes sette,
That man shal yelde to his wyf hir dette?
Now wher-with sholde he make his payement,
If he ne used his sely instrument?
Than were they maad up-on a creature,
To purge uryne, and eek for engendrure.

But I seye noght that every wight is holde,
That hath swich harneys as I to yow tolde,
To goon and usen hem in engendrure;
Than sholde men take of chastitee no cure.
Crist was a mayde, and shapen as a man,
And many a seint, sith that the world bigan,
Yet lived they ever in parfit chastitee.

> sely] good.

THE WIFE OF BATH'S PROLOGUE

I nil envye no virginitee;
Lat hem be breed of pured whete-seed,
And lat us wyves hoten barly-breed;
And yet with barly-breed, Mark telle can,
Our lord Jesu refresshed many a man.
In swich estaat as god hath cleped us
I wol persevere, I nam nat precious.
In wyfhode I wol use myn instrument
As frely as my maker hath it sent.
If I be daungerous, god yeve me sorwe!
Myn housbond shal it have bothe eve and morwe,
Whan that him list com forth and paye his dette.
An housbonde I wol have, I nil nat lette,
Which shal be bothe my dettour and my thral,
And have his tribulacioun with-al
Up-on his flessh, whyl that I am his wyf.
I have the power duringe al my lyf
Up-on his propre body, and noght he.
Right thus th'apostel tolde it un-to me;
And bad our housbondes for to love us weel.
Al this sentence me lyketh every-deel—

.   .   .   .

I shal seye sooth, tho housbondes that I hadde,
As three of hem were gode and two were badde.
The three men were gode, and riche, and olde;
Unnethe mighte they the statut holde
In which that they were bounden un-to me.
Ye woot wel what I mene of this, pardee!
As help me god, I laughe whan I thinke
How pitously a-night I made hem swinke;

> hoten] be called.   precious] scrupulous.
>   daungerous] grudging.

And by my fey, I tolde of it no stoor.
They had me yeven hir gold and hir tresoor;
Me neded nat do lenger diligence
To winne hir love, or doon hem reverence.
They loved me so wel, by god above,
That I ne tolde no deyntee of hir love!
A wys womman wol sette hir ever in oon
To gete hir love, ther as she hath noon.
But sith I hadde hem hoolly in myn hond,
And sith they hadde me yeven all hir lond,
What sholde I taken hede hem for to plese,
But it were for my profit and myn ese?
I sette hem so a-werke, by my fey,
That many a night they songen "weilawey!"
The bacoun was nat fet for hem, I trowe,
That som men han in Essex at Dunmowe.
I governed hem so wel, after my lawe,
That ech of hem ful blisful was and fawe
To bringe me gaye thinges fro the fayre.
They were ful glad whan I spak to hem fayre;
For god it woot, I chidde hem spitously.

 . . . . . .

 Lordinges, right thus, as ye have understonde,
Bar I stifly myne olde housbondes on honde,
That thus they seyden in hir dronkenesse;
And al was fals, but that I took witnesse
On Janekin and on my nece also.
O lord, the peyne I dide hem and the wo,
Ful giltelees, by goddes swete pyne!
For as an hors I coude byte and whyne.

   tolde of it no stoor] took no account of it.
    deyntee] value. fawe] glad.

THE WIFE OF BATH'S PROLOGUE

I coude pleyne, thogh I were in the gilt,
Or elles often tyme hadde I ben spilt.
Who-so that first to mille comth, first grint;
I pleyned first, so was our werre y-stint.
They were ful glad t'excusen hem ful blyve
Of thing of which they never agilte hir lyve.

Of wenches wolde I beren him on honde,
Whan that for syk unnethes mighte he stonde.
Yet tikled it his herte, for that he
Wende that I hadde of him so greet chiertee.
I swoor that al my walkinge out by nighte
Was for t'espye wenches that he dighte;
Under that colour hadde I many a mirthe.
For al swich wit is yeven us in our birthe;
Deceite, weping, spinning god hath yive
To wommen kindely, whyl they may live.
And thus of o thing I avaunte me,
Atte ende I hadde the bettre in ech degree,
By sleighte, or force, or by som maner thing,
As by continuel murmur or grucching;
Namely a-bedde hadden they meschaunce,
Ther wolde I chyde and do hem no plesaunce;
I wolde no lenger in the bed abyde,
If that I felte his arm over my syde,
Til he had maad his raunson un-to me;
Than wolde I suffre him do his nycetee.
And ther-fore every man this tale I telle,
Winne who-so may, for al is for to selle.
With empty hand men may none haukes lure;
For winning wolde I al his lust endure,

chiertee] fondness.   dighte] lay with.   kindely]
naturally.   Namely] especially.   winne] profit.

And make me a feyned appetyt;
And yet in bacon hadde I never delyt;
That made me that ever I wolde hem chyde.
For thogh the pope had seten hem bisyde,
I wolde nat spare hem at hir owene bord.
For by my trouthe, I quitte hem word for word.
As help me verray god omnipotent,
Thogh I right now sholde make my testament,
I ne owe hem nat a word that it nis quit.
I broghte it so aboute by my wit,
That they moste yeve it up, as for the beste;
Or elles hadde we never been in reste.
For thogh he loked as a wood leoun,
Yet sholde he faille of his conclusioun.

Thanne wolde I seye, 'gode lief, tak keep
How mekely loketh Wilkin oure sheep;
Com neer, my spouse, lat me ba thy cheke!
Ye sholde been al pacient and meke,
And han a swete spyced conscience,
Sith ye so preche of Jobes pacience.
Suffreth alwey, sin ye so wel can preche;
And but ye do, certein we shal yow teche
That it is fair to have a wyf in pees.
Oon of us two moste bowen, doutelees;
And sith a man is more resonable
Than womman is, ye moste been suffrable.
What eyleth yow to grucche thus and grone?
Is it for ye wolde have my queynte allone?
Why taak it al, lo, have it every-deel;
Peter! I shrewe yow but ye love it weel!

wood] mad.　ba] kiss.　spyced] scrupulous.　queynte]
pudendum.

For if I wolde selle my *bele chose*,
I coude walke as fresh as is a rose;
But I wol kepe it for your owene tooth.
Ye be to blame, by god, I sey yow sooth.'
   Swiche maner wordes hadde we on honde.
Now wol I speken of my fourthe housbonde.
   My fourthe housbonde was a revelour,
This is to seyn, he hadde a paramour;
And I was yong and ful of ragerye,
Stiborn and strong, and joly as a pye.
Wel coude I daunce to an harpe smale,
And singe, y-wis, as any nightingale,
Whan I had dronke a draughte of swete wyn.
Metellius, the foule cherl, the swyn,
That with a staf birafte his wyf hir lyf,
For she drank wyn, thogh I hadde been his wyf,
He sholde nat han daunted me fro drinke;
And, after wyn, on Venus moste I thinke:
For al so siker as cold engendreth hayl,
A likerous mouth moste han a likerous tayl.
In womman vinolent is no defence,
This knowen lechours by experience.
   But, lord Crist! whan that it remembreth me
Up-on my yowthe, and on my jolitee,
It tikleth me aboute myn herte rote.
Unto this day it dooth myn herte bote
That I have had my world as in my tyme.
But age, allas! that al wol envenyme,
Hath me biraft my beautee and my pith;
Lat go, fare-wel, the devel go therwith!

ragerye] wantonness.   siker] sure.   likerous] greedy.
vinolent] full of wine.

The flour is goon, ther is na-more to telle,
The bren, as I best can, now moste I selle;
But yet to be right mery wol I fonde.
Now wol I tellen of my fourthe housbonde.

I seye, I hadde in herte greet despyt
That he of any other had delyt.
But he was quit, by god and by seint Joce!
I made him of the same wode a croce;
Nat of my body in no foul manere,
But certeinly, I made folk swich chere,
That in his owene grece I made him frye
For angre, and for verray jalousye.
By god, in erthe I was his purgatorie,
For which I hope his soule be in glorie.
For god it woot, he sat ful ofte and song
Whan that his shoo ful bitterly him wrong.
Ther was no wight, save god and he, that wiste,
In many wyse, how sore I him twiste.
He deyde whan I cam fro Jerusalem,
And lyth y-grave under the rode-beem,
Al is his tombe noght so curious
As was the sepulcre of him, Darius,
Which that Appelles wroghte subtilly;
It nis but wast to burie him preciously.
Lat him fare-wel, god yeve his soule reste,
He is now in the grave and in his cheste.

My fifthe housbonde, god his soule blesse!
Which that I took for love and no richesse,
He som-tyme was a clerk of Oxenford,
And had left scole, and wente at hoom to bord

bren] bran.   fonde] try.

With my gossib, dwellinge in oure toun,
God have hir soule! hir name was Alisoun.
She knew myn herte and eek my privetee
Bet than our parisshe-preest, so moot I thee!
To hir biwreyed I my conseil al.
For had myn housbonde pissed on a wal,
Or doon a thing that sholde han cost his lyf,
To hir, and to another worthy wyf,
And to my nece, which that I loved weel,
I wolde han told his conseil every-deel.
And so I dide ful often, god it woot,
That made his face ful often reed and hoot
For verray shame, and blamed him-self for he
Had told to me so greet a privetee.

But now sir, lat me see, what I shal seyn?
A! ha! by god, I have my tale ageyn.

Whan that my fourthe housbond was on bere,
I weep algate, and made sory chere,
As wyves moten, for it is usage,
And with my coverchief covered my visage;
But for that I was purveyed of a make,
I weep but smal, and that I undertake.

To chirche was myn housbond born a-morwe
With neighebores, that for him maden sorwe;
And Jankin oure clerk was oon of tho.
As help me god, whan that I saugh him go
After the bere, me thoughte he hadde a paire
Of legges and of feet so clene and faire,
That al myn herte I yaf un-to his hold.
He was, I trowe, a twenty winter old,
And I was fourty, if I shal seye sooth;
But yet I hadde alwey a coltes tooth.

Gat-tothed I was, and that bicam me weel;
I hadde the prente of sëynt Venus seel.
As help me god, I was a lusty oon,
And faire and riche, and yong, and wel bigoon;
And trewely, as myne housbondes tolde me,
I had the beste *quoniam* mighte be.
For certes, I am al Venerien
In felinge, and myn herte is Marcien.
Venus me yaf my lust, my likerousnesse,
And Mars yaf me my sturdy hardinesse.
Myn ascendent was Taur, and Mars ther-inne.
Allas! allas! that ever love was sinne!
I folwed ay myn inclinacioun
By vertu of my constellacioun;
That made me I coude noght withdrawe
My chambre of Venus from a good felawe.
Yet have I Martes mark up-on my face,
And also in another privee place.
For, god so wis be my savacioun,
I ne loved never by no discrecioun,
But ever folwede myn appetyt,
Al were he short or long, or blak or whyt;
I took no kepe, so that he lyked me,
How pore he was, ne eek of what degree.

What sholde I seye, but, at the monthes ende,
This joly clerk Jankin, that was so hende,
Hath wedded me with greet solempnitee,
And to him yaf I al the lond and fee
That ever was me yeven ther-bifore;
But afterward repented me ful sore.

gat-tothed] gap-toothed.   wel bigoon] happy.
hende] courteous.

He nolde suffre nothing of my list.
By god, he smoot me ones on the list,
For that I rente out of his book a leef,
That of the strook myn ere wex al deef.

. . . .

And with his fist he smoot me on the heed,
That in the floor I lay as I were deed.
And when he saugh how stille that I lay,
He was agast, and wolde han fled his way,
Til atte laste out of my swogh I breyde:
'O! hastow slayn me, false theef?' I seyde,
'And for my land thus hastow mordred me?
Er I be deed, yet wol I kisse thee.'

And neer he cam, and kneled faire adoun,
And seyde, 'dere suster Alisoun,
As help me god, I shal thee never smyte;
That I have doon, it is thy-self to wyte.
Foryeve it me, and that I thee biseke'—
And yet eft-sones I hitte him on the cheke,
And seyde, 'theef, thus muchel am I wreke;
Now wol I dye, I may no lenger speke.'
But atte laste, with muchel care and wo,
We fille acorded, by us selven two.
He yaf me al the brydel in myn hond
To han the governance of hous and lond,
And of his tonge and of his hond also,
And made him brenne his book anon right tho.
And whan that I hadde geten un-to me,
By maistrie, al the soveraynetee,
And that he seyde, 'myn owene trewe wyf,
Do as thee lust the terme of al thy lyf,

list] (1) desire (2) ear.   breyde] started.   wyte] blame.

Keep thyn honour, and keep eek myn estaat'—
After that day we hadden never debaat.

GEOFFREY CHAUCER

4   *Haylle, comly and clene*

Primus Pastor

HAYLLE, comly and clene: haylle, yong child!
  Haylle, maker, as I meyne, of a madyn so mylde.
Thou has waryd, I weyne, the warlo so wylde,
The fals gyler of teyn, now goys he begylde.
    Lo, he merys;
Lo, he laghys, my swetyng,
A wel fare metyng,
I have holden my hetyng,
    Have a bob of cherys.

Secundus Pastor

Haylle, sufferan savyoure, for thou has us soght:
Haylle, frely foyde and floure, that alle thyng has wroght.
Haylle, full of favoure, that made alle of noght!
Haylle! I kneylle and I cowre. A byrd have I broght
    To my barne.
Haylle, lytylle tyné mop,
Of oure crede thou art crop:
I wold drynk on thy cop,
    Lytylle day starne.

  waryd] cursed.   warlo] wizard.   gyler] beguiler.
teyn] sorrow.   merys] grows merry.   hetyng] promise.
frely foyde] noble child.   mop] young creature.   crop]
head.   cop] cup.

HAYLLE, COMLY AND CLENE

Tertius Pastor

Haylle, derlyng dere, fulle of godhede,
I pray the be nere when that I have nede.
Haylle! swete is thy chere: My hart wold blede
To se the sytt here in so poore wede,
    With no pennys.
Haylle! put furth thy dalle,
I bryng the bot a balle:
Have and play the with-alle,
    And go to the tenys.   ANON.

5   *The Tournament of Tottenham*

OF all thes kene conquerours to carpe it were kynde;
    Of fele feyhtyng folk ferly we fynde,
The Turnament of Totenham have we in mynde;
It were harme sych hardynes were holden byhynde,
    In story as we rede,
        Of Hawkyn, of Harry,
        Of Tomkyn, of Terry,
        Of them that were dughty
        And stalworth in dede.

If befel in Totenham on a dere day,
Ther was mad a shurtyng be the hy-way:
Theder com al the men of the contray,
Of Hyssylton, of Hy-gate, and of Hakenay.

dalle] hand.   carpe] speak.   kynde] fitting.   fele]
many.   ferly] a marvel.   dere] sad.   shurtyng]
sport.

41

And all the swete swynkers.
  Ther hopped Hawkyn,
  Ther daunsed Dawkyn,
  Ther trumped Tomkyn,
    And all were trewe drynkers.

Tyl the day was gon and evyn-song past,
That thay schuld rekyn the scot and ther contes cast,
Perkyn the potter into the press past,
And sayd, Randol the refe, a dohter thou hast,
  Tyb the dere:
    Therfor wyt wold I,
    Whych of all thys bachelery
    Were best worthy
      To wed hur to hys fere.

Upstyrt thos gadelyngys wyth ther lang staves,
And sayd, Randol the refe, lo! thys lad raves;
Baldely amang us thy dohter he craves;
And we er rycher men than he, and more god haves
    Of catell and corn;
    Then sayd Perkyn, to Tybbe I have hyht
    That I schal be alway redy in my ryht,
    If that it schuld be thys day sevenyht,
      Or elles yet tomorn.

Then sayd Randolfe the refe, Ever be he waryed,
That about thys carpyng lenger wold be taryed:
I wold not my dohter, that scho were miscaryed,
But at hur most worschyp I wold scho were maryed;

swynkers] labourers. scot] payment. contes] accounts.
wyt wold I] would I know. to hys fere] as his mate.
gadelyngys] fellows. hyht] promised. waryed] cursed.
most worschyp] best advantage.

42

THE TOURNAMENT OF TOTTENHAM

Therfor a Turnament schal begynne
    Thys day sevenyht
    Wyth a flayl for to fyht:
    And he that is of most myght
        Schall brouke hur wyth wynne.

Whoso berys hym best in the turnament,
Hym schal be granted the gre be the common assent,
Forto wynne my dohter wyth dughtynesse of dent,
And Coppell my brode-henne that was broht out of Kent,
    And my donnyd kowe.
        For no spens wyl I spare,
        For no catell wyl I care,
        He schal have my gray mare,
          And my spottyd sowe.

There was many bold lad ther bodyes to bede:
Than thay toke thayr leve, and homward thay yede;
And all the weke afterward thay graythed ther wede,
Tyll it come to the day, that they schuld do ther dede.
    Thay armed ham in matts;
        Thay set on ther nollys,
        For to kepe ther pollys,
        Gode blake bollys,
          For batryng of batts.

Thay sowed tham in schepeskynnes, for thay schuld not
    brest:
Ilkan toke a blak hat, in sted of a crest:

brouke] enjoy.   wynne] pleasure.   gre] prize.   dent]
blow.   donnyd] dun.   catell] money.   bede] offer.   graythed
ther wede] prepared their armour.   nollys] heads.   for
batryng of batts] as a defence against clubs.   brest] burst.

THE TOURNAMENT OF TOTTENHAM

A harow brod as a fanne above on ther brest,
And a flayle in ther hande; for to fyght prest,
    Furth gon thay fare:
      Ther was kyd mekyl fors,
      Who schuld best fend hys cors:
      He that had no gode hors,
        He gat hym a mare.

Sych another gadryng have I not sene oft,
When all the gret company com rydand to the croft:
Tyb on a gray mare was set upon loft
On a sek ful of fedyrs for scho schuld syt soft,
    And led hur to the gap.
      For crying of al the men
      Forther wold not Tyb then,
      Tyl scho had hur gode brode hen
        Set in hur lap.

A gay gyrdyl Tyb had on, borowed for the nonys,
And a garland on hur hed ful of rounde bonys,
And a broche on hur brest ful of safer stonys,
Wyth the holy-rode tokenyng, was wretyn for the
    nonys;
    No catel was ther spared.
      When joly Gyb saw hur thare,
      He gyrd so hys gray mare,
      That scho lete a faucon fare
        At the rereward.

    prest] ready.   kyd] shown.   fend hys cors] defend his
body.   safer] sapphire.

THE TOURNAMENT OF TOTTENHAM

I vow to God, quoth Herry, I schal not lefe behynde,
May I mete wyth Bernard on Bayard the blynde,
Ich man kepe hym out of my wynde,
For whatsoever that he be, before me I fynde,
    I wot I schall hym greve.
       Wele sayd, quoth Hawkyn.
       And I vow, quoth Dawkyn,
       May I mete wyth Tomkyn,
         Hys flayl hym reve.

I vow to God, quoth Hud, Tyb, soon schal thou se,
Whych of al this bachelery granted is the gre:
I schal scomfet thaym all, for the love of the;
In what place so I come thay schal have dout of me,
    Myn armes ar so clere:
       I bere a reddyl, and a rake,
       Poudred wyth a brenand drake,
       And three cantells of a cake
         In ych a cornere.

I vow to God, quoth Hawkyn, yf I have the gowt,
Al that I fynde in the felde persand here aboute,
Have I twyes or thryes redyn thurgh the route,
In ych a stede ther thay me se, of me thay schal have doute,
    When I begyn to play.
       I make avowe that I ne schall,
       But yf Tybbe wyl me call,
       Or I be thryes don fall,
         Ryht onys com away.

dout] fear.   reddyl] riddle.   poudred] ornamented.
cantells] slices.   don fall] made to fall.

THE TOURNAMENT OF TOTTENHAM

Then sayd Terry, and swore be hys crede;
Saw thou never yong boy forth hys body bede,
For when thay fyht fastest and most ar in drede,
I schall take Tyb by the hand, and hur away lede:
 I am armed at the full;
  In myn armys I bere wele
  A dog trogh, and a pele,
  A sadyll wythouten a panell,
   Wyth a fles of woll.

I vow to God, quoth Dudman, and swor be the stra,
Whyls me ys left my mare, thou gets hur not swa;
For scho ys wele schapen, and lyht as the ra,
Ther ys no capul in thys myle befor hur schal ga;
 Sche wul ne noht begyle:
  Sche wyl me bere, I dar wele say,
  On a lang somerys day,
  Fro Hyssylton to Hakenay,
   Noht other half myle.

I vow to God, quoth Perkyn, thow speks of cold rost,
I schal wyrch wyselyer withouten any bost:
Five of the best capullys that ar in thys ost,
I wot I schal thaym wynne, and bryng thaym to my cost,
 And here I grant tham Tybbe.
  Wele, boyes, here ys he,
  That wyl fyht, and not fle,
  For I am in my jolyte,
   Wyth so forth, Gybbe!

dog trogh] dough trough.   pele] baker's shovel.
panell] saddle cloth. ra] roe. capul] horse.

THE TOURNAMENT OF TOTTENHAM

When thay had ther vowes made, furth on thay hie,
Wyth flayles, and hornes, and trumpes mad of tre:
Ther were all the bachelerys of that contre;
Thay were dyht in aray, as thamselfe wold be:
> Thayr baners were ful bryht
>> Of an old rotten fell;
>> The cheveron of a plow-mell;
>> And the schadow of a bell,
>>> Poudred wyth mone lyht.

I wot yt was no chylder game, whan thay togedyr met,
When ich a freke in the feld on hys felaw bet.
And layd on styfly, for nothying wold thay let,
And faght ferly fast, tyll ther horses swet,
> And fewe wordys spoken.
>> Ther were flayles al to slatred,
>> Ther were scheldys al to flatred,
>> Bollys and dysches all to schatred,
>>> And many hedys brokyn.

Ther was clynkyng of cart-sadellys, and clatteryng of
cannes;
Of fele frekys in the feld brokyn were their fannes;
Of sum were the hedys brokyn, of sum the brayn pannes,
And yll were thay besene, er thay went thens
> Wyth swyppyng of swepyllys.
>> The boyes were so wery for-foght,
>> Thay myht not fyht mare oloft,
>> But creped about in the croft,
>>> As thay were croked crepyllis.

---

fell] hide. plow-mell] plough-hammer. freke] man.
to slatred] splintered in pieces. besene] treated. swyppyng
of swepyllys] striking of flails. crepyllis] cripples.

Perkyn was so wery, that he began to loute;
Help, Hud, I am ded in thys ylk rowte:
A hors for forty pens, a gode and a stoute!
That I may lyhtly come of my noye out,
    For no cost wyl I spare.
      He styrt up as a snayle,
      And hent a capul be the tayle,
      And raft Dawkins hys flayle,
        And wan there a mare.

Perkyn wan five, and Hud wan twa:
Glad and blythe thay ware, that they had don sa;
Thay wold have tham to Tyb, and present hur with tha:
The capullys were so wery, that thay myht not ga,
    But styl gon thay stand.
      Allas! quoth Hudde, my joye I lese;
      Mee had lever then a ston of chese,
      That dere Tyb had al these,
        And wyst it were my sand.

Perkyn turnyd hym about in that ych thrang,
Among thos wery boyes he wrest and he wrang;
He threw tham doun to the erth, and thrast than
    amang,
When he saw Tyrry away with Tyb fang,
    And after hym ran;
      Of his horse he hym drogh,
      And gaf hym of hys flayl inogh:
      We te he! quoth Tyb, and lugh,
        Ye er a dughty man.

    loute] bellow.   sand] gift.   lugh] laughed.

THE TOURNAMENT OF TOTTENHAM

Thus thay tugged, and rugged, tyl yt was nere nyht:
All the wyves of Tottenham came to se that syht
Wyth wyspes, and kexis, and ryschys there lyht,
To fech hom ther husbandes, that were tham trouth plyht;
    And sum broht gret harows,
      Ther husbandes hom to fech,
      Sum on dores, and sum on hech,
      Sum on hyrdyllys, and som on crech,
        And som on whele-barows.

Thay gaderyd Perkyn about, everych syde,
And grant hym ther the gre, the more was hys pryde:
Tyb and he, wyth gret merthe, homward con thay ryde,
And were al nyht togedyr, tyl the morn tyde;
    And thay ifere assent.
      So wele hys nedys he has sped,
      That dere Tyb he had wed;
      The prayse-folk, that hur led,
        Were of the turnament.

To that ylk fest com many for the nones;
Sum come hyphalt, and sum tryppand on the stonys:
Sum a staf in hys hand, and sum two at onys;
Of sum were the hedes broken, and sum the schulder
   bonys;
    With sorrow com thay thedyr.
      Wo was Hawkyn, wo was Herry,
      Wo was Tomkyn, wo was Terry.
      And so was all the bachelary,
        When thay met togedyr.

wyspes, and kexis] torches and sticks.   hech] lower half of a door.   crech] rack.

At that fest thay wer servyd with a ryche aray.
Every fyve & fyve had a cokenay;
And so thay sat in jolyte al the lang day;
And at the last thay went to bed with ful gret deray:
 Mekyl merthe was them among;
  In every corner of the hous
  Was melody delycyus
  For to here precyus
   Of six menys song.   ANON.

6   *Adam lay ibowndyn*

ADAM lay ibowndyn,
  bowndyn in a bond
fowr thowsand wynter
 thowt he not to long;
and al was for an appil,
 an appil that he tok,
as clerkes fyndyn
 wretyn in here book.
ne hadde the appil take ben,
 the appil taken ben,
ne hadde never our lady
 a ben Hevene qwen.
blyssid be the tyme
 that appil take was!
therfore we mown syngyn
 Deo gracias.

         ANON.

cokenay] egg. deray] disorder. here] their.
mown] may well.

50

The gentle Cock

I HAVE a gentil cok
    crowyt me day,
he doth me rysyn erly
    my matyins for to say.

I have a gentil cok,
    comyn he is of gret,
his comb is of red corel,
    his tayl is of get.

I have a gentyl cok,
    comyn he is of kynde,
his comb is of red corel,
    his tayl is of inde;

his legges ben of asour,
    so geintil and so smale,
his spores arn of sylver quyt
    into the wortewale;

his eyyn arn of cristal,
    lokyn al in aumbyr,
and every nyht he perchit hym
    in myn ladyis chaumbyr.

ANON.

comyn he is of gret] he is sprung of great stock.   get]
jet.   kynde] high lineage.   inde] indigo.   asour] azure.
quyt] white.   wortewale] root.

51

SEYNT STEVENE was a clerk in Kyng Herowdes halle.
And servyd him of bred and cloth, as every kyng befalle.

Stevyn out of kechone cam, wyth boris hed on honde;
He saw a sterre was fayr and bryht over Bedlem stonde.

He kyst adoun the boris hed and went into the halle.
'I forsak the, Kyng Herowdes, and thi werkes alle.

I forsak the, Kyng Herowdes, and thi werkes alle;
Ther is a chyld in Bedlem born is beter than we alle.'

'Quat eylyt the, Stevene? quat is the befalle?
Lakkyt the eyther mete or drynk in Kyng Herowdes halle?'

'Lakit me neyther mete ne drynk in Kyng Herowdes
halle;
Ther is a chyld in Bedlem born is beter than we alle.'

'Quat eylyt the, Stevyn? art thu wod, or thu gynnyst to
brede?
Lakkyt the eyther gold or fe, or ony ryche wede?'

'Lakyt me neyther gold ne fe, ne non ryche wede;
Ther is a chyld in Bedlem born schal helpyn us at our nede.'

'That is al so soth, Stevyn, al so soth, iwys,
As this capoun crowe schal that lyth here in myn dysh.'

That word was not so sone seyd, that word in that halle,
The capoun crew *Cristus natus est!* among the lordes alle.

kyst] cast.   wod] mad.   brede] start out of your mind.
schal] shall.

'Rysyt up, myn turmentowres, be to and als be on
And ledyt Stevyn out of this town, and stonyt hym wyth
　　　ston!'

Tokyn he Stevene, and stonyd hym in the way,
And therfore is his evyn on Crystes owyn day.

ANON.

9　　　　　*Jolly Jankyn*

'KYRIE, so kyrie,'
　　　Jankyn syngyt merie,
　　With 'aleyson'.

As I went on Yol Day in owre prosessyon,
Knew I joly Jankyn be his mery ton.
　　　　　Kyrieleyson.

Jankyn began the Offys on the Yol Day,
And yyt me thynkyt it dos me good, so merie gan he say,
　　　　　'Kyrieleyson.'

Jankyn red the Pystyl ful fayre and ful wel,
And yyt me thinkyt it dos me good, as evere have I sel.
　　　　　Kyrieleyson.

Jankyn at the Sanctus crakit a merie note,
And yyt me thinkyt it dos me good: I payid for his
　　cote.
　　　　　Kyrieleyson.

　be to and als be on] as one man.　　he] they.　　Pystyl]
Epistle.　　sel] good fortune.

53

Jankyn crakit notes, an hunderid on a knot,
And yyt he hakkyt hem smallere than wortes to the pot.
Kyrieleyson.

Jankyn at the Agnus beryt the paxbrede;
He twynkelid, but sayd nowt, and on myn fot he trede.
Kyrieleyson.

Benedicamus Domino: Cryst fro schame me schylde;
Deo gracias therto: alas, I go with chylde!
Kyrieleyson.   ANON.

10   *Love without Longing*

I HAVE a yong suster
        fer beyondyn the se;
Many be the drowryis
        that sche sente me.

Sche sente me the cherye,
        withoutyn ony ston,
And so sche dede the dowe,
        withoutyn ony bon.

Sche sente me the brere,
        withoutyn ony rynde,
Sche bad me love my lemman
        withoute longyng.

How schulde ony cherye
        be withoute ston?
And how schulde ony dowe
        ben withoute bon?

wortes] vegetables.   paxbrede] disk used in giving the
'kiss of peace' to the congregation.   drowryis] presents.
dowe] dove.

LOVE WITHOUT LONGING

How schulde any brere
  ben withoute rynde?
How schulde I love my lemman
  without longyng?

Quan the cherye was a flour,
  than hadde it non ston;
Quan the dowe was an ey,
  than hadde it non bon.

Quan the brere was onbred,
  than hadde it non rynd;
Quan the mayden hayt that sche lovit,
  sche is without longyng.

                  ANON.

11   *Song for my Lady*

NOW wolde I fayne sum merthis mak,
  Al only for my ladis sak,
    When I her se;
But nowe I am so far fro her
    It wilnot be.

Thow I be far out of her siht,
I am her man both day and nyght,
    And so wol be.
Therefore wolde as I love her
    She lovyd me.

brere] briar.   rynde] bark.   ey] egg.   onbred]
unopened.   hayt] has.

SONG FOR MY LADY

Whan she is mery, than am I gladde,
Whan she is sory, than am I sadde,
    And cause is whye,
For he levyth not that lovyd
    So wel as I.

She seith that she hath seen it write
That seldyn seyn is sone forgeit;
    Yt is not so,
For yn good feith, save only her,
    I love no mo.

Wherfor I pray bothe nyght and day
That she may cast alle care away,
    And leve in rest,
And evermore wherever she be
    To love me best.

And I to her to be so trewe,
And never to chaunge for no newe
    Unto my ende
And that I may in her service
    Ever to amend.   A. GODWIN.

M Y Gudame wes a gay wif, bot scho wes rycht
     gend,
   Scho duelt furth fer in to France, apon Falkland fellis;
Thay callit her Kynd Kittok, quhasa hir weill kend:
   Scho wes like a caldrone cruke cler under kellis;
Thay threpit that scho deit of thrist, and maid a gud end.

   Efter hir dede, scho dredit nought in hevin for to duell;
And sa to hevin the hieway driedless scho wend,
   Yit scho wanderit, and yeid by to ane elriche well.
      Scho met thar, as I wene,
        Ane ask rydand on a snaill,
        And cryit, 'Ourtane fallow, haill!'
        And raid ane inche behind the taill,
      Till it wes neir evin.

Sa scho had hap to be horsit to hir herbry,
   Att ane ailhous neir hevin, it nyghttit thaim thare;
Scho deit of thrist in this warld, that gert hir be so dry,
   Scho neuer eit, bot drank our mesur and mair.
Scho slepit quhill the morne at none, and rais airly;
   And to the yettis of hevin fast can the wif fair,
And by Sanct Petir, in at the yet, scho stall prevely:
   God lukit and saw hir lattin in, and lewch his hert sair.
      And than, yeris sevin
        Scho lewit a gud life,
        And wes our Ladyis hen wif:
        And held Sanct Petir at stryfe,
      Ay quhill scho wes in hevin.

cler under kellis] fair under her head-dress.   gert] caused
to be.   lewch] laughed.

THE BALLAD OF KYND KITTOK

Sche lukit out on a day, and thoght ryght lang
   To se the ailhous beside, in till an euill hour;
And out of hevin the hie gait cowth the wif gang
    For to get hir ane fresche drink, ye aill of hevin wes
     sour.
Scho come againe to hevinnis yet, quhen the bell rang,
   Sanct Petir hat hir with a club, quhill a gret clour
Rais in hir heid, becaus the wif yeid wrang.
    Whan to the ailhous agane scho ran, the pycharis to
    pour,
       And for to brew, and baik.
        Frendis, I pray you hertfully,
        Gif ye be thristy or dry,
        Drink with my Guddame, as ye ga by,
      Anys for my saik.

WILLIAM DUNBAR.

13   *Quod Dunbar to Kennedy*

THE erd sould trymbill, the firmament sould schaik,
   And all the air in vennamus suddane stink,
And all the diuillis of hell for redour quaik,
   To heir quhat I sould wryt, with pen and ynk;
   For and I flyt sum sege for schame sould sink,
The se sould birn, the mone sould thoill ecclippis,
Rochis sould ryfe, the warld sould hald no grippis,
   Sa loud of cair the commoun bell sould clynk.

   clour] lump.   redour] harsh treatment.   thoill] endure.

QUOD DUNBAR TO KENNEDY

Irsche brybour baird, wyle beggar with thy brattis,
 Cuntbittin crawdoun Kennedy, coward of kynd,
Evill farit and dryit, as Denseman on the rattis,
 Lyke as the gleddis had on thy gulesnowt dynd;
 Mismaid monstour, ilk mone owt of thy mynd,
Renunce, rebald, thy ryming, thow bot royis,
 Thy trechour tung hes tane ane heland strynd;
Ane lawland ers wald mak a bettir noyis.

Thow Lazarus, thow laithly lene tramort,
 To all the warld thow may example be,
To luk upoun thy gryslie peteous port,
 For hiddowis, haw, and holkit is thyne ee;
 Thy cheik bane bair, and blaiknit is thy ble;
Thy choip, thy choll, garris men for to leif chest;
 Thy gane it garris us think that we mon de:
I conjure the, thow hungert heland gaist.

The larbar lukis of thy lang lene craig,
 Thy pure pynit thrott, peilit and owt of ply,
Thy skolderit skin, hewd lyk ane saffrone bag,
 Garris men dispyt thar flesche, thow Spreit of Gy:
 Fy! feyndly front; fy! tykis face, fy! fy!
Ay loungand, lyk ane loikman on ane ledder;
 With hingit luik ay wallowand upone wry,
Lyke to ane stark theif glowrand in ane tedder.

tramort] dead body. haw and holkit] livid and hollow.
blaiknit] pallid. ble] complexion. choip] jaw. choll]
jowl. garris] causes. chest] wrangling. gane] face.
heland] highland. larbar] weak. craig] neck. pure
pynit] quite shrivelled up. peilit] bare. ply] condition.
skolderit] scorched. dispyt] despise. Gy] Guido
de Corvo. loungand] lounging. loikman] hangman.
glowrand] staring. tedder] noose.

QUOD DUNBAR TO KENNEDY

Nyse nagus, nipcaik, with thy schulderis narrow,
   Thow lukis lowsy, loun of lownis aw;
Hard hurcheoun, hirpland, hippit as ane harrow,
   Thy rigbane rattillis, and thy ribbis on raw,
Thy hanchis hirklis with hukebanis harth and haw,
Thy laithly lymis are lene as ony treis;
   Obey, theif baird, or I sall brek thy gaw,
Fowll carrybald, cry mercy on thy kneis.

Thow purehippit, ugly averill,
   With hurkland banis, holkand throw thy hyd,
Reistit and crynit as hangitman on hill,
   And oft beswakkit with ane ourhie tyd,
   Quhilk brewis mekle barret to thy bryd;
Hir cair is all to clenge thy cabroch howis,
   Quhair thow lyis sawsy in saphron, bak and syd,
Powderit with prymros, savrand all with clowis.

Forworthin wirling, I warne the it is wittin,
   How, skyttand skarth, thow hes the hurle behind;
Wan wraiglane wasp, ma wormis hes thow beschittin
   Nor thair is gers on grund or leif on lind;

nyse nagus] strange miser.   nipcaik] mean person.   aw]
all.   hurcheoun] hedgehog.   hirpland] limping.   rigbane]
backbone.   hirklis] contract.   hukebanis] haunch
bones.   harth] hard.   gaw] gall-bladder.   carrybald]
monster.   averill] old horse.   hurkland] coming together.
holkand] piercing.   reistit and crynit] dried and shrivelled
up.   beswakkit] splashed.   barret] trouble.   clenge]
cleanse.   cabroch] scraggy.   howis] houghs.   clowis]
cloves.   forworthin wirling] worthless little wretch.   wittin]
known.   skyttand skarth] excreting cormorant.   hurle]
diarrhoea.   wraiglane] wriggling.   nor] than.   gers]
grass.

QUOD DUNBAR TO KENNEDY

Thocht thow did first sic foly to my fynd,
Thow sall agane with ma witnes than I;
   Thy gulsoch gane dois on thy back it bind,
Thy hostand hippis lattis nevir thy hos go dry.

Thow held the burch lang with ane borrowit goun,
   And ane caprowsy barkit all with sweit,
And quhen the laidis saw the sa lyk a loun,
   Thay bickerit the with mony bae and bleit:
   Now upaland thow leivis on rubbit quheit,
Oft for ane caus thy burdclaith neidis no spredding,
   For thow hes nowthir for to drink nor eit,
Bot lyk ane berdles baird that had no bedding.

Strait Gibbonis air, that nevir ourstred ane hors,
   Bla berfute berne, in bair tyme wes thow borne;
Thow bringis the Carrik clay to Edinburgh Cors
   Upoun thy botingis, hobland, hard as horne;
   Stra wispis hingis owt, quhair that the wattis ar worne:
Cum thow agane to skar us with thy strais,
   We sall gar scale our sculis all the to scorne,
And stane the up the calsay quhair thow gais.

Off Edinburch the boyis as beis owt thrawis,
   And cryis owt ay, 'Heir cumis our awin queir Clerk!'
Than fleis thow lyk ane howlat chest with crawis,
   Quhill all the bichis at thy botingis dois bark:

gulsoch] jaundiced. hostand] coughing. caprowsy]
cape (?). barkit] hardened. bickerit] assailed. bae] baa.
rubbit quheit] rubbed wheat. air] heir. bair] needy.
Carrik] Ayrshire. botingis] boots. wattis] welts. skar]
scare. scale] dismiss. calsay] pavement. howlat] owl.

F

QUOD DUNBAR TO KENNEDY

Than carlingis cryis, 'Keip curches in the merk,
Our gallowis gaipis; lo! quhair ane greceles gais.'
    Ane uthir sayis, 'I se him want ane sark,
I reid yow, cummer, tak in your lynning clais.'

Than rynis thow doun the gait with gild of boyis,
    And all the toun tykis hingand in thy heilis;
Of laidis and lownis thair rysis sic ane noyis,
    Quhill runsyis rynis away with cairt and quheilis,
    And cager aviris castis bayth coillis and creilis,
For rerd of the and rattling of thy butis;
    Fische wyvis cryis, Fy! and castis doun skillis and skeilis;
Sum claschis the, sum cloddis the on the cutis.

Loun lyk Mahoun, be boun me till obey,
    Theif, or in greif mischeif sall the betyd;
Cry grace, tykis face, or I the chece and sley;
    Oule, rare and yowle, I sall defowll thy pryd;
    Peilet gled, baith fed and bred of bichis syd,
And lyk ane tyk, purspyk, quhat man settis by the!
    Forflittin, countbittin, beschittin, barkit hyd,
Clym ledder, fyle tedder, foule edder, I defy the.

Mauch muttoun, vyle buttoun, peilit gluttoun, air to
    Hilhouse;
    Rank beggar, ostir dregar, foule fleggar, in the flet;

carlingis] old women.   curches] kerchiefs.   cummer]
friend.   rynis] runnest.   gait] street.   runsyis] horses.
cager aviris] cart-horses.   coillis] coals.   creilis] wicker
baskets.   butis] boots.   skillis and skeilis] baskets and
pails.   claschis] slap hard.   cloddis] pelt.   cutis] ankles.
Mahoun] i.e. the devil.   mischeif] misfortune.   rare and
yowle] roar and howl.   peilet gled] plucked kite.   purspyk]
pickpocket.   ledder] ladder.   edder] adder.   ostir] oyster.

QUOD DUNBAR TO KENNEDY

Chittirlilling, ruch rilling, lik schilling in the milhouse;
  Baird rehator, theif of natour, fals tratour, feyndis gett;
   Filling of tauch, rak sauch, cry crauch, thow art our sett;
Muttoun dryver, girnall ryver, yadswyvar, fowll fell the:
  Herretyk, lunatyk, purspyk, carlingis pet,
Rottin crok, dirtin dok, cry cok, or I sall quell the.
      Quod Dunbar to Kennedy.

                WILLIAM DUNBAR.

14   *Care away*

    Care away away away
    care away for ever more

A LL that I may swynk or swet,
  my wyfe it wyll both drynk and ete,
and I sey ouht she wyl me bete.
  carfull ys my hart therfor.

If I sey ouht of hyr but good,
she loke on me as she war wod
and wyll me clouht abouht the hod.
  carfull ys my hart therfor.

If she wyll to the gud ale ryd,
me must trot all by hyr syd
and whan she drynk I must abyd.
  carfull ys my hart therfor.

If I say, it shal be thus,
she sey, Thou lyyst charll, Iwous,
wenest thou to overcome me thus?
  carfull ys my hart therfor.

and] if.   wod] mad.   Iwous] assuredly.

63

If ony man have such a wyfe to lede,
he shal know how *judicare* cam in the creed;
of hys penans God do hym meed.

    carfull ys my hart therfor.   ANON.

15   *Phyllyp Sparowe*

*P*LA *ce bo*,
  Who is there, who?
Di le xi,
Dame Margery;
Fa, re, my, my,
Wherfore and why, why?
For the sowle of Philip Sparowe,
That was late slayn at Carowe,
Among the Nones Blake,
For that swete soules sake,
And for all sparowes soules,
Set in our bederolles,
Pater noster qui,
With an *Ave Mari*,
And with the corner of a Crede,
The more shalbe your mede.

  Whan I remembre agayn
How mi Philyp was slayn,
Neuer halfe the payne
Was betwene you twayne,
Pyramus and Thesbe,
As than befell to me:
I wept and I wayled,
The tearys downe hayled;
But nothynge it auayled

64

PHYLLYP SPAROWE

To call Phylyp agayne,
Whom Gyb our cat hath slayne.

.   .   .   .   .   .

It was so prety a fole,
It wold syt on a stole,
And lerned after my scole
For to kepe his cut,
With, Phyllyp, kepe your cut!
It had a veluet cap,
And wold syt vpon my lap,
And seke after small wormes,
And somtyme white bred crommes;
And many tymes and ofte
Betwene my brestes softe
It wolde lye and rest;
It was propre and prest.
Somtyme he wolde gaspe
Whan he sawe a waspe;
A fly or a gnat,
He wolde flye at that;
And prytely he wold pant
Whan he saw an ant;
Lord, how he wolde pry
After the butterfly!
Lorde, how he wolde hop
After the gressop!
And whan I sayd, Phyp, Phyp,
Than he wold lepe and skyp,
And take me by the lyp.

fole] fool.   kepe his cut] keep his distance.   propre
and prest] pretty and lively.   gressop] grasshopper.

Alas, it wyll me slo,
That Phillyp is gone me fro!
  Si in i qui ta tes,
Alas, I was euyll at ease!
De pro fun dis cla ma vi,
Whan I sawe my sparowe dye!
     .   .   .

  For it wold come and go,
And fly so to and fro;
And on me it wolde lepe
Whan I was aslepe,
And his fethers shake
Wherewith he wolde make
Me often for to wake,
And for to take him in
Vpon my naked skyn;
God wot, we thought no syn:
What though he crept so lowe?
It was no hurt, I trowe,
He dyd nothynge, perde,
But syt vpon my kne:
Phyllyp, though he were nyse,
In him it was no vyse;
Phyllyp had leue to go
To pyke my lytell too;
Phillip myght be bolde
And do what he wolde;
Phillip wolde seke and take
All the flees blake
That he coulde there espye
With his wanton eye.
     .   .   .   .   .

  slo] kill.   nyse] wanton.   too] toe.

That vengeaunce I aske and crye,
By way of exclamacyon,
On all the hole nacyon
Of cattes wylde and tame;
God send them sorowe and shame!
That cat specyally
That slew so cruelly
My lytell prety sparowe
That I brought vp at Carowe.
   O cat of carlyshe kynde,
The fynde was in thy mynde
Whan thou my byrde vntwynde!
I wold thou haddest ben blynde!
The leopardes sauage,
The lyons in theyr rage,
Myght catche the in theyr pawes,
And gnawe the in theyr jawes!
The serpentes of Lybany
Myght stynge the venymously!
The dragones with their tonges
Might poyson thy lyuer and longes!
The mantycors of the montaynes
Myght fede them on thy braynes!
   Melanchates, that hounde
That plucked Acteon to the grounde,
Gaue hym his mortall wounde,
Chaunged to a dere,
The story doth appere,
Was chaunged to an harte:
So thou, foule cat that thou arte,

carlyshe kynde] churlish nature.   untwynde] de-
stroyed.   mantycors] human-headed monsters.

The selfe same hounde
Myght the confounde,
That his owne lord bote,
Myght byte asondre thy throte!
  Of Inde the gredy grypes
Myght tere out all thy trypes!
Of Arcady the beares
Might plucke awaye thyne eares!
The wylde wolfe Lycaon
Byte asondre thy backe bone!
Of Ethna the brennynge hyll,
That day and night brenneth styl,
Set in thy tayle a blase,
That all the world may gase
And wonder vpon the,
From Occyan the greate se
Vnto the Iles of Orchady,
From Tyllbery fery
To the playne of Salysbery!
So trayterously my byrde to kyll
That neuer ought the euyll wyll!

  Was neuer byrde in cage
More gentle of corage
In doynge his homage
Vnto his souerayne.
Alas, I say agayne,
Deth hath departed vs twayne!
The false cat hath the slayne:
Farewell, Phyllyp, adew!
Our Lorde thy soule reskew!

bote] bit.   grypes] griffins.   ought] owed.

PHYLLYP SPAROWE

Farewell without restore,
Farewell for euermore!

    .   .   .   .   .

    Kyrie, eleison,
    Christe, eleison,
    Kyrie, eleison!
For Phylyp Sparowes soule,
Set in our bederolle,
Let vs now whysper
A *Pater noster*.
Lauda, anima mea, Dominum!
To wepe with me loke that ye come,
All maner of byrdes in your kynd;
Se none be left behynde.
To mornynge loke that ye fall
With dolorous songes funerall,
Some to synge, and some to say,
Some to wepe, and some to pray,
Euery byrde in his laye.

    .   .   .   .   .

    But for the egle doth flye
Hyest in the skye,
He shall be the sedeane,
The quere to demeane,
As prouost pryncypall,
To teach them theyr ordynall;
Also the noble fawcon,
With the gerfawcon,

    sedeane] subdean.   demeane] rule.
           ordynall] ritual.

The tarsell gentyll,
They shall morne soft and styll
In theyr amysse of gray;
The sacre with them shall say
Dirige for Phyllyppes soule;
The goshauke shall haue a role
The queresters to controll;
The lanners and the marlyons
Shall stand in their morning gounes;
The hobby and the muskette
The sensers and the crosse shall fet;
The kestrell in all this warke
Shall be holy water clarke.

And now the darke cloudy nyght
Chaseth away Phebus bryght,
Taking his course toward the west,
God sende my sparoes sole good rest!
Requiem aeternam dona eis, Domine!
Fa, fa, fa, my, re, re,
A por ta in fe ri,
Fa, fa, fa, my, my.
    Credo videre bona Domini,
I pray God, Phillip to heuen may fly!
Domine, exaudi orationem meam!
To heuen he shall, from heuen he cam!
    Do mi nus vo bis cum!
Of al good praiers God send him sum!
        Oremus.
Deus, cui proprium est misereri et parcere,
On Phillips soule haue pyte!

sacre, lanners, marlyons, hobby, muskette, kestrell] various
kinds of hawks.

For he was a prety cocke,
And came of a gentyll stocke,
And wrapt in a maidenes smocke,
And cherysshed full dayntely,
Tyll cruell fate made him to dy:
Alas, for dolefull desteny!
But whereto shuld I
Lenger morne or crye?
To Jupyter I call,
Of heuen emperyall,
That Phyllyp may fly
Aboue the starry sky,
To treade the prety wren,
That is our Ladyes hen:
Amen, amen, amen!   JOHN SKELTON.

16   *To Maystres Isabell Pennell*

B Y saynt Mary, my lady,
    Your mammy and your dady
Brought forth a godely babi!
   My mayden Isabell,
Reflaring rosabell,
The flagrant camamell;
   The ruddy rosary,
The souerayne rosemary,
The praty strawbery;
   The columbyne, the nepte,
The ieloffer well set,
The propre vyolet;

reflaring rosabell] sweet smelling fair-rose.   flagrant]
fragrant.   rosary] rosebush.   nepte] catmint.   ieloffer]
gillyflower.   propre] pretty.

71

TO MAYSTRES ISABELL PENNELL

Enuwyd your colowre
Is lyke the dasy flowre
After the Aprill showre;
    Sterre of the morow gray,
The blossom on the spray,
The fresshest flowre of May;
    Maydenly demure,
Of womanhode the lure;
Wherfore I make you sure,
    It were an heuenly helth,
It were an endeles welth,
A lyfe for God hymselfe,
    To here this nightingale,
Amonge the byrdes smale,
Warbelynge in the vale,
Dug, dug,
Iug, iug,
Good yere and good luk,
With chuk, chuk, chuk, chuk!   John Skelton.

17   *Gup, Scot!*

GUP, Scot,
    Ye blot:
Laudate
Caudate,
Set in better
Thy pentameter.
This Dundas,
This Scottishe as,
He rymes and railes
That Englishmen haue tailes.

    enuwyd] tinted.   Gup] gee-up!

GUP, SCOT!

Skeltonus laureatus,
Anglicus natus,
Provocat Musas
Contra Dundas
Spurcissimum Scotum,
Undique notum,
Rustice fotum,
Vapide potum.
Skelton laureat
After this rate
Defendeth with his pen
All Englysh men
Agayn Dundas,
That Scottishe asse.
Shake thy tayle, Scot, lyke a cur,
For thou beggest at euery mannes dur:
Tut, Scot, I sey,
Go shake thy dog, hey!
Dundas of Galaway
With thy versyfyeng rayles
How they haue tayles.
By Jesu Christ,
Fals Scot, thou lyest:
But behynd in our hose
We bere there a rose
For thy Scottyshe nose,
A spectacle case
To couer thy face,
With tray deux ase.
A tolman to blot,
A rough foted Scot!

tray deux ase] trey, deuce, ace.   tolman] penman (?)

Dundas, sir knaue,
Why doste thow depraue
This royall reame,
Whose radiant beame
And relucent light
Thou hast in despite,
Thou donghyll knyght?
But thou lakest might,
Dundas, dronken and drowsy,
Skabed, scuruy, and lowsy,
Of vnhappy generacion
And most vngracious nacion.
Dundas,
That dronke asse,
That ratis and rankis,
That prates and prankes
On Huntley bankes,
Take this our thankes;
Dunde, Dunbar,
Walke, Scot,
Walke, sot,
Rayle not to far.   JOHN SKELTON.

18   *Speke, Parrot*

MY name is Parrot, a byrd of paradyse,
  By nature deuysed of a wonderous kynde,
Dyentely dyeted with dyuers dylycate spyce,
    Tyl Euphrates, that flode, dryueth me into Inde;
    Where men of that countrey by fortune me fynd,
And send me to greate ladyes of estate:
Then Parot must haue an almond or a date;

SPEKE, PARROT

A cage curyously caruen, with syluer pyn,
    Properly paynted, to be my couertowre;
A myrrour of glasse, that I may toote therin;
      These maidens ful mekely with many a diuers flowre
      Freshly they dresse, and make swete my bowre,
With, Speke, Parrot, I pray you, full curtesly they say;
Parrot is a goodly byrd, a pretty popagey:

With my becke bent, my lyttyl wanton eye,
    My fedders freshe as is the emrawde grene,
About my neck a cyrculet lyke the ryche rubye,
    My lyttyll leggys, my feet both fete and clene,
    I am a mynyon to wayt vppon a quene;
My proper Parrot, my lyttyl pretty foole;
With ladyes I lerne, and go with them to scole.

Hagh, ha, ha, Parrot, ye can laugh pretyly!
    Parrot hath not dyned of al this long day:
Lyke your pus cate, Parrot can mute and cry
    In Lattyn, in Ebrew, Araby, and Caldey;
    In Greke tong Parrot can bothe speke and say,
As Percyus, that poet, doth reporte of me,
Quis expedivit psittaco suum chaire?

Dowse French of Parryse Parrot can lerne,
    Pronounsynge my purpose after my properte,
With, *Perliez byen, Parrot, ou perlez rien*;
    With Douch, with Spanysh, my tong can agre;
    In Englysh to God Parrot can supple,
Cryst saue Kyng Henry the viii., our royall kyng,
The red rose in honour to florysh and sprynge!

      toote] peep.   mute] mew.   dowse] soft.

With Kateryne incomparable, our ryall quene also,
    That pereles pomegarnet, Chryst saue her noble grace!
Parrot, *saves habler Castiliano,*
      With *fidasso de cosso* in Turkey and in Trace;
      Vis consilii expers, as techith me Horace,
    Mole ruit sua, whose dictes ar pregnaunte,
    Souentez foys, Parrot, *en souenaunte.*

My lady maystres, dame Philology,
    Gaue me a gyfte in my nest whan I laye,
To lerne all language, and it to spake aptely:
    Now *pandez mory,* wax frantycke, some men saye;
    Phroneses for Freneses may not holde her way.
An almond now for Parrot, dilycatly drest;
In *Salve festa dies, toto* theyr doth best.

Moderata juvant, but *toto* doth excede;
    Dyscressyon is moder of noble vertues all;
Myden agan in Greke tonge we rede;
    But reason and wyt wantyth theyr prouyncyall
    When wylfulnes is vycar generall.
Haec res acu tangitur, Parrot, *par ma foy:*
Ticez vous, Parrot, *tenez vous coye.*

Besy, besy, besy, and besynes agayne!
    Que pensez voz, Parrot? what meneth this besynes?
Vitulus in Oreb troubled Arons brayne,
    Melchisedeck mercyfull made Moloc mercyles;
    To wyse is no vertue, to medlyng, to restles;
In mesure is tresure, *cum sensu maturato;*
Ne tropo sanno, no tropo mato.

     .   .   .   .   .   .

What is this to purpose? 'Ouer in a whynny meg!'
   Hop Lobyn of Lowdeon wald haue e byt of bred;
The iebet of Baldock was made for Jack Leg;
   An arrow vnfethered and without an hed,
   A bagpype without blowynge standeth in no sted:
Some run to far before, some run to far behynde,
Some be to churlysshe, and some be to kynde.

  .   .   .   .

But ware the cat, Parot, ware the fals cat!
   With, Who is there? a mayd? nay, nay, I trow:
Ware ryat, Parrot, ware ryot, ware that!
   Mete, mete for Parrot, mete, I say, how!
   Thus dyuers of language by lernyng I grow:
With, Bas me, swete Parrot, bas me, swete swete;
To dwell amonge ladyes Parrot is mete.

Parrot, Parrot, Parrot, praty popigay!
   With my beke I can pyke my lyttel praty too;
My delyght is solas, pleasure, dysporte, and pley;
   Lyke a wanton, whan I wyll, I rele to and froo:
   Parot can say, *Caesar, ave*, also;
But Parrot hath no fauour to Esebon:
Aboue all other byrdis, set Parrot alone.

Ulula, Esebon, for Ieromy doth wepe!
   Sion is in sadnes, Rachell ruly doth loke;
Madionita Ietro, our Moyses kepyth his shepe;
Gedeon is gon, that Zalmane vndertoke,
Oreb *et* Zeb, of *Judicum* rede the boke;
Now Geball, Amon, and Amaloch,—harke, harke!
Parrot pretendith to be a bybyll clarke.

  .   .   .   .   .   .

iebet] gibbet.   ryat, ryot] riot.   bas] kiss.   ruly] ruefully.

G

SPEKE, PARROT

Monon calon agaton,
Quod Parato
In Graeco.

Let Parrot, I pray you, haue lyberte to prate,
  For *aurea lingua Graeca* ought to be magnyfyed,
Yf it were cond perfytely, and after the rate,
  As *lingua Latina,* in scole matter occupyed;
  But our Grekis theyr Greke so well haue applyed,
That they cannot say in Greke, rydynge by the way,
How, hosteler, fetche my hors a botell of hay!

·   ·   ·   ·   ·   ·

For Parot is no churlish chowgh, nor no flekyd pye,
  Parrot is no pendugum, that men call a carlyng,
Parrot is no woodecocke, nor no butterfly,
  Parrot is no stameryng stare, that men call a starlyng;
  But Parot is my owne dere harte and my dere derling;
Melpomene, that fayre mayde, she burneshed his beke:
I pray you, let Parrot haue lyberte to speke.

Parrot is a fayre byrd for a lady;
  God of his goodnes him framed and wrought;
When Parrot is ded, she dothe not putrefy:
  Ye, all thyng mortall shall torne vnto nought,
  Except mannes soule, that Chryst so dere bought;
That neuer may dye, nor neuer dye shall:
Make moche of Parrot, the popegay ryall.

For that pereles prynce that Parrot dyd create,
  He made you of nothynge by his magistye:
Poynt well this probleme that Parrot doth prate,

  pendugum] penguin (?)   **carlyng**] old woman.
  78

SPEKE, PARROT

And remembre amonge how Parrot and ye
  Shall lepe from this lyfe, as mery as we be;
Pompe, pryde, honour, ryches, and worldly lust,
Parrot sayth playnly, shall tourne all to dust.

   .   .   .   .   .

Le dereyn Lenveoy

Prepayre yow, Parrot, breuely your passage to take,
  Of Mercury vndyr the trynall aspecte,
And sadlye salute ower solen syre Sydrake,
  And shewe hym that all the world dothe coniecte,
  How the maters he mellis in com to small effecte;
For he wantythe of hys wyttes that all wold rule alone;
Hyt is no lytyll bordon to bere a grete mylle stone:

To bryng all the see into a cheryston pytte,
  To nombyr all the sterrys in the fyrmament,
To rule ix realmes by one mannes wytte,
  To suche thynges ympossybyll reason cannot consente:
Muche money, men sey, there madly he hathe spente:
Parrot, ye may prate thys vndyr protestacion,
Was neuyr suche a senatour syn Crystes incarnacion.

Wherfor he may now come agayne as he wente,
  Non sine postica sanna, as I trowe,
From Calys to Dovyr, to Caunterbury in Kente,
  To make reconyng in the resseyte how Robyn loste hys
    bowe,
  To sowe corne in the see sande, ther wyll no crope
    growe.
Thow ye be tauntyd, Parotte, with tonges attayntyd,
Yet your problemes ar preignaunte, and with loyalte
  acquayntyd.   JOHN SKELTON.

trynall] threefold.   solen] sullen.   coniecte] conjecture.

'A, MY dere, a, my dere Son,'
   Seyd Mary, 'A, my dere;
A, my dere, a, my dere Son,'
   Seyd Mary, 'A, my dere;
Kys thy moder, Jhesu,
Kys thi moder, Jhesu,
   With a lawghyng chere.'

This endurs nyght
I sawe a syght
   All in my slepe:
Mary, that may,
She sang lullay
   And sore did wepe.
To kepe she sought
Full fast about
   Her Son from colde;
Joseph seyd, 'Wiff,
My joy, my lyff,
   Say what ye wolde.'
'Nothyng, my spowse,
Is in this howse
   Unto my pay;
My Sone, a Kyng
That made all thyng,
Lyth in hay.'

'My moder dere,
Amend your chere,
   And now be still;

This endurs nyght] a night or two ago.   may] maiden.
pay] liking.

Thus for to lye,
It is sothely
   My Fadirs will.
Derision,
Gret passion
Infynytly, infynytely,
As it is fownd,
Many a wownd
   Suffyr shall I.
On Calvery,
That is so hye,
   Ther shall I be,
Man to restore,
Naylit full sore
   Uppon a tre.'

ANON.

20   *Under the Leaves green*

WHO shall have my fayre lady?
   Who shall have my faire lady?
Who but I, who but I, who but I?
  Under the levys grene,
  Under the levys grene.

The fayrest man
That best love can,
Dandirly, dandirly, dandirly dan,
  Under the levys grene,
  Under the levys grene.

ANON.

81

MY lady is a prety on,
　　A prety, prety, prety on,
My lady is a prety on
　　As ever I saw.

She is gentyll and also wyse;
Of all other she berith the price
　　That ever I saw.

To here hir syng, to se her dance!
She wyll the best herselfe advance
　　That ever I saw.

To se her fyngers that be so small!
In my consail she passeth all
　　That ever I saw.

Nature in her hath wonderly wroght;
Crist never sych another bowght
　　That ever I saw.

I have sene many that have bewty;
Yet is ther non lyk to my lady
　　That ever I saw.

Therfor I dare this boldly say:
I shall have the best and farest may
　　That ever I saw.

ANON.

berith the price] has the pre-eminence.

THE maidens came
   When I was in my mother's bower,
I had all that I would.
   The bailey beareth the bell away;
   The lily, the rose, the rose I lay.
The silver is white, red is the gold;
The robes they lay in fold.
   The bailey beareth the bell away;
   The lily, the rose, the rose I lay.
And through the glass windows shines the sun.
How should I love, and I so young?
   The bailey beareth the bell away;
   The lily, the rose, the rose I lay.   ANON.

23   *Little John Nobody*

IN december, when the days draw to be short,
   After november, when the nights wax noisome and long;
As I past by a place privily at a port,
I saw one sit by himself making a song:
His last talk of trifles, who told with his tongue
That few were fast i' th' faith. I freyned that freak,
Whether he wanted wit, or some had done him wrong.
   He said, he was little John Nobody, that durst not
      speak.

John Nobody, quoth I, what news? thou soon note and tell
What manner men thou mean, thou art so mad.
He said, These gay gallants, that will construe the gospel,
As Solomon the sage, with semblance full sad;

         freyned] asked.   freak] man.

LITTLE JOHN NOBODY

To discuss divinity they nought adread;
More meet it were for them to milk kye at a fleyk.
Thou liest, quoth I, thou losel, like a lewd lad.
    He said he was little John Nobody, that durst not
    speak.

It is meet for every man on this matter to talk,
And the glorious gospel ghostly to have in mind;
It is sooth said, that sect but much unseemly skalk,
As boys babble in books, that in scripture are blind:
Yet to their fancy soon a cause will find;
As to live in lust, in lechery to leyk:
Such caitives count to become of Cain's kind;
    But that I, little John Nobody durst not speak.

For our reverend father hath set forth an order,
Our service to be said in our seignour's tongue;
As Solomon the sage set forth the scripture;
Our suffrages, and services, with many a sweet song,
With homilies, and godly books us among,
That no stiff, stubborn stomachs we should freyk:
But wretches nere worse to do poor men wrong;
    But that I little John Nobody dare not speak.

For bribery was never so great, since born was our Lord,
And whoredom was never less hated, sith Christ harrowed
      hell,
And poor men are so sore punished commonly through the
      world,
That it would grieve any one, that good is, to hear tell.

    fleyk] stall.   losel] scoundrel.   leyk] play.   freyk]
indulge.   nere] were never.

LITTLE JOHN NOBODY

For al the homilies and good books, yet their hearts be so
    quell,
That if a man do amiss, with mischief they will him
    wreak;
The fashion of these new fellows is so vile and fell:
    But that I little John Nobody dare not speak.

Thus to live after their lust, that life would they have,
And in lechery to leyk al their long life;
For all the preaching of Paul, yet many a proud knave
Wil move mischief in their mind both to maid and wife
To bring them in advoutry, or else, they wil strife,
And in brawling about bawdry, God's commandments
    break:
But of these frantic ill fellows, few of them do thrife;
    Though I little John Nobody dare not speak.

If thou company with them, they will currishly carp, and
    not care
According to their foolish fantasy; but fast will they
    naught:
Prayer with them is but prating; therefore they it forbear:
Both alms deeds, and holiness, they hate it in their thought:
Therefore pray we to that prince, that with his blood us
    bought,
That he will mend that is amiss: for many a manful freyk
Is sorry for these sects, though they say little or nought;
    And that I little John Nobody dare not once speak.

Thus in no place, this Nobody, in no time I met,
Where no man, ne nought was, nor nothing did appear;
Through the sound of a synagogue for sorrow I swet,
That *Aeolus* through the echo did cause me to hear.

        advoutry] adultery.

85

Then I drew me down into a dale, whereas the dumb deer
Did shiver for a shower, but I shunted from a freyk:
For I would no wight in this world wist who I were,
    But little John Nobody, that dare not once speak.

ANON.

24   *A Maid of Kent*

THERE was a maid come out of Kent,
    Dainty love, dainty love;
There was a maide came out of Kent,
    Dangerous be:
There was a maid came out of Kent,
Fair, proper, small and gent,
As ever upon the ground went,
    For so should it be.   ANON.

25   *I had a little Nut-tree*

I HAD a little nut-tree, nothing would it bear
    But a golden nutmeg and a silver pear;
The King of Spain's daughter came to visit me,
And all for the sake of my little nut-tree.
I skipp'd over water, I danced over sea,
And all the birds in the air couldn't catch me.

ANON.

26   *Hey diddle diddle*

SING hey diddle diddle, the cat and the fiddle,
    The cow jumped over the moon;
The little dog laughed to see such craft,
    And the dish ran away with the spoon. ANON.

27 *Prayer*

MATTHEW, Mark, Luke, and John,
    Bless the bed that I lie on,
Four corners to my bed,
Four angels round my head,
One to watch, one to pray,
And two to bear my soul away.   ANON.

28 *A Nonsense Carol*

MY heart of gold as true as steel,
    As I me leanéd to a bough,
In faith but if ye love me well,
    Lord, so Robin lough!

My lady went to Canterbury,
    The saint to be her boot:
She met with Kate of Malmesbury:
    Why sleepest thou in an apple root?

Nine mile to Michaelmas,
    Our dame began to brew;
Michael set his mare to grass,
    Lord, so fast it snew!

For you, love, I brake my glass,
    Your gown is furred with blue;
The devil is dead, for there I was;
    Iwis it is full true.

And if ye sleep, the cock will crow,
    True heart, think what I say;
Jackanapes will make a mow;
    Look who dare say him nay.

lough] laughed.   snew] snowed.   look] take care.

I pray you have me now in mind,
    I tell you of the matter;
He blew his horn against the wind;
    The crow goeth to the water.

Yet I tell you mickle more;
    The cat lieth in the cradle;
I pray you keep true heart in store;
    A penny for a ladle.

I swear by Saint Katharine of Kent,
    The goose goeth to the green;
All our doggés tail is brent,
    It is not as I ween.

Tirlery lorpin, the laverock sang,
    So merrily pipes the sparrow,
The cow brake loose, the rope ran home,
    Sir, God give you good-morrow!   ANON.

29   *King Orfeo*

A Shetland Ballad

I

DER lived a king inta da aste,
    Scowan ürla grün
Der lived a lady in da wast.
    Whar giorten han grün oarlac.

II

Dis king he has a huntin gaen,
He's left his Lady Isabel alane.

aste] east.   *Scowan, &c.*] Early green's the wood (?)   *Whar
giorten, &c.*] Where the hart goes yearly (?)

88

KING ORFEO

'Oh I wis ye'd never gaen away,
For at your hame is döl an wae.

IV

'For da king o Ferrie we his daert,
Has pierced your lady to da hert.'

.   .   .   .   .   .

V

And aifter dem da king has gaen,
But when he cam it was a grey stane.

VI

Dan he took oot his pipes ta play,
Bit sair his hert wi döl an wae.

VII

And first he played da notes o noy,
An dan he played da notes o joy.

VIII

An dan he played da göd gabber reel,
Dat meicht ha made a sick hert hale.

IX

'Noo come ye in inta wir ha',
An come ye in among wis a'.'

X

Now he's gaen in inta der ha',
An he's gaen in among dem a'.

döl] grief.   noy] grief.   da göd gabber reel] the rollick-
ing dance-tune.   wir] our.   wis] us.

XI

Dan he took out his pipes to play,
Bit sair his hert wi döl an wae.

XII

An first he played da notes o noy,
An dan he played da notes o joy.

XIII

An dan he played da göd gabber reel,
Dat meicht ha made a sick hert hale.

XIV

'Noo tell to us what ye will hae:
What sall we gie you for your play?'—

XV

'What I will hae I will you tell,
An dat's me Lady Isabel.'—

XVI

'Yees tak your lady, an yees gaeng hame,
An yees be king ower a' your ain.'

XVII

He's taen his lady, an he's gaen hame,
An noo he's king ower a' his ain.   ANON.

30   *My dancing Day*

TO-MORROW shall be my dancing day:
    I would my true love did so chance
To see the legend of my play,
    To call my true love to my dance:
        Sing O my love, O my love, my love, my love;
        This have I done for my true love.

90

MY DANCING DAY

Then was I born of a virgin pure,
    Of her I took fleshly substánce;
Thus was I knit to man's natúre,
    To call my true love to my dance:

In a manger laid and wrapped I was,
    So very poor, this was my chance,
Betwixt an ox and a silly poor ass,
    To call my true love to my dance:

Then afterwards baptized I was;
    The Holy Ghost on me did glance,
My Father's voice heard from above,
    To call my true love to my dance:

Into the desert I was led,
    Where I fasted without substánce;
The devil bade me make stones my bread,
    To have me break my true love's dance:

The Jews on me they made great suit,
    And with me made great variance,
Because they loved darkness rather than light,
    To call my true love to my dance:

For thirty pence Judas me sold,
    His covetousness for to advance;
'Mark whom I kiss, the same do hold,'
    The same is he shall lead the dance:

Before Pilate the Jews me brought,
    Where Barabbas had deliveránce;
They scourged me and set me at nought,
    Judged me to die to lead the dance:

Then on the cross hangéd I was,
  Where a spear to my heart did glance;
There issued forth both water and blood,
  To call my true love to my dance:

Then down to hell I took my way
  For my true love's deliveránce,
And rose again on the third day,
  Up to my true love and the dance:

Then up to heaven I did ascend,
  Where now I dwell in sure substánce,
On the right hand of God, that man
  May come unto the general dance.   ANON.

31 *The Bailiff's Daughter of Islington*

I

THERE was a youth, and a well-belovéd youth,
  And he was an esquire's son,
He loved the bailiff's daughter dear,
  That lived in Islington.

II

But she was coy, and she would not believe
  That he did love her so,
No, nor at any time she would
  Any countenance to him show.

III

But when his friends did understand
  His fond and foolish mind,
They sent him up to fair London,
  An apprentice for to bind.

IV

And when he had been seven long years,
  And his love he had not seen;
'Many a tear have I shed for her sake
  When she little thought of me.'

V

All the maids of Islington
  Went forth to sport and play;
All but the bailiff's daughter dear;
  She secretly stole away.

VI

She put off her gown of grey,
  And put on her puggish attire;
She's up to fair London gone,
  Her true-love to require.

VII

As she went along the road,
  The weather being hot and dry,
There was she aware of her true-love,
  At length came riding by.

VIII

She stept to him, as red as any rose,
  And took him by the bridle-ring:
'I pray you, kind sir, give me one pennỳ,
  To ease my weary limb.'—

IX

'I prithee, sweetheart, canst thou tell me
  Where that thou wast born?'—
'At Islington, kind sir,' said she,
  'Where I have had many a scorn.'—

puggish] tramp's.

X

'I prithee, sweetheart, canst thou tell me
  Whether thou dost know
The bailiff's daughter of Islington?'—
  'She's dead, sir, long ago.'—

XI

'Then will I sell my goodly steed,
  My saddle and my bow;
I will into some far countrey,
  Where no man doth me know.'—

XII

'Oh stay, Oh stay, thou goodly youth!
  She's alive, she is not dead;
Here she standeth by thy side,
  And is ready to be thy bride.'—

XIII

'Oh farewell grief, and welcome joy,
  Ten thousand times and o'er!
For now I have seen my own true-love,
  That I thought I should have seen no more.'

ANON.

32 *Jennifer gentle and Rosemary*

THERE was a knicht riding frae the east,
    Jennifer gentle an' rosemaree.
Who had been wooing at monie a place,
    As the doo flies owre the mulberry tree.

He cam' unto a widow's door,
And speird whare her three dochters were.

94

JENNIFER GENTLE AND ROSEMARY

'The auldest ane's to a washing gane,
The second's to a baking gane.

The youngest ane's to a wedding gane,
And it will be nicht or she be hame.'

He sat him doun upon a stane,
Till thir three lasses cam' tripping hame.

The auldest ane she let him in,
And pinned the door wi' a siller pin.

The second ane she made his bed,
And laid saft pillows unto his head.

The youngest ane was bauld and bricht,
And she tarried for words wi' this unco knicht.—

'Gin ye will answer me questions ten,
The morn ye sall be made my ain:—

'O what is higher nor the tree?
And what is deeper nor the sea?

'Or what is heavier nor the lead?
And what is better nor the bread?

'Or what is whiter nor the milk?
Or what is safter nor the silk?

'Or what is sharper nor a thorn?
Or what is louder nor a horn?

'Or what is greener nor the grass?
Or what is waur nor a woman was?'

'O heaven is higher nor the tree,
And hell is deeper nor the sea.

'O sin is heavier nor the lead,
The blessing's better nor the bread.

'The snaw is whiter nor the milk,
And the down is safter nor the silk.

'Hunger is sharper nor a thorn,
And shame is louder nor a horn.

'The pies are greener nor the grass,
And Clootie's waur nor a woman was.'

As sune as she the fiend did name,
 Jennifer gentle an' rosemaree,
He flew awa' in a blazing flame,
 As the doo flies owre the mulberry tree.

ANON.

33   *Sir John Graeme and Barbara Allan*

IT was in and about the Martinmas time,
 When the green leaves were a falling;
That Sir John Graeme o' the west country,
 Fell in love wi' Barbara Allan.

He sent his men down through the town,
 To the place wher she was dwelling;
'O haste and come to my master dear,
 Gin ye be Barbara Allan.'

O hooly, hooly rose she up,
 To the place wher he was lying;
And when she drew the curtain by,
 'Young man, I think ye're dying.'

'O it's I'm sick, and very very sick,
    And 'tis a' for Barbara Allan.'
'O the better for me ye's never be,
    Though your hearts blood were a spilling.

'O dinna ye mind, young man,' said she,
    'When ye war in the tavern a drinking;
How ye made the healths gae round and round,
    And slighted Barbara Allan?'

He turn'd his face unto the wall,
    And death was with him dealing;
'Adieu! adieu! my dear friends all,
    And be kind to Barbara Allan.'

And slowly, slowly raise she up,
    And slowly, slowly left him;
And sighing said, she could not stay,
    Since death of life had reft him.

She had not gane a mile but twa,
    When she heard the dead-bell ringing,
And every jow the dead-bell geid,
    It cry'd, woe to Barbara Allan!

'O mither, mither, mak my bed,
    O mak it saft and narrow:
Since my love died for me to-day,
    I'll die for him to-morrow.'   ANON.

34   *Bonny George Campbell*

I

HIE upon Hielands,
    And laigh upon Tay,
Bonny George Campbell
    Rade out on a day

Saddled and bridled,
 Sae gallant to see,
Hame cam' his gude horse,
 But never cam' he.

II

Down ran his auld mither,
 Greetin' fu' sair;
Out ran his bonny bride,
 Reaving her hair;
'My meadow lies green,
 And my corn is unshorn,
My barn is to bigg,
 And my babe is unborn.'

III

Saddled and bridled,
 And booted rade he:
A plume in his helmet,
 A sword at his knee;
But toom cam' his saddle
 A' bluidy to see,
O hame cam' his gude horse,
 But never cam' he!   ANON.

35 *The Fause Knicht upon the Road*

'O WHARE are ye gaun?'
 Quo' the fause knicht upon the road;
'I'm gaun to the scule,'
Quo' the wee boy, and still he stude.

  bigg] build. toom] empty.

THE FAUSE KNICHT UPON THE ROAD

'What is that upon your back?'
Quo' the fause knicht upon the road;
'Atweel it is my bukes,'
Quo' the wee boy, and still he stude.

'What's that ye've got in your arm?'
Quo' the fause knicht upon the road;
'Atweel it is my peit,'
Quo' the wee boy, and still he stude.

'Wha's aucht they sheep?'
Quo' the fause knicht upon the road;
'They're mine and my mither's,'
Quo' the wee boy, and still he stude.

'How monie o' them are mine?'
Quo' the fause knicht upon the road;
'A' they that hae blue tails,'
Quo' the wee boy, and still he stude.

'I wiss ye were on yon tree:'
Quo' the fause knicht upon the road;
'And a gude ladder under me,'
Quo' the wee boy, and still he stude.

'And the ladder for to break,'
Quo' the fause knicht upon the road;
'And you for to fa' down,'
Quo' the wee boy, and still he stude.

'I wiss ye were in yon sie,'
Quo' the fause knicht upon the road;
'And a gude bottom under me,'
Quo' the wee boy, and still he stude.

peit] a peat carried to school as a contribution to the firing.

'And the bottom for to break,'
Quo' the fause knicht upon the road;
'And ye to be drowned,'
Quo' the wee boy, and still he stude.   ANON.

36   *The Cherry-tree Carol*

JOSEPH was an old man,
  and an old man was he,
When he wedded Mary,
  in the land of Galilee.

Joseph and Mary walked
  through an orchard good,
Where was cherries and berries,
  so red as any blood.

Joseph and Mary walked
  through an orchard green,
Where was berries and cherries,
  as thick as might be seen.

O then bespoke Mary,
  so meek and so mild:
'Pluck me one cherry, Joseph,
  for I am with child.'

O then bespoke Joseph,
  with words most unkind:
'Let him pluck thee a cherry
  that brought thee with child.'

O then bespoke the babe,
  within his mother's womb:
'Bow down then the tallest tree,
  for my mother to have some.'

THE CHERRY-TREE CAROL

Then bowèd down the highest tree
  unto his mother's hand;
Then she cried, 'See, Joseph,
  I have cherries at command.'

'O eat your cherries, Mary,
  O eat your cherries, now;
O eat your cherries, Mary,
  that grow upon the bough.'

As Joseph was a walking,
  he heard an angel sing:
'This night shall be born
  our heavenly king.

'He neither shall be born
  in housen nor in hall,
Nor in the place of Paradise,
  but in an ox's stall.

'He neither shall be clothed
  in purple nor in pall,
But all in fair linen,
  as were babies all.

'He neither shall be rocked
  in silver nor in gold,
But in a wooden cradle,
  that rocks on the mould.

'He neither shall be christened
  in white wine nor red,
But with fair spring water,
  with which we were christened.'

Then Mary took her babe,
    and sat him on her knee,
Saying, 'My dear son, tell me
    what this world will be.'

'O I shall be as dead, mother,
    as the stones in the wall;
O the stones in the streets, mother,
    shall mourn for me all.

'Upon Easter-day, mother,
    my uprising shall be;
O the sun and the moon, mother,
    shall both rise with me.'   ANON.

37   *Song of Sixpence*

SING a song o' sixpence,
    A bagful of rye;
Four and twenty blackbirds,
    Baked in a pie.
And when the pie was opened,
    The birds began to sing,
And was not this a dainty dish
    To set before a king?

The king was in the parlour,
    Counting o'er his money;
The queen was in the kitchen,
    Eating bread and honey;
The maid was in the garden,
    Laying out the clothes,
Up came a magpie
    And bit off her nose.   ANON.

AS I sat on a sunny bank,
A sunny bank, a sunny bank,
As I sat on a sunny bank
On Christmas Day in the morning.

I saw three ships come sailing by,
Come sailing by, come sailing by,
I saw three ships come sailing by,
On Christmas Day in the morning.

And who d'you think were on the ship,
Were on the ship, were on the ship,
And who d'you think were on the ship
But Joseph and his Fair Lady.

O he did whistle and she did sing,
And all the bells on earth did ring
For joy our Saviour Christ was born
On Christmas Day in the morning.

ANON.

39 *Blow the Winds, I-ho!*

THERE was a shepherd's son,
He kept sheep on yonder hill;
He laid his pipe and his crook aside,
And there he slept his fill.
And blow the winds, I-ho!
Sing, blow the winds, I-ho!
Clear away the morning dew,
And blow the winds, I-ho!

BLOW THE WINDS, I-HO!

He lookéd east, he lookéd west,
    He took another look,
And there he spied a lady gay,
    Was dipping in a brook.

She said, 'Sir, don't touch my mantle,
    Come, let my clothes alone,
I will give you as much white money
    As you can carry home.'

'I will not touch your mantle,
    I'll let your clothes alone,
I'll take you out of the water clear,
    My dear, to be my own.'

He did not touch her mantle,
    He let her clothes alone,
But he took her from the clear water,
    And all to be his own.

He set her on a milk-white steed,
    Himself upon another,
And there they rode along the road,
    Like sister and like brother.

And as they rode along the road,
    He spied some cocks of hay;
'Yonder,' he says, 'is a lovely place
    For men and maids to play.'

And when they came to her father's gate,
    She pulléd at a ring,
And ready was the proud porter
    For to let the lady in.

And when the gates were opened,
   This lady jumpéd in;
She says, 'You are a fool without,
   And I'm a maid within.

'Good morrow, to you, modest boy,
   I thank you for your care,
If you had been what you should have been,
   I would not have left you there.

'There is a horse in my father's stable,
   He stands behind the thorn,
He shakes his head above the trough,
   But dares not prie the corn.

'There is a bird in my father's flock,
   A double comb he wears,
He flaps his wings and crows full loud,
   But a capon's crest he bears.

'There is a flower in my father's garden,
   They call it marygold,
The fool that will not when he may
   He shall not when he wold.'

Said the shepherd's son, as he doft his shoon,
   'My feet they shall run bare,
But if ever I meet another maid,
   I rede that maid beware.'   Anon.

40   *Willie Macintosh*

I

'TURN, Willie Macintosh,
   Turn, I bid you;
Gin ye burn Auchindown,
   Huntly will head you.'—

II

'Head me or hang me,
    That canna fley me;
I'll burn Auchindown
    Ere the life lea' me.'

III

Coming down Deeside,
    In a clear morning,
Auchindown was in flame,
    Ere the cock-crawing.

IV

But coming o'er Cairn Croom,
    And looking down, man,
I saw Willie Macintosh
    Burn Auchindown, man.

V

'Bonnie Willie Macintosh,
    Whare left ye your men?'—
'I left them in the Stapler,
    But they'll never come hame.'

VI

'Bonny Willie Macintosh,
    Whare now is your men?'—
'I left them in the Stapler,
    Sleeping in their sheen.'   ANON.

    fley] frighten.

I

ALL the trees they are so high,
  The leaves they are so green,
The day is past and gone, sweet-heart,
  That you and I have seen.
    It is cold winter's night,
    You and I must bide alone:
      Whilst my pretty lad is young
      And is growing.

II

In a garden as I walked,
  I heard them laugh and call;
There were four and twenty playing there,
  They played with bat and ball.
    O the rain on the roof,
    Here and I must make my moan:
      Whilst my pretty lad is young
      And is growing.

III

I listen'd in the garden,
  I lookèd o'er the wall;
'Midst five and twenty gallants there
  My love exceeded all.
    O the wind on the thatch,
    Here and I alone must weep:
      Whilst my pretty lad is young
      And is growing.

IV

O father, father dear,
　Great wrong to me is done,
That I should married be this day,
　Before the set of sun.
　　　At the huffle of the gale,
　　　Here I toss and cannot sleep:
　　　　Whilst my pretty lad is young
　　　　And is growing.

V

My daughter, daughter dear,
　If better be, more fit,
I'll send him to the court awhile,
　To point his pretty wit.
　　　But the snow, snowflakes fall,
　　　O and I am chill as dead:
　　　　Whilst my pretty lad is young
　　　　And is growing.

VI

To let the lovely ladies know
　They may not touch and taste,
I'll bind a bunch of ribbons red
　About his little waist.
　　　But the raven hoarsely croaks,
　　　And I shiver in my bed;
　　　　Whilst my pretty lad is young
　　　　And is growing.

VII

I married was, alas,
  A lady high to be,
In court and stall and stately hall,
  And bower of tapestry.
      But the bell did only knell,
        And I shuddered as one cold:
          When I wed the pretty lad
            Not done growing.

VIII

At fourteen he wedded was,
  A father at fifteen,
At sixteen's face was white as milk,
  And then his grave was green;
      And the daisies were outspread,
        And buttercups of gold,
          O'er my pretty lad so young
            Now ceased growing.

ANON.

42 *The Lion and the Unicorn*

THE lion and the unicorn,
      Fighting for the crown,
The lion beat the unicorn
  All thro' the town,
And when he had beat him out,
  He beat him in again;
He beat him three times over,
  His power to maintain.

ANON.

I

UNHAPPY Verse, the witness of my unhappy state,
  Make thyself flutt'ring wings of thy fast flying
    Thought, and fly forth unto my Love, wheresoever
      she be:
Whether lying restless in heavy bed, or else
  Sitting so cheerless at the cheerful board, or else
  Playing alone careless on her heavenly virginals.
If in bed, tell her, that my eyes can take no rest;
  If at board, tell her, that my mouth can eat no meat;
  If at her virginals, tell her, I can hear no mirth.
Askéd, why? say: Waking love suffereth no sleep:
  Say, that raging love doth appal the weak stomach:
  Say, that lamenting love marreth the musical.
Tell her, that her pleasures were wont to lull me asleep:
  Tell her, that her beauty was wont to feed mine eyes:
  Tell her, that her sweet tongue was wont to make me
    mirth.
Now do I nightly waste, wanting my kindly rest:
  Now do I daily starve, wanting my lively food:
  Now do I always die, wanting thy timely mirth.
And if I waste, who will bewail my heavy chance?
  And if I starve, who will record my curséd end?
  And if I die, who will say: 'This was, Immerito'?

                  EDMUND SPENSER.

44   *Bethsabe's Song*

HOT sun, cool fire, tempered with sweet air,
  Black shade, fair nurse, shadow my white hair:
Shine, sun; burn, fire; breathe, air, and ease me;
Black shade, fair nurse, shroud me and please me:

Shadow, my sweet nurse, keep me from burning,
Make not my glad cause cause of mourning.
    Let not my beauty's fire
    Inflame unstaid desire,
    Nor pierce any bright eye
    That wandereth lightly.

GEORGE PEELE.

45   *Song*

WHEN as the rye reach to the chin,
    And chopcherry, chopcherry ripe within,
Strawberries swimming in the cream,
And school-boys playing in the stream;
    Then O, then O, then O my true love said,
      Till that time come again,
    She could not live a maid.

GEORGE PEELE.

46   *A Voice speaks from the Well*

FAIR maiden, white and red,
    Comb me smooth, and stroke my head;
And thou shalt have some cockle bread.
Gently dip, but not too deep,
For fear thou make the golden beard to weep.
Fair maid, white and red,
Comb me smooth, and stroke my head;
And every hair a sheave shall be,
And every sheave a golden tree.

GEORGE PEELE.

FROM the hag and hungry goblin
    That into rags would rend ye
And the spirit that stan' by the naked man
In the Book of Moons defend ye!
That of your five sound senses
You never be forsaken
Nor travel from yourselves with Tom
Abroad to beg your bacon.
    Nor never sing 'Any food, any feeding,
    Money, drink or clothing':
    Come dame or maid, be not afraid,
    Poor Tom will injure nothing.

Of thirty bare years have I
Twice twenty been enragéd
And of forty bin three times fifteen
In durance soundly cagéd
In the lordly lofts of Bedlam
On stubble soft and dainty,
Brave bracelets strong, sweet whips ding dong,
With wholesome hunger plenty.
    And now I sing &c.

With a thought I took for Maudlin
And a cruse of cockle pottage
With a thing thus—tall, (sky bless you all),
I fell into this dotage.
I slept not since the conquest,
Till then I never wakéd
Till the roguish boy of love where I lay
Me found and stripped me naked.
    And made me sing &c.

TOM O' BEDLAM

When short I have shorn my sowce face
And swigged my hornéd barrel
In an oaken inn do I pawn my skin
As a suit of gilt apparel.
The moon's my constant mistress
And the lonely owl my marrow
The flaming drake and the night-crow make
Me music to my sorrow.
    While there I sing &c.

The palsy plague these pounces,
When I prig your pigs or pullen,
Your culvers take, or mateless make
Your chanticlere, and sullen.
When I want provant with Humfrey
I sup, and when benighted
To repose in Paul's with waking souls
I never am affrighted.
    But still do I sing &c.

I know more than Apollo,
For oft when he lies sleeping
I behold the stars at mortal wars
And the wounded welkin weeping;
The moon embrace her shepherd
And the queen of love her warrior,
While the first doth horn the star of the morn
And the next the heavenly Farrier.
    While I do sing &c.

The Gipsy Snap and Tedro
Are none of Tom's comrados.
The punk I scorn and the cutpurse sworn
And the roaring-boys bravadoes.

pullen] chickens.   culvers] doves.   provant] provender.

The sober, white, and gentle,
Me trace, or touch, and spare not;
But those that cross Tom's Rhinoceros
Do what the panther dare not.
   Although I sing &c.

With an host of furious fancies
Whereof I am commander
With a burning spear, and a horse of air,
To the wilderness I wander.
By a knight of ghosts and shadows
I summoned am to tourney
Ten leagues beyond the wide world's end.
Me thinks it is no journey.
   All while I sing &c.

ANON.

48   *Of Treason*

TREASON doth never prosper; what's the reason?
For if it prosper, none dare call it treason.

SIR JOHN HARINGTON.

49   *The Fairy Blessing*

NOW the hungry lion roars,
   And the wolf behowls the moon;
Whilst the heavy ploughman snores,
   All with weary task fordone.
Now the wasted brands do glow,
   Whilst the screech-owl, screeching loud,
Puts the wretch that lies in woe
   In remembrance of a shroud.

THE FAIRY BLESSING

Now it is the time of night
   That the graves, all gaping wide,
Every one lets forth his sprite,
   In the church-way paths to glide:
And we fairies, that do run
   By the triple Hecate's team,
From the presence of the sun,
   Following darkness like a dream,
Now are frolic; not a mouse
Shall disturb this hallow'd house:
I am sent with broom before,
To sweep the dust behind the door.

Through the house give glimmering light
   By the dead and drowsy fire;
Every elf and fairy sprite
   Hop as light as bird from brier;
And this ditty after me,
Sing and dance it trippingly.

First, rehearse your song by rote,
To each word a warbling note:
Hand in hand, with fairy grace,
Will we sing, and bless this place.

Now, until the break of day,
   Through this house each fairy stray.
To the best bride-bed will we,
Which by us shall blesséd be;
And the issue there create
Ever shall be fortunate!
So shall all the couples three
Ever true in loving be;

And the blots of Nature's hand
Shall not in their issue stand:
Never mole, hare-lip, nor scar,
Nor mark prodigious, such as are
Despiséd in nativity,
Shall upon their children be.
With this field-dew consecrate,
Every fairy take his gait,
And each several chamber bless,
Through this palace, with sweet peace;
And the owner of it blest
Ever shall in safety rest.

WILLIAM SHAKESPEARE.

50 *Feste's Song*

WHEN that I was and a little tiny boy,
   With hey, ho, the wind and the rain;
A foolish thing was but a toy,
   For the rain it raineth every day.

But when I came to man's estate,
   With hey, ho, the wind and the rain;
'Gainst knaves and thieves men shut their gate,
   For the rain it raineth every day.

But when I came, alas! to wive,
   With hey, ho, the wind and the rain;
By swaggering could I never thrive,
   For the rain it raineth every day.

But when I came unto my beds,
   With hey, ho, the wind and the rain;
With toss-pots still had drunken heads,
   For the rain it raineth every day.

FESTE'S SONG

A great while ago the world begun,
    With hey, ho, the wind and the rain;
But that's all one, our play is done,
    And we'll strive to please you every day.

WILLIAM SHAKESPEARE.

51   *The Pedlar's Song*

WHEN daffodils begin to peer,
    With heigh! the doxy, over the dale,
Why, then comes in the sweet o' the year;
    For the red blood reigns in the winter's pale.

The white sheet bleaching on the hedge,
    With heigh! the sweet birds, O, how they sing!
Doth set my pugging tooth on edge;
    For a quart of ale is a dish for a king.

The lark, that tirra-lira chants,
    With, heigh! with, heigh! the thrush and the jay,
Are summer songs for me and my aunts,
    While we lie tumbling in the hay.

WILLIAM SHAKESPEARE.

52   *Madrigals*

I

SINCE Bonny-boots was dead, that so divinely
  Could toot and foot it, (O he did it finely!)
    We ne'er went more a-Maying
    Nor had that sweet fa-laing.

ANTONY AND WILLIAM HOLBORNE.

pugging] thieving (?)

MADRIGALS

II

O I do love, then kiss me;
   And after I'll not miss thee
With bodies' lovely meeting
To dally, pretty sweeting.
Though I am somewhat agéd,
Yet is not love assuagéd;
But with sweet ardent clips,
I'll lay thee on the lips,
And make thee ever swear:
Farewell, old bachelor.   Robert Jones.

III

AY me, alas, heigh ho, heigh ho!
   Thus doth Messalina go
Up and down the house a-crying,
For her monkey lies a-dying.
Death, thou art too cruel
To bereave her jewel,
Or to make a seizure
Of her only treasure.
If her monkey die,
She will sit and cry,
Fie fie fie fie fie!   Thomas Weelkes.

IV

HA ha! ha ha! This world doth pass
   Most merrily I'll be sworn,
For many an honest Indian ass
   Goes for a unicorn.
       Fara diddle dyno,
       This is idle fyno.

MADRIGALS

Tie hie! tie hie! O sweet delight!
  He tickles this age that can
Call Tullia's ape a marmasyte
  And Leda's goose a swan.
      Fara diddle dyno,
      This is idle fyno.

So so! so so! Fine English days!
  For false play's no reproach,
For he that doth the coachman praise
  May safely use the coach.
      Fara diddle dyno,
      This is idle fyno.

THOMAS WEELKES.

V

Hawking for the Partridge

SITH sickles and the shearing scythe
  Hath shorn the fields of late,
Now shall our hawks and we be blithe.
  Dame Partridge ware your pate!
      Our murdering kites
      In all their flights
      Will seld or never miss
To truss you ever and make your bale our bliss.

Whurr ret $\left\{\begin{array}{l}\text{Quando}\\\text{Duty}\\\text{Jew}\\\text{Travel}\end{array}\right.$ Whurr ret $\left\{\begin{array}{l}\text{Nimble}\\\text{Beauty}\\\text{Damsel}\\\text{Trover}\end{array}\right.$
      Hey dogs hey!

MADRIGALS

Ware haunt hey
Wanton	ret	Sugar	ret	Mistress
Sempster		Faver		Minx
Callis		Dover		Sant
Dancer		Jerker		Quoy

ret
Tricker	ret	Crafty	ret	Minion
Dido		Civil		Lemmon
Cherry		Carver		Courtier
Stately		Ruler		German whurr! let fly!

O well flown, eager kite, mark!
We falconers thus make sullen kites
   Yield pleasure fit for kings,
And sport with them in those delights,
   And oft in other things.

Thomas Ravenscroft.

VI

MY mistress is as fair as fine,
   Milk-white fingers, cherry nose.
Like twinkling day-stars looks her eyne,
   Lightening all things where she goes.
Fair as Phoebe, though not so fickle,
Smooth as glass, though not so brickle.

My heart is like a ball of snow
   Melting at her lukewarm sight;
Her fiery lips like night-worms glow,
   Shining clear as candle-light.
Neat she is, no feather lighter;
Bright she is, no daisy whiter.

Thomas Ravenscroft.

VII

M Y mistress frowns when she should play;
I'll please her with a Fa la la.
Sometimes she chides, but I straightway
Present her with a Fa la la.

You lovers that have loves astray
May win them with a Fa la la.
Quick music's best, for still they say
None pleaseth like your Fa la la.   JOHN HILTON.

53   *First Love*

S ILLY boy, 'tis full moon yet, thy night as day shines
clearly;
Had thy youth but wit to fear, thou couldst not love so
dearly.
Shortly wilt thou mourn when all thy pleasures are
bereaved;
Little knows he how to love that never was deceived.

This is thy first maiden flame, that triumphs yet un-
stained;
All is artless now you speak, not one word yet is feigned;
All is heaven that you behold, and all your thoughts are
blessèd;
But no spring can want his fall, each Troilus hath his
Cressid.

Thy well-ordered locks ere long shall rudely hang
neglected;
And thy lively pleasant cheer read grief on earth dejected.

Much then wilt thou blame thy Saint, that made thy heart
 so holy,
And with sighs confess, in love that too much faith is folly.

Yet be just and constant still! Love may beget a wonder,
Not unlike a summer's frost, or winter's fatal thunder.
He that holds his sweetheart true, unto his day of dying,
Lives of all that ever breathed most worthy the envying.

Thomas Campion.

54 *Shall I come, sweet Love, to thee?*

SHALL I come, sweet love, to thee,
 When the evening beams are set?
Shall I not excluded be?
 Will you find no feignèd let?
Let me not, for pity, more,
Tell the long hours at your door!

Who can tell what thief or foe,
 In the covert of the night,
For his prey will work my woe,
 Or through wicked foul despite:
So may I die unredrest,
Ere my long love be possest.

But to let such dangers pass,
 Which a lover's thoughts disdain,
'Tis enough in such a place
 To attend love's joys in vain.
Do not mock me in thy bed,
While these cold nights freeze me dead.

Thomas Campion.

SIMON: O Mine own sweet heart,
 and when wilt thou be true;
Or when will the time come
 that I shall marry you,
That I may give you kisses,
 one, two or three,
More sweeter than the honey,
 that comes from the bee.

SUSAN: My Father is unwilling
 that I should marry thee,
Yet I could wish in heart,
 that so the same might be:
For now me thinks thou seemest,
 more lovely unto me:
And fresher than the blossoms,
 that blooms on the tree.

SIMON: Thy mother is most willing,
 and will consent I know,
Then let us to thy Father
 now both together go:
Where if he give us his good will,
 and to our match agree:
'Twill be sweeter than the honey
 that comes from the bee.

SUSAN: Come go, for I am willing,
 good fortune be our guide:
From that which I have promised,
 dear heart, I'll never slide:

SIMON AND SUSAN

If that he do but smile,
   and I the same may see,
'Tis better than the blossoms,
   that blooms upon the tree.

SIMON: But stay, here comes thy Mother,
       we'll talk with her a word:
     I doubt not but some comfort,
       to us she may afford:
     If comfort she will give us,
       that we the same may see,
     'Twill be sweeter than the honey,
       that comes from the bee.

SUSAN: O Mother we are going
       my Father for to pray,
     That he will give me his good will,
       for long I cannot stay.
     A young man I have chosen
       a fitting match for me,
     More fairer than the blossoms
       that blooms on the tree.

MOTHER: Daughter thou art old enough
       to be a wedded wife,
     You maidens are desirous
       to lead a married life.
     Then my consent good daughter
       shall to thy wishes be,
     For young thou art as blossoms
       that bloom upon the tree.

SIMON AND SUSAN

SIMON: Then mother you are willing
          Your daughter I shall have:
And Susan thou art welcome
          I'll keep thee fine and brave.
And have those wishéd blessings
          bestowéd upon thee,
More sweeter than the honey
          that comes from the bee.

SUSAN: Yet Simon I am minded
          to lead a merry life,
And be as well maintainéd
          as any City wife:
And live a gallant mistress
          of maidens that shall be
More fairer than the blossoms
          that bloom upon the tree.

SIMON: Thou shalt have thy Caudles,
          before thou dost arise:
For churlishness breeds sickness
          and danger therein lies.
Young lasses must be cherished
          with sweets that dainty be,
Far sweeter than the honey
          that cometh from the bee.

MOTHER: Well said good Son and Daughter,
          this is the only diet
To please a dainty young wife,
          and keep the house in quiet.

K

SIMON AND SUSAN

But stay, here comes your Father,
    his words I hope will be
More sweeter than the blossoms
    that bloom upon the tree.

FATHER: Why how now daughter Susan
    do you intend to marry?
Maidens in the old time
    did twenty winters tarry.
Now in the teens no sooner
    but you a wife will be
And lose the sweetest blossom
    that blooms upon thy tree.

SUSAN: It is for my preferment
    good Father say not nay,
For I have found a husband kind
    and loving every way:
That still unto my fancy
    will evermore agree,
Which is more sweet than honey
    that comes from the bee.

MOTHER: Hinder not your daughter,
    good husband, lest you bring
Her loves consuming sickness,
    or else a worser thing.
Maidens youngly married
    loving wives will be
And sweet as is the honey
    which comes from the bee.

SIMON AND SUSAN

SIMON: Good Father be not cruel,
        your daughter is mine own:
Her mother hath consented
        and is to liking grown.
And if your self will give then,
        her gentle hand to me,
'Twill sweeter be than honey
        that comes from the bee.

FATHER: God give thee joy dear Daughter,
        there is no reason I
Should hinder thy proceeding,
        and thou a maiden die:
And after to lead apes in hell,
        as maidens dooméd be:
That fairer are than blossoms
        that bloom upon the tree.

SIMON: Then let's unto the Parson
        and Clerk to say Amen:

SUSAN: With all my heart good Simon,
        we are concluded then,
My father and mother both
        do willingly agree
My Simon's sweet as honey
        that comes from the bee.

All together sing:
        You Maidens and Bachelors
        we hope will lose no time,
        Which learn it by experience
        that youth is in the prime,

And daily in their hearts desire
  young married folks to be
More sweeter than the blossoms
  that bloom upon the tree.   ANON.

56   *The Masque of Christmas*

NOW God preserve, as you well do deserve,
  Your majesties all two there;
Your highness small, with my good lords all,
  And ladies, how do you do there?

Give me leave to ask, for I bring you a masque
  From little, little, little London;
Which say the king likes, I have passed the pikes,
  If not, old Christmas is undone.

Our dance's freight is a matter of eight,
  And two, the which are wenches:
In all they be ten, four cocks to a hen,
  And will swim to the tune like tenches.

Each hath his knight for to carry his light,
  Which some would say are torches;
To bring them here, and to lead them there,
  And home again to their own porches.

Now their intent, is above to present,
  ,With all the appurtenances,
A right Christmas, as of old it was,
  To be gathered out of the dances.

Which they do bring, and afore the king,
  The queen, and prince, as it were now
Drawn here by love; who over and above,
  Doth draw himself in the gear too.

THE MASQUE OF CHRISTMAS

Hum drum, sauce for a coney;
  No more of your martial music;
Even for the sake o' the next new stake,
  For there I do mean to use it.

And now to ye, who in place are to see,
  With roll and farthingale hoopéd:
I pray you know, though he want his bow,
  By the wings, that this is Cupid.

He might go back for to cry, What you lack?
  But that were not so witty:
His cap and coat are enough to note,
  That he is the Love o' the city.

And he leads on, though he now be gone,
  For that was only his-rule:
But now comes in, Tom of Bosoms-inn,
  And he presenteth Mis-rule.

Which you may know, by the very show,
  Albeit you never ask it:
For there you may see, what his ensigns be,
  The rope, the cheese, and the basket.

This Carol plays, and has been in his days
  A chirping boy, and a kill-pot:
Kit cobbler it is, I'm a father of his,
  And he dwells in the lane call'd Fill-pot.

But who is this? O, my daughter Cis,
  Minced-pie; with her do not dally
On pain o' your life: she's an honest cook's wife,
  And comes out of Scalding Alley.

THE MASQUE OF CHRISTMAS

Next in the trace, comes Gambol in place;
    And, to make my tale the shorter,
My son Hercules, ta'en out of Distaff Lane,
    But an active man, and a porter.

Now Post and Pair, old Christmas's heir,
    Doth make and a jingling sally;
And wot you who, 'tis one of my two
    Sons, card-makers in Pur Alley.

Next in a trice, with his box and his dice,
    Mac'-pipin my son, but younger,
Brings Mumming in; and the knave will win,
    For he is a costermonger.

But New Year's Gift, of himself makes shift,
    To tell you what his name is:
With orange on head, and his ginger-bread,
    Clem Wasp of Honey Lane 'tis.

This, I you tell, is our jolly Wassel,
    And for Twelfth-night more meet too:
She works by the ell, and her name is Nell,
    And she dwells in Threadneedle Street too.

Then Offering, he, with his dish and his tree,
    That in every great house keepeth,
Is by my son, young Little-worth, done,
    And in Penny-rich Street he sleepeth.

Last, Baby-cake, that an end doth make
    Of Christmas' merry, merry vein-a,
Is child Rowlan, and a straight young man,
    Though he come out of Crooked Lane-a.

There should have been, and a dozen I ween,
    But I could find but one more
Child of Christmas, and a Log it was,
    When I them all had gone o'er.

I prayéd him, in a time so trim,
    That he would make one to prance it:
And I myself would have been the twelfth,
    O but Log was too heavy to dance it.

BEN JONSON.

57   *Inviting a Friend to Supper*

TO-NIGHT, grave sir, both my poor house and I
    Do equally desire your company:
Not that we think us worthy such a guest,
    But that your worth will dignify our feast,
With those that come; whose grace may make that seem
    Something, which, else, could hope for no esteem.
It is the fair acceptance, Sir, creates
    The entertainment perfect: not the cates.
Yet shall you have, to rectify your palate,
    An olive, capers, or some better salad
Ushering the mutton; with a short-legged hen,
    If we can get her, full of eggs, and then,
Lemons, and wine for sauce: to these, a coney
    Is not to be despaired of, for our money;
And, though fowl, now, be scarce, yet there are clerks,
    The sky not falling, think we may have larks.
I'll tell you of more, and lie, so you will come:
    Of partridge, pheasant, wood-cock, of which some
May yet be there; and godwit, if we can:
    Knat, rail, and ruff too. How so e'er, my man

Shall read a piece of VIRGIL, TACITUS,
   LIVY, or of some better book to us,
Of which we'll speak our minds, amidst our meat;
   And I'll profess no verses to repeat:
To this, if ought appear, which I know not of,
   That will the pastry, not my paper, show of.
Digestive cheese, and fruit there sure will be;
   But that, which most doth take my *Muse*, and me,
Is a pure cup of rich *Canary*-wine,
   Which is the *Mermaid's*, now, but shall be mine:
Of which had HORACE, or ANACREON tasted,
   Their lives, as do their lines, till now had lasted.
Tobacco, Nectar, or the *Thespian* spring,
   Are all but LUTHER's beer, to this I sing.
Of this we will sup free, but moderately,
   And we will have no *Pooly*, or *Parrot* by;
Nor shall our cups make any guilty men:
   But, at our parting, we will be, as when
We innocently met. No simple word,
   That shall be uttered at our mirthful board,
Shall make us sad next morning: or affright
   The liberty, that we'll enjoy to-night.

BEN JONSON.

58   *Song to Sleep*

CARE charming sleep, thou easer of all woes,
   Brother to death, sweetly thy self dispose
On this afflicted Prince, fall like a cloud
In gentle showers, give nothing that is loud,
Or painful to his slumbers; easy, light,
And as a purling stream, thou son of night,

Pass by his troubled senses; sing his pain
Like hollow murmuring wind, or silver rain,
Into this Prince gently, Oh gently slide,
And kiss him into slumbers like a bride.

JOHN FLETCHER.

59   *Art thou gone in Haste?*

ART thou gone in haste?
  I'll not forsake thee!
Runn'st thou ne'er so fast,
  I'll o'ertake thee!
O'er the dales or the downs,
  Through the green meadows,
From the fields, through the towns,
  To the dim shadows!

All along the plain,
  To the low fountains;
Up and down again,
  From the high mountains:
Echo, then, shall again
  Tell her I follow,
And the floods to the woods
  Carry my holla.
    Holla!
Ce! la! ho! ho! hu!   ANON.

60   *Great Tom*

BE dumb ye infant chimes, thump not the metal
  That ne'er outrung a tinker and his kettle,
Cease all your petty larums, for to-day
Is young Tom's resurrection from the clay:

And know, when Tom shall ring his loudest knells
The big'st of you'll be thought but dinner bells . . .
Rejoice with Christ Church—look higher Oseney,
Of giant bells the famous treasury;
The base vast thundering Clock of Westminster,
Grave Tom of Lincoln and huge Excester
Are but Tom's eldest brothers, and perchance
He may call cousin with the bell of France.

RICHARD, BISHOP CORBET.

61 *A Proper New Ballad, intituled The Fairies
Farewell; or, God-a-Mercy Will*

FAREWELL rewards and Fairies,
   Good housewives now may say,
For now foul sluts in Dairies
   Do fare as well as they.
And though they sweep their hearths no less
   Than maids were wont to do,
Yet who of late for cleanliness,
   Finds Sixpence in her shoe?

Lament, lament, old Abbeys,
   The Fairies lost command;
They did but change Priest's babies,
   But some have chang'd your land:
And all your children stol'n from thence
   Are now grown puritans;
Who live as changelings ever since
   For love of your demains.

At morning and at evening both
   You merry were and glad,
So little care of sleep and sloth
   These pretty Ladies had;

A PROPER NEW BALLAD

When Tom came home from labour,
　　Or Ciss to milking rose,
Then merrily merrily went their Tabor,
　　And nimbly went their Toes.

Witness those rings and roundelayes
　　Of theirs, which yet remain,
Were footed in Queen Mary's days
　　On many a grassy plain;
But since of late, Elizabeth,
　　And later James came in,
They never danced on any heath
　　As when the time hath been.

By which we note the Fairies
　　Were of the old profession;
Their songs were Ave Maries,
　　Their dances were procession:
But now, alas! they all are dead
　　Or gone beyond the Seas,
Or further for Religion fled,
　　Or else they take their ease.

A tell-tale in their company
　　They never could endure,
And whoso kept not secretly
　　Their mirth was punished sure;
It was a just and Christian deed
　　To pinch such black and blue:
O how the Common-wealth doth need
　　Such Justices as you!

Now they have left our Quarters
   A Register they have,
Who looketh to their Charters,
   A Man both wise and grave;
An hundred of their merry pranks
   By one that I could name
Are kept in store, con twenty thanks
   To William for the same.

To William Churne of Staffordshire,
   Give laud and praises due;
Who every meal can mend your cheer,
   With tales both old and true;
To William all give audience,
   And pray you for his noddle;
For all the Fairies' evidence
   Were lost, if it were addle.

RICHARD, BISHOP CORBET.

62   *The Distracted Puritan*

AM I mad, O noble Festus,
   When zeal and godly knowledge
Have put me in hope
To deal with the Pope,
As well as the best in the college?
   Boldly I preach, hate a cross, hate a surplice,
     Mitres, copes, and rotchets;
   Come hear me pray nine times a day,
     And fill your heads with crochets.

THE DISTRACTED PURITAN

In the house of pure Emanuel
I had my education,
   Where my friends surmise
   I dazzl'd my eyes
With the light of revelation.
   Boldly I preach, &c.

They bound me like a bedlam,
They lash'd my four poor quarters;
   Whilst this I endure,
   Faith makes me sure
To be one of Fox's martyrs.
   Boldly I preach, &c.

These injuries I suffer
Through Anti-Christ's persuasion:
   Take off this chain,
   Neither Rome nor Spain
Can resist my strong invasion.
   Boldly I preach, &c.

Of the beast's ten horns (God bless us!)
I have knock'd off three already;
   If they let me alone
   I'll leave him none:
But they say I am too heady.
   Boldly I preach, &c.

When I sack'd the Seven-hill'd City,
I met the great red Dragon;
   I kept him aloof
   With the armour of proof,
Though here I have never a rag on.
   Boldly I preach, &c.

THE DISTRACTED PURITAN

With a fiery sword and target,
There fought I with this monster:
    But the sons of pride
    My zeal deride,
And all my deeds misconster.
    Boldly I preach, &c.

I unhors'd the Whore of Babel,
With the lance of Inspiration;
    I made her stink,
    And spill the drink
In the cup of abominations.
    Boldly I preach, &c.

I have seen two in a vision
With a flying book between them.
    I have been in despair
    Five times a year,
And been cur'd by reading Greenham.
    Boldly I preach, &c.

I observ'd in Perkin's Tables
The black lines of damnation;
    Those crooked veins
    So stuck in my brains,
That I fear'd my reprobation.
    Boldly I preach, &c.

In the holy tongue of Canaan
I plac'd my chiefest pleasure:
    Till I prick'd my foot
    With an Hebrew root,
That I bled beyond all measure.
    Boldly I preach, &c.

I appear'd before the archbishop,
And all the high commission;
  I gave him no grace,
  But told him to his face,
That he favour'd superstition.
  Boldly I preach, hate a cross, hate a surplice,
    Mitres, copes, and rotchets:
  Come hear me pray nine times a day,
    And fill your heads with crotchets.

RICHARD, BISHOP CORBET.

63   *She smiled like a Holiday*

SWEET she was, as kind a love
  As ever fetter'd swain;
Never such a dainty one
  Shall man enjoy again:
Set a thousand on a row
  I forbid that any show
Ever the like of her,
  Hey nonny nonny noe.
Face she had of filbert hue,
  And bosom'd like a swan;
Back she had of bended yew,
  And waisted by a span.
Hair she had as black as crow
  From the head unto the toe,
Down, down, all over her,
  Hey nonny nonny noe.
She smiled like a holy-day
  And simper'd like the spring;
She prank'd it like a popinjay
  And like a swallow sing;

She trip'd it like a barren doe,
  She strutted like a gor-crow,
Which made the men so fond of her,
  Hey nonny nonny noe.

ANON.

64   *Upon a Maid*

HERE she lies (in bed of spice)
  Fair as Eve in Paradise:
For her beauty it was such
Poets could not praise too much.
Virgins come, and in a ring
Her supremest requiem sing;
Then depart, but see ye tread
Lightly, lightly o'er the dead.

ROBERT HERRICK.

65   *An Epitaph upon a Virgin*

HERE a solemn fast we keep,
  While all beauty lies asleep
Hushed be all things; (no noise here)
But the toning of a tear:
Or a sigh of such as bring
Cowslips for her covering.

ROBERT HERRICK.

66   *His Prayer to Ben Jonson*

WHEN I a verse shall make,
  Know I have prayed thee,
For old religion's sake,
  Saint Ben, to aid me.

Make the way smooth for me,
   When I, thy Herrick,
Honouring thee, on my knee
   Offer my lyric.

Candles I'll give to thee,
   And a new altar;
And thou, Saint Ben, shalt be
   Writ in my psalter.
                              ROBERT HERRICK.

67   *Anacreontic*

BORN I was to be old,
   And for to die here:
After that, in the mould
   Long for to lie here.
But before that day comes,
   Still I be bousing;
For I know, in the tombs
   There's no carousing.
                              ROBERT HERRICK.

68   *Lovers how they come and part*

A GYGES' ring they bear about them still,
   To be, and not seen when and where they will.
They tread on clouds, and though they sometimes fall,
They fall like dew, but make no noise at all.
So silently they one to th'other come,
As colours steal into the pear or plum,
And air-like, leave no pression to be seen
Where e'er they met, or parting place has been.
                              ROBERT HERRICK.

HIC, hoc, the carrion crow,
    For I have shot something too low:
I have quite missed my mark,
And shot the poor sow to the heart;
Wife, bring treacle in a spoon,
Or else the poor sow's heart will down.

ANON.

70   *The constant Lover*

THOUGH regions far divided
    And tedious tracts of time,
By my misfortune guided,
    Make absence thought a crime;
Though we were set asunder
    As far, as East from West,
Love still would work this wonder,
    Thou shouldst be in my breast.

How slow, alas, are paces,
    Compared to thoughts that fly
In moment back to places
    Whole ages scarce descry.
The body must have pauses;
    The mind requires no rest;
Love needs no second causes
    To guide thee to my breast.

Accept in that poor dwelling
    But welcome, nothing great,
With pride no turrets swelling,
    But lowly as the seat

THE CONSTANT LOVER

Where, though not much delighted,
   In peace thou mayst be blest,
Unfeasted yet unfrighted
   By rivals, in my breast.

But this is not the diet
   That doth for glory strive;
Poor beauties seek in quiet
   To keep one heart alive.
The price of his ambition,
   That looks for such a guest,
Is hopeless of fruition,
   To beat an empty breast.

See then my last lamenting:
   Upon a cliff I'll sit,
Rock Constancy presenting,
   Till I grow part of it;
My tears a quicksand feeding,
   Whereon no foot can rest,
My sighs a tempest breeding
   About my stony breast.

Those arms, wherein wide open
   Love's fleet was wont to put,
Shall laid across betoken
   That haven's mouth is shut.
Mine eyes no light shall cherish
   For ships at sea distressed,
But darkling let them perish
   Or split against my breast.

Yet if I can discover
  When thine before it rides,
To show I was thy lover
  I'll smooth my rugged sides;
And so much better measure
  Afford thee than the rest,
Thou shalt have no displeasure
  By knocking at my breast.

AURELIAN TOWNSEND.

71   *The Siege*

'TIS now since I sat down before
    That foolish fort, a heart;
(Time strangely spent) a year, and more,
  And still I did my part:

Made my approaches, from her hand
  Unto her lip did rise,
And did already understand
  The language of her eyes.

Proceeding on with no less art,
  My tongue was engineer;
I thought to undermine the heart
  By whispering in the ear.

When this did nothing, I brought down
  Great cannon-oaths, and shot
A thousand thousand to the town,
  And still it yielded not.

I then resolved to starve the place
  By cutting off all kisses,
Praising and gazing on her face,
  And all such little blisses.

144

THE SIEGE

To draw her out, and from her strength,
    I drew all batteries in:
And brought myself to lie at length,
    As if no siege had been.

When I had done what man could do
    And thought the place mine own,
The enemy lay quiet too,
    And smiled at all was done.

I sent to know from whence, and where,
    These hopes, and this relief?
A spy informed, Honour was there,
    And did command in chief.

March, march (quoth I) the word straight give,
    Let's lose no time, but leave her:
That giant upon air will live,
    And hold it out for ever.

To such a place our camp remove
    As will no siege abide;
I hate a fool that starves her love
    Only to feed her pride.

SIR JOHN SUCKLING.

72   *Sonnet*

OF thee (kind boy) I ask no red and white
    To make up my delight,
      No odd becoming graces,
Black eyes, or little know-not-whats, in faces;

Make me but mad enough, give me good store
Of Love, for her I court,
                    I ask no more,
'Tis love in love that makes the sport.

There's no such thing as that we beauty call,
          It is mere cosenage all;
          For though some long ago
Liked certain colours mingled so and so,
That doth not tie me now from choosing new,
If I a fancy take
                    To black and blue,
That fancy doth it beauty make.

'Tis not the meat, but 'tis the appetite
          Makes eating a delight,
          And if I like one dish
More than another, that a pheasant is;
What in our watches, that in us is found,
So to the height and nick
                    We up be wound,
No matter by what hand or trick.

                              SIR JOHN SUCKLING.

73 *A Prognostication on Will Laud, late*
     Archbishop of Canterbury

MY little lord, methinks 'tis strange,
     That you should suffer such a change,
          In such a little space.
You, that so proudly t'other day,
          Did rule the king, and country sway,
          Must budge to 'nother place.

A PROGNOSTICATION ON WILL LAUD

Remember now from whence you came,
And that your grandsires of your name,
 Were dressers of old cloth.
Go, bid the dead men bring their shears,
And dress your coat to save your ears,
 Or pawn your head for both.

The wind shakes cedars that are tall,
An haughty mind must have a fall,
 You are but low I see;
And good it had been for you still,
If both your body, mind, and will,
 In equal shape should be.

The king by heark'ning to your charms,
Hugg'd our destruction in his arms,
 And gates to foes did ope;
Your staff would strike his sceptre down,
Your mitre would o'ertop the crown,
 If you should be a Pope.

But you that did so firmly stand,
To bring in Popery in this land,
 Have miss'd your hellish aim;
Your saints fall down, your angels fly,
Your crosses on yourself do lie,
 Your craft will be your shame.

We scorn that Popes with crozier staves,
Mitres, or keys, should make us slaves,
 And to their feet to bend:
The Pope and his malicious crew,
We hope to handle all, like you,
 And bring them to an end.

A PROGNOSTICATION ON WILL LAUD

The silenc'd clergy, void of fear,
In your damnation will bear share,
   And speak their mind at large:
Your cheese-cake cap and magpie gown,
That make such strife in ev'ry town,
   Must now defray your charge.

Within this six years six ears have
Been cropped off worthy men and grave,
   For speaking what was true;
But if your subtle head and ears
Can satisfy those six of theirs,
   Expect but what's your due.

Poor people that have felt your rod,
Yield *laud* to the devil, praise to God,
   For freeing them from thrall;
Your little *grace*, for want of grace,
Must lose your patriarchal place,
   And have no grace at all.

Your white lawn sleeves that were the wings
Whereon you soared to lofty things,
   Must be your fins to swim;
Th'Archbishop's *see* by Thames must go,
With him unto the Tower below,
   There to be rack'd like him.

Your oath cuts deep, your lies hurt sore,
Your *canons* made Scot's cannons roar,
   But now I hope you'll find,
That there are cannons in the Tower,
Will quickly batter down your power,
   And sink your haughty mind.

A PROGNOSTICATION ON WILL LAUD

The Commonalty have made a vow,
No oath, no canons to allow,
    No Bishop's *Common Prayer*;
No lazy prelates that shall spend
Such great revenues to no end,
    But virtue to impair.

Dumb dogs that wallow in such store,
That would suffice above a score
    Pastors of upright will;
Now they'll make all the bishops teach,
And you must in the pulpit preach,
    That stands on Tower Hill.

When the young lads to you did come,
You knew their meaning by the drum,
    You had better yielded then;
Your head and body then might have
One death, one burial, and one grave,
    By boys—but two by men.

But you that by your judgments clear
Will make five quarters in a year
    And hang them on the gates,
That head shall stand upon the bridge,
When your's shall under Traitor's trudge,
    And smile on your miss'd pates.

The little *Wren* that soar'd so high
Thought on his wings away to fly,
    Like *Finch*, I know not whither;
But now the subtle whirly-*Wind-
Debanke* hath left the bird behind,
    You two must flock together.

A bishop's head, a deputy's breast,
A *Finch's* tongue, a *Wren* from's nest,
   Will set the Devil on foot;
He's like to have a dainty dish,
At once both flesh and fowl and fish,
   And *Duck* and *Lamb* to boot.

But this I say, that your lewd life
Did fill both Church and State with strife,
   And trample on the Crown;
Like a bless'd martyr you will die,
For Church's good; she rises high,
   When such as you fall down.   ANON.

74   *When the King enjoys his own again*

WHAT Booker can prognosticate,
   Concerning king's or kingdom's fate?
I think myself to be as wise
   As he that gazeth on the skies:
     My skill goes beyond
     The depth of a Pond,
Or Rivers in the greatest rain;
     Whereby I can tell,
     All things will be well,
When the king enjoys his own again.

There's neither Swallow, Dove nor Dade,
   Can soar more high, nor deeper wade;
Nor show a reason from the stars,
   What causeth peace or civil wars:
     The man in the moon
     May wear out his shoon,

WHEN THE KING ENJOYS HIS OWN AGAIN

By running after Charles his wain;
But all's to no end,
For the times will not mend,
Till the king enjoys his own again.

Though for a time we see Whitehall
With cobwebs hanging on the wall,
Instead of silk and silver brave,
Which formerly it used to have;
With rich perfume
In every room,
Delightful to that princely train,
Which again you shall see,
When the time it shall be,
That the king enjoys his own again.

Full forty years the royal crown
Hath been his father's and his own;
And is there any one but he
That in the same should sharer be?
For who better may
The sceptre sway,
Than he that hath such right to reign?
Then let's hope for a peace,
For the wars will not cease,
Till the king enjoys his own again.

Till then upon Ararat's hill
My Hope shall cast her anchor still,
Until I see some peaceful dove
Bring home the branch she dearly love:
Then will I wait,
Till the waters abate,

Which now disturb my troubled brain,
　　Else never rejoice,
　　Till I hear the voice,
That the king enjoys his own again.
　　　　　　　　　　　　Martin Parker.

75　　　*A Free Parliament Litany*

MORE Ballads!—here's a spick and span new Sup-
　　plication,
By order of a Committee for the Reformation
To be read in all churches and chapels of this nation,
Upon pain of slavery and sequestration.
　　From Fools and Knaves, in our Parliament free,
　　Libera nos, Domine!

From those that ha' more Religion and less conscience
　　than their fellows;
From a Representative that's fearful and jealous;
From a starting jadish people that's troubled with the
　　yellows,
And a priest that blows the coal (a crack in his bellows).
　　From Fools and Knaves, &c.

From shepherds that lead their flocks into the briars,
And then fleece'um—From Vow-breakers and King-triers;
—Of Church and Crown lands, from both sellers and
　　buyers;
From the children of him that's the Father of Liars.
　　From Fools and Knaves, &c.

From the Doctrine and Discipline of Now and anon:
Preserve us and our wives; from John T. and Saint John,

A FREE PARLIAMENT LITANY

Like Master, like Man, every way but one:
The Master has a large conscience, and the Man has none.
    From Fools and Knaves, &c.

From Major-Generals, Army-Officers, and that fanatic
    crew;
From the parboil'd pimp Scot, and from Goodface, the Jew;
From old Mildmay, that in Cheapside mistook his cue;
And from him that won't pledge—give the Devil his due.
    From Fools and Knaves, &c.

From long-winded speeches and not a wise word;
From a Gospel ministry settled by the sword;
From the act of a Rump, that stinks when it is stirr'd;
From a Knight of the Post, and a Cobbling Lord.
    From Fools and Knaves, &c.

From all the rich people that ha' made us poor;
From a Speaker that creeps to the House by a back-door;
From that badger, Robinson (that limps and bites sore);
And that dog in a doublet, Arthur—that will do so no
    more.
    From Fools and Knaves, &c.

From a certain sly Knave with a beastly name;
From a Parliament that's wild, and a people that's tame;
From Skippon, Titchbourne, Ireton,—and another of the
    same;
From a dung-hill Cock, and a Hen of the Game.
    From Fools and Knaves, &c.

From all those that sat in the High Court of Justice;
From Usurpers that style themselves 'the People's Trustees';
From an old Rump, in which neither profit nor gust is;
And from the recovery of that which now in the dust is.
    From Fools and Knaves, &c.

A FREE PARLIAMENT LITANY

From a backsliding Saint that pretends to acquiesce;
From crossing of proverbs (let 'um hang that confess);
From a snivelling cause, in a pontifical dress;
Two Lawyers, with the Devil and his dam in a mess.
    From Fools and Knaves, &c.

From those that trouble the waters, to mend the fishing,
And fight 'the Lord's battles' under the Devil's commission;
Such as eat up the Nation, whilst the Government's
    a-dishing:
And from a people when it should be doing, stands wishing.
    From Fools and Knaves, &c.

From an everlasting Mock-Parliament—and from none;
From Strafford's old friends—Harry, Jack, and John;
From the Solicitor's Wolf-law deliver our King's son;
And from the Resurrection of the Rump that is dead and
    gone.
    From Fools and Knaves, &c.

From foreign invasion and commotions at home;
From our present distraction, and from work to come;
From the same hand again, Smectymnuus or the Bum,
And from taking Geneva in our way to Rome.
    From Fools and Knaves, &c.

From a hundred thousand Pound Tax, to maintain knaves
    and whores;
(But it is well given to These that turn'd Those out of
    doors);
From undoing ourselves in plaistering old sores;
He that set them a-work, let him pay their scores.
    From Fools and Knaves, &c.

A FREE PARLIAMENT LITANY

From Saints and Tender-Consciences in Buff;
From Mounson in a foam, and Haslerigg in a huff;
From both men and women that think they never have
    enough;
And from a fool's head that looks thro' a chain and a ruff.
   From Fools and Knaves, &c.

From those that would divide the General and the City;
From Harry Martin's whore, that was neither sound nor
    pretty;
From a Faction that has neither brain nor pity;
From the Mercy of a fanatic Committee.
   From Fools and Knaves, &c.

Preserve us, good Heaven, from entrusting those
That ha' Much to get, and little to lose;
That murther'd the Father, and the Son would depose;
(Sure they can't be our friends that are their Country's
    foes).
   From Fools and Knaves, &c.

From Bradshaw's presumption, and from Hoyle's de-
    spairs,
From rotten members, blind guides, preaching aldermen,
    and false may'rs;
From Long knives, Long ears, Long Parliaments, and
    Long pray'rs;
In mercy to this Nation—Deliver us and our heirs.
   From Fools and Knaves, in our Parliament free,
   Libera nos, Domine!

                            ANON.

YE merry hearts that love to play
  At Cards, see who hath won the day;
You that once did sadly sing
'The Knave o' th' Clubs hath won the King';
    Now more happy times ye have,
    The King hath overcome the Knave,
    The King hath overcome the Knave.

Not long ago a Game was play'd,
When three Crowns at the stake were laid;
England had no cause to boast,
Knaves won that which Kings had lost;
    Coaches gave the way to carts,
    And Clubs were better cards than Hearts,
    And Clubs were better cards than Hearts.

Old Noll was the Knave o' th' Clubs,
And Dad of such as preach in tubs,
Bradshaw, Ireton, and Pride,
Were three other Knaves beside;
    And they play'd with half the Pack,
    Throwing out all cards but Black,
    Throwing out all cards but Black.

But the just Fates threw these four out,
Which made the Loyal Party shout;
The Pope would fain have had the Stock,
And with these cards have whipt his dock;
    But soon the Devil these cards snatches,
    To dip in brimstone, and make matches,
    To dip in brimstone, and make matches.

WIN AT FIRST AND LOSE AT LAST

But still the sport for to maintain,
Lambert, Haslerigg, and Vane,
With one-eyed Hewson, took their places,
Knaves were better cards than Aces;
  But Fleetwood he himself did save,
  Because he was more fool than Knave,
  Because he was more fool than Knave.

Cromwell, tho' he so much had won,
Yet he had an unlucky son;
He sits still, and not regards,
Whilst cunning gamesters set the Cards;
  And thus, alas, poor silly Dick,
  He play'd awhile but lost the trick,
  He play'd awhile but lost the trick.

The Rumpers that had won whole Towns,
The spoils of martyrs and of Crowns,
Were not contented, but grew rough,
As though they had not won enough;
  They kept the cards still in their hands,
  To play for Tithes and College lands,
  To play for Tithes and College lands.

The Presbyters began to fret,
That they were like to lose the set;
Unto the Rump they did appeal,
And said it was their turn to deal;
  Then dealt the Presbyterians, but
  The Army sware that they will cut,
  The Army sware that they will cut.

WIN AT FIRST AND LOSE AT LAST

The Foreign Lands began to wonder,
To see what gallants we liv'd under,
That they, which Christmas did forswear,
Should follow gaming all the year—
      Nay more, which was the strangest thing,
      To play so long without a King!
      To play so long without a King!

The bold Fanatics present were,
Like butlers with their boxes there;
Not doubting but that every game
Some profit would redound to them;
      Because they were the gamesters' minions,
      And every day broach'd new opinions,
      And every day broach'd new opinions.

But Cheshire men (as stories say)
Began to shew them gamesters' play;
Brave Booth, and all his army, strives
To save the stakes, or lose their lives;
      But, O sad fate! they were undone,
      By playing of their Cards too soon,
      By playing of their Cards too soon.

Thus all the while a Club was trump,
There's none could ever beat the Rump;
Until a noble General came,
And gave the cheaters a clear slam;
      His finger did outwit their noddy,
      And screw'd up poor Jack Lambert's body,
      And screw'd up poor Jack Lambert's body.

WIN AT FIRST AND LOSE AT LAST

Then Haslerigg began to scowl,
And said the General play'd foul;
'Look to him, partners, for I tell ye,
This Monk has got a King in 's belly:'
    'Not so,' quoth Monk, 'but I believe,
    Sir Arthur has a Knave in 's sleeve,
    Sir Arthur has a Knave in 's sleeve.'

When General Monk did understand
The Rump were peeping into 's hand,
He wisely kept his cards from sight,
Which put the Rump into a fright;
    He saw how many were betray'd,
    That shew'd their Cards before they play'd,
    That shew'd their Cards before they play'd.

At length, quoth he, 'Some cards we lack,
I will not play with half a pack;
What you cast out I will bring in,
And a new game we will begin:'
    With that the standers-by did say,
    They never yet saw fairer play.
    They never yet saw fairer play.

But presently this game was past,
And for a second Knaves were cast;
All new cards, not stain'd with spots,
As was the Rumpers and the Scots—
    Here good gamesters play'd their parts,
    And turn'd up the King of Hearts,
    And turn'd up the King of Hearts.

After this game was done, I think,
The standers-by had cause to drink,
And all loyal subjects sing,
Farewell Knaves, and welcome King:
    For, till we saw the King return'd,
    We wish'd the Cards had all been burn'd,
    We wish'd the Cards had all been burn'd.
                      LAURENCE PRICE.

77   *Sir Walter Raleigh sailing in the*
Low-lands

SIR Walter Raleigh has built a Ship
           in the Neatherlands,
Sir Walter Raleigh has built a Ship
           in the Neatherlands,
And it is called the sweet Trinity,
And was taken by the false Gallaly,
              sailing in the Low-lands.

Is there never a seaman bold
           in the Neatherlands?
Is there never a seaman bold
           in the Neatherlands?
That will go take this false Gallaly,
And to redeem the sweet Trinity,
              sailing in the Low-lands.

Then spoke the little Ship boy
           in the Neatherlands,
Then spoke the little Ship boy
           in the Neatherlands,

SAILING IN THE LOW-LANDS

Master, Master, what will you give me?
And I will take this false Gallaly,
And release the sweet Trinity,
                   sailing in the Low-lands.

I'll give thee gold, and I'll give thee fee,
                   in the Neatherlands,
I'll give thee gold and I'll give thee fee,
                   in the Neatherlands,
And my eldest daughter thy wife shall be,
                   sailing in the Low-lands.

He set his breast, and away he did swim,
                   in the Neatherlands,
He set his breast, and away he did swim,
                   in the Neatherlands,
Until he came to the false Gallaly
                   sailing in the Low-lands.

He had an augur fit for the nonce,
                   in the Neatherlands,
He had an augur fit for the nonce,
                   in the Neatherlands,
The which will bore fifteen good holes at once,
                   sailing in the Low-lands.

Some were at cards, and some at dice,
                   in the Neatherlands,
Some were at cards, and some at dice,
                   in the Neatherlands,
Until the salt water flashed in their eyes,
                   sailing in the Low-lands.

SAILING IN THE LOW-LANDS

Some cut their hats and some their caps,
      in the Neatherlands,
Some cut their hats and some their caps,
      in the Neatherlands,
For to stop the salt-water gaps,
      sailing in the Low-lands.

He set his breast and away did swim,
      in the Neatherlands,
He set his breast and away did swim,
      in the Neatherlands,
Until he came to his own Ship again,
      sailing in the Low-lands.

I have done the work I have promised to do,
      in the Neatherlands,
I have done the work I have promised to do,
      in the Neatherlands,
For I have sunk the false Gallaly,
And released the sweet Trinity,
      sailing in the Low-lands.

You promised me gold, and you promised me fee,
      in the Neatherlands.
You promised me gold and you promised me fee,
      in the Neatherlands.
Your eldest daughter my Wife she must be,
      sailing in the Low-lands.

You shall have gold, and you shall have fee,
      in the Neatherlands,
You shall have gold, and you shall have fee,
      in the Neatherlands,
But my eldest daughter your Wife shall never be,
      sailing in the Low-lands.

Then fare you well, you cozening Lord,
    in the Neatherlands.
Then fare you well, you cozening Lord,
    in the Neatherlands.
Seeing you are not as good as your word,
    for sailing in the Low-lands.

And thus I shall conclude my Song,
    of the sailing in the Low-lands,
And thus I shall conclude my Song,
    of the sailing in the Low-lands.
Wishing happiness to all Seamen, old or young,
    in their sailing in the Low-lands.
        ANON.

78   *The Careless Gallant*

LET us drink and be merry, dance, joke, and rejoice,
 With claret and sherry, theorbo and voice,
The changeable world to our joy is unjust,
All treasure's uncertain, then down with your dust;
 In frolics dispose your pounds, shillings, and pence,
 For we shall be nothing a hundred years hence.

We'll sport and be free with Frank, Betty, and Dolly,
Have lobsters and oysters to cure melancholy,
Fish dinners will make a man spring like a flea,
Dame Venus, love's lady, was born of the sea,
 With her and with Bacchus we'll tickle the sense,
 For we shall be past it a hundred years hence.

Your beautiful bit, that hath all eyes upon her,
That her honesty sells for a hogo of honour,

THE CARELESS GALLANT

Whose lightness and brightness doth cast such a splendour,
That none are thought fit but the stars to attend her;
    Though now she seems pleasant and sweet to the sense,
    Will be damnably mouldy a hundred years hence.

Your usurer that in the hundred takes twenty,
Who wants in his wealth, and pines in his plenty,
Lays up for a season which he shall ne'er see,
The year of one thousand, eight hundred and three,
    Shall have changed all his bags, his houses and rents,
    For a worm-eaten coffin a hundred years hence.

Your Chancery-lawyer who by subtlety thrives,
In spinning a suit to the length of three lives,
A suit which the client doth wear out in slavery,
Whilst pleader makes conscience a cloak for his knavery,
    Can boast of his cunning but i' th' present tense,
    For *non est inventus* a hundred years hence.

Then why should we turmoil in cares and in fears,
And turn our tranquillity to sighs and tears?
Let's eat, drink and play, ere the worms do corrupt us,
For I say that, *Post mortem nulla voluptas*;
    Let's deal with our Damsels, that we may from thence
    Have broods to succeed us a hundred years hence.

I never could gain satisfaction upon
Your dreams of a bliss when we're cold as a stone,
The Sages call us Drunkards, Gluttons, and Wenchers,
But we find such morsels, upon their own trenchers:
    For Abigail, Hannah, and sister Prudence,
    Will simper to nothing a hundred years hence.

THE CARELESS GALLANT

The butterfly courtier, that pageant of state,
The mouse-trap of honour and May-game of fate,
With all his ambitions, intrigues, and his tricks,
Must die like a clown, and then drop into Styx,
    His plots against death are too slender a fence,
    For he'll be out of place a hundred years hence.

Yea, the poet himself that so loftily sings,
As he scorns any subjects, but heroes or kings,
Must to the capricios of fortune submit,
And often be counted a fool for his wit,
    Thus beauty, wit, wealth, law, learning and sense,
    All comes to nothing a hundred years hence.

THOMAS JORDAN.

79   *Hudibras, the Presbyterian Knight*

HE was in logic a great critic,
    Profoundly skill'd in analytic.
He could distinguish, and divide
A hair 'twixt South and South-West side:
On either which he would dispute,
Confute, change hands, and still confute.
He'd undertake to prove by force
Of argument, a man's no horse.
He'd prove a buzzard is no fowl,
And that a lord may be an owl,
A calf an Alderman, a goose a Justice,
And rooks Committee-men, and Trustees;
He'd run in debt by disputation,
And pay with ratiocination.
All this by syllogism, true
In mood and figure, he would do.

For rhetoric he could not ope
His mouth, but out there flew a trope:
And when he happened to break off
I' th' middle of his speech, or cough,
H' had hard words, ready to shew why,
And tell what rules he did it by.
Else when with greatest art he spoke,
You'd think he talk'd like other folk,
For all a rhetorician's rules,
Teach nothing but to name his tools,
His ordinary rate of speech
In loftiness of sound was rich,
A Babylonish dialect,
Which learned pedants much affect.
It was a parti-colour'd dress
Of patch'd and pyball'd languages:
'Twas English cut on Greek and Latin,
Like fustian heretofore on satin.
It had an odd promiscuous tone,
As if h' had talk'd three parts in one.
Which made some think when he did gabble,
Th' had heard three labo'rers of Babel;
Or Cerberus himself pronounce
A leash of languages at once.
This he as volubly would vent
As if his stock would ne'er be spent.
And truly to support that charge
He had supplies as vast and large.
For he could coin or counterfeit
New words with little or no wit:
Words so debas'd and hard, no stone
Was hard enough to touch them on.

And when with hasty noise he spoke 'em,
The ignorant for current took 'em.
That had the orator who once,
Did fill his mouth with pebble stones
When he harangu'd, but known his phrase,
He would have us'd no other ways.

.   .   .   .

Beside he was a shrewd philosopher,
And had read every text and gloss over:
What e'er the crabbed'st author hath
He understood b' implicit faith,
What ever sceptic could inquire for;
For every why he had a wherefore;
Knew more than forty of them do,
As far as words and terms could go.
All which he understood by rote,
And as occasion serv'd, would quote;
No matter whether right or wrong:
They might be either said or sung.
His notions fitted things so well,
That which was which he could not tell;
But oftentimes mistook th' one
For th' other, as great clerks have done.
He could reduce all things to acts,
And knew their natures by abstracts,
Where entity and quiddity
The ghosts of defunct bodies fly;
Where truth in person does appear,
Like words congeal'd in northern air.
He knew what's what, and that's as high
As metaphysic wit can fly,

In school divinity as able
As he that hight Irrefragable;
Profound in all the nominal
And real ways beyond them all;
And with as delicate a hand,
Could twist as tough a rope of sand,
And weave fine cobwebs, fit for skull
That's empty when the moon is full;
Such as take lodgings in a head
That's to be let unfurnished.
He could raise scruples dark and nice,
And after solve 'em in a trice:
As if divinity had catch'd
The itch, of purpose to be scratch'd;
Or, like a mountebank, did wound
And stab her self with doubts profound,
Only to shew with how small pain
The sores of faith are cur'd again;
Although by woeful proof we find,
They always leave a scar behind.
He knew the seat of Paradise,
Could tell in what degree it lies:
And as he was dispos'd, could prove it,
Below the moon, or else above it.
What Adam dreamt of when his bride
Came from her closet in his side:
Whether the Devil tempted her
By a High Dutch interpreter:
If either of them had a navel;
Who first made music malleable:
Whether the serpent at the fall
Had cloven feet, or none at all.

All this without a gloss or comment,
He would unriddle in a moment:
In proper terms, such as men smatter
When they throw out and miss the matter.
For his religion it was fit
To match his learning and his wit:
'Twas Presbyterian true blue,
For he was of that stubborn crew
Of errant saints, whom all men grant
To be the true Church Militant:
Such as do build their faith upon
The holy text of pike and gun;
Decide all controversies by
Infallible artillery;
And prove their doctrine orthodox
By apostolic blows and knocks;
Call fire and sword and desolation,
A godly-thorough-Reformation,
Which always must be carry'd on,
And still be doing, never done:
As if religion were intended
For nothing else but to be mended.
A sect, whose chief devotion lies
In odd perverse antipathies;
In falling out with that or this,
And finding somewhat still amiss:
More peevish, cross, and splenetic,
Than dog distract, or monkey sick.
That with more care keep Holy-day
The wrong, than others the right way:
Compound for sins, they are inclin'd to;
By damning those they have no mind to;

Still so perverse and opposite,
As if they worshipp'd God for spite,
The self-same thing they will abhor
One way, and long another for.
Free-will they one way disavow,
Another, nothing else allow.
All piety consists therein
In them, in other men all sin.
Rather than fail, they will defy
That which they love most tenderly,
Quarrel with minc'd pies, and disparage
Their best and dearest friend, plum-porridge;
Fat pig and goose itself oppose,
And blaspheme custard through the nose.
Th' Apostles of this fierce Religion,
Like Mahomet's, were ass and widgeon,
To whom our Knight, by fast instinct
Of wit and temper was so linked,
As if hypocrisy and non-sense
Had got th' advowson of his conscience.

SAMUEL BUTLER.

80 *Sidrophel, the Rosicrucian Conjurer*

THIS said, he turned about his steed,
And eftsoons on th' adventure rid;
Where leave we him and Ralph a while,
And to the conjurer turn our style,
To let our reader understand
What's useful of him beforehand.
He had been long t'wards mathematics,
Optics, philosophy, and statics,

SIDROPHEL, THE ROSICRUCIAN CONJURER

Magic, horoscopy, astrology,
And was old dog at physiology;
But as a dog that turns the spit
Bestirs himself, and plies his feet
To climb the wheel, but all in vain,
His own weight brings him down again:
And still he's in the self-same place
Where at his setting out he was;
So in the circle of the arts
Did he advance his nat'ral parts,
Till falling back still, for retreat,
He fell to juggle, cant, and cheat:
For as those fowls that live in water
Are never wet, he did but smatter;
Whate'er he laboured to appear,
His understanding still was clear;
Yet none a deeper knowledge boasted,
Since old Hodge Bacon, and Bob Grosted.
Th' intelligible world he knew,
And all men dream on't to be true:
That in this world there's not a wart
That has not there a counterpart;
Nor can there, on the face of ground
An individual beard be found
That has not, in that foreign nation,
A fellow of the self-same fashion;
So cut, so coloured, and so curl'd,
As those are in th' inferior world.
H' had read Dee's Prefaces before
The Dev'l, and Euclid, o'er and o'er;
And all th' intrigues 'twixt him and Kelly,
Lescus and th' Emperor would tell ye:

SIDROPHEL, THE ROSICRUCIAN CONJURER

But with the moon was more familiar
Than e'er was almanac well-willer;
Her secrets understood so clear,
That some believ'd he had been there;
Knew when she was in fittest mood
For cutting corns, or letting blood;
When for anointing scabs or itches,
Or to the burn applying leeches;
When sows and bitches may be spay'd,
And in what sign best cider's made.
Whether the wane be, or increase,
Best to set garlic, or sow peas;
Who first found out the man i' th' moon,
That to the ancients was unknown;
How many dukes, and earls, and peers,
Are in the planetary spheres,
Their airy empire, and command,
Their sev'ral strengths by sea and land;
What factions th' have, and what they drive at
In public vogue, or what in private;
With what designs and interests
Each party manages contests.
He made an instrument to know
If the moon shine at full or no;
That would, as soon as e'er she shone, straight
Whether 'twere day or night demonstrate;
Tell what her d'ameter t'an inch is,
And prove that she's not made of green cheese.
It would demonstrate, that the Man in
The Moon's a sea Mediterranean;
And that it is no dog nor bitch
That stands behind him at his breech,

But a huge Caspian sea, or lake,
With arms, which men for legs mistake;
How large a gulf his tail composes,
And what a goodly bay his nose is;
How many German leagues by th' scale
Cape-snout's from promontory-tail.
He made a planetary gin,
Which rats would run their own heads in,
And come o' purpose to be taken,
Without th' expense of cheese or bacon;
With lute-strings he would counterfeit
Maggots, that crawl on dish of meat,
Quote moles and spots on any place
O' th' body, by the index-face:
Detect lost maidenheads, by sneezing,
Or breaking wind of dames, or pissing;
Cure warts and corns, with application
Of med'cines, to th' imagination.
Fright agues into dogs, and scare,
With rhymes the tooth-ache and catarrh.
Chase evil spirits away by dint
Of sickle, horseshoe, hollow-flint.
Spit fire out of a walnut-shell,
Which made the Roman slaves rebel;
And fire a mine in China, here,
With sympathetic gunpowder.
He knew whats'ever's to be known,
But much more than he knew, would own.
What med'cine 'twas that Paracelsus
Could make a man with, as he tells us;
What figur'd slates are best to make,
On wat'ry surface, duck or drake.

173

N

What bowling-stones, in running race
Upon a board, have swiftest pace.
Whether a pulse beat in the black
List of a dappl'd louse's back.
If Systole or Diastole move
Quickest, when he's in wrath, or love:
When two of them do run a race,
Whether they gallop, trot, or pace,
How many scores a flea will jump,
Of his own length, from head to rump;
Which Socrates, and Chaerephon
In vain, essay'd so long agone;
Whether his snout a perfect nose is,
And not an elephant's proboscis;
How many different specieses
Of maggots breed in rotten cheese,
And which are next of kin to those
Engendered in a chandler's nose;
Or those not seen, but understood,
That live in vinegar and wood.

SAMUEL BUTLER.

81   *The Mower to the Glow-Worms*

YE living lamps, by whose dear light
    The nightingale does sit so late,
And studying all the summer-night,
Her matchless songs does meditate;

Ye country comets, that portend
No war, nor princes funeral,
Shining unto no higher end
Than to presage the grass's fall;

THE MOWER TO THE GLOW-WORMS

Ye glow-worms, whose officious flame
To wand'ring mowers shows the way,
That in the night have lost their aim,
And after foolish fires do stray;

Your courteous lights in vain you waste,
Since Juliana here is come,
For she my mind hath so displac'd
That I shall never find my home.

ANDREW MARVELL.

82   *Upon Appleton House*

OH thou, that dear and happy isle,
The garden of the world erewhile,
Thou Paradise of four seas,
Which Heaven planted us to please,
But, to exclude the world, did guard
With watery if not flaming sword;
What luckless apple did we taste,
To make us mortal, and thee waste?

Unhappy! shall we never more
That sweet militia restore,
When gardens only had their towers,
And all the garrisons were flowers,
When roses only arms might bear,
And men did rosy garlands wear?
Tulips, in several colours barred,
Were then the Switzers of our guard.

The gardener had the soldier's place,
And his more gentle forts did trace.
The nursery of all things green
Was then the only magazine.

The winter quarters were the stoves,
Where he the tender plants removes,
But war all this doth overgrow:
We ordnance plant, and powder sow.

And yet there walks one on the sod
Who, had it pleasèd him and God,
Might once have made our gardens spring
Fresh as his own, and flourishing.
But he preferred to the Cinque Ports
These five imaginary forts:
And, in those half-dry trenches, spanned
Power which the ocean might command.

For he did, with his utmost skill,
Ambition weed, but conscience till.
Conscience, that heaven-nursèd plant,
Which most our earthly gardens want.
A prickling leaf it bears, and such
As that which shrinks at every touch;
But flowers eternal, and divine,
That in the crowns of Saints do shine.

The sight does from these bastions ply,
The invisible artillery;
And at proud Cawood Castle seems
To point the battery of its beams.
As if it quarrelled in the seat
The ambition of its prelate great.
But o'er the meads below it plays,
Or innocently seems to gaze.

UPON APPLETON HOUSE

And now to the abyss I pass
Of that unfathomable grass,
Where men like grasshoppers appear,
But grasshoppers are giants there:
They, in their squeaking laugh, contemn
Us as we walk more low than them:
And, from the precipices tall
Of the green spires, to us do call.

To see men through this meadow dive,
We wonder how they rise alive.
As, under water, none does know
Whether he fall through it or go.
But, as the mariners that sound,
And show upon their lead the ground,
They bring up flowers so to be seen,
And prove they've at the bottom been.

No scene that turns with engines strange
Does oftener than these meadows change.
For when the sun the grass hath vexed,
The tawny mowers enter next;
Who seem like Israelites to be,
Walking on foot through a green sea.
To them the grassy deeps divide,
And crowd a lane to either side.

With whistling scythe and elbow strong,
These massacre the grass along.

.   .   .   .   .

The mower now commands the field;
In whose new traverse seemeth wrought
A camp of battle newly fought:

Where, as the meads with hay, the plain
Lies quilted o'er with bodies slain:
The women that with forks it fling,
Do represent the pillaging.

And now the careless victors play,
Dancing the triumphs of the hay;
Where every mower's wholesome heat
Smells like an Alexander's sweat.
Their females fragrant as the mead
Which they in fairy circles tread:
When at their dance's end they kiss,
Their new-made hay not sweeter is.

When, after this, 'tis piled in cocks,
Like a calm sea it shews the rocks:
We wondering in the river near
How boats among them safely steer.
Or, like the desert Memphis' sand,
Short pyramids of hay do stand.
And such the Roman camps do rise
In hills for soldiers' obsequies.

This scene again withdrawing brings
A new and empty face of things;
A levelled space, as smooth and plain,
As clothes for Lilly stretched to stain.
The world when first created sure
Was such a table rase and pure;
Or rather such is the Toril,
Ere the bulls enter at Madril.

For to this naked equal flat,
Which levellers take pattern at,

UPON APPLETON HOUSE

The villagers in common chase
Their cattle, which it closer rase;
And what below the scythe increased
Is pinched yet nearer by the beast.
Such, in the painted world, appeared
Davenant, with the universal herd.

They seem within the polished grass
A landscape drawn in looking-glass.
And shrunk in the huge pasture show
As spots, so shaped, on faces do.
Such fleas, ere they approach the eye,
In multiplying glasses lie.
They feed so wide, so slowly move,
As constellations do above.

Then, to conclude these pleasant acts,
Denton sets ope its cataracts;
And makes the meadow truly be
(What it but seemed before) a sea.
For, jealous of its Lord's long stay,
It tries to invite him thus away.
The river in itself is drowned,
And isles the astonished cattle round.

Let others tell the paradox,
How eels now bellow in the ox;
How horses at their tails do kick,
Turned as they hang to leeches quick;
How boats can over bridges sail;
And fishes do the stables scale.
How salmons trespassing are found;
And pikes are taken in the pound.

But I, retiring from the flood,
Take sanctuary in the wood.

．　　　．　　　．　　　．　　　．

When first the eye this forest sees
It seems indeed as wood not trees:
As if their neighbourhood so old
To one great trunk them all did mould.
There the huge bulk takes place, as meant
To thrust up a fifth element;
And stretches still so closely wedged,
As if the night within were hedged.

Dark all without it knits; within
It opens passable and thin;
And in as loose an order grows,
As the Corinthian porticos.
The arching boughs unite between
The columns of the temple green;
And underneath the wingèd quires
Echo about their tunèd fires.

The nightingale does here make choice
To sing the trials of her voice.
Low shrubs she sits in, and adorns
With music high the squatted thorns.
But highest oaks stoop down to hear,
And listening elders prick the ear;
The thorn, lest it should hurt her, draws
Within the skin its shrunken claws.

But I have for my music found
A sadder, yet more pleasing sound:
The stock-doves, whose fair necks are graced
With nuptial rings, their ensigns chaste;

Yet always, for some cause unknown,
Sad pair unto the elms they moan.
O why should such a couple mourn,
That in so equal flames do burn!

Then as I careless on the bed
Of gelid strawberries do tread,
And through the hazels thick espy
The hatching throstle's shining eye,
The heron, from the ash's top,
The eldest of its young lets drop,
As if it stork-like did pretend
That tribute to its Lord to send.

But most the hewel's wonders are,
Who here has the holtfelster's care,
He walks still upright from the root,
Measuring the timber with his foot;
And all the way, to keep it clean,
Doth from the bark the wood-moths glean,
He, with his beak, examines well
Which fit to stand and which to fell.

The good he numbers up, and hacks;
As if he marked them with the axe.
But where he, tinkling with his beak,
Does find the hollow oak to speak,
That for his building he designs,
And through the tainted side he mines.
Who could have thought the tallest oak
Should fall by such a feeble stroke?

Nor would it, had the tree not fed
A traitor worm, within it bred,
(As first our flesh, corrupt within,
Tempts impotent and bashful sin,)
And yet that worm triumphs not long,
But serves to feed the hewel's young,
While the oak seems to fall content,
Viewing the treason's punishment.

Thus I, easy philosopher,
Among the birds and trees confer;
And little now to make me, wants
Or of the fowls, or of the plants.
Give me but wings as they, and I
Straight floating on the air shall fly:
Or turn me but, and you shall see
I was but an inverted tree.

Already I begin to call
In their most learned original:
And where I language want, my signs
The bird upon the bough divines;
And more attentive there doth sit
Than if she were with lime-twigs knit.
No leaf does tremble in the wind
Which I returning cannot find.

Out of these scattered Sibyls' leaves
Strange prophecies my fancy weaves:
And in one history consumes,
Like Mexique paintings, all the plumes.

What Rome, Greece, Palestine, e'er said,
I in this light mosaic read.

ANDREW MARVELL.

83   *The Old Woman who lived in a Shoe*

THERE was an old woman and she lived in a shoe,
She had so many children, she didn't know what to
do.
She crumm'd 'em some porridge without any bread
And she borrowed a beetle, and she knocked 'em all on the
head.
Then out went the old woman to bespeak 'em a coffin
And when she came back she found 'em all a-loffing.

ANON.

84   *I saw a Peacock*

I SAW a peacock with a fiery tail
I saw a blazing comet drop down hail
I saw a cloud with ivy circled round
I saw a sturdy oak creep on the ground
I saw a pismire swallow up a whale
I saw a raging sea brim full of ale
I saw a Venice glass sixteen foot deep
I saw a well full of men's tears that weep
I saw their eyes all in a flame of fire
I saw a house as big as the moon and higher
I saw the sun even in the midst of night
I saw the Man that saw this wondrous sight.

ANON.

85 *Lucy Locket and Kitty Fisher*

LUCY LOCKET lost her pocket,
    Kitty Fisher found it,
But the devil a penny was there in it
    Except the binding round it.

ANON.

86 *London Bridge*

LONDON Bridge is broken down,
        Dance o'er my lady lee,
London Bridge is broken down,
        With a gay lady.

How shall we build it up again?
        Dance o'er my lady lee,
How shall we build it up again?
        With a gay lady.

Build it up with silver and gold,
        Dance o'er my lady lee,
Build it up with silver and gold,
        With a gay lady.

Silver and gold will be stole away,
        Dance o'er my lady lee,
Silver and gold will be stole away,
        With a gay lady.

Build it up with iron and steel,
        Dance o'er my lady lee,
Build it up with iron and steel,
        With a gay lady.

LONDON BRIDGE

Iron and steel will bend and bow,
    Dance o'er my lady lee,
Iron and steel will bend and bow,
    With a gay lady.

Build it up with wood and clay,
    Dance o'er my lady lee,
Build it up with wood and clay,
    With a gay lady.

Wood and clay will wash away,
    Dance o'er my lady lee,
Wood and clay will wash away,
    With a gay lady.

Build it up with stone so strong,
    Dance o'er my lady lee,
Huzza! 'twill last for ages long,
    With a gay lady.

ANON.

87   *The cauld Lad of Hilton*

WAE's me! wae's me!
    The acorn's not yet
Fallen from the tree
That's to grow the wood,
That's to make the cradle,
That's to rock the bairn,
That's to grow to a man,
That's to lay me.

ANON.

THE Moon, in her pride, once glanced aside
        Her eyes and espied the day;
As unto his bed, in waistcoat of red,
Fair Phoebus him led the way;
Such changes of thought, in her chastity wrought,
That thus she besought the boy,
O tarry, and marry the Starry Diana,
That will be thy Gem and Joy.

I will be as bright at noon as at night,
If that may delight the day;
Come hither and join thy glories with mine,
Together we'll shine for aye.
The night shall be noon, and every moon
As pleasant as June or May;
O tarry, and marry the Starry Diana,
That will be thy Gem and Joy.

Enamour'd of none, I live chaste and alone,
Though courted of one, some say;
And true if it were so frivolous fear
Let never my dear dismay;
I'll change my opinion, and turn my old Minion,
The Sleepy Endimion away,
O tarry, and marry the Starry Diana,
That will be thy Gem and Joy.

And but that the night should have wanted her light,
Or lovers in sight should play,
Or Phoebus should shame to bestow such a dame
(With a dow'r of his flame) on a boy,

Or day should appear, eternally here,
And night otherwhere, the day
Had tarry'd and marry'd the starry'd Diana,
And she been his Gem and Joy.

ANON.

89   *The Hunting of the Gods*

SONGS of Shepherds and rustical roundelays
Formed of fancies, and whistled on reeds,
Sung to solace young nymphs upon holy days
Are too unworthy for wonderful deeds.
Phoebus ingenious or winged Cylenius
His lofty Genius, may seem to declare,
In verse better coined and voice more refined.
How States devined, once hunted the hare.

Stars enamour'd with pastimes Olympical,
Stars and planets that beautiful shone;
Would no longer that earthly men only shall
Swim in pleasure, and they but look on.
Round about horned Lucina they swarmed,
And her informed how minded they were;
Each god and goddess, to take human bodies,
As lords and ladies, to follow the hare.

Chaste Diana applauded the motion,
And pale Proserpina, set in her place,
Lights the welkin, and governs the ocean,
While she conducted her nephews in chase,
And by her example, her father to trample

187

THE HUNTING OF THE GODS

The old and ample earth, leave the air,
Neptune the water, the wine Liber Pater,
And Mars the slaughter, to follow the hare.

Light god Cupid was hors'd upon Pegasus,
Borrow'd of Muses with kisses and prayers,
Strong Alcides upon cloudy Caucasus,
Mounts a Centaur that proudly him bears.
Postilion of the sky, light heel'd Mercury,
Makes his coursers fly fleet as the air,
Yellow Apollo, the kennel doth follow,
With whoop and hollow after the hare.

Hymen ushers the ladies; Astraea
The just, took hands with Minerva the bold,
Ceres the brown, with bright Cytherea,
With Thetis the wanton, Bellona the old;
Shamefac'd Aurora, with subtle Pandora;
And May with Flora, did company bear;
Juno was stated, too high to be mated,
But yet she hated not hunting the hare.

Drown'd Narcissus, from his Metamorphosis,
Rais'd by echo, new manhood did take;
Snoring Somnus upstarted in Cineris,
That this thousand year was not awake.
To see club-footed old Mulciber booted,
And Pan promoted on Chiron's mare;
Proud Faunus pouted, and Aeolus shouted,
And Momus flouted, but follow'd the hare.

Deep Melampus and cunning Ichnobates,
Nape and tiger, and harpy, the skies
Rend with roaring, whilst huntsman-like Hercules
Winds the plentiful horn to their cries,

THE HUNTING OF THE GODS

Till with varieties, to solace their pieties,
The weary deities repos'd them where
We shepherds were seated, and there we repeated,
What we conceited of their hunting the hare.

Young Amintas suppos'd the gods came to breathe
(After some battles) themselves on the ground,
Thirsis thought the stars came to dwell here beneath,
And that hereafter the earth would go round.
Coridon aged, with Phyllis engaged,
Was much enraged with jealous despair;
But fury faded, and he was persuaded,
When I thus applauded the hunting the hare.

Stars but shadows were, state were but sorrow,
Had they no motion, nor that no delight;
Joys are jovial, delight is the marrow
Of life, and action the axle of might.
Pleasure depends upon no other friends,
And yet freely lends to each virtue a share;
Only as measures the jewel of pleasures,
Of pleasure the treasures of hunting the hare.

Three broad bowls to the Olympical Rector,
His Troy-borne eagle he brings on his knee,
Jove to Phoebus carouses in nectar,
And he to Hermes, and Hermes to me;
Wherewith infused, I pip'd and I mused,
In songs unused this sport to declare;
And that the rouse of Jove, round as his sphere may move,
Health to all that love hunting the hare.

ANON.

COME lasses and lads, take leave of your dads,
  And away to the Maypole hey;
For every he has got a she
  With a Minstrel standing by:
  For Willy has gotten his Jill,
  And Johnny has got his Joan,
To jigg it, jigg it, jigg it, jigg it, jigg it up and down.

Y' are out,' says Dick, ' 'Tis a lie,' says Nick,
  'The fiddler played it false';
'Tis true,' says Hugh, and so says Sue,
  And so says nimble Alice.
    The fiddler then began
    To play the tune agen,
And every girl did trip it, trip it, trip it to the men.

Yet there they sat, until it was late
  And tired the fiddler quite,
With singing and playing, without any paying
  From morning until night.
    They told the fiddler then
    They'd pay him for his play,
And each a twopence, twopence, twopence, gave him and
      went away.

'Good night' says Tom, and so says John,
  'Good night', says Dick to Will,
'Good night' says Sis, 'Good night' says Pris,
  'Good night', says Peg to Nell.

Some run, some went, some stayed
Some dallied by the way,
And bound themselves by kisses twelve to meet next
holiday.

ANON.

91 *Lilli Burlero*

HO! broder Teague, dost hear de decree?
   Lilli Burlero, bullen a-la.
Dat we shall have a new deputie,
   Lilli Burlero, bullen a-la.
   Lero lero, lilli burlero, lero, lero, bullen a-la,

Ho! by Shaint Tyburn, it is de Talbote:
   Lilli, &c.
And he will cut de Englishman's troate.
   Lilli, &c.

Dough by my shoul de English do praat,
De law's on dare side, and Creish knows what

But if dispence do come from de Pope,
We'll hang Magna Charta and dem in a rope.

For de good Talbot is made a lord,
And with brave lads is coming abroad:

Who all in France have taken a sware,
Dat dey will have no Protestant heir.

Ara! but why does he stay behind?
Ho! by my shoul 'tis a Protestant wind.

But see de Tyrconnel is now come ashore,
And we shall have commissions gillore,

And he dat will not go to de mass,
Shall be turn out, and look like an ass,

Now, now de heretics all go down,
By Chris and Shaint Patric, de nation's our own.

Dare was an old phrophecy found in a bog,
'Ireland shall be rul'd by an ass and a dog.'

And now dis prophecy is come to pass,
For Talbot's de dog, and James is de ass.

THOMAS LORD WHARTON.

92   *Song of Venus*

FAIREST isle, all isles excelling,
    Seat of pleasures, and of loves;
Venus here will choose her dwelling,
    And forsake her Cyprian Groves.

Cupid, from his fav'rite nation,
    Care and envy will remove;
Jealousy that poisons passion,
    And despair that dies for love.

Gentle murmurs, sweet complaining,
    Sighs that blow the fire of love;
Soft repulses, kind disdaining,
    Shall be all the pains you prove.

Ev'ry swain shall pay his duty,
    Grateful ev'ry nymph shall prove;
And as these excel in beauty,
    Those shall be renown'd for love.

JOHN DRYDEN.

OUR author by experience finds it true,
  'Tis much more hard to please himself than you;
And out of no feign'd modesty, this day,
Damns his laborious trifle of a play;
Not that it's worse than what before he writ,
But he has now another taste of Wit;
And, to confess a truth (though out of time,)
Grows weary of his long-loved mistress Rhyme.
Passion's too fierce to be in fetters bound,
And Nature flies him like enchanted ground:
What verse can do he has perform'd in this,
Which he presumes the most correct of his;
But spite of all his pride, a secret shame
Invades his breast at Shakespeare's sacred name:
Aw'd when he hears his godlike Romans rage,
He in a just despair would quit the stage;
And to an age less polished, more unskilled,
Does with disdain the foremost honours yield.
As with the greater dead he dares not strive,
He would not match his verse with those who live:
Let him retire, betwixt two ages cast,
The first of this, and hindmost of the last.
A losing gamester, let him sneak away;
He bears no ready money from the play.
The fate which governs poets, thought it fit,
He should not raise his fortunes by his Wit.
The clergy thrive, and the litigious bar;
Dull heroes fatten with the spoils of war:
All southern vices, Heaven be praised, are here;
But Wit's a luxury you think too dear.

When you to cultivate the plant are loth,
'Tis a shrewd sign 'twas never of your growth:
And Wit in northern climates will not blow,
Except, like orange-trees, 'tis hous'd from snow.
There needs no care to put a play-house down,
'Tis the most desert place of all the town:
We and our neighbours, to speak proudly, are
Like monarchs, ruined with expensive war;
While, like wise English, unconcerned you sit,
And see us play the tragedy of Wit.   JOHN DRYDEN.

94   *Mac Flecknoe*

ALL human things are subject to decay,
    And, when Fate summons, monarchs must obey:
This Flecknoe found, who, like Augustus, young
Was called to empire and had governed long:
In prose and verse was owned, without dispute
Through all the realms of Nonsense, absolute.
This aged prince now flourishing in peace,
And blest with issue of a large increase,
Worn out with business, did at length debate
To settle the succession of the state;
And pond'ring which of all his sons was fit
To reign, and wage immortal war with wit,
Cried, ''Tis resolved; for Nature pleads that he
Should only rule, who most resembles me:
Shadwell' alone my perfect image bears,
Mature in dulness from his tender years;
Shadwell alone of all my sons is he
Who stands confirmed in full stupidity.
The rest to some faint meaning make pretence,
But Shadwell never deviates into sense.

MAC FLECKNOE

Some beams of wit on other souls may fall,
Strike through and make a lucid interval;
But Shadwell's genuine night admits no ray,
His rising fogs prevail upon the day:
Besides, his goodly fabric fills the eye
And seems designed for thoughtless Majesty:
Thoughtless as Monarch Oaks that shade the plain,
And, spread in solemn state, supinely reign.
Heywood and Shirley were but types of thee,
Thou last great prophet of tautology:
Even I, a dunce of more renown than they,
Was sent before but to prepare thy way:
And coarsely clad in Norwich drugget came
To teach the nations in thy greater name.
My warbling lute, the lute I whilom strung,
When to King John of Portugal I sung,
Was but the prelude to that glorious day,
When thou on silver Thames did'st cut thy way,
With well timed oars before the Royal Barge,
Swelled with the pride of thy celestial charge;
And, big with Hymn, commander of an host,
The like was ne'er in Epsom blankets tost.
Methinks I see the new Arion sail,
The lute still trembling underneath thy nail.
At thy well sharpened thumb from shore to shore
The treble squeaks for fear, the basses roar:
Echoes from Pissing-Alley, Shadwell call,
And Shadwell they resound from Aston hall.
About thy boat the little fishes throng,
As at the morning toast that floats along.
Sometimes as prince of thy harmonious band,
Thou wield'st thy papers in thy threshing hand.

St. André's feet ne'er kept more equal time,
Not ev'n the feet of thy own Psyche's rhyme:
Though they in number as in sense excel,
So just, so like tautology they fell
That, pale with envy, Singleton forswore
The lute and sword which he in triumph bore,
And vowed he ne'er would act Villerius more.'
Here stopped the good old sire; and wept for joy,
In silent raptures of the hopeful boy.
All arguments, but most his plays, persuade
That for anointed dulness he was made.

   Close to the walls which fair Augusta bind,
(The fair Augusta much to fears inclin'd)
An ancient fabric raised t'inform the sight,
There stood of yore, and Barbican it hight:
A watch tower once, but now, so fate ordains,
Of all the pile an empty name remains.
From its old ruins brothel-houses rise,
Scenes of lewd loves, and of polluted joys,
Where their vast courts the mother-strumpets keep,
And, undisturb'd by watch, in silence sleep.
Near these a Nursery erects its head,
Where queens are formed, and future heroes bred:
Where unfledged actors learn to laugh and cry,
Where infant punks their tender voices try,
And little Maximins the gods defy.
Great Fletcher never treads in buskins here,
Nor greater Jonson dares in socks appear.
But gentle Simkin just reception finds
Amid this monument of vanished minds;
Pure clinches, the suburbian Muse affords;
And Panton waging harmless war with words.

MAC FLECKNOE

Here Flecknoe, as a place to fame well known,
Ambitiously designed his Shadwell's throne.
For ancient Decker prophesied long since,
That in this pile should reign a mighty prince,
Born for a scourge of wit, and flail of sense,
To whom true dulness should some Psyches owe,
But worlds of misers from his pen should flow;
Humorists and hypocrites it should produce,
Whole Raymond families and tribes of Bruce.

Now Empress Fame had published the renown
Of Shadwell's coronation through the town.
Rous'd by report of fame, the nations meet,
From near Bun-Hill and distant Watling-Street,
No Persian carpets spread th' imperial way,
But scattered limbs of mangled poets lay;
From dusty shops neglected authors come,
Martyrs of pies and relics of the bum.
Much Heywood, Shirley, Ogleby there lay,
But loads of Shadwell almost choked the way.
Bilked stationers for yeomen stood prepar'd
And Herringman was captain of the guard.
The hoary prince in majesty appear'd,
High on a throne of his own labours rear'd.
At his right hand our young Ascanius sat
Rome's other hope and pillar of the state.
His brows thick fogs, instead of glories, grace,
And lambent dulness played around his face.
As Hannibal did to the altars come,
Sworn by his sire a mortal foe to Rome;
So Shadwell swore, nor should his vow be vain,
That he till death true dulness would maintain;
And, in his father's right, and realm's defence.

MAC FLECKNOE

Ne'er to have peace with wit, nor truce with sense.
The king himself the sacred unction made,
As king by office, and as priest by trade:
In his sinister hand, instead of ball,
He placed a mighty mug of potent ale;
Love's kingdom to his right he did convey,
At once his sceptre and his rule of sway;
Whose righteous lore the prince had practis'd young
And from whose loins recorded Psyche sprung.
His temples, last, with poppies were o'erspread,
That nodding seemed to consecrate his head:
Just at that point of time, if fame not lie,
On his left hand twelve reverend owls did fly.
So Romulus, 'tis sung, by Tiber's Brook,
Presage of sway from twice six vultures took.
Th'admiring throng loud acclamations make
And omens of his future empire take.
The sire then shook the honours of his head,
And from his brows damps of oblivion shed
Full on the filial dulness: long he stood,
Repelling from his breast the raging god;
At length burst out in his prophetic mood:
   'Heavens bless my son, from Ireland let him reign
To far Barbadoes on the western main;
Of his dominion may no end be known,
And greater than his father's be his throne.
Beyond love's kingdom let him stretch his pen';
He paused, and all the people cried 'Amen'.
Then thus continued he, 'My son, advance
Still in new impudence, new ignorance.
Success let others teach, learn thou from me
Pangs without birth, and fruitless industry.

MAC FLECKNOE

Let Virtuosos in five years be writ;
Yet not one thought accuse thy toil of wit.
Let gentle George in triumph tread the stage,
Make Dorimant betray, and Loveit rage;
Let Cully, Cockwood, Fopling, charm the pit,
And in their folly show the writer's wit.
Yet still thy fools shall stand in thy defence
And justify their author's want of sense.
Let 'em be all by thy own model made
Of dulness and desire no foreign aid,
That they to future ages may be known,
Not copies drawn, but issue of thy own.
Nay let thy men of wit too be the same,
All full of thee, and differing but in name;
But let no alien Sedley interpose
To lard with wit thy hungry Epsom prose.
And when false flowers of rhetoric thou would'st cull,
Trust Nature, do not labour to be dull;
But write thy best, and top; and in each line
Sir Formal's oratory will be thine.
Sir Formal, though unsought, attends thy quill,
And does thy northern dedications fill.
Nor let false friends seduce thy mind to fame,
By arrogating Jonson's hostile name,
Let Father Flecknoe fire thy mind with praise
And Uncle Ogleby thy envy raise.
Thou art my blood, where Jonson has no part:
What share have we in Nature or in Art?
Where did his wit on learning fix a brand
And rail at arts he did not understand?
Where made he love in Prince Nicander's vein,
Or swept the dust in Psyche's humble strain?

Where sold he bargains, "Whip-stich, kiss my arse,"
Promis'd a play and dwindled to a farce?
When did his muse from Fletcher scenes purloin,
As thou whole Etheredge dost transfuse to thine?
But so transfused as oils on waters flow,
His always floats above, thine sinks below.
This is thy province, this thy wondrous way,
New humours to invent for each new play:
This is that boasted bias of thy mind,
By which one way, to dulness, 'tis inclined.
Which makes thy writings lean on one side still,
And, in all changes, that way bends thy will.
Nor let thy mountain belly make pretence
Of likeness: thine's a tympany of sense.
A tun of man in thy large bulk is writ,
But sure thou'rt but a kilderkin of wit.
Like mine thy gentle numbers feebly creep;
Thy tragic muse gives smiles, thy comic sleep.
With whate'er gall thou sett'st thy self to write,
Thy inoffensive satires never bite.
In thy felonious heart though venom lies,
It does but touch thy Irish pen, and dies.
Thy genius calls thee not to purchase fame
In keen iambics, but mild anagram:
Leave writing plays, and choose for thy command
Some peaceful province in acrostic land.
There thou mayest wings display, and altars raise,
And torture one poor word ten thousand ways;
Or, if thou would'st thy different talents suit,
Set thy own songs, and sing them to thy lute.'
He said, but his last words were scarcely heard,
For Bruce and Longvil had a trap prepar'd,

And down they sent the yet declaiming bard,
Sinking he left his drugget robe behind,
Borne upwards by a subterranean wind,
The mantle fell to the young prophet's part
With double portion of his father's art.

JOHN DRYDEN.

95   *Prologue to Love Triumphant*

SO now, this poet, who forsakes the stage
  Intends to gratify the present age.
One warrant shall be signed for every man;
All shall be wits that will; and beaux that can:
He dies, at least to us, and to the stage,
And what he has he leaves this noble age.
He leaves you, first, all plays of his inditing,
The whole estate which he has got by writing.
The beaux may think this nothing but vain praise;
They'll find it something, the testator says;
For half their love is made from scraps of plays.
To his worst foes, he leaves his honesty,
That they may thrive upon't as much as he.
He leaves his manners to the roaring boys,
Who come in drunk, and fill the house with noise.
He leaves to the dire critics of his wit
His silence and contempt of all they writ.
To Shakespeare's critic, he bequeaths the curse,
To find his faults, and yet himself make worse;
Last, for the fair, he wishes you may be
From your dull critics, the lampooners free.
Tho' he pretends no legacy to leave you,
An old man may at least good wishes give you.

JOHN DRYDEN.

I SOWED the seeds of love, it was all in the spring,
　In April, May, and June, likewise, when small birds
　　they do sing;
My garden's well planted with flowers everywhere,
Yet I had not the liberty to choose for myself the flower
　　that I loved so dear.

My gardener he stood by, I asked him to choose for me,
He chose me the violet, the lily and pink, but those I
　　refused all three;
The violet I forsook, because it fades so soon,
The lily and the pink I did o'erlook, and I vowed I'd stay
　　till June.

In June there's a red rose-bud, and that's the flower for
　　me!
But often have I plucked at the red rose-bud till I gained
　　the willow-tree;
The willow-tree will twist, and the willow-tree will
　　twine—,
O! I wish I was in the dear youth's arms that once had the
　　heart of mine.

My gardener he stood by, he told me to take great care,
For in the middle of a red rose-bud there grows a sharp
　　thorn there;
I told him I'd take no care till I did feel the smart,
And often I plucked at the red rose-bud till I pierced it to
　　the heart.

THE SEEDS OF LOVE

I'll make me a posy of hyssop,—no other I can touch,—
That all the world may plainly see I love one flower too
    much;
My garden is run wild! where shall I plant anew—
For my bed, that once was covered with thyme, is all
    overrun with rue?

            (Mrs. Fleetwood Habergham?)

97   *Upon drinking in a Bowl*

    VULCAN contrive me such a cup
       As Nestor us'd of old:
Shew all thy skill to trim it up;
   Damask it round with gold.

Make it so large, that, fill'd with sack
   Up to the swelling brim,
Vast toasts, on the delicious lake,
   Like ships at sea, may swim.

Engrave not battle on his cheek;
   With war I've nought to do:
I'm none of those that took Mastrick,
   Nor Yarmouth Leaguer knew.

Let it no name of planets tell,
   Fixed stars, or constellations:
For I am no Sir Sidrophel,
   Nor none of his relations.

But carve thereon a spreading vine;
   Then add two lovely boys;
Their limbs in amorous folds intwine,
   The type of future joys.

UPON DRINKING IN A BOWL

Cupid and Bacchus my saints are;
   May drink and love still reign:
With wine I wash away my cares,
   And then to love again.

JOHN WILMOT, EARL OF ROCHESTER.

98   *I'll sail upon the Dog-star*

I'LL sail upon the Dog-star,
   And then pursue the morning;
I'll chase the Moon till it be noon,
But I'll make her leave her horning.

I'll climb the frosty mountain,
And there I'll coin the weather;
I'll tear the rainbow from the sky
And tie both ends together.

The stars pluck from their orbs too,
And crowd them in my budget;
And whether I'm a roaring boy,
Let all the nation judge it.

THOMAS DURFEY.

99   *Humpty Dumpty*

HUMPTY Dumpty sat on a wall,
   Humpty Dumpty had a great fall;
Threescore men and threescore more
Cannot place Humpty Dumpty as he was before.

ANON.

The House that Jack built

THIS is the knife with a handle of horn,
That killed the cock that crowed in the morn,
That wakened the priest all shaven and shorn,
That married the man all tattered and torn
Unto the maiden all forlorn,
That milked the cow with a crumpled horn
That tossed the dog over the barn,
That worried the cat
That killed the rat
That ate the malt
That lay in the house that Jack built.   ANON.

101 *Rock, Ball, Fiddle*

HE that lies at the stock,
Shall have the gold rock;
He that lies at the wall,
Shall have the gold ball;
He that lies in the middle,
Shall have the gold fiddle.   ANON.

102 *This is the Key*

THIS is the key of the kingdom:
In that kingdom there is a city.
In that city there is a town.
In that town there is a street.
In that street there is a lane.
In that lane there is a yard.
In that yard there is a house.
In that house there is a room.

P

In that room there is a bed.
On that bed there is a basket.
In that basket there are some flowers.

Flowers in a basket.
Basket in the bed.
Bed in the room.
Room in the house.
House in the yard.
Yard in the lane.
Lane in the street.
Street in the town.
Town in the city.
City in the kingdom.
Of the kingdom this is the key.   ANON.

103   *The twelve Days of Christmas*

THE twelfth day of Christmas,
    My true love gave me
Twelve lords a leaping,
Eleven ladies dancing,
Ten pipers piping,
Nine drummers drumming,
Eight maids a milking,
Seven swans a swimming,
Six geese a laying,
Five gold rings,
Four colly birds,
Three French hens,
Two turtle doves, and
A partridge in a pear-tree.   ANON.

I'LL sing you twelve O
   Green grow the rushes O
What are your twelve O?
Twelve for the twelve apostles
Eleven for the eleven that went up to heaven
Ten for the ten commandments
Nine for the nine bright shiners
Eight for the eight bold rainers
Seven for the seven stars in the sky
Six for the six proud walkers
Five for the symbol at your door
Four for the Gospel makers
Three, three for the rivals
Two, two for the lily-white boys
Clothed all in green O
One is one and all alone
And evermore shall be so.   ANON.

105   *Hallo My Fancy*

IN melancholic fancy,
   Out of myself,
In the vulcan dancy,
All the world surveying,
Nowhere staying,
Just like a fairy elf;
Out o'er the tops of highest mountains skipping,
Out o'er the hill, the trees and valleys tripping,
Out o'er the ocean seas, without an oar or shipping,—
   Hallo my fancy, whither wilt thou go?

207

HALLO MY FANCY

Amidst the misty vapours
Fain would I know
What doth cause the tapers;
Why the clouds benight us
And affright us,
While we travel here below;
Fain would I know what makes the roaring thunder,
And what these lightnings be that rend the clouds asunder,
And what these comets are on which we gaze and wonder—
Hallo my fancy, whither wilt thou go?

Fain would I know the reason
Why the little ant,
All the summer season,
Layeth up provision
On condition
To know no winter's want.
And how housewives, that are so good and painful,
Do unto their husbands prove so good and gainful;
And why the lazy drones to them do prove disdainful—
Hallo my fancy, whither wilt thou go?

.   .   .   .   .

Amidst the foamy ocean,
Fain would I know
What doth cause the motion,
And returning
In its journeying,
And doth so seldom swerve?
And how the little fishes that swim beneath salt waters,
Do never blind their eye; methinks it is a matter
An inch above the reach of old Erra Pater!—
Hallo my fancy, whither wilt thou go?

HALLO MY FANCY

Fain would I be resolvèd
How things are done;
And where the bull was calvèd
Of bloody Phalaris,
And where the tailor is
That works to the man i' the moon!
Fain would I know how Cupid aims so rightly;
And how the little fairies do dance and leap so lightly,
And where fair Cynthia makes her ambles nightly—
Hallo my fancy, whither wilt thou go?

In conceit like Phaeton
I'll mount Phoebus' chair
Having ne'er a hat on,
All my hair's a-burning
In my journeying;
Hurrying through the air.
Fain would I hear his fiery horses neighing
And see how they on foamy bits are playing,
All the stars and planets I will be surveying!—
Hallo my fancy, whither wilt thou go?

O from what ground of nature
Doth the pelican,
That self-devouring creature
Prove so froward
And untoward,
Her vitals for to restrain!
And why the subtle fox, while in death-wounds is lying,
Do not lament his pangs by howling and by crying,
And why the milk-swan doth sing when she's a-dying—
Hallo my fancy, whither wilt thou go?

HALLO MY FANCY

Fain would I conclude this,
At least make essay;
What similitude is:
Why fowls of a feather
Flock and fly together,
And lambs know beasts of prey;
How Nature's alchemists, these small laborious creatures,
Acknowledge still a prince in ordering their matters,
And suffer none to live who slothing lose their features—
Hallo my fancy, whither wilt thou go?

.　　.　　.　　.　　.　　.

To know this world's centre
Height, depth, breadth, and length,
Fain would I adventure
To search the hid attractions
Of magnetic actions
And adamantine strength.
Fain would I know, if in some lofty mountain,
Where the moon sojourns, if there be tree or fountain;
If there be beasts of prey, or yet be fields to hunt in—
Hallo my fancy, whither wilt thou go? ...

Hallo my fancy, hallo,
Stay, stay at home with me,
I can no longer follow,
For thou hast betrayed me,
And bewrayed me;
It is too much for thee.
Stay, stay at home with me, leave off thy lofty soaring;
Stay then at home with me, and on thy books be poring;
For he that goes abroad, lays little up in storing—
Thou'rt welcome my fancy, welcome home to me.

William Cleland.

GOOD people, what, will you of all be bereft—
Will you never learn wit while a penny is left?
You are all like the dog in the fable betray'd,
To let go the substance and snatch at the shade;
With specious pretences, and foreign expenses,
　　We war for Religion, and waste all our chink,
'Tis nipped, and 'tis clipped, 'tis lent, and 'tis spent,
　　Till 'tis gone, 'tis gone to the Devil I think.

We pay for our new-born, we pay for our dead,
We pay if we're single, we pay if we're wed;
To show that our merciful senate don't fail,
They begin at our head and tax down to the tail.
We pay through the nose by subjecting foes,
　　Yet for all our expenses get nothing but blows;
At home we are cheated, abroad we're defeated,
　　But the end on't, the end on't—the Lord above knows!

We parted with all our old money, to shew
We foolishly hope for a plenty of new;
But might have remember'd, when we came to the push,
That a bird in the hand is worth two in the bush:
We now like poor wretches are kept under hatches,
　　At rack and at manger like beasts in the ark,
Since our burgesses and knights make us pay for our lights—
　　Why should we, why should we be kept in the dark?

EDWARD WARD.

D ISTRACTED with care,
    For Phillis the fair;
Since nothing could move her,
Poor Damon, her lover,
Resolves in despair
No longer to languish,
Nor bear so much anguish;
But, mad with his love,
To a precipice goes;
Where, a leap from above
Would soon finish his woes.

When in rage he came there,
Beholding how steep
The sides did appear,
And the bottom how deep;
His torments projecting,
And sadly reflecting,
That a lover forsaken
A new love may get;
But a neck, when once broken,
Can never be set:
And, that he could die
Whenever he would;
But, that he could live
But as long as he could;
How grievous soever
The torment might grow,
He scorn'd to endeavour
To finish it so.

But bold, unconcern'd
At thoughts of the pain,
He calmly return'd
To his cottage again.

WILLIAM WALSH.

108   *The Maunder's Praise of his*
      strowling Mort

DOXY, oh! thy glaziers shine
   As glimmar; by the Salomon!
No gentry mort hath prats like thine,
   No cove e'er wap'd with such a one.

White thy fambles, red thy gan,
   And thy quarrons dainty is;
Couch a hogshead with me then,
   In the darkmans clip and kiss. . . .

ANON.

109   *A Paraphrase from the French*

IN grey-haired Celia's withered arms
   As mighty Louis lay,
She cried 'If I have any charms,
   My dearest, let's away!
For you, my love, is all my fear,
   Hark how the drums do rattle;
Alas, sir! what should you do here
   In dreadful day of battle?
Let little Orange stay and fight,
   For danger's his diversion;
The wise will think you in the right
   Not to expose your person,

213

A PARAPHRASE FROM THE FRENCH

Nor vex your thoughts how to repair
    The ruins of your glory:
You ought to leave so mean a care
    To those who pen your story.
Are not Boileau and Corneille paid
    For panegyric writing?
They know how heroes may be made,
    Without the help of fighting.
When foes too saucily approach,
    'Tis best to leave them fairly;
Put six good horses in your coach,
    And carry me to Marly.
Let Boufflers, to secure your fame,
    Go take some town, or buy it;
Whilst you, great sir, at Notre Dame,
    Te Deum sing in quiet!'

MATTHEW PRIOR.

110   *Mary the Cook-maid's Letter
to Doctor Sheridan*

WELL; if ever I saw such another man, since my
    mother bound my head,
You a gentleman! Marry come up, I wonder where you
    were bred?
I am sure such words do not become a man of your cloth,
I would not give such language to a dog, faith and troth.
Yes, you called my master a knave, Fie. Mr. Sheridan, 'tis
    a shame
For a parson, who should know better things, to come out
    with such a name.

MARY THE COOK-MAID'S LETTER

Knave in your teeth, Mr. Sheridan, 'tis both a shame and
a sin,
And the dean my master is an honester man than you and
all your kin:
He has more goodness in his little finger, than you have in
your whole body,
My master is a parsonable man, and not a spindle-shanked
hoddy doddy.
And now whereby I find you would fain make an excuse,
Because my master one day in anger called you goose.
Which, and I am sure I have been his servant four years
since October,
And he never called me worse than sweetheart drunk or sober:
Not that I know his Reverence was ever concerned to my
knowledge,
Though you and your come-rogues keep him out so late
in your College.

You say you will eat grass on his grave: a Christian eat
grass!
Whereby you now confess yourself to be a goose or an ass:
But that's as much as to say, that my master should die
before ye,
Well, well, that's as God pleases, and I don't believe that's
a true story,
And so say I told you so, and you may go tell my master;
what care I?
And I don't care who knows it, 'tis all one to Mary.
Everybody knows, that I love to tell truth and shame the
Devil,
I am but a poor servant, but I think gentlefolks should be
civil.

Besides, you found fault with our vittles one day that you
    was here,
I remember it was upon a Tuesday, of all days in the year.
And Saunders the man says, you are always jesting and
    mocking,
Mary (said he, one day as I was mending my master's
    stocking,)
My master is so fond of that minister that keeps the
    school;
I thought my master a wise man, but that man makes him
    a fool.
Saunders, said I, I would rather than a quart of ale,
He would come into our kitchen, and I would pin a dish-
    clout to his tail.

And now I must go, and get Saunders to direct this letter,
For I write but a sad scrawl, but my sister Marget she
    writes better.
Well, but I must run and make the bed before my master
    comes from prayers,
And see now, it strikes ten, and I hear him coming upstairs:
Whereof I could say more to your verses, if I could write
    written hand,
And so I remain in a civil way, your servant to command,
                          Mary.
                          JONATHAN SWIFT.

III   *A new Song of Wood's Halfpence*

YE people of Ireland, both country and city,
    Come listen with patience and hear out my ditty:
At this time I'll choose to be wiser than witty:
        Which nobody can deny.

A NEW SONG OF WOOD'S HALFPENCE

The halfpence are coming, the nation's undoing,
There's an end of your ploughing, and baking and
    brewing,
In short, you must all go to wreck and to ruin:
      Which nobody can deny.

Both high men and low men, and thick men and tall men,
And rich men and poor men, and free men and thrall men,
Will suffer; and this man, and that man, and all men:
      Which nobody can deny.

The soldier is ruin'd, poor man, by his pay;
His five pence will prove but a farthing a day,
For meat, or for drink, or he must run away:
      Which nobody can deny.

When he pulls out his twopence, the tapster says not,
That ten times as much he must pay for his shot;
And thus the poor soldier must soon go to pot:
      Which nobody can deny.

If he goes to the baker, the baker will huff,
And twenty pence have for a twopenny loaf,
Then 'dog, rogue, and rascal,' and so kick and cuff:
      Which nobody can deny.

Again, to the market whenever he goes,
The butcher and soldier must be mortal foes,
One cuts off an ear, and the other a nose:
      Which nobody can deny.

The butcher is stout and he values no swagger;
A cleaver 's a match any time for a dagger,
And a blue sleeve may give such a cuff as may stagger:
      Which nobody can deny.

A NEW SONG OF WOOD'S HALFPENCE

The squire who has got him twelve thousand a year,
O Lord! what a mountain his rents would appear!
Should he take them, he would not have house-room, I
    fear:
        Which nobody can deny.

Though at present he lives in a very large house,
There would then not be room in it left for a mouse;
But the squire is too wise, he will not take a souse:
        Which nobody can deny.

The farmer who comes with his rent in this cash,
For taking these counters and being so rash,
Will be kick'd out of doors both himself and his trash:
        Which nobody can deny.

For in all the leases that ever we hold,
We must pay our rent in good silver and gold,
And not in brass tokens of such a base mould:
        Which nobody can deny.

The wisest of lawyers all swear, they will warrant
No money but silver and gold can be current;
And, since they will swear it, we all may be sure on't:
        Which nobody can deny.

And I think, after all, it would be very strange,
To give current money for base in exchange,
Like a fine lady swapping her moles for the mange:
        Which nobody can deny.

But read the king's patent, and there you will find
That no man need take them but who has a mind,
For which we must say that his Majesty 's kind:
        Which nobody can deny.

A NEW SONG OF WOOD'S HALFPENCE

Now God bless the Drapier who open'd our eyes!
I'm sure, by his book, that the writer is wise;
He shows us the cheat from the end to the rise:
    Which nobody can deny.

Nay, farther, he shows it a very hard case,
That this fellow Wood, of a very bad race,
Should of all the fine gentry of Ireland take place:
    Which nobody can deny.

That he and his halfpence should come to weigh down
Our subjects so loyal and true to the crown;
But I hope, after all, that they will be his own:
    Which nobody can deny.

This book, I do tell you, is writ for your goods,
And a very good book 'tis against Mr. Wood's,
If you stand true together, he's left in the suds:
    Which nobody can deny.

Ye shopmen and tradesmen, and farmers, go read it,
For I think in my soul at this time that you need it;
Or, egad, if you don't, there's an end of your credit:
    Which nobody can deny.

                     JONATHAN SWIFT (?).

112   *Verses on the Death of Dr. Swift*

    Written by Himself: Nov. 1731

THE time is not remote, when I
   Must by the course of nature die:
When I foresee my special friends,
Will try to find their private ends:

Though it is hardly understood,
Which way my death can do them good;
Yet, thus methinks, I hear them speak:
'See, how the Dean begins to break;
Poor gentleman, he droops apace,
You plainly find it in his face:
That old vertigo in his head
Will never leave him, till he's dead:
Besides, his memory decays,
He recollects not what he says;
He cannot call his friends to mind;
Forgets the place where last he din'd:
Plies you with stories o'er and o'er,
He told them fifty times before.
How does he fancy we can sit,
To hear his out-of-fashion'd wit?
But he takes up with younger folks,
Who for his wine will bear his jokes:
Faith, he must make his stories shorter,
Or change his comrades once a quarter:
In half the time, he talks them round;
There must another set be found.

'For poetry, he's past his prime,
He takes an hour to find a rhyme:
His fire is out, his wit decay'd,
His fancy sunk, his Muse a jade.
I'd have him throw away his pen;—
But there's no talking to some men.'

And then their tenderness appears,
By adding largely to my years:

'He's older than he would be reckon'd,
And well remembers Charles the Second.

'He hardly drinks a pint of wine;
And that, I doubt, is no good sign.
His stomach too begins to fail:
Last year we thought him strong and hale;
But now, he's quite another thing;
I wish he may hold out till spring.'
Then hug themselves, and reason thus:
'It is not yet so bad with us.'
    In such a case they talk in tropes,
And, by their fears express their hopes:
Some great misfortune to portend,
No enemy can match a friend;
With all the kindness they profess,
The merit of a lucky guess,
(When daily Howd'y's come of course,
And servants answer; 'Worse and worse')
Would please them better than to tell,
That, 'God be prais'd, the Dean is well.'
Then he who prophesied the best,
Approves his foresight to the rest:
'You know, I always fear'd the worst,
And often told you so at first:'
He'd rather choose that I should die,
Than his prediction prove a lie.
Not one foretells I shall recover;
But all agree to give me over.

. . . . . .

    Behold the fatal day arrive!
'How is the Dean?' 'He's just alive.'

Q

Now the departing prayer is read;
'He hardly breathes.' 'The Dean is dead.'
   Before the passing-bell begun,
The news through half the town has run.
'O, may we all for death prepare!
What has he left? and who's his heir?
I know no more than what the news is,
'Tis all bequeath'd to public uses.
To public use! A perfect whim!
What had the public done for him!
Mere envy, avarice, and pride!
He gave it all:—but first he died.
And had the Dean, in all the nation,
No worthy friend, no poor relation?
So ready to do strangers good,
Forgetting his own flesh and blood?'

   Now Grub-Street wits are all employ'd;
With elegies the town is cloy'd:
Some paragraph in every paper,
To curse the Dean, or bless the Drapier.

   The doctors, tender of their fame,
Wisely on me lay all the blame:
'We must confess his case was nice;
But he would never take advice:
Had he been rul'd, for aught appears,
He might have liv'd these twenty years:
For when we open'd him we found,
That all his vital parts were sound.'

   From Dublin soon to London spread,
'Tis told at court, 'The Dean is dead.'

Kind Lady Suffolk in the spleen,
Runs laughing up to tell the Queen.
The Queen, so gracious, mild, and good,
Cries, 'Is he gone! 'tis time he should.
He's dead you say; why let him rot;
I'm glad the medals were forgot.
I promis'd him, I own; but when?
I only was the Princess then;
But now, as Consort of the King,
You know, 'tis quite a different thing.'

   .   .   .   .   .   .

Now Curll his shop from rubbish drains;
Three genuine tomes of Swift's remains.
And then to make them pass the glibber,
Revis'd by Tibbalds, Moore, and Cibber.
He'll treat me as he does my betters.
Publish my Will, my Life, my Letters.
Revive the libels born to die;
Which Pope must bear, as well as I.

Here shift the scene, to represent
How those I love, my death lament.
Poor Pope will grieve a month, and Gay
A week; and Arbuthnot a day.
St. John himself will scarce forbear,
To bite his pen, and drop a tear.
The rest will give a shrug and cry,
'I'm sorry; but we all must die.'
Indifference clad in Wisdom's guise,
All fortitude of mind supplies:
For how can stony bowels melt,
In those who never pity felt;

When *we* are lash'd, *they* kiss the rod,
Resigning to the will of God.

The fools, my juniors by a year,
Are tortur'd with suspense and fear.
Who wisely thought my age a screen,
When death approach'd, to stand between:
The screen removed, their hearts are trembling,
They mourn for me without dissembling.

My female friends, whose tender hearts
Have better learn'd to act their parts,
Receive the news in doleful dumps,
'The Dean is dead, (and what is trumps?)
Then, Lord have mercy on his soul.
(Ladies, I'll venture for the vole.)
Six deans they say must bear the pall.
(I wish I knew what king to call.)
Madam, your husband will attend
The funeral of so good a friend.
No madam, 'tis a shocking sight,
And he's engag'd to-morrow night!
My lady Club would take it ill,
If he should fail her at quadrille.
He lov'd the Dean. (I lead a heart.)
But dearest friends, they say, must part.
His time was come; he ran his race;
We hope he's in a better place.'

Why do we grieve that friends should die?
No loss more easy to supply.
One year is past; a different scene!
No further mention of the Dean;

Who now, alas, no more is missed,
Than if he never did exist.
Where's now the favourite of Apollo?
Departed; and his Works must follow:
Must undergo the common fate;
His kind of wit is out of date.
Some country squire to Lintot goes,
Inquires for Swift in verse and prose:
Says Lintot, 'I have heard the name:
He died a year ago.' 'The same.'
He searcheth all his shop in vain;
'Sir, you may find them in Duck Lane:
I sent them with a load of books,
Last Monday to the pastry-cook's.
To fancy they could live a year!
I find you're but a stranger here.
The Dean was famous in his time;
And had a kind of knack at rhyme;
His way of writing now is past;
The town has got a better taste:
I keep no antiquated stuff;
But, spick and span I have enough.
Pray, do but give me leave to shew 'em;
Here's Colley Cibber's birthday poem.'

.   .   .   .   .   .

Suppose me dead; and then suppose
A club assembled at the Rose;
Where from discourse of this and that,
I grow the subject of their chat:
And, while they toss my name about,
With favour some, and some without;

One quite indifferent in the cause,
My character impartial draws:

   'The Dean, if we believe report,
Was never ill received at court:
As for his works in verse and prose,
I own myself no judge of those:
Nor can I tell what critics thought 'em;
But this I know, all people bought 'em;
As with a moral view design'd
To cure the vices of mankind:
His vein, ironically grave,
Expos'd the fool, and lash'd the knave:
To steal a hint was never known,
But what he writ was all his own.

   'He never thought an honour done him,
Because a duke was proud to own him:
Would rather slip aside, and choose
To talk with wits in dirty shoes:
Despis'd the fools with stars and garters,
So often seen caressing Chartres.
He never courted men in station,
Nor persons had in admiration;
Of no man's greatness was afraid,
Because he sought for no man's aid.
Though trusted long in great affairs,
He gave himself no haughty airs:
Without regarding private ends,
Spent all his credit for his friends:
And only chose the wise and good;
No flatterers; no allies in blood;

But succour'd virtue in distress,
And seldom fail'd of good success;
As numbers in their hearts must own,
Who, but for him, had been unknown.

'With princes kept a due decorum,
But never stood in awe before 'em:
He follow'd David's lesson just,
In princes never put thy trust.
And, would you make him truly sour;
Provoke him with a slave in power:
The Irish senate, if you nam'd,
With what impatience he declaim'd!
Fair LIBERTY was all his cry;
For her he stood prepar'd to die;
For her he boldly stood alone;
For her he oft expos'd his own.
Two kingdoms, just as faction led,
Had set a price upon his head;
But not a traitor could be found,
To sell him for six hundred pound.

'Had he but spar'd his tongue and pen,
He might have rose like other men:
But power was never in his thought;
And wealth he valu'd not a groat:
Ingratitude he often found,
And pitied those who meant the wound:
But kept the tenour of his mind,
To merit well of humankind:
Nor made a sacrifice of those
Who still were true, to please his foes.

He labour'd many a fruitless hour
To reconcile his friends in power;
Saw mischief by a faction brewing,
While they pursu'd each other's ruin.
But, finding vain was all his care,
He left the court in mere despair.

'And, oh! how short are human schemes!
Here ended all our golden dreams.
What St. John's skill in state affairs,
What Ormond's valour, Oxford's cares,
To save their sinking country lent,
Was all destroy'd by one event.
Too soon that precious life was ended,
On which alone, our weal depended.

.   .   .   .   .   .

'Perhaps I may allow, the Dean
Had too much satire in his vein;
And seem'd determin'd not to starve it,
Because no age could more deserve it.
Yet, malice never was his aim;
He lash'd the vice but spar'd the name.
No individual could resent,
Where thousands equally were meant.
His satire points at no defect,
But what all mortals may correct;
For he abhorred that senseless tribe,
Who call it humour when they gibe:
He spar'd a hump, or crooked nose,
Whose owners set not up for beaux.
True genuine dulness mov'd his pity,
Unless it offer'd to be witty.

Those, who their ignorance confessed,
He ne'er offended with a jest;
But laughed to hear an idiot quote
A verse from Horace, learn'd by rote.

'He knew a hundred pleasant stories,
With all the turns of Whigs and Tories:
Was cheerful to his dying day,
And friends would let him have his way.

'He gave the little wealth he had,
To build a house for fools and mad:
And showed by one satiric touch,
No nation wanted it so much:
That kingdom he hath left his debtor,
I wish it soon may have a better.'

JONATHAN SWIFT.

113 *The Sluggard*

'TIS the voice of the sluggard; I heard him complain,
  'You have wak'd me too soon, I must slumber again.'
As the door on its hinges, so he on his bed,
Turns his sides and his shoulders and his heavy head.

'A little more sleep, and a little more slumber;'
Thus he wastes half his days and his hours without number;
And when he gets up, he sits folding his hands,
Or walks about saunt'ring, or trifling he stands.

I pass'd by his garden, and saw the wild briar,
The thorn and the thistle grow broader and higher;
The clothes that hang on him are turning to rags;
And his money still wastes, till he starves or he begs.

I made him a visit, still hoping to find
He had took better care for improving his mind:
He told me his dreams, talk'd of eating and drinking;
But he scarce reads his Bible, and never loves thinking.

ISAAC WATTS.

114   *Song*

MACHEATH. WERE I laid on Greenland's coast,
      And in my arms embrac'd my lass;
     Warm amidst eternal frost,
     Too soon the half year's night would pass.
  POLLY. Were I sold on Indian soil,
     Soon as the burning day was clos'd,
     I could mock the sultry toil
     When on my charmer's breast repos'd.
MACHEATH. And I would love you all the day,
  POLLY. Every night would kiss and play,
MACHEATH. If with me you'd fondly stray
  POLLY. Over the hills and far away.

JOHN GAY.

115   *Mr. Pope's Welcome from Greece*

Upon his having finished his translation of Homer's Iliad

LONG hast thou, friend! been absent from thy soil,
  Like patient Ithacus at siege of Troy;
I have been witness of thy six years' toil,
  Thy daily labours, and thy night's annoy,
Lost to thy native land, with great turmoil,
  On the wide sea, oft threat'ning to destroy:
Methinks with thee I've trod Sigæan ground,
And heard the shores of Hellespont resound.

MR. POPE'S WELCOME FROM GREECE

Did I not see thee when thou first sett'st sail
  To seek adventures fair in Homer's land?
Did I not see thy sinking spirits fail,
  And wish thy bark had never left the strand?
Ev'n in mid ocean often didst thou quail,
  And oft lift up thy holy eye and hand,
Praying the Virgin dear, and saintly choir,
Back to the port to bring thy bark entire.

Cheer up, my friend, thy dangers now are o'er;
  Methinks—nay, sure the rising coasts appear;
Hark how the guns salute from either shore,
  As thy trim vessel cuts the Thames so fair:
Shouts answ'ring shouts, from Kent and Essex roar,
  And bells break loud thro' every gust of air:
Bonfires do blaze, and bones and cleavers ring,
As at the coming of some mighty king.

Now pass we Gravesend with a friendly wind,
  And Tilbury's white fort, and long Blackwall;
Greenwich, where dwells the friend of human kind,
  More visited than or her park or hall,
Withers the good, and (with him ever join'd)
  Facetious Disney, greet thee first of all:
I see his chimney smoke, and hear him say,
Duke! that's the room for Pope, and that for Gay.

Come in, my friends, here shall ye dine and lie,
  And here shall breakfast, and here dine again;
And sup, and breakfast on, (if ye comply)
  For I have still some dozens of champagne:

His voice still lessens as the ship sails by;
　　He waves his hand to bring us back in vain;
For now I see, I see proud London's spires;
Greenwich is lost, and Deptford dock retires.

Oh, what a concourse swarms on yonder key!
　　The sky re-echoes with new shouts of joy:
By all this show, I ween, 'tis Lord May'r's day,
　　I hear the voice of trumpet and hautboy.—
No, now I see them near—oh, these are they
　　Who come in crowds to welcome thee from Troy.
Hail to the bard whom long as lost we mourn'd,
From siege, from battle, and from storm return'd!

　　　.　　　.　　　.　　　.　　　.

See generous Burlington, with goodly Bruce,
　　(But Bruce comes wafted in a soft sedan)
Dan Prior next, belov'd by every muse,
　　And friendly Congreve, unreproachful man!
(Oxford by Cunningham hath sent excuse)
　　See hearty Watkins comes with cup and can;
And Lewis, who has never friend forsaken;
And Laughton whisp'ring asks—Is Troy town taken?

Earl Warwick comes, of free and honest mind;
　　Bold, gen'rous Craggs, whose heart was ne'er disguis'd:
Ah why, sweet St. John, cannot I thee find?
　　St. John for ev'ry social virtue priz'd.—
Alas! to foreign climates he's confin'd,
　　Or else to see thee here I well surmiz'd:
Thou too, my Swift, dost breathe Bœotian air;
When wilt thou bring back wit and humour here?

MR. POPE'S WELCOME FROM GREECE

Harcourt I see for eloquence renown'd,
 The mouth of justice, oracle of law!
Another Simon is beside him found,
 Another Simon, like as straw to straw.
How Lansdowne smiles, with lasting laurel crown'd!
 What mitred prelate there commands our awe?
See Rochester approving nods his head,
And ranks one modern with the mighty dead.

Carlton and Chandos thy arrival grace;
 Hanmer, whose eloquence th' unbiass'd sways;
Harley, whose goodness opens in his face,
 And shews his heart the seat where virtue stays.
Ned Blount advances next, with busy pace,
 In haste, but saunt'ring, hearty in his ways:
I see the friendly Carylls come by dozens,
Their wives, their uncles, daughters, sons, and cousins.

Arbuthnot there I see, in physic's art,
 As Galen learn'd, or famed Hippocrate;
Whose company drives sorrow from the heart,
 As all disease his medicines dissipate:
Kneller amid the triumph bears his part,
 Who could (were mankind lost) a new create:
What can th' extent of his vast soul confine?
A painter, critic, engineer, divine!

Thee Jervas hails, robust and debonair,
 Now have we conquer'd Homer, friends, he cries:
Dartneuf, grave joker, joyous Ford is there,
 And wond'ring Maine, so fat with laughing eyes:

MR. POPE'S WELCOME FROM GREECE

(Gay, Maine, and Cheney, boon companions dear,
 Gay fat, Maine fatter, Cheney huge of size)
Yea Dennis, Gildon, (hearing thou hast riches)
And honest, hatless Cromwell, with red breeches.

O Wanley, whence com'st thou with shorten'd hair,
 And visage from thy shelves with dust besprent?
'Forsooth (quoth he) from placing Homer there,
 For ancients to compyle is myne entente:
Of ancients only hath Lord Harley care;
 But hither me hath my meeke lady sent:—
In manuscript of Greeke rede we thilke same,
But book yprint best plesyth myn gude dame.'

Yonder I see, among th' expecting crowd,
 Evans with laugh jocose, and tragic Young;
High-buskin'd Booth, grave Mawbert, wand'ring Frowd,
 And Titcomb's belly waddles slow along.
See Digby faints at Southern talking loud,
 Yea Steele and Tickell mingle in the throng;
Tickell whose skiff (in partnership they say)
Set forth for Greece, but founder'd in the way.

 . . . . . .

How lov'd! how honour'd thou! yet be not vain;
 And sure thou art not, for I hear thee say,
All this, my friends, I owe to Homer's strain,
 On whose strong pinions I exalt my lay.
What from contending cities did he gain;
 And what rewards his grateful country pay?
None, none were paid—why then all this for me?
These honours, Homer, had been just to thee.

JOHN GAY.

Written by Colley Cibber, Esq., Poet Laureate

GOD prosper long our gracious King,
    Now sitting on the throne;
Who leads this nation in a string,
    And governs all but one.

This is the day when, right or wrong,
    I, Colley Bays, Esquire,
Must for my sack indite a song,
    And thrum my venal lyre.

Not he who ruled great Judah's realm,
    Y'clyped Solomon,
Was wiser than Our's at the helm,
    Or had a wiser son.

He raked up wealth to glut his till,
    In drinking, w—s, and houses;
Which wiser George can save to fill
    His pocket, and his spouse's.

His head with wisdom deep is fraught,
    His breast with courage glows;
Alas, how mournful is the thought,
    He ever should want foes!

For, in his heart he loves a drum,
    As children love a rattle;
If not in field, in drawing-room,
    He daily sounds to battle.

AN ODE FOR THE NEW YEAR

The Queen, I also pray, God save!
    His consort plump and dear;
Who, just as he is wise and brave,
    Is pious and sincere.

She's courteous, good, and charms all folks,
    Loves one as well as t'other;
Of Arian and of Orthodox
    Alike the nursing-mother.

Oh! may she always meet success
    In every scheme and job;
And still continue to caress,
    That honest statesman, Bob.

God send the Prince, that babe of grace
    A little w— and horse;
A little meaning in his face,
    And money in his purse.

Heav'n spread o'er all his family
    That broad illustrious glare,
Which shines so flat in ev'ry eye,
    And makes them all so stare.

All marry gratis, boy and miss,
    And still increase their store;
'As in beginning was, now is,
    And shall be ever more.'

But oh! ev'n Kings must die, of course,
    And to their heirs be civil;
We poets, too, on wingéd-horse,
    Must soon post to the devil:

Then, since I have a son, like you,
  May he Parnassus rule;
So shall the Crown and Laurel, too,
  Descend from Fool to Fool!

JOHN GAY (?).

117 *The Rape of the Lock*

CANTO III

CLOSE by those meads, for ever crowned with flowers,
  Where Thames with pride surveys his rising towers,
There stands a structure of majestic frame,
Which from the neighb'ring Hampton takes its name.
Here Britain's statesmen oft the fall foredoom
Of foreign tyrants and of nymphs at home;
Here thou, great ANNA! whom three realms obey,
Dost sometimes counsel take—and sometimes tea.

  Hither the heroes and the nymphs resort,
To taste awhile the pleasures of a court;
In various talk th' instructive hours they past,
Who gave the ball, or paid the visit last;
One speaks the glory of the British queen,
And one describes a charming Indian screen;
A third interprets motions, looks, and eyes;
At every word a reputation dies.
Snuff, or the fan, supply each pause of chat,
With singing, laughing, ogling, *and all that*.

  Meanwhile, declining from the noon of day,
The sun obliquely shoots his burning ray;

237

R

The hungry judges soon the sentence sign,
And wretches hang that jury-men may dine;
The merchant from th' Exchange returns in peace,
And the long labours of the toilet cease.
Belinda now, whom thirst of fame invites,
Burns to encounter two advent'rous knights,
At Ombre singly to decide their doom;
And swells her breast with conquests yet to come.
Straight the three bands prepare in arms to join,
Each band the number of the sacred nine.
Soon as she spreads her hand, th' aërial guard
Descend, and sit on each important card:
First Ariel perched upon a Matadore,
Then each, according to the rank they bore;
For Sylphs, yet mindful of their ancient race,
Are, as when women, wondrous fond of place.

Behold, four Kings in majesty revered,
With hoary whiskers and a forky beard;
And four fair Queens whose hands sustain a flower,
Th' expressive emblem of their softer power;
Four Knaves in garbs succinct, a trusty band,
Caps on their heads, and halberts in their hand;
And particoloured troops, a shining train,
Draw forth to combat on the velvet plain.

The skilful Nymph reviews her force with care:
Let Spades be trumps! she said, and trumps they were.

Now move to war her sable Matadores,
In show like leaders of the swarthy Moors.
Spadillio first, unconquerable Lord!
Led off two captive trumps, and swept the board.
As many more Manillio forced to yield,
And marched a victor from the verdant field.

Him Basto followed, but his fate more hard
Gained but one trump and one Plebeian card.
With his broad sabre next, a chief in years,
The hoary Majesty of Spades appears,
Puts forth one manly leg, to sight revealed,
The rest, his many-coloured robe concealed.
The rebel Knave, who dares his prince engage,
Proves the just victim of his royal rage.
Even mighty Pam, that kings and queens o'erthrew
And mowed down armies in the fights of Lu,
Sad chance of war! now destitute of aid,
Falls undistinguished by the victor spade!

Thus far both armies to Belinda yield;
Now to the Baron fate inclines the field.
His warlike Amazon her host invades,
Th' imperial consort of the crown of Spades.
The Club's black tyrant first her victim died,
Spite of his haughty mien, and barb'rous pride:
What boots the regal circle on his head,
His giant limbs, in state unwieldy spread;
That long behind he trails his pompous robe,
And, of all monarchs, only grasps the globe?

The Baron now his Diamonds pours apace;
Th' embroidered King who shows but half his face,
And his refulgent Queen, with powers combined,
Of broken troops an easy conquest find.
Clubs, Diamonds, Hearts, in wild disorder seen,
With throngs promiscuous strew the level green.
Thus when dispersed a routed army runs,
Of Asia's troops, and Afric's sable sons,
With like confusion different nations fly,
Of various habit, and of various dye,

The pierced battalions disunited fall,
In heaps on heaps; one fate o'erwhelms them all.
   The Knave of Diamonds tries his wily arts,
And wins (oh shameful chance!) the Queen of Hearts.
At this, the blood the virgin's cheek forsook,
A livid paleness spreads o'er all her look;
She sees, and trembles at th' approaching ill,
Just in the jaws of ruin, and Codille.
And now (as oft in some distempered State)
On one nice trick depends the general fate.
An Ace of Hearts steps forth: the King unseen
Lurked in her hand, and mourned his captive Queen:
He springs to vengeance with an eager pace,
And falls like thunder on the prostrate Ace.
The Nymph exulting fills with shouts the sky;
The walls, the woods, and long canals reply.
   Oh thoughtless mortals! ever blind to fate,
Too soon dejected, and too soon elate.
Sudden, these honours shall be snatched away,
And cursed for ever this victorious day.
   For lo! the board with cups and spoons is crowned,
The berries crackle, and the mill turns round;
On shining altars of Japan they raise
The silver lamp; the fiery spirits blaze:
From silver spouts the grateful liquors glide,
While China's earth receives the smoking tide:
At once they gratify their scent and taste,
And frequent cups prolong the rich repast.
Straight hover round the Fair her airy band;
Some, as she sipped, the fuming liquor fanned,
Some o'er her lap their careful plumes displayed,
Trembling, and conscious of the rich brocade.

THE RAPE OF THE LOCK

Coffee, (which makes the politician wise,
And see through all things with his half-shut eyes)
Sent up in vapours to the Baron's brain
New stratagems, the radiant Lock to gain.
Ah cease, rash youth! desist ere 'tis too late,
Fear the just Gods, and think of Scylla's fate!
Changed to a bird, and sent to flit in air,
She dearly pays for Nisus' injured hair!

But when to mischief mortals bend their will,
How soon they find fit instruments of ill!
Just then, Clarissa drew with tempting grace
A two-edged weapon from her shining case:
So ladies in romance assist their knight,
Present the spear, and arm him for the fight.
He takes the gift with rev'rence, and extends
The little engine on his fingers' ends;
This just behind Belinda's neck he spread,
As o'er the fragrant steams she bends her head.
Swift to the Lock a thousand Sprites repair,
A thousand wings, by turns, blow back the hair;
And thrice they twitched the diamond in her ear;
Thrice she looked back, and thrice the foe drew near.
Just in that instant, anxious Ariel sought
The close recesses of the Virgin's thought;
As on the nosegay in her breast reclined,
He watched th' ideas rising in her mind,
Sudden he viewed, in spite of all her art,
An earthly lover lurking at her heart.
Amazed, confused, he found his power expired,
Resigned to fate, and with a sigh retired.

The Peer now spreads the glitt'ring Forfex wide,
T'inclose the Lock; now joins it, to divide.

Even then, before the fatal engine closed,
A wretched Sylph too fondly interposed;
Fate urged the shears, and cut the Sylph in twain,
(But airy substance soon unites again)
The meeting points the sacred hair dissever
From the fair head, for ever, and for ever!

ALEXANDER POPE.

118   *To a Lady*

Of the Characters of Women

NOTHING so true as what you once let fall,
   'Most women have no characters at all.'
   How many pictures of one nymph we view,
All how unlike each other, all how true!
Arcadia's Countess, here, in ermined pride,
Is, there, Pastora by a fountain side.
Here Fannia, leering on her own good man,
And there, a naked Leda with a swan.
Let then the fair one beautifully cry,
In Magdalen's loose hair, and lifted eye,
Or dressed in smiles of sweet Cecilia shine,
With simp'ring angels, palms, and harps divine;
Whether the charmer sinner it, or saint it,
If folly grow romantic, I must paint it.
   Come then, the colours and the ground prepare!
Dip in the rainbow, trick her off in air;
Choose a firm cloud, before it fall, and in it
Catch, ere she change, the Cynthia of this minute,
   Rufa, whose eye quick-glancing o'er the park,
Attracts each light gay meteor of a spark,

242

TO A LADY

Agrees as ill with Rufa studying Locke,
As Sappho's diamonds with her dirty smock;
Or Sappho at her toilet's greasy task,
With Sappho fragrant at an evening masque:
So morning insects that in muck begun,
Shine, buzz, and fly-blow in the setting-sun.

How soft is Silia! fearful to offend;
The frail one's advocate, the weak one's friend:
To her, Calista proved her conduct nice;
And good Simplicius asks of her advice.
Sudden, she storms! she raves! You tip the wink,
But spare your censure; Silia does not drink.
All eyes may see from what the change arose,
All eyes may see—a pimple on her nose.

Papillia, wedded to her am'rous spark,
Sighs for the shades—'How charming is a park!'
A park is purchased, but the fair he sees
All bathed in tears—'Oh, odious, odious trees!'

Ladies, like variegated tulips, show;
'Tis to their changes half their charms we owe;
Fine by defect, and delicately weak,
Their happy spots the nice admirer take,
'Twas thus Calypso once each heart alarmed,
Awed without virtue, without beauty charmed;
Her tongue bewitched as oddly as her eyes,
Less wit than mimic, more a wit than wise;
Strange graces still, and stranger flights she had,
Was just not ugly, and was just not mad;
Yet ne'er so sure our passion to create,
As when she touched the brink of all we hate.

Narcissa's nature, tolerably mild,
To make a wash, would hardly stew a child;

TO A LADY

Has even been proved to grant a lover's prayer,
And paid a tradesman once to make him stare;
Gave alms at Easter, in a Christian trim,
And made a widow happy, for a whim.
Why then declare good-nature is her scorn,
When 'tis by that alone she can be borne?
Why pique all mortals, yet affect a name?
A fool to pleasure, yet a slave to fame:
Now deep in Taylor and the Book of Martyrs,
Now drinking citron with his Grace and Chartres:
Now conscience chills her, and now passion burns;
And atheism and religion take their turns;
A very heathen in the carnal part,
Yet still a sad, good Christian at her heart.

　　See sin in state, majestically drunk;
Proud as a peeress, prouder as a punk;
Chaste to her husband, frank to all beside,
A teeming mistress, but a barren bride.
What then? let blood and body bear the fault,
Her head's untouched, that noble seat of thought:
Such this day's doctrine—in another fit
She sins with poets through pure love of wit.
What has not fired her bosom or her brain?
Cæsar and Tall-boy, Charles and Charlemagne.
As Helluo, late Dictator of the Feast,
The nose of Hautgout, and the tip of taste,
Critic'd your wine, and analysed your meat,
Yet on plain pudding deigned at home to eat;
So Philomedé, lect'ring all mankind
On the soft passion, and the taste refined,
Th' address, the delicacy—stoops at once,
And makes her hearty meal upon a dunce.

TO A LADY

Flavia's a wit, has too much sense to pray;
To toast our wants and wishes, is her way;
Nor asks of God, but of her stars, to give
The mighty blessing, 'while we live, to live.'
Then all for death, that opiate of the soul!
Lucretia's dagger, Rosamonda's bowl.
Say, what can cause such impotence of mind?
A spark too fickle, or a spouse too kind.
Wise wretch! with pleasures too refined to please;
With too much spirit to be e'er at ease;
With too much quickness ever to be taught;
With too much thinking to have common thought:
You purchase pain with all that joy can give,
And die of nothing but a rage to live.

Turn then from wits; and look on Simo's mate,
No ass so meek, no ass so obstinate.
Or her, that owns her faults, but never mends,
Because she's honest, and the best of friends.
Or her, whose life the Church and scandal share,
For ever in a passion, or a prayer.
Or her, who laughs at Hell, but (like her Grace)
Cries, 'Ah! how charming, if there's no such place!'
Or who in sweet vicissitude appears
Of mirth and opium, ratafie and tears,
The daily anodyne, and nightly draught,
To kill those foes to fair ones, time and thought.
Woman and fool are two hard things to hit;
For true no-meaning puzzles more than wit.

But what are these to great Atossa's mind?
Scarce once herself, by turns all womankind!
Who, with herself, or others, from her birth
Finds all her life one warfare upon earth:

245

TO A LADY

Shines in exposing knaves, and painting fools,
Yet is, whate'er she hates and ridicules.
No thought advances, but her eddy brain
Whisks it about, and down it goes again.
Full sixty years the world has been her trade,
The wisest fool much time has ever made.
From loveless youth to unrespected age,
No passion gratified except her rage.
So much the fury still out-ran the wit,
The pleasure missed her, and the scandal hit.
Who breaks with her, provokes revenge from Hell,
But he's a bolder man who dares be well.
Her every turn with violence pursued,
Nor more a storm her hate than gratitude:
To that each passion turns, or soon or late;
Love, if it makes her yield, must make her hate:
Superiors? death! and equals? what a curse!
But an inferior not dependent? worse.
Offend her, and she knows not to forgive;
Oblige her, and she'll hate you while you live:
But die, and she'll adore you—then the bust
And temple rise—then fall again to dust.
Last night, her lord was all that's good and great;
A knave this morning, and his will a cheat.
Strange! by the means defeated of the ends,
By spirit robbed of power, by warmth of friends,
By wealth of followers! without one distress
Sick of herself through very selfishness!
Atossa, cursed with every granted prayer,
Childless with all her children, wants an heir.
To heirs unknown descends th' unguarded store,
Or wanders, Heaven-directed, to the poor.

TO A LADY

Pictures like these, dear Madam, to design,
Asks no firm hand, and no unerring line;
Some wand'ring touches, some reflected light,
Some flying stroke alone can hit 'em right:
For how should equal colours do the knack?
Chameleons who can paint in white and black?
    'Yet Chloe sure was formed without a spot'—
Nature in her then erred not, but forgot.
'With every pleasing, every prudent part,
Say, what can Chloe want?'—She wants a heart.
She speaks, behaves, and acts just as she ought;
But never, never, reached one gen'rous thought.
Virtue she finds too painful an endeavour,
Content to dwell in decencies for ever.
So very reasonable, so unmoved,
As never yet to love, or to be loved.
She, while her lover pants upon her breast,
Can mark the figures on an Indian chest;
And when she sees her friend in deep despair,
Observes how much a chintz exceeds mohair.
Forbid it Heaven, a favour or a debt
She e'er should cancel—but she may forget.
Safe is your secret still in Chloe's ear;
But none of Chloe's shall you ever hear.
Of all her dears she never slandered one,
But cares not if a thousand are undone.
Would Chloe know if you're alive or dead?
She bids her footman put it in her head.
Chloe is prudent—Would you too be wise?
Then never break your heart when Chloe dies.

ALEXANDER POPE.

P. SHUT, shut the door, good John! fatigued, I said,
    Tie up the knocker, say I'm sick, I'm dead.
The Dog-star rages! nay 'tis past a doubt,
All Bedlam, or Parnassus, is let out:
Fire in each eye, and papers in each hand,
They rave, recite, and madden round the land.

    What walls can guard me, or what shades can hide?
They pierce my thickets, through my Grot they glide;
By land, by water, they renew the charge;
They stop the chariot, and they board the barge.
No place is sacred, not the Church is free;
Even Sunday shines no Sabbath-day to me;
Then from the Mint walks forth the man of rhyme,
Happy to catch me just at dinner-time.

    Is there a parson, much bemused in beer,
A maudlin poetess, a rhyming peer,
A clerk, foredoomed his father's soul to cross,
Who pens a stanza, when he should engross?
Is there, who, locked from ink and paper, scrawls
With desp'rate charcoal round his darkened walls?
All fly to TWIT'NAM, and in humble strain
Apply to me, to keep them mad or vain.
Arthur, whose giddy son neglects the laws,
Imputes to me and my damned works the cause:
Poor Cornus sees his frantic wife elope,
And curses wit, and poetry, and Pope.

    Friend to my life! (which did not you prolong,
The world had wanted many an idle song)
What drop or nostrum can this plague remove?
Or which must end me, a fool's wrath or love?

TO DR. ARBUTHNOT

A dire dilemma! either way I'm sped,
If foes, they write, if friends, they read me dead.
Seized and tied down to judge, how wretched I!
Who can't be silent, and who will not lie.
To laugh, were want of goodness and of grace,
And to be grave, exceeds all power of face.
I sit with sad civility, I read
With honest anguish, and an aching head;
And drop at last, but in unwilling ears,
This saving counsel, 'Keep your piece nine years.'

'Nine years!' cries he, who, high in Drury-lane,
Lulled by soft zephyrs through the broken pane,
Rhymes ere he wakes, and prints before term ends,
Obliged by hunger, and request of friends:
'The piece, you think, is incorrect? why, take it,
I'm all submission, what you'd have it, make it.'

Three things another's modest wishes bound,
My friendship, and a prologue, and ten pound.

Pitholeon sends to me: 'You know his Grace,
I want a patron; ask him for a place.'
'Pitholeon libelled me,'—'but here's a letter
Informs you, Sir, 'twas when he knew no better.
Dare you refuse him? Curll invites to dine,
He'll write a journal, or he'll turn divine.'

Bless me! a packet.—''Tis a stranger sues,
A virgin tragedy, an orphan muse.'
If I dislike it, 'Furies, death and rage!'
If I approve, 'Commend it to the stage.'
There (thank my stars) my whole commission ends,
The players and I are, luckily, no friends.
Fired that the house reject him, ''Sdeath I'll print it,
And shame the fools—Your int'rest, Sir, with Lintot!'

'Lintot, dull rogue! will think your price too much:'
'Not, Sir, if you revise it, and retouch.'
All my demurs but double his attacks;
At last he whispers, 'Do; and we go snacks.'
Glad of a quarrel, straight I clap the door,
'Sir, let me see your works and you no more.'

'Tis sung, when Midas' ears began to spring,
(Midas, a sacred person and a king)
His very minister who spied them first,
(Some say his queen) was forced to speak, or burst.
And is not mine, my friend, a sorer case,
When every coxcomb perks them in my face?
A. Good friend, forbear! you deal in dang'rous things.
I'd never name queens, ministers, or kings;
Keep close to ears, and those let asses prick;
'Tis nothing— P. Nothing? if they bite and kick?
Out with it, Dunciad! let the secret pass,
That secret to each fool, that he's an ass:
The truth once told (and wherefore should we lie?)
The Queen of Midas slept, and so may I.

You think this cruel? take it for a rule,
No creature smarts so little as a fool.
Let peals of laughter, Codrus! round thee break,
Thou unconcerned canst hear the mighty crack:
Pit, box, and gall'ry in convulsions hurled,
Thou stand'st unshook amidst a bursting world.
Who shames a scribbler? break one cobweb through,
He spins the slight, self-pleasing thread anew:
Destroy his fib or sophistry, in vain,
The creature's at his dirty work again,
Throned in the centre of his thin designs,
Proud of a vast extent of flimsy lines!

TO DR. ARBUTHNOT

Whom have I hurt? has poet yet, or peer,
Lost the arched eye-brow, or Parnassian sneer?
And has not Colley still his lord, and whore?
His butchers Henley, his free-masons Moore?
Does not one table Bavius still admit?
Still to one bishop Philips seem a wit?
Still Sappho— A. Hold! for God's sake—you'll offend,
No Names!—be calm!—learn prudence of a friend!
I too could write, and I am twice as tall;
But foes like these— P. One flatt'rer's worse than all.
Of all mad creatures, if the learned are right,
It is the slaver kills, and not the bite.
A fool quite angry is quite innocent:
Alas! 'tis ten times worse when they repent.

One dedicates in high heroic prose,
And ridicules beyond a hundred foes:
One from all Grubstreet will my fame defend,
And, more abusive, calls himself my friend.
This prints my letters, that expects a bribe,
And others roar aloud, 'Subscribe, subscribe.'

There are, who to my person pay their court:
I cough like Horace, and, though lean, am short,
Ammon's great son one shoulder had too high,
Such Ovid's nose, and 'Sir! you have an eye'—
Go on, obliging creatures, make me see
All that disgraced my betters, met in me.
Say for my comfort, languishing in bed,
'Just so immortal Maro held his head:'
And when I die, be sure you let me know
Great Homer died three thousand years ago.

Why did I write? what sin to me unknown
Dipped me in ink, my parents', or my own?

TO DR. ARBUTHNOT

As yet a child, nor yet a fool to fame,
I lisped in numbers, for the numbers came.
I left no calling for this idle trade,
No duty broke, no father disobeyed.
The Muse but served to ease some friend, not wife,
To help me through this long disease, my life,
To second, ARBUTHNOT! thy art and care,
And teach the being you preserved, to bear.

But why then publish? Granville the polite,
And knowing Walsh, would tell me I could write;
Well-natured Garth inflamed with early praise;
And Congreve loved, and Swift endured my lays;
The courtly Talbot, Somers, Sheffield read;
Even mitred Rochester would nod the head,
And St. John's self (great Dryden's friends before)
With open arms received one poet more.
Happy my studies, when by these approved!
Happier their author, when by these beloved!
From these the world will judge of men and books,
Not from the Burnets, Oldmixons, and Cookes.

Soft were my numbers; who could take offence,
While pure description held the place of sense?
Like gentle Fanny's was my flowery theme,
A painted mistress, or a purling stream.
Yet then did Gildon draw his venal quill;—
I wished the man a dinner, and sat still.
Yet then did Dennis rave in furious fret;
I never answered,—I was not in debt.
If want provoked, or madness made them print,
I waged no war with Bedlam or the Mint.

Did some more sober critic come abroad;
If wrong, I smiled; if right, I kissed the rod.

TO DR. ARBUTHNOT

Pains, reading, study, are their just pretence,
And all they want is spirit, taste, and sense.
Commas and points they set exactly right,
And 'twere a sin to rob them of their mite.
Yet ne'er one sprig of laurel graced these ribalds,
From slashing Bentley down to pidling Tibalds:
Each wight, who reads not, and but scans and spells,
Each word-catcher, that lives on syllables,
Even such small critics some regard may claim,
Preserved in Milton's or in Shakespeare's name.
Pretty! in amber to observe the forms
Of hairs, or straws, or dirt, or grubs, or worms!
The things, we know, are neither rich nor rare,
But wonder how the devil they got there.

Were others angry, I excused them too;
Well might they rage, I gave them but their due.
A man's true merit 'tis not hard to find;
But each man's secret standard in his mind,
That casting-weight pride adds to emptiness,
This, who can gratify? for who can guess?
The bard whom pilfered pastorals renown,
Who turns a Persian tale for half a crown,
Just writes to make his barrenness appear,
And strains, from hard-bound brains, eight lines a year;
He, who still wanting, though he lives on theft,
Steals much, spends little, yet has nothing left:
And He, who now to sense, now nonsense leaning,
Means not, but blunders round about a meaning:
And He, whose fustian's so sublimely bad,
It is not poetry, but prose run mad:
All these, my modest satire bade translate,
And owned that nine such poets made a Tate.

How did they fume, and stamp, and roar, and chafe!
And swear, not ADDISON himself was safe.
   Peace to all such! but were there One whose fires
True genius kindles, and fair fame inspires;
Blest with each talent and each art to please,
And born to write, converse, and live with ease:
Should such a man, too fond to rule alone,
Bear, like the Turk, no brother near the throne.
View him with scornful, yet with jealous eyes,
And hate for arts that caused himself to rise;
Damn with faint praise, assent with civil leer,
And without sneering, teach the rest to sneer;
Willing to wound, and yet afraid to strike,
Just hint a fault, and hesitate dislike;
Alike reserved to blame, or to commend,
A tim'rous foe, and a suspicious friend;
Dreading even fools, by flatt'rers besieged,
And so obliging, that he ne'er obliged;
Like Cato, give his little Senate laws,
And sit attentive to his own applause;
While wits and Templars every sentence raise,
And wonder with a foolish face of praise:—
Who but must laugh, if such a man there be?
Who would not weep, if ATTICUS were he?

      ·   ·   ·   ·   ·   ·

   Cursed be the verse, how well soe'er it flow,
That tends to make one worthy man my foe,
Give virtue scandal, innocence a fear,
Or from the soft-eyed virgin steal a tear!
But he who hurts a harmless neighbour's peace,
Insults fallen worth, or beauty in distress,

TO DR. ARBUTHNOT

Who loves a lie, lame slander helps about,
Who writes a libel, or who copies out:
That fop, whose pride affects a patron's name,
Yet absent, wounds an author's honest fame:
Who can your merit selfishly approve,
And show the sense of it without the love;
Who has the vanity to call you friend,
Yet wants the honour, injured, to defend;
Who tells whate'er you think, whate'er you say,
And, if he lie not, must at least betray:
Who to the Dean and silver bell can swear,
And sees at Canons what was never there;
Who reads, but with a lust to misapply,
Make satire a lampoon, and fiction, lie.
A lash like mine no honest man shall dread,
But all such babbling blockheads in his stead.

  Let Sporus tremble— A. What? that thing of silk,
Sporus, that mere white curd of ass's milk?
Satire or sense, alas! can Sporus feel?
Who breaks a butterfly upon a wheel?
P. Yet let me flap this bug with gilded wings,
This painted child of dirt, that stinks and stings;
Whose buzz the witty and the fair annoys,
Yet wit ne'er tastes, and beauty ne'er enjoys:
So well-bred spaniels civilly delight
In mumbling of the game they dare not bite.
Eternal smiles his emptiness betray,
As shallow streams run dimpling all the way.
Whether in florid impotence he speaks,
And, as the prompter breathes, the puppet squeaks;
Or at the ear of Eve, familiar toad,
Half froth, half venom, spits himself abroad,

TO DR. ARBUTHNOT

In puns, or politics, or tales, or lies,
Or spite, or smut, or rhymes, or blasphemies.
His wit all see-saw, between that and this,
Now high, now low, now master up, now miss,
And he himself one vile antithesis.
Amphibious thing! that acting either part,
The trifling head or the corrupted heart,
Fop at the toilet, flatt'rer at the board,
Now trips a lady, and now struts a lord.
Eve's tempter thus the Rabbins have expressed,
A cherub's face, a reptile all the rest;
Beauty that shocks you, parts that none will trust;
Wit that can creep, and pride that licks the dust.

Not fortune's worshipper, nor fashion's fool,
Not lucre's madman, nor ambition's tool,
Not proud, nor servile;—be one poet's praise,
That, if he pleased, he pleased by manly ways:
That flatt'ry, even to kings, he held a shame,
And thought a lie in verse or prose the same.
That not in fancy's maze he wandered long,
But stooped to truth, and moralized his song:
That not for fame, but virtue's better end,
He stood the furious foe, the timid friend,
The damning critic, half approving wit,
The coxcomb hit, or fearing to be hit;
Laughed at the loss of friends he never had,
The dull, the proud, the wicked, and the mad;
The distant threats of vengeance on his head
The blow unfelt, the tear he never shed;
The tale revived, the lie so oft o'erthrown,
Th' imputed trash, and dulness not his own;
The morals blackened when the writings scape,

TO DR. ARBUTHNOT

The libelled person, and the pictured shape;
Abuse, on all he loved, or loved him, spread,
A friend in exile, or a father, dead;
The whisper, that to greatness still too near,
Perhaps, yet vibrates on his Sov'REIGN's ear:—
Welcome for thee, fair Virtue! all the past;
For thee, fair Virtue! welcome even the last!

.   .   .   .   .

O Friend! may each domestic bliss be thine!
Be no unpleasing melancholy mine:
Me, let the tender office long engage,
To rock the cradle of reposing age,
With lenient arts extend a Mother's breath,
Make languor smile, and smooth the bed of death,
Explore the thought, explain the asking eye,
And keep a while one parent from the sky!
On cares like these if length of days attend,
May Heaven, to bless those days, preserve my friend,
Preserve him social, cheerful, and serene,
And just as rich as when he served a QUEEN.
A. Whether that blessing be denied or given,
Thus far was right, the rest belongs to Heaven.

                                        ALEXANDER POPE.

120 *Engraved on the Collar of a Dog, which
      I gave to His Royal Highness*

I AM his Highness' dog at Kew;
Pray tell me, sir, whose dog are you?

                                        ALEXANDER POPE,

121   *Robin and Richard*

ROBIN and Richard were two pretty men,
   They lay in bed till the clock struck ten:
Then up starts Robin, and looks at the sky,
'Oh! brother Richard, the sun's very high,
The bull's in the barn threshing the corn;
The cock's on the dunghill blowing his horn.
The cat's at the fire frying of fish,
The dog's in the pantry breaking his dish.
You go before, with the bottle and bag,
And I will come after, on little Jack Nag.'   ANON.

122   *How many Miles to Barley-Bridge?*

'HOW many miles to Barley-Bridge?'
    'Three score and ten.'
'Can I get there by candle-light?'
   'Yes, if your legs be long.'

'A courtesy to you, and a courtesy to you,
If you please will you let the King's horses through?'
    'Through and through shall they go,
      For the king's sake;
But the one that is hindmost
    Will meet with a great mistake.'   ANON.

123   *Ride a Cock-Horse*

RIDE a cock-horse to Banbury-Cross,
   To see an old woman get up on her horse.
Rings on her fingers, and bells on her toes,
And so she makes music wherever she goes.   ANON.

GAY go up, and gay go down,
   To ring the bells of London town.

Bull's eyes and targets,
Say the bells of St. Marg'ret's.

Brickbats and tiles,
Say the bells of St. Giles'.

Halfpence and farthings
Say the bells of St. Martin's.

Oranges and lemons,
Say the bells of St. Clement's.

Pancakes and fritters,
Say the bells of St. Peter's.

Two sticks and an apple,
Say the bells at Whitechapel.

Old Father Baldpate,
Say the slow bells at Aldgate.

Maids in white aprons,
Say the bells of St. Cath'rine's.

Pokers and tongs,
Say the bells at St. John's.

Kettles and pans,
Say the bells at St. Ann's.

You owe me ten shillings,
Say the bells at St. Helen's.

When will you pay me?
Say the bells at Old Bailey.

When I grow rich,
Say the bells at Fleetditch.

259

When will that be?
Say the bells at Stepney.

I am sure I don't know,
Says the great bell at Bow.

When I am old,
Say the bells at St. Paul's.

Here comes a candle to light you to bed,
And here comes a chopper to chop off your head.

ANON.

125   *The Vicar of Bray*

IN good King Charles's golden days,
   When loyalty no harm meant;
A furious high-church man I was,
   And so I gain'd preferment.
Unto my flock I daily preach'd,
   Kings are by God appointed,
And damn'd are those who dare resist,
   Or touch the Lord's anointed.
      And this is law, I will maintain
        Unto my dying day, Sir,
      That whatsoever King shall reign,
        I will be Vicar of Bray, Sir!

When Royal James possessed the crown,
   And popery grew in fashion;
The penal law I houted down,
   And read the declaration:
The Church of Rome, I found would fit,
   Full well my constitution,
And I had been a Jesuit,
   But for the Revolution.
      And this is law, &c.

THE VICAR OF BRAY

When William our deliverer came,
    To heal the nation's grievance,
I turned the cat in pan again,
    And swore to him allegiance:
Old principles I did revoke,
    Set conscience at a distance,
Passive obedience is a joke,
    A jest is non-resistance.
        And this is law, &c.

When glorious Ann became our Queen,
    The Church of England's glory,
Another face of things was seen,
    And I became a Tory:
Occasional conformists base,
    I damn'd, and moderation,
And thought the church in danger was,
    From such prevarication.
        And this is law, &c.

When George in pudding time came o'er,
    And moderate men looked big, Sir,
My principles I chang'd once more,
    And so became a Whig, Sir:
And thus preferment I procur'd,
    From our Faith's Great Defender,
And almost every day abjur'd
    The Pope, and the Pretender.
        And this is law, &c.

The illustrious House of Hanover,
    And Protestant succession,
To these I lustily will swear,
    Whilst they can keep possession:

For in my faith, and loyalty,
   I never once will falter,
But George, my lawful King shall be,
   Except the times should alter.
     And this is law, &c.

ANON.

126   *Hunting Song*

THE dusky night rides down the sky,
   And ushers in the morn;
The hounds all join in glorious cry,
   The huntsman winds his horn:
     And a-hunting we will go.

The wife around her husband throws
   Her arms, and begs his stay;
My dear, it rains, and hails, and snows,
   You will not hunt to-day.
     But a-hunting we will go.

A brushing fox in yonder wood,
   Secure to find we seek;
For why, I carried sound and good
   A cartload there last week.
     And a-hunting we will go.

Away he goes, he flies the rout,
   Their steeds all spur and switch;
Some are thrown in, and some thrown out,
   And some thrown in the ditch:
     But a-hunting we will go.

At length his strength to faintness worn,
   Poor Renard ceases flight;
Then hungry, homeward we return,
   To feast away the night:
     Then a-drinking we will go.
            HENRY FIELDING.

127   *Hunting Song*

THE sun from the east tips the mountains with gold:
   The meadows all spangled with dew-drops behold!
Hear! the lark's early matin proclaims the new day,
And the horn's cheerful summons rebukes our delay.
   With the sports of the field there's no pleasure can vie,
   While jocund we follow the hounds in full cry.

Let the drudge of the town still make riches his sport,
The slave of the state hunt the smiles of a court;
No care and ambition our pastime annoy,
But innocence still gives a zest to our joy.

Mankind are all hunters in various degree;
The priest hunts a living—the lawyer a fee,
The doctor a patient—the courtier a place,
Though often, like us, he's flung out in the chase.

The cit hunts a plumb—while the soldier hunts fame,
The poet a dinner—the patriot a name;
And the practis'd coquette, tho' she seems to refuse,
In spite of her airs, still her lover pursues.

Let the bold and the busy hunt glory and wealth;
All the blessing we ask is the blessing of health,

With hound and with horn thro' the woodlands to roam,
And, when tired abroad, find contentment at home.
  With the sports of the field there's no pleasure can vie,
  While jocund we follow our hounds in full cry.

PAUL WHITEHEAD.

128 *Heart of Oak*

COME, cheer up, my lads! 'tis to glory we steer,
  To add something more to this wonderful year;
To honour we call you, not press you like slaves,
For who are so free as we sons of the waves.

> Heart of oak are our ships,
> Heart of oak are our men,
> We always are ready,
> Steady! Boys! steady!

We'll fight and we'll conquer again and again.

We ne'er see our foes but we wish them to stay,
They never see us but they wish us away;
If they run, why we follow and run them ashore,
For if they won't fight us, we cannot do more.
  Heart of oak, &c.

They swear they'll invade us, these terrible foes;
They frighten our women, our children, and beaux;
But should their flat-bottoms in darkness get o'er,
Still Britons they'll find to receive them on shore.
  Heart of oak, &c.

We'll still make them run, and we'll still make them sweat,
In spite of the devil and Brussels Gazette,
Then cheer up, my lads, with one heart let us sing,
Our soldiers, our sailors, our statesmen, and king.
  Heart of oak, &c.

DAVID GARRICK.

OF old, when Scarron his companions invited,
    Each guest brought his dish, and the feast was united;
If our landlord supplies us with beef, and with fish,
Let each guest bring himself, and he brings the best dish:
Our Dean shall be venison, just fresh from the plains;
Our Burke shall be tongue, with a garnish of brains;
Our Will shall be wild-fowl, of excellent flavour,
And Dick with his pepper shall heighten their savour:
Our Cumberland's sweet-bread its place shall obtain,
And Douglas is pudding, substantial and plain:
Our Garrick's a salad; for in him we see
Oil, vinegar, sugar, and saltness agree:
To make out the dinner, full certain I am,
That Ridge is anchovy, and Reynolds is lamb;
That Mickey's a capon, and by the same rule,
Magnanimous Goldsmith a gooseberry fool.
At a dinner so various, at such a repast,
Who'd not be a glutton, and stick to the last?
Here, waiter! more wine, let me sit while I'm able,
Till all my companions sink under the table;
Then, with chaos and blunders encircling my head,
Let me ponder, and tell what I think of the dead.

    Here lies the good Dean, re-united to earth,
Who mixed reason with pleasure, and wisdom with mirth:
If he had any faults, he has left us in doubt,
At least, in six weeks, I could not find 'em out;
Yet some have declared, and it can't be denied 'em,
That sly-boots was cursedly cunning to hide 'em.

    Here lies our good Edmund, whose genius was such,
We scarcely can praise it, or blame it too much;

RETALIATION

Who, born for the universe, narrowed his mind,
And to party gave up what was meant for mankind.
Though fraught with all learning, yet straining his throat
To persuade Tommy Townshend to lend him a vote;
Who, too deep for his hearers, still went on refining,
And thought of convincing, while they thought of dining;
Though equal to all things, for all things unfit,
Too nice for a statesman, too proud for a wit:
For a patriot, too cool; for a drudge, disobedient;
And too fond of the right to pursue the expedient.
In short, 'twas his fate, unemployed, or in place, Sir,
To eat mutton cold, and cut blocks with a razor.

Here lies honest William, whose heart was a mint,
While the owner ne'er knew half the good that was in 't;
The pupil of impulse, it forced him along,
His conduct still right, with his argument wrong;
Still aiming at honour, yet fearing to roam,
The coachman was tipsy, the chariot drove home;
Would you ask for his merits? alas! he had none;
What was good was spontaneous, his faults were his own.

Here lies honest Richard, whose fate I must sigh at;
Alas, that such frolic should now be so quiet!
What spirits were his! what wit and what whim!
Now breaking a jest, and now breaking a limb;
Now wrangling and grumbling to keep up the ball,
Now teasing and vexing, yet laughing at all!
In short, so provoking a devil was Dick,
That we wished him full ten times a day at Old Nick;
But, missing his mirth and agreeable vein,
As often we wished to have Dick back again.

RETALIATION

Here Cumberland lies, having acted his parts,
The Terence of England, the mender of hearts;
A flattering painter, who made it his care
To draw men as they ought to be, not as they are.
His gallants are all faultless, his women divine,
And comedy wonders at being so fine;
Like a tragedy queen he has dizened her out,
Or rather like tragedy giving a rout.
His fools have their follies so lost in a crowd
Of virtues and feelings, that folly grows proud;
And coxcombs, alike in their failings alone,
Adopting his portraits, are pleased with their own.
Say, where has our poet this malady caught?
Or, wherefore his characters thus without fault?
Say, was it that vainly directing his view
To find out men's virtues, and finding them few,
Quite sick of pursuing each troublesome elf,
He grew lazy at last, and drew from himself?

Here Douglas retires, from his toils to relax,
The scourge of impostors, the terror of quacks:
Come, all ye quack bards, and ye quacking divines,
Come, and dance on the spot where your tyrant re-
        clines:
When satire and censure encircled his throne,
I feared for your safety, I feared for my own;
But now he is gone, and we want a detector,
Our Dodds shall be pious, our Kenricks shall lecture;
Macpherson write bombast, and call it a style,
Our Townshend make speeches, and I shall compile;
New Lauders and Bowers the Tweed shall cross over,
No countryman living their tricks to discover;

Detection her taper shall quench to a spark,
And Scotchman meet Scotchman, and cheat in the dark.

Here lies David Garrick, describe me, who can,
An abridgement of all that was pleasant in man;
As an actor, confessed without rival to shine:
As a wit, if not first, in the very first line:
Yet, with talents like these, and an excellent heart,
The man had his failings, a dupe to his art.
Like an ill-judging beauty, his colours he spread,
And beplastered with rouge his own natural red.
On the stage he was natural, simple, affecting;
'Twas only that when he was off he was acting.
With no reason on earth to go out of his way,
He turned and he varied full ten times a day.
Though secure of our hearts, yet confoundedly sick
If they were not his own by finessing and trick,
He cast off his friends, as a huntsman his pack,
For he knew when he pleased he could whistle them
      back.
Of praise a mere glutton, he swallowed what came,
And the puff of a dunce he mistook it for fame;
Till his relish grown callous, almost to disease,
Who peppered the highest was surest to please.
But let us be candid, and speak out our mind,
If dunces applauded, he paid them in kind.
Ye Kenricks, ye Kellys, and Woodfalls so grave,
What a commerce was yours, while you got and you gave !
How did Grub Street re-echo the shouts that you raised,
While he was be-Rosciused, and you were be-praised !
But peace to his spirit, wherever it flies,
To act as an angel, and mix with the skies:

RETALIATION

Those poets, who owe their best fame to his skill,
Shall still be his flatterers, go where he will.
Old Shakespeare, receive him, with praise and with love,
And Beaumonts and Bens be his Kellys above.

Here Mickey reclines, a most blunt, pleasant creature,
And slander itself must allow him good nature:
He cherished his friend, and he relished a bumper;
Yet one fault he had, and that one was a thumper.
Perhaps you may ask if the man was a miser?
I answer, no, no, for he always was wiser:
Too courteous, perhaps, or obligingly flat?
His very worst foe can't accuse him of that:
Perhaps he confided in men as they go,
And so was too foolishly honest? Ah no!
Then what was his failing? come, tell it, and burn ye!
He was, could he help it?—a special attorney.

Here Reynolds is laid, and, to tell you my mind,
He has not left a better or wiser behind:
His pencil was striking, resistless, and grand;
His manners were gentle, complying, and bland;
Still born to improve us in every part,
His pencil our faces, his manners our heart:
To coxcombs averse, yet most civilly steering,
When they judged without skill he was still hard of
    hearing:
When they talked of their Raphaels, Correggios, and stuff,
He shifted his trumpet, and only took snuff.

OLIVER GOLDSMITH.

T

I

HERE lies the body of Richard Hind,
Who was neither ingenious, sober, nor kind.

II. *In St. Olave's Church, Southwark, on Mr. Munday*

HALLOWED be the Sabbaoth,
And farewell all worldly Pelfe;
The Weeke begins on Tuesday,
For Munday hath hang'd himselfe.

III. *In Christ Church, Bristol, on Thomas Turner, twice master of the Company of Bakers*

LIKE to a Baker's oven is the grave,
Wherein the bodies of the faithful have
A setting in, and where they do remain
In hopes to rise, and to be drawn again:
Blessed are they who in the Lord are dead;
Though set like dough, they shall be drawn like bread.

IV. *On Peter Robinson*

HERE lies the preacher, judge, and poet, Peter
Who broke the laws of God, and man, and metre.
                   LORD JEFFREY.

V. *On Prince Frederick*

HERE lies Fred
Who was alive and is dead.
Had it been his father,
I had much rather;

Had it been his brother,
Still better than another;
Had it been his sister,
No one would have missed her;
Had it been the whole generation,
So much the better for the nation;
But since 'tis only Fred
Who was alive and is dead,
Why, there's no more to be said.   ANON.

131   *Epigrams*

I. *On a Clergyman's Horse biting him*

THE steed bit his master;
    How came this to pass?
He heard the good pastor
    Cry, 'All flesh is grass'.   ANON.

II. *The Mother's Choice*

THESE panting damsels, dancing for their lives,
Are only maidens waltzing into wives.
Those smiling matrons are appraisers sly,
Who regulate the dance, the squeeze, the sigh,
And each base cheapening buyer having chid,
Knock down their daughters to the noblest bid!
                              ANON.

III. *Epigram on an academic Visit to the Continent*

I WENT to Frankfort, and got drunk
With that most learn'd professor—Brunck:
I went to Worts, and got more drunken
With that more learn'd professor—Ruhncken.
                    RICHARD PORSON.

EPIGRAMS

IV. *On Inclosures*

'Tis bad enough in man or woman
To steal a goose from off a common;
But surely he's without excuse
Who steals the common from the goose.   Anon.

V. *Forensic Jocularities. The History of a Case
shortly reported by a Master in Chancery*

A Chancery Suit

Mr. Leach made a speech,
　　Angry, neat, but wrong;
Mr. Hart, on the other part,
　　Was prosy, dull, and long.

Mr. Bell spoke very well,
　　Though nobody knew about what;
Mr. Trower talk'd for an hour,
　　Sat down, fatigued, and hot.

Mr. Parker made the case darker,
　　Which was dark enough without;
Mr. Cooke quoted his book,
　　And the Chancellor said, I doubt.   Anon.

VI. *The Dutch*

In matters of commerce the fault of the Dutch
Is offering too little and asking too much.
　　　　　　　　　　　　　　George Canning.

132　　*The Royal Tour*

He reaches Weymouth—treads the Esplanade—
　Hark, hark, the jingling bells! the cannonade!
Drums beat, the hurdigurdies grind the air;
Dogs, cats, old women, all upon the stare:

THE ROYAL TOUR

All Weymouth gapes with wonder—hark! huzzas!
The roaring welcome of a thousand jaws!

.   .   .   .

Lo, Pitt arrives! alas, with lantern face!
'What, hæ, Pitt, hæ—what, Pitt, hæ, more disgrace?'

'Ah, Sire, bad news! a second dire defeat!
Vendée undone, and all the Chouans beat!'

'Hæ, hæ—what, what?—beat, beat?—what, beat agen?
Well, well, more money—raise more men, more men.
But mind, Pitt, hæ—mind, huddle up the news,
Coin something, and the growling land amuse:
Make all the Sans-culottes to Paris caper,
And Rose shall print the vict'ry in his Paper.
Let's hear no more, no more of Cornish tales—
I shan't refund a guinea, Pitt, to Wales:
I can't afford it, no—I can't afford:
Wales cost a deal in pocket-cash and board.
Pitt, Pitt, there's Frost, my bailiff Frost—see, see!
Well, Pitt, go back, go back again—b'ye, b'ye:
Keep London still—no matter how they carp—
Well, well, go back, and bid Dundas look sharp.
Must not lose France—no, France must wear a crown:
If France won't swallow, ram a monarch down.
Some crowns are scarce worth sixpences—hæ, Pitt?—'
The Premier smil'd, and left the Royal Wit.

Now Frost approaches—'Well, Frost, well, Frost, pray,
How, how went sheep a score?—how corn and hay?'
'An't please your Majesty—a charming price:
Corn very soon will be as dear as spice.'

'Thank God! but say, say, do the poor complain?
Hæ, hæ, will wheat be sixpence, Frost, a grain?'

'I hope not, Sire; for great were then my fears,
That Windsor would be pull'd about our ears.'

'Frost, Frost, no politics—no, no, Frost, no:
You, you talk politics! oho, oho!
Windsor come down about our ears! what, what?
D'ye think, hæ, hæ, that I'm afraid of that?
What, what are soldiers good for, but obey?
Macmanus, Townsend, Jealous, hæ, hæ, hæ?
Pull Windsor down? hæ, what?—a pretty job!
Windsor be pull'd to pieces by the mob!
Talk, talk of farming, that's your fort, d'ye see;
And mind, mind, politics belong to me.
Go back, go back, and watch the Windsor chaps;
Count all the poultry; set, set well the traps.
See, see! see! Stacie—here, here, Stacie, here—
Going to market, Stacie?—dear, dear, dear!
I get all my provision by the mail—
Hæ, money plenty, Stacie? don't fear jail.
Rooms, rooms all full? hæ, hæ? no beds to spare?
What, what! give trav'lers, hæ, good fare, good fare?
Good sign, good sign, to have no empty beds!
Shows, shows that people like to see Crown'd Heads.'

The Mail arrives! hark! hark! the cheerful horn,
To Majesty announcing oil and corn;
Turnips and cabbages, and soap and candles;
And lo, each article Great Caesar handles!
Bread, cheese, salt, catchup, vinegar, and mustard,
Small beer, and bacon, apple-pie and custard:

THE ROYAL TOUR

All, all, from Windsor greets his frugal Grace,
For Weymouth is a d—mn'd expensive place.

Sal'sb'ry appears, the Lord of stars and strings;
Presents his poem to the best of Kings.
Great Caesar reads it—feels a laughing fit,
And wonders Sal'sb'ry should become a wit.
A batch of bullocks! see Great Caesar run:
He stops the Drover—bargain is begun.
He feels their ribs and rumps—he shakes his head—
'Poor, Drover, poor—poor, very poor indeed.'
Caesar and Drover haggle—diff'rence split—
How much?—a shilling! what a royal hit!
A load of hay in sight! Great Caesar flies—
Smells—shakes his head—'Bad hay—sour hay—' he buys.
'Smell, Courtown—smell—good bargain—lucky load—
Smell, Courtown—sweeter hay was never mow'd.'

A herd of swine goes by!—'Whose hogs are these?
Hæ, Farmer, hæ?'—'Yours, Measter, if yow pleaze.'
'Poor, Farmer, poor—lean, lousy, very poor—
Sell, sell, hæ, sell?'—'Iss, Measter, to be zure:
My pigs were made for zale, but what o' that?
Yow caall mun lean; now, Zur, I caall mun vat—
Measter, I baant a starling—can't be cort;
You think, agosh, to ha the pigs vor nort.'
Lo! Caesar buys the pigs—he slily winks—
'Hæ, Gwinn, the fellow is not caught, he thinks—
Fool, not to know the bargain I have got!
Hæ, Gwinn—nice bargain—lucky, lucky lot!'

Enter the dancing dogs! they take their stations;
They bow, they curtsey to the Lord of Nations.

They dance, they skip, they charm the K— of Fun,
While Courtiers see themselves almost outdone.

Lord Paulet enters on his hands and knees,
Joining the hunts of hares with hunts of fleas.
Enter Sir Joseph! gladd'ning royal eyes!
What holds his hand? a box of butterflies,
Grubs, nests, and eggs of humming-birds, to please;
Newts, tadpoles, brains of beetles, stings of bees.
The noble President without a bib on,
To sport the glories of his blushing ribbon!
The fishermen! the fishermen behold!
A shoal of fish! the men their nets unfold;
Surround the scaly fry—they drag to land:
Caesar and Co. rush down upon the sand;
The fishes leap about—Gods! what a clatter!
Caesar, delighted, jumps into the water—
He marvels at the fish with fins and scales—
He plunges at them—seizes heads and tails;
Enjoys the draught—he capers—laughs aloud,
And shows his captives to the gaping crowd.
He orders them to Glo'ster Lodge—they go:
But are the fishermen rewarded?—NO!!!

Caesar spies Lady Cathcart with a book;
He flies to know what 'tis—he longs to look.
'What's in your hand, my Lady? let me know.'
'A book, an't please your M—y.' 'Oho!
Book's a good thing—good thing—I like a book.
Very good thing, my Lady—let me look—
War of America! my Lady, hæ?
Bad thing, my Lady!—fling, fling that away.'

THE ROYAL TOUR

A sailor pops upon the Royal Pair,
On crutches borne—an object of despair:
His squalid beard, pale cheek, and haggard eye,
Though silent, pour for help a piercing cry.

'Who, who are you? what, what? hæ, what are you?'

'A man, my Liege, whom Kindness never knew.'

'A sailor! sailor, hæ? you've lost a leg.'

'I know it, Sir—which forces me to beg.
I've nine poor children, Sir, besides a wife—
God bless them! the sole comforts of my life.'

'Wife and nine children, hæ?—all, all alive?
No, no, no wonder that you cannot thrive.
Shame, shame, to fill your hut with such a train!
Shame to get brats for others to maintain!
Get, get a wooden leg, or one of cork:
Wood's cheapest—yes, get wood, and go to work.
But mind, mind Sailor—hæ, hæ, hæ—hear, hear—
Don't go to Windsor, mind, and cut one there:
That's dangerous, dangerous—there I place my traps—
Fine things, fine things, for legs of thieving chaps:
Best traps, my traps—take care—they bite, they bite,
And sometimes catch a dozen legs a night.'

'Oh! had I money, Sir, to buy a leg!'

'No money, hæ? nor I—go beg—go beg.'—

How sweetly kind to bid the cripple mump,
And cut from other people's trees a stump!

THE ROYAL TOUR

How vastly like our kind Archbishop M——re,
Who loves not beggar tribes at Lambeth door,
Of meaner parsons bids them ask relief——
There, carry their coarse jugs for broth and beef!
'Mine Gote! your Mashesty!——don't hear such stuff.
De Workhouse always geefs de poor enough.
Why make bout dirty leg sush wond'rous fuss?——
And 'den, what impudence for beg of Us!
In Strelitz, O mine Gote! de beggar skip:
Dere, for a sharity, we geefs a whip.
Money make subshects impudent, I'm sure——
Respect be always where de peepel's poor.'

'How, Sailor, did you lose your leg?——hæ, hæ?'

'I lost it, please your Majesty, at sea,
Hard fighting for my country and my King.'

'Hæ, what?——that's common, very common thing.
Hæ! lucky fellow, that you were not drill'd:
Some lose their heads, and many men are kill'd.
Your parish? where's your parish? hæ——where, where?'

'I serv'd my 'prenticeship in Manchester.'

'Fine town, fine town——full, full of trade and riches——
Hæ, Sailor, hæ, can you make leather breeches?
These come from Manchester——there, there I got 'em!'
On which Great Caesar claps his buckskin bottom.

'Must not encourage vagrants——no, no, no——
Must not make laws, my lad, and break 'em too.
Where, where's your parish, hæ? and where's your pass?
Well, make haste home——I've got, I've got no brass.'

JOHN WOLCOT (PETER PINDAR).

HERE, a sheer hulk, lies poor Tom Bowling,
   The darling of our crew;
No more he'll hear the tempest howling,
   For death has broach'd him to.
His form was of the manliest beauty,
   His heart was kind and soft,
Faithful below he did his duty,
   And now he's gone aloft.

Tom never from his word departed,
   His virtues were so rare,
His friends were many, and true-hearted,
   His Poll was kind and fair:
And then he'd sing so blithe and jolly,
   Ah many's the time and oft!
But mirth is turn'd to melancholy,
   For Tom is gone aloft.

Yet shall Poor Tom find pleasant weather,
   When he who all commands
Shall give, to call life's crew together,
   The word to pipe all hands.
Thus death, who Kings and Tars dispatches,
   In vain Tom's life has doff'd,
For, though his body's under hatches,
   His soul is gone aloft.

CHARLES DIBDIN.

DID you ever hear of Captain Wattle?—
He was all for love, and a little for the bottle.
We know not, though pains we have taken to inquire,
If gunpowder he invented, or the Thames set on fire;
If to him was the centre of gravity known,
The longitude, or the philosopher's stone;
Or whether he studied from Bacon or Boyle,
Copernicus, Locke, Katerfelto, or Hoyle:
But this we have learnt, with great labour and pain,
That he loved Miss Roe, and she loved him again.

Than sweet Miss Roe none e'er looked fiercer,
She had but one eye, and that was a piercer.
We know not, for certainty, her education;
If she wrote, mended stockings, or settled the nation;
At cards, if she liked whist, and swabbers or voles;
Or at dinner lov'd pig, or a steak on the coals;
Whether most of the Sappho she was, or Thalestris,
Or if dancing was taught her by Hopkins or Vestris;
But, for your satisfaction, this good news we obtain,
That she loved Captain Wattle, and he loved her again,

When wedded he became lord and master, depend on't;
He had but one leg, but he'd a foot at the end on't,
Which of government when she would fain hold the
    bridle,
He took special caution should never lie idle;
So, like most married folk, 'twas 'My plague and my
    chicken!'
And sometimes a kissing and sometimes a kicking;

Then, for comfort, a cordial she'd now and then try,
Alternately piping or bunging her eye;
And these facts of this couple the history contain;
For when he kicked Miss Roe, she kicked him again.

CHARLES DIBDIN.

135 *Come, let's to Bed*

COME, let's to bed,
    Says Sleepy-head;
Sit up a while, says Slow;
Hang on the pot,
Says Greedy-gut,
Let's sup before we go.

ANON.

136 *There was a King*

THERE was a King and he had three daughters,
    And they all lived in a basin of water;
        The basin bended,
        My story's ended.
If the basin had been stronger
My story would have been longer.

ANON.

137 *Peter White*

PETER WHITE will ne'er go right,
    Would you know the reason why?
He follows his nose where'er he goes,
And that stands all awry.

ANON.

138   *Solomon Grundy*

SOLOMON GRUNDY,
  Born on a Monday,
Christened on Tuesday,
Married on Wednesday,
Took ill on Thursday,
Worse on Friday,
Died on Saturday,
Buried on Sunday.
This is the end
Of Solomon Grundy.   ANON.

139   *As I went to Bonner*

AS I went to Bonner,
  I met a pig
    Without a wig,
Upon my word and honour.   ANON.

140   *There was a crooked Man*

THERE was a crooked man, and he went a crooked
    mile,
He found a crooked sixpence against a crooked stile:
He bought a crooked cat which caught a crooked mouse,
And they all lived together in a little crooked house.

     ANON.

141   *Doctor Foster*

DOCTOR FOSTER went to Glo'ster
  In a shower of rain;
He stepped in a puddle up to his middle,
  And wouldn't go there again.   ANON.

142   *Gray Goose and Gander*

GRAY goose and gander,
   Waft your wings together,
And carry the good King's daughter
   Over the one strand river.   ·   ANON.

143   *A Cat may look at a King*

A CAT may look at a king,
   And sure I may look at an ugly thing.
                       ANON.

144   *The Man in the Moon*

THE man in the moon came tumbling down,
   And asked his way to Norwich;
He went to the south, and burnt his mouth
   With supping hot pease-porridge.

                       ANON.

145   *A New Year Carol*

HERE we bring new water
   from the well so clear,
For to worship God with,
   this happy New Year.

Sing levy dew, sing levy dew,
   the water and the wine;
The seven bright gold wires
   and the bugles that do shine.

Sing reign of Fair Maid,
   with gold upon her toe,—
Open you the West Door,
   and turn the Old Year go.

A NEW YEAR CAROL

Sing reign of Fair Maid,
    with gold upon her chin,—
Open you the East Door,
    and let the New Year in.

Sing levy dew, sing levy dew,
    the water and the wine;
The seven bright gold wires
    and the bugles that do shine.   ANON.

146   *Jack and Gill*

JACK and Gill went up the hill
    To fetch a bottle of water;
Jack fell down and broke his crown,
    And Gill came tumbling after.

Then up Jack got, and home did trot,
    As fast as he could caper,
Dame Gill did the job to plaster his nob
    With vinegar and brown paper.
                ANON.

147 *The Death and Burial of Cock Robbin*

HERE lies Cock Robbin dead and cold:
    His end this book will soon unfold!

'Who did kill Cock Robbin?'
'I' said the sparrow, 'with my bow and arrow,
I did kill Cock Robbin.'

'Who did see him die?'
'I' said the fly, 'with my little eye,
And I did see him die.'

284

'And who catch'd his blood?'
'I' said the fish, 'with my little dish,
And I catch'd his blood.'

'And who did make his shroud?'
'I' said the beetle, 'with my little needle,
And I did make his shroud.'

'Who'll dig his grave?'
'I' said the owl,
'With my spade and show'l,
And I'll dig his grave.'

'Who'll be the parson?'
'I' said the rook,
'With my little book,
And I'll be the parson.'

'Who'll be the clerk?'
'I' said the lark,
'If 'tis not in the dark,
And I'll be the clerk.'

'Who'll carry him to the grave?'
'I' said the kite,
'If 'tis not in the night,
And I'll carry him to the grave.'

'Who'll carry the link?'
'I' said the linnet,
'I'll fetch it in a minute,
And I'll carry the link.'

'Who'll be chief mourner?'
'I' said the swan,
'I'm sorry he's gone,
And I'll be chief mourner.'

U

'Who'll bear the pall?'
'We' said the wren,
 Both the cock and the hen,
'And we'll bear the pall.'

'Who'll run before?'
'I' said the deer,
'I run fast for fear,
And I'll run before.'

'Who'll sing a psalm?'
'I' said the thrush,
As she sat in a bush,
'And I'll sing a psalm.'

'Who'll throw in the dirt?'
'I' said the fox,
'Though I steal hens and cocks,
I'll throw in the dirt.'

'And who'll toll the bell?'
'I' said the bull,
'Because I can pull,
And so, Cock Robbin, farewell!'

All the birds of the air
Fell to sighing and sobbing,
When they heard the bell toll
For poor Cock Robbin.   ANON.

148   *Scarborough Fair*

WHERE are you going? To Scarborough Fair?
    Parsley, sage, rosemary and thyme,
Remember me to a bonny lass there,
For once she was a true lover of mine.

Tell her to make me a cambric shirt,
Parsley, sage, rosemary and thyme,
Without any needle or thread work'd in it,
And she shall be a true lover of mine.

Tell her to wash it in yonder well,
Parsley, sage, rosemary and thyme,
Where water ne'er sprung nor a drop of rain fell,
And she shall be a true lover of mine.

Tell her to plough me an acre of land,
Parsley, sage, rosemary and thyme,
Between the sea and the salt sea strand,
And she shall be a true lover of mine.

Tell her to plough it with one ram's horn,
Parsley, sage, rosemary and thyme,
And sow it all over with one peppercorn,
And she shall be a true lover of mine.

Tell her to reap it with a sickle of leather,
Parsley, sage, rosemary and thyme,
And tie it all up with a tom tit's feather,
And she shall be a true lover of mine.

Tell her to gather it all in a sack,
Parsley, sage, rosemary and thyme,
And carry it home on a butterfly's back,
And then she shall be a true lover of mine.   ANON.

149   *A Man of Words and not of Deeds*

A MAN of words and not of deeds
  Is like a garden full of weeds;
And when the weeds begin to grow,
It's like a garden full of snow;

And when the snow begins to fall,
It's like a bird upon the wall;
And when the bird away does fly,
It's like an eagle in the sky;
And when the sky begins to roar,
It's like a lion at the door;
And when the door begins to crack,
It's like a stick across your back;
And when your back begins to smart,
It's like a penknife in your heart;
And when your heart begins to bleed,
You're dead, and dead, and dead, indeed.

ANON.

150   *Song*

HERE'S to the maiden of bashful fifteen;
    Here's to the widow of fifty;
Here's to the flaunting extravagant quean,
    And here's to the housewife that's thrifty.

Chorus
    Let the toast pass,—
    Drink to the lass,
I'll warrant she'll prove an excuse for the glass.

Here's to the charmer whose dimples we prize;
    Now to the maid who has none, sir:
Here's to the girl with a pair of blue eyes,
    And here's to the nymph with but *one*, sir.

Here's to the maid with a bosom of snow;
    Now to her that's as brown as a berry:
Here's to the wife with a face full of woe,
    And now to the girl that is merry.

For let 'em be clumsy, or let 'em be slim,
   Young or ancient, I care not a feather;
So fill a pint bumper quite up to the brim,
   And let us e'en toast them together.
                RICHARD BRINSLEY SHERIDAN.

151 *Come, Landlord, fill the flowing Bowl*

COME, landlord, fill the flowing bowl
   Until it doth run over;
For to-night we'll merry merry be,
   To-morrow we'll be sober.

The man who drinketh small beer
   And goes to bed quite sober,
Fades as the leaves do fade
   That drop off in October.

But he who drinks just what he likes
   And getteth half-seas over,
Will live until he dies perhaps,
   And then lie down in clover.

The man who kisses a pretty girl
   And goes and tells his mother,
Ought to have his lips cut off,
   And never kiss another.   ANON.

152   *The British Grenadiers*

SOME talk of Alexander, and some of Hercules,
  Of Conon and Lysander, and some Miltiades;
But of all the world's brave heroes, there's none that can
    compare,
With a tow, row, row, row, row, to the British Grenadiers.
   Chorus. But of all the world's brave heroes, &c.

None of those ancient heroes e'er saw a cannon ball,
Or knew the force of powder to slay their foes withal;
But our brave boys do know it, and banish all their fears,
With a tow, row, row, row, row, the British Grenadiers.
    Chorus. But our brave boys, &c.

When e'er we are commanded to storm the palisades,
Our leaders march with fusees and we with hand
    grenades;
We throw them from the glacis about our enemies' ears,
With a tow, row, row, row, row, the British Grenadiers.
    Chorus. We throw them, &c.

The God of War was pleased and great Bellona smiles,
To see these noble heroes of our British Isles;
And all the Gods celestial, descending from their spheres,
Beheld with admiration the British Grenadiers.
    Chorus. And all the Gods celestial, &c.

Then let us crown a bumper, and drink a health to those
Who carry caps and pouches, that wear the looped
    clothes;
May they and their commanders live happy all their years,
With a tow, row, row, row, row, the British Grenadiers.
    Chorus. May they and their commanders, &c.

                            Anon.

153   *Auguries of Innocence*

A ROBIN redbreast in a cage
  Puts all Heaven in a rage.
A dove-house fill'd with doves and pigeons
Shudders Hell thro' all its regions.
A dog starv'd at his master's gate
Predicts the ruin of the State.

AUGURIES OF INNOCENCE

A horse misus'd upon the road
Calls to Heaven for human blood.
Each outcry of the hunted hare
A fibre from the brain does tear.
A skylark wounded in the wing,
A cherubim does cease to sing.
The game-cock clipped and arm'd for fight
Does the rising sun affright.
Every wolf's and lion's howl
Raises from Hell a Human soul.
The wild deer, wandering here and there,
Keeps the Human soul from care.
The lamb misus'd breeds public strife,
And yet forgives the butcher's knife.
He who shall hurt the little wren
Shall never be belov'd by men.
He who the ox to wrath has mov'd
Shall never be by woman lov'd.
The wanton boy that kills the fly
Shall feel the spider's enmity.
He who torments the chafer's sprite
Weaves a bower in endless night.
The caterpillar on the leaf
Repeats to thee thy mother's grief.
Kill not the moth nor butterfly,
For the Last Judgement draweth nigh.
He who shall train the horse to war
Shall never pass the polar bar.
The beggar's dog and widow's cat,
Feed them, and thou wilt grow fat.
The bat that flits at close of eve
Has left the brain that won't believe.

AUGURIES OF INNOCENCE

The owl that calls upon the night
Speaks the unbeliever's fright.
The gnat that sings his summer's song
Poison gets from Slander's tongue.
The poison of the snake and newt
Is the sweat of Envy's foot.
The poison of the honey-bee
Is the artist's jealousy.
A truth that's told with bad intent
Beats all the lies you can invent.

Joy and woe are woven fine,
A clothing for the soul divine;
Under every grief and pine
Runs a joy with silken twine.
It is right it should be so;
Man was made for joy and woe;
And when this we rightly know,
Thro' the world we safely go.

The babe is more than swaddling-bands;
Throughout all these human lands
Tools were made, and born were hands,
Every farmer understands.
Every tear from every eye
Becomes a babe in Eternity;
This is caught by Females bright,
And return'd to its own delight.
The bleat, the bark, bellow, and roar,
Are waves that beat on Heaven's shore.
The babe that weeps the rod beneath
Writes revenge in realms of death.

AUGURIES OF INNOCENCE

He who mocks the infant's faith
Shall be mock'd in Age and Death.
He who shall teach the child to doubt
The rotting grave shall ne'er get out.
He who respects the infant's faith
Triumphs over Hell and Death.

The child's toys and the old man's reasons
Are the fruits of the two seasons.
The questioner, who sits so sly,
Shall never know how to reply.
He who replies to words of Doubt
Doth put the light of knowledge out.
A riddle, or the cricket's cry,
Is to Doubt a fit reply.
The emmet's inch and eagle's mile
Make lame Philosophy to smile.
He who doubts from what he sees
Will ne'er believe, do what you please.
If the sun and moon should doubt,
They'd immediately go out.

The prince's robes and beggar's rags
Are toadstools on the miser's bags.
The beggar's rags, fluttering in air,
Does to rags the heavens tear.
The poor man's farthing is worth more
Than all the gold on Afric's shore.
One mite wrung from the labourer's hands
Shall buy and sell the miser's lands;
Or, if protected from on high,
Does that whole nation sell and buy.

The soldier, arm'd with sword and gun,
Palsied strikes the summer's sun.
The strongest poison ever known
Came from Caesar's laurel crown.
Nought can deform the human race
Like to armour's iron brace.
When gold and gems adorn the plough
To peaceful arts shall Envy bow.
To be in a passion you good may do,
But no good if a passion is in you.
The whore and gambler, by the state
Licensed, build that nation's fate.
The harlot's cry from street to street
Shall weave Old England's winding-sheet.
The winner's shout, the loser's curse,
Dance before dead England's hearse.

WILLIAM BLAKE.

154   *Epigrams*

An Answer to the Parson

'WHY of the sheep do you not learn peace?'
'Because I don't want you to shear my fleece.'

Sir Joshua Reynolds

WHEN Sir Joshua Reynolds died
All Nature was degraded;
The King dropped a tear into the Queen's ear,
And all his pictures faded.

To English Connoisseurs

You must agree that Rubens was a fool,
And yet you make him master of your school,

And give more money for his slobberings
Than you will give for Raphael's finest things.
I understood Christ was a carpenter
And not a brewer's servant, my good Sir.

To Flaxman

I MOCK thee not, though I by thee am mockèd;
Thou call'st me madman, but I call thee blockhead.

To Hunt

You think Fuseli is not a Great Painter. I'm glad:
This is one of the best compliments he ever had.

A Character

HER whole life is an epigram, smart, smooth, and neatly
    penned,
Platted quite neat to catch applause, with a hang-noose at
    the end.

Marriage

WHEN a man has married a wife, he finds out whether
Her knees and elbows are only glued together.

                   WILLIAM BLAKE.

155   The Yankeys' Return from Camp

FATHER and I went down to camp,
  Along with Cap'n Gooding;
And there we saw the men and boys,
  As thick as hasty pudding.
  Chorus: Yankey Doodle, keep it up,
          Yankey Doodle Dandy;
       Mind the music and the step.
       And with the girls be handy.

And there we see a thousand men,
    As rich as Squire David;
And what they wasted every day,
    I wish it could be savèd.
    Chorus: Yankey Doodle, &c.

And there was Cap'n Wellington,
    And gentle folks about him;
They say he's grown so 'tarnal proud,
    He will not ride without 'em.
    Chorus: Yankey Doodle, &c.

I saw another snarl of men
    A-digging graves, they told me;
So 'tarnal long, so 'tarnal deep,
    They 'tended they should hold me.
    Chorus: Yankey Doodle, &c.

It scared me so, I hooked it off,
    Nor stopped, as I remember;
Nor turned about till I got home,
    Locked up in mother's chamber.
    Chorus: Yankey Doodle, &c.   ANON.

156   *I once was a Maid*

I ONCE was a maid, tho' I cannot tell when,
  And still my delight is in proper young men:
Some one of a troop of dragoons was my daddie,
No wonder I'm fond of a sodger laddie.
      Sing, lal de lal, &c.

The first of my loves was a swaggering blade,
To rattle the thundering drum was his trade;
His leg was so tight, and his cheek was so ruddy,
Transported I was with my sodger laddie.

But the godly old chaplain left him in the lurch;
The sword I forsook for the sake of the church:
He ventur'd the soul, and I risked the body,
'Twas then I proved false to my sodger laddie.

Full soon I grew sick of my sanctified sot,
The regiment at large for a husband I got;
From the gilded spontoon to the fife I was ready,
I askèd no more but a sodger laddie.

But the peace it reduc'd me to beg in despair,
Till I met my old boy in a Cunningham fair;
His rags regimental, they flutter'd so gaudy,
My heart it rejoic'd at a sodger laddie.

And now I have liv'd—I know not how long,
And still I can join in a cup and a song;
But whilst with both hands I can hold the glass
    steady,
Here's to thee, my hero, my sodger laddie!

                                    ROBERT BURNS.

157   *The Poet's Welcome to his love-
            begotten Daughter*

THOU 's welcome, wean! mishanter fa' me,
    If ought of thee, or of thy mammy,
Shall ever daunton me, or awe me,
            My sweet wee lady,
Or if I blush when thou shalt ca' me
            Tit-ta or daddy.

WELCOME TO HIS DAUGHTER

Wee image of my bonnie Betty,
I fatherly will kiss and daut thee,
As dear an' near my heart I set thee
      Wi' as guid will,
As a' the priests had seen me get thee
      That's out o' hell.

What tho' they ca' me fornicator,
An' tease my name in kintra clatter:
The mair they talk I'm kent the better,
      E'en let them clash;
An auld wife's tongue's a feckless matter
      To gie ane fash.

Welcome, my bonnie, sweet wee dochter—
Tho' ye come here a wee unsought for,
An' tho' your comin' I hae fought for
      Baith kirk an' queir;
Yet, by my faith, ye're no unwrought for!
      That I shall swear!

Sweet fruit o' mony a merry dint,
My funny toil is now a' tint,
Sin' thou came to the warl asklent,
      Which fools may scoff at;
In my last plack thy part's be in't—
      The better half o't.

An' if thou be what I wad hae thee,
An' tak the counsel I shall gie thee,
A lovin' father I'll be to thee,
      If thou be spar'd;
Thro' a' thy childish years I'll ee thee,
      An' think't weel war'd.

Tho' I should be the waur bested,
Thou's be as braw an' bienly clad,
An' thy young years as nicely bred
      Wi' education,
As ony brat o' wedlock's bed
      In a' thy station.

Gude grant that thou may aye inherit
Thy mither's person, grace, an' merit,
An' thy poor worthless daddy's spirit,
      Without his failins;
'Twill please me mair to see and hear o't,
      Than stockit mailins.

ROBERT BURNS.

158   *Holy Willie's Prayer*

O THOU, wha in the Heavens dost dwell,
  Wha, as it pleases best thysel',
Sends ane to heaven and ten to hell,
      A' for thy glory,
And no for ony guid or ill
      They've done afore thee!

I bless and praise thy matchless might,
Whan thousands thou hast left in night,
That I am here afore thy sight,
      For gifts an' grace
A burnin' an' a shinin' light,
      To a' this place.

What was I, or my generation,
That I should get sic exaltation?

HOLY WILLIE'S PRAYER

I, wha deserve most just damnation,
   For broken laws,
Sax thousand years 'fore my creation,
   Thro' Adam's cause.

When frae my mither's womb I fell,
Thou might hae plungèd me in hell,
To gnash my gums, to weep and wail,
   In burnin' lakes,
Where damnèd devils roar and yell,
   Chain'd to their stakes;

Yet I am here a chosen sample,
To show thy grace is great and ample;
I'm here a pillar in thy temple,
   Strong as a rock,
A guide, a buckler, an example
   To a' thy flock.

O Lord, thou kens what zeal I bear,
When drinkers drink, and swearers swear,
And singin' there and dancin' here,
   Wi' great an' sma':
For I am keepit by thy fear
   Free frae them a'.

But yet, O Lord! confess I must
At times I'm fash'd wi' fleshly lust;
An' sometimes too, in warldly trust,
   Vile self gets in;
But thou remembers we are dust,
   Defil'd in sin.

HOLY WILLIE'S PRAYER

O Lord! yestreen, thou kens, wi' Meg—
Thy pardon I sincerely beg;
O! may 't ne'er be a livin' plague
      To my dishonour,
An' I'll ne'er lift a lawless leg
      Again upon her.

Besides I farther maun allow,
Wi' Lizzie's lass, three times I trow—
But, Lord, that Friday I was fou,
      When I cam near her,
Or else thou kens thy servant true
      Wad never steer her.

May be thou lets this fleshly thorn
Beset thy servant e'en and morn
Lest he owre high and proud should turn,
      That he's sae gifted;
If sae, thy hand maun e'en be borne
      Until thou lift it.

Lord, bless thy chosen in this place,
For here thou hast a chosen race;
But God confound their stubborn face,
      And blast their name,
Wha bring thy elders to disgrace
      An' public shame.

Lord, mind Gawn Hamilton's deserts,
He drinks, an' swears, an' plays at cartes,
Yet has sae mony takin' arts
      Wi' grit an' sma',
Frae God's ain priest the people's hearts
      He steals awa'.

X

HOLY WILLIE'S PRAYER

An' when we chasten'd him therefor,
Thou kens how he bred sic a splore
As set the warld in a roar
       O' laughin' at us;
Curse thou his basket and his store,
       Kail and potatoes.

Lord, hear my earnest cry an' pray'r,
Against that presbyt'ry o' Ayr;
Thy strong right hand, Lord, make it bare
       Upo' their heads;
Lord, weigh it down, and dinna spare,
       For their misdeeds.

O Lord my God, that glib-tongu'd Aiken,
My very heart and soul are quakin',
To think how we stood sweatin', shakin',
       An' piss'd wi' dread,
While he, wi' hingin' lips and snakin',
       Held up his head.

Lord, in the day of vengeance try him;
Lord, visit them wha did employ him,
And pass not in thy mercy by them,
       Nor hear their pray'r:
But, for thy people's sake, destroy them,
       And dinna spare.

But, Lord, remember me and mine
Wi' mercies temp'ral and divine,
That I for gear and grace may shine
       Excell'd by nane,
And a' the glory shall be thine,
       Amen, Amen!

ROBERT BURNS.

A Ballad

ORTHODOX, Orthodox, wha believe in John
Knox,
    Let me sound an alarm to your conscience:
There's a heretic blast has been blawn i' the wast,
    'That what is not sense must be nonsense.'

Dr. Mac, Dr. Mac, you should stretch on a rack,
    To strike evil-doers wi' terror;
To join faith and sense upon ony pretence,
    Is heretic, damnable error.

Town of Ayr, town of Ayr, it was mad, I declare,
    To meddle wi' mischief a-brewing;
Provost John is still deaf to the church's relief,
    And orator Bob is its ruin.

D'rymple mild, D'rymple mild, tho' your heart's like a
child,
    And your life like the new driven snaw,
Yet that winna save ye, auld Satan must have ye,
    For preaching that three's ane and twa.

Rumble John, Rumble John, mount the steps wi' a
groan,
    Cry the book is wi' heresy cramm'd;
Then lug out your ladle, deal brimstane like adle,
    And roar ev'ry note of the damn'd.

THE KIRK'S ALARM

Simper James, Simper James, leave the fair Killie dames,
    There's a holier chase in your view;
I'll lay on your head, that the pack ye'll soon lead,
    For puppies like you there's but few.

Singet Sawney, Singet Sawney, are ye herding the penny,
    Unconscious what evils await?
Wi' a jump, yell, and howl, alarm every soul,
    For the foul thief is just at your gate.

Daddy Auld, Daddy Auld, there's a tod in the fauld,
    A tod meikle waur than the clerk;
Tho' ye can do little skaith, ye'll be in at the death,
    And gif ye canna bite, ye may bark.

Davie Bluster, Davie Bluster, if for a saint ye do muster,
    The corps is no nice of recruits:
Yet to worth let's be just, royal blood ye might boast,
    If the ass was the king of the brutes.

Jamie Goose, Jamie Goose, ye hae made but toom
    roose,
    In hunting the wicked Lieutenant;
But the Doctor's your mark, for the Lord's haly ark,
    He has cooper'd and ca'd a wrang pin in 't.

Poet Willie, Poet Willie, gie the Doctor a volley,
    Wi' your 'liberty's chain' and your wit;
O'er Pegasus' side ye ne'er laid a stride,
    Ye but smelt, man, the place where he shit.

304

THE KIRK'S ALARM

Andro Gouk, Andro Gouk, ye may slander the book,
    And the book no the waur, let me tell ye!
Ye are rich, and look big, but lay by hat and wig,
    And ye'll hae a calf's head o' sma' value.

Barr Steenie, Barr Steenie, what mean ye? what mean ye?
    If ye'll meddle nae mair wi' the matter.
Ye may hae some pretence to havins and sense,
    Wi' people wha ken ye nae better.

Irvine Side, Irvine Side, wi' your turkeycock pride,
    Of manhood but sma' is your share;
Ye've the figure, 'tis true, even your faes will allow,
    And your friends they dare grant you nae mair.

Muirland Jock, Muirland Jock, when the Lord makes a
    rock
    To crush common sense for her sins,
If ill manners were wit, there's no mortal so fit
    To confound the poor Doctor at ance.

Holy Will, Holy Will, there was wit i' your skull,
    When ye pilfer'd the alms o' the poor;
The timmer is scant when ye're ta'en for a saint,
    Wha should swing in a rape for an hour.

Calvin's sons, Calvin's sons, seize your sp'ritual guns,
    Ammunition you never can need;
Your hearts are the stuff will be powther enough,
    And your skulls are storehouses o' lead.

THE KIRK'S ALARM

Poet Burns, Poet Burns, wi' your priest-skelping turns,
  Why desert ye your auld native shire?
Your muse is a gipsy, e'en tho' she were tipsy
  She cou'd ca' us nae waur than we are.

ROBERT BURNS.

160 *Whistle, and I'll come to you, my Lad*

O WHISTLE, and I'll come to you, my lad;
  O whistle, and I'll come to you, my lad:
Tho' father and mither and a' should gae mad,
O whistle, and I'll come to you, my lad.

But warily tent, when ye come to court me,
And come na unless the back-yett be a-jee;
Syne up the back-stile, and let naebody see,
And come as ye were na comin' to me.
And come as ye were na comin' to me.

At kirk, or at market, whene'er ye meet me,
Gang by me as tho' that ye car'd na a flee:
But steal me a blink o' your bonnie black ee,
Yet look as ye were na lookin' at me.
Yet look as ye were na lookin' at me.

Aye vow and protest that ye care na for me,
And whiles ye may lightly my beauty a wee;
But court na anither, tho' jokin' ye be,
For fear that she wyle your fancy frae me.
For fear that she wyle your fancy frae me.

ROBERT BURNS.

O WHA my babie-clouts will buy?
　　O wha will tent me when I cry?
Wha will kiss me whare I lie?
　　The rantin' dog, the daddie o't.

Wha will own he did the faut?
'Wha will buy the groanin' maut?
Wha will tell me how to ca't?
　　The rantin' dog, the daddie o't.

When I mount the creepie-chair,
Wha will sit beside me there?
Gie me Rob, I seek nae mair,
　　The rantin' dog, the daddie o't.

Wha will crack to me my lane?
Wha will mak me fidgin' fain?
Wha will kiss me o'er again?
　　The rantin' dog, the daddie o't.
　　　　　　　　　　　　　ROBERT BURNS.

The Parson's Looks

THAT there is falsehood in his looks
　　I must and will deny;
They say their master is a knave—
　　And sure they do not lie.

Lord Galloway

BRIGHT ran thy line, O Galloway,
　　Thro' many a far-fam'd sire;
So ran the far-famed Roman way,
　　So ended in a mire!
　　　　　　　　　　　　　ROBERT BURNS.

OH Boney's on the sea
   Says the Shan Van Vocht,
Oh Boney's on the sea,
He'll be here the first of May,
And the Orange will decay
   Says the Shan Van Vocht.

Oh Boney's on the shore
   Says the Shan Van Vocht,
Oh Boney's on the shore,
Don't you hear his cannons roar?
We'll be Orangemen no more
   Says the Shan Van Vocht.

Oh Boney's on dry land
   Says the Shan Van Vocht,
Oh Boney's on dry land,
He's a sword in every hand,
He's a loyal Ribbon man,
   Says the Shan Van Vocht.   ANON.

164   *The Wearing of the Green*

OH Paddy dear, and did you hear the news that's
   going round?
The shamrock is forbid by law to grow on Irish ground:
Saint Patrick's day no more we'll keep, his colour can't be
   seen,
For there's a cruel law agin the wearing of the Green.
I met with Napper Tandy and he took me by the hand,
And said he, How's poor old Ireland, and how does she
   stand?

She's the most distressful country that ever yet was seen;
They're hanging men and women for the wearing of the
    Green.

Then since the colour we must wear is England's cruel
    Red,
'Twill serve us to remind us of the blood that has been shed;
You may take the shamrock from your hat and cast it on
    the sod,
But never fear, 'twill take root there, though underfoot 'tis
    trod.
When laws can stop the blades of grass from growing as
    they grow,
And when the leaves in summertime their verdure dare not
    show,
Then I will change the colour that I wear in my caubeen;
But till that day, please God, I'll stick to wearing of the
    Green.   ANON.

165   *The Croppy Boy*

IT was early, early in the spring,
  The birds did whistle and sweetly sing,
Changing their notes from tree to tree,
And the song they sang was Old Ireland free.

It was early, early in the night,
The yeoman cavalry gave me a fright;
The yeoman cavalry was my downfall
And taken was I by Lord Cornwall.

'Twas in the guard-house where I was laid
And in a parlour where I was tried;
My sentence passed and my courage low
When to Dungannon I was forced to go.

THE CROPPY BOY

As I was passing my father's door
My brother William stood at the door,
My aged father stood at the door
And my tender mother her hair she tore.

As I was walking up Wexford Street
My own first cousin I chanced to meet;
My own first cousin did me betray,
And for one bare guinea swore my life away.

My sister Mary heard the express,
She ran upstairs in her morning-dress—
Five hundred guineas I will lay me down,
To see my brother safe in Wexford town.

As I was walking up Wexford Hill,
Who could blame me to cry my fill?
I looked behind and I looked before,
But my tender mother I shall ne'er see more.

As I was mounted on the platform high,
My aged father was standing by;
My aged father did me deny,
And the name he gave me was the Croppy Boy.

It was in Dungannon this young man died,
And in Dungannon his body lies;
And you good Christians that do pass by,
Just shed a tear for the Croppy Boy.   ANON.

166   *The ould Orange Flute*

IN the County Tyrone, in the town of Dungannon,
Where many a ruction myself had a han' in,
Bob Williamson lived, a weaver to trade,
And as all of us thought a stout Orange blade.

THE OULD ORANGE FLUTE

On the twelfth of July, as it yearly did come,
Bob played on the flute to the sound of the drum;
And although you may talk of the harp or the lute,
There was nothing could sound like Bob's ould Orange
    flute.

But this treacherous scoundrel he took us all in,
For he married a Paypish called Bridget M'Ginn;
And turned Paypish himself, and forsook the ould cause
That gave us our freedom, religion and laws.
Now, the boys in the townland made some stir upon it,
And Bob had to fly to the province of Connacht.
He fled with his wife and his fixings to boot,
And along with the rest went the ould Orange flute.

At chapel on Sundays to atone for past deeds,
He said Pater and Ave, and counted his beads,
Till, after some time, at the priest's own desire,
He went with his ould flute to play in the choir.
He went with his ould flute to play in the Mass,
And the instrument shivered and sighed, 'Oh, alas!'
And blow as he would, though it made a great noise,
The flute would play only the 'Protestant Boys'.

Bob jumped, humphed and started and got in a splutter,
And threw his ould flute in the blest Holy Water;
He thought that this charm would bring some other
    soun'
And he blew it but then it played 'Croppies Lie Down!'
And all he could whistle, and finger, and blow,
To play Paypish music the flute would not go;
'Kick the Pope', 'The Boyne Water', it always would
    sound,
But one Paypish squeak in it could not be found.

At a council of priests that was held the next day
They prepared to administer auto-da-fay;
For they couldn't knock heresy out of its head,
And they bought Bob another to play in its stead.
So the ould flute was doomed, and its fate was pathetic,
It was fastened and burned at the stake as heretic.
And while the flames roared they all heard a strange noise,
'Twas the ould flute still playin' the 'Protestant Boys'!

ANON.

167 *The Groves of Blarney*

THE groves of Blarney they look so charming,
  Down by the purling of sweet, silent streams,
Being banked with posies that spontaneous grow there,
Planted in order by the sweet rock close.
'Tis there's the daisy and the sweet carnation,
The blooming pink and the rose so fair,
The daffodowndilly, likewise the lily,
All flowers that scent the sweet, fragrant air.
        O, ullagoane.

'Tis Lady Jeffers that owns this station;
Like Alexander, or Queen Helen fair,
There's no commander in all the nation,
For emulation, can with her compare.
Such walls surround her, that no nine-pounder
Could dare to plunder her place of strength;
But Oliver Cromwell he did her pommell,
And made a breach in her battlement.
        O, ullagoane.

THE GROVES OF BLARNEY

There's gravel walks there for speculation
And conversation in sweet solitude.
'Tis there the lover may hear the dove, or
The gentle plover in the afternoon;
And if a lady would be so engaging
As to walk alone in those shady bowers,
'Tis there the courtier he may transport her
Into some fort, or all under ground.
       O, ullagoane.

'Tis there's the kitchen hangs many a flitch in
With the maids a stitching upon the stair;
The bread and biske', the beer and whisky,
Would make you frisky if you were there.
'Tis there you'd see Peg Murphy's daughter
A washing praties forenent the door,
With Roger Cleary, and Father Healy,
All blood relations to my Lord Donoughmore.
       O, ullagoane.

For 'tis there's a cave where no daylight enters,
But cats and badgers are for ever bred;
Being mossed by nature, that makes it sweeter
Than a coach-and-six or a feather bed.
'Tis there the lake is, well stored with perches,
And comely eels in the verdant mud;
Besides the leeches, and groves of beeches,
Standing in order for to guard the flood.
       O, ullagoane.

There's statues gracing this noble place in—
All heathen gods and nymphs so fair;
Bold Neptune, Plutarch, and Nicodemus,
All standing naked in the open air!

So now to finish this brave narration,
Which my poor geni' could not entwine;
But were I Homer, or Nebuchadnezzar,
'Tis in every feature I would make it shine.
O, ullagoane.

R. A. MILLIKEN.

168   *Galway Races*

IT'S there you'll see confectioners with sugar sticks and
dainties,
The lozenges and oranges, lemonade and the raisins;
The gingerbread and spices to accommodate the ladies,
And a big crubeen for threepence to be picking while
you're able.

It's there you'll see the gamblers, the thimbles and the
garters,
And the sporting Wheel of Fortune with the four and
twenty quarters,
There was others without scruple pelting wattles at poor
Maggy,
And her father well contented and he looking at his
daughter.

It's there you'll see the pipers and fiddlers competing,
And the nimble-footed dancers and they tripping on the
daisies.
There was others crying segars and lights, and bills of all
the races,
With the colour of the jockeys, the prize and horses'
ages.

It's there you'd see the jockeys and they mounted on most
    stately,
The pink and blue, the red and green, the Emblem of our
    nation,
When the bell was rung for starting, the horses seemed
    impatient,
Though they never stood on ground, their speed was so
    amazing.

There was half a million people there of all denominations,
The Catholic, the Protestant, the Jew and Prespetarian.
There was yet no animosity, no matter what persuasion,
But failte and hospitality, inducing fresh acquaintance.

ANON.

169   *Johnny's the Lad I love*

AS I roved out on a May morning,
    Being in the youthful spring,
I leaned my back close to the garden wall
To hear the small birds sing;

And to hear two lovers talk, my dear,
To know what they would say,
That I might know a little of her mind
Before I would go away.

'Come sit you down, my heart,' he says,
'All on this pleasant green,
It's full three-quarters of a year and more
Since together you and I have been.'

'I will not sit on the grass,' she said,
'Now nor any other time,
For I hear you're engaged with another maid,
And your heart is no more of mine.

315

'Oh, I'll not believe what an old man says,
For his days are well nigh done,
Nor will I believe what a young man says,
For he's fair to many a one.

'But I will climb a high, high tree,
And rob a wild bird's nest,
And I'll bring back whatever I do find
To the arms I love the best,' she said,
'To the arms I love the best.'   ANON.

170   *Johnny, I hardly knew ye*

WHILE going the road to sweet Athy,
        Hurroo! Hurroo!
While going the road to sweet Athy,
        Hurroo! Hurroo!
While going the road to sweet Athy,
A stick in my hand and a drop in my eye,
A doleful damsel I heard cry:—
        'Och, Johnny, I hardly knew ye!
With drums and guns, and guns and drums
        The enemy nearly slew ye,
        My darling dear, you look so queer,
        Och, Johnny, I hardly knew ye!

'Where are your eyes that looked so mild?
        Hurroo! Hurroo!
Where are your eyes that looked so mild?
        Hurroo! Hurroo!
Where are your eyes that looked so mild
When my poor heart you first beguiled?
Why did you run from me and the child?
        Och, Johnny, I hardly knew ye!
With drums, &c.

316

JOHNNY, I HARDLY KNEW YE

'Where are the legs with which you run?
    Hurroo! Hurroo!
Where are the legs with which you run?
    Hurroo! Hurroo!
Where are the legs with which you run
When you went to carry a gun?—
Indeed your dancing days are done!
    Och, Johnny, I hardly knew ye!
With drums, &c.

'It grieved my heart to see you sail,
    Hurroo! Hurroo!
It grieved my heart to see you sail,
    Hurroo! Hurroo!
It grieved my heart to see you sail
Though from my heart you took leg bail,—
Like a cod you're doubled up head and tail.
    Och, Johnny, I hardly knew ye!
With drums, &c.

'You haven't an arm and you haven't a leg,
    Hurroo! Hurroo!
You haven't an arm and you haven't a leg,
    Hurroo! Hurroo!
You haven't an arm and you haven't a leg,
You're an eyeless, noseless, chickenless egg;
You'll have to be put in a bowl to beg;
    Och, Johnny, I hardly knew ye!
With drums, &c.

'I'm happy for to see you home,
    Hurroo! Hurroo!

Y

JOHNNY, I HARDLY KNEW YE

I'm happy for to see you home,
 Hurroo! Hurroo!
I'm happy for to see you home,
All from the island of Sulloon,
So low in flesh, so high in bone,
 Och, Johnny, I hardly knew ye!
With drums, &c.

'But sad as it is to see you so,
 Hurroo! Hurroo!
But sad as it is to see you so,
 Hurroo! Hurroo!
But sad as it is to see you so,
And to think of you now as an object of woe,
Your Peggy'll still keep ye on as her beau;
 Och, Johnny, I hardly knew ye!
With drums and guns, and guns and drums
  The enemy nearly slew ye,
  My darling dear, you look so queer,
  Och, Johnny, I hardly knew ye!'   ANON.

171 *The Night before Larry was stretched*

THE night before Larry was stretched,
 The boys they all paid him a visit;
A bit in their sacks, too, they fetched;
 They sweated their duds till they riz it;
For Larry was ever the lad,
 When a boy was condemned to the squeezer,
Would fence all the duds that he had
 To help a poor friend to a sneezer,
And warm his gob 'fore he died.

THE NIGHT BEFORE LARRY WAS STRETCHED

The boys they came crowding in fast,
They drew all their stools round about him,
Six glims round his trap-case were placed,
He couldn't be well waked without 'em.
When one of us asked could he die
Without having truly repented,
Says Larry, 'That's all in my eye,
And first by the clargy invented,
To get a fat bit for themselves.'

'I'm sorry, dear Larry,' says I,
'To see you in this situation;
And, blister my limbs if I lie,
I'd as lieve it had been my own station.'
'Ochone! it's all over,' says he,
'For the neck-cloth I'll be forced to put on,
And by this time to-morrow you'll see
Your poor Larry as dead as a mutton,
Because why, his courage was good.

'And I'll be cut up like a pie,
And my nob from my body be parted.'
'You're in the wrong box, then,' says I,
'For blast me if they're so hard-hearted;
A chalk on the back of your neck
Is all that Jack Ketch dares to give you;
Then mind not such trifles a feck,
For why should the likes of them grieve you?
And now, boys, come tip us the deck.'

The cards being called for, they played,
Till Larry found one of them cheated;
A dart at his napper he made
(The boy being easily heated);

THE NIGHT BEFORE LARRY WAS STRETCHED

'O, by the hokey, you thief,
I'll scuttle your nob with my daddle!
You cheat me because I'm in grief,
But soon I'll demolish your noddle,
And leave you your claret to drink.'

Then the clargy came in with his book,
He spoke him so smooth and so civil;
Larry tipped him a Kilmainham look,
And pitched his big wig to the devil;
Then sighing, he threw back his head,
To get a sweet drop of the bottle,
And pitiful sighing, he said:
'Oh, the hemp will be soon round my throttle,
And choke my poor windpipe to death.'

'Though sure it's the best way to die,
O! the devil a better a-livin'!
For when the gallows is high
Your journey is shorter to heaven:'
But what harasses Larry the most,
And makes his poor soul melancholy,
Is that he thinks of the time when his ghost
Will come in a sheet to sweet Molly;
'O, sure it will kill her alive!'

So moving these last words he spoke,
We all vented our tears in a shower;
For my part, I thought my heart broke,
To see him cut down like a flower.
On his travels we watched him next day;
O! the throttler, I thought I could kill him;

But Larry not one word did say,
Nor changed till he came to King William,
Then, musha, his colour grew white.

When we came to the numbing chit,
He was tucked up so neat and so pretty,
The rumbler jogged off from his feet,
And he died with his face to the city;
He kicked, too—but that was all pride,
For soon you might see 'twas all over;
Soon after the noose was untied,
And at darkee we waked him in clover,
And sent him to take a ground sweat.

ANON.

172   *The Reverie of Poor Susan*

AT the corner of Wood Street, when daylight appears,
Hangs a Thrush that sings loud, it has sung for three
years:
Poor Susan has passed by the spot, and has heard
In the silence of morning the song of the bird.

'Tis a note of enchantment; what ails her? She sees
A mountain ascending, a vision of trees;
Bright volumes of vapour through Lothbury glide,
And a river flows on through the vale of Cheapside.

Green pastures she views in the midst of the dale
Down which she so often has tripped with her pail;
And a single small cottage, a nest like a dove's,
The one only dwelling on earth that she loves.

She looks, and her heart is in heaven: but they fade,
The mist and the river, the hill and the shade;
The stream will not flow, and the hill will not rise,
And the colours have all passed away from her eyes!

WILLIAM WORDSWORTH.

173   *Bonny Dundee*

TO the Lords of Convention 'twas Claver'se who
     spoke,
'Ere the King's crown shall fall, there are crowns to be
     broke;
So let each Cavalier who loves honour and me,
Come follow the bonnet of Bonny Dundee.

   Chorus:
      Come fill up my cup, come fill up my can,
      Come saddle your horses, and call up your men;
      Come open the West Port and let me gang free,
      And it's room for the bonnets of Bonny Dundee!'

Dundee he is mounted, he rides up the street,
The bells are rung backward, the drums they are beat;
But the Provost, douce man, said, 'Just e'en let him be,
The Gude Town is weel quit of that Deil of Dundee.'

'Away to the hills, to the caves, to the rocks—
Ere I own a usurper, I'll couch with the fox—
And tremble, false Whigs, in the midst of your glee,
You have not seen the last of my bonnet and me!'

He waved his proud hand, and the trumpets were blown,
The kettle-drums clashed, and the horsemen rode on,
Till on Ravelston's cliffs, and on Clermiston's lee,
Died away the wild war-notes of Bonny Dundee.

BONNY DUNDEE

Chorus:

Come fill up my cup, come fill up my can.
Come saddle the horses and call up the men,
Come open your gates, and let me gae free,
For it's up with the bonnets of Bonny Dundee.

SIR WALTER SCOTT.

174 *The Devil's Thoughts*

FROM his brimstone bed at break of day
A-walking the Devil is gone,
To visit his little snug farm the earth
And see how his stock goes on.

Over the hill and over the dale,
And he went over the plain,
And backward and forward he switched his long tail
As a gentleman switches his cane.

And how then was the Devil dressed?
Oh! he was in his Sunday best:
His jacket was red and his breeches were blue,
And there was a hole where the tail came through.

He saw a Lawyer killing a Viper
On a dunghill hard by his own stable;
And the Devil smiled, for it put him in mind
Of Cain and his brother, Abel.

He saw an Apothecary on a white horse
Ride by on his vocations,
And the Devil thought of his old Friend
Death in the Revelations.

He saw a cottage with a double coach-house,
A cottage of gentility!
And the Devil did grin, for his darling sin
Is pride that apes humility.

He peeped into a rich bookseller's shop,
Quoth he! we are both of one college,
For I sat myself like a cormorant once
Hard by the tree of knowledge.

Down the river did glide, with wind and tide,
A pig, with vast celerity,
And the Devil looked wise as he saw how the while,
It cut its own throat. 'There!' quoth he with a smile,
'Goes "England's commercial prosperity". '

As he went through Cold-Bath fields he saw
A solitary cell;
And the Devil was pleased, for it gave him a hint
For improving his prisons in Hell.

General —'s burning face
He saw with consternation,
And back to hell his way did he take,
For the Devil thought by a slight mistake
It was general conflagration.

SAMUEL TAYLOR COLERIDGE.

175 *Free Thoughts on several eminent
Composers*

SOME cry up Haydn, some Mozart,
Just as the whim bites; for my part,
I do not care a farthing candle
For either of them, or for Handel.—

FREE THOUGHTS ON EMINENT COMPOSERS

Cannot a man live free and easy,
Without admiring Pergolesi?
Or thro' the world with comfort go,
That never heard of Doctor Blow?
So help me God, I hardly have;
And yet I eat, and drink, and shave,
Like other people, if you watch it,
And know no more of Stave or Crotchet,
Than did the primitive Peruvians;
Or those old ante-queer-Diluvians
That lived in the unwash'd world with Tubal,
Before that dirty blacksmith Jubal
By stroke on anvil, or by summ'at,
Found out, to his great surprise, the gamut.
I care no more for Cimarosa,
Than he did for Salvator Rosa,
Being no painter; and bad luck
Be mine, if I can bear that Gluck!
Old Tycho Brahe, and modern Herschel,
Had something in 'em; but who's Purcel?
The devil, with his foot so cloven,
For aught I care, may take Beethoven;
And, if the bargain does not suit,
I'll throw him Weber in to boot.
There's not the splitting of a splinter
To choose 'twixt him last named, and Winter.
Of Doctor Pepusch old queen Dido
Knew just as much, God knows, as I do.
I would not go four miles to visit
Sebastian Bach (or Batch, which is it?);
No more I would for Bononcini.
As for Novello, or Rossini,

I shall not say a word to grieve 'em,
Because they're living; so I leave 'em.

CHARLES LAMB.

176   *A Farewell to Tobacco*

MAY the Babylonish curse
  Straight confound my stammering verse,
If I can a passage see
In this word-perplexity,
Or a fit expression find,
Or a language to my mind,
(Still the phrase is wide and scant)
To take leave of thee, GREAT PLANT!
Or in any terms relate
Half my love, or half my hate:
For I hate, yet love, thee so,
That, whichever thing I show,
The plain truth will seem to be
A constrain'd hyperbole,
And the passion to proceed
More from a mistress than a weed.

Sooty retainer to the vine,
Bacchus' black servant, negro fine;
Sorcerer, that mak'st us dote upon
Thy begrimed complexion,
And, for thy pernicious sake,
More and greater oaths to break
Than reclaimèd lovers take
'Gainst women: thou thy siege dost lay
Much too in the female way,
While thou suck'st the lab'ring breath
Faster than kisses or than death.

A FAREWELL TO TOBACCO

Thou in such a cloud dost bind us,
That our worst foes cannot find us,
And ill fortune, that would thwart us,
Shoots at rovers, shooting at us;
While each man, through thy height'ning steam,
Does like a smoking Etna seem,
And all about us does express
(Fancy and wit in richest dress)
A Sicilian fruitfulness.

Thou through such a mist dost show us,
That our best friends do not know us,
And, for those allowèd features,
Due to reasonable creatures,
Liken'st us to fell Chimeras,
Monsters that, who see us, fear us;
Worse than Cerberus or Geryon,
Or, who first loved a cloud, Ixion.

Bacchus we know, and we allow
His tipsy rites. But what art thou
That but by reflex canst show
What his deity can do,
As the false Egyptian spell
Aped the true Hebrew miracle?
Some few vapours thou may'st raise,
The weak brain may serve to amaze,
But to the reins and nobler heart
Canst nor life nor heat impart.

Brother of Bacchus, later born,
The old world was sure forlorn,
Wanting thee, that aidest more
The god's victories than before

A FAREWELL TO TOBACCO

All his panthers, and the brawls
Of his piping Bacchanals.
These, as stale, we disallow,
Or judge of *thee* meant: only thou
His true Indian conquest art;
And, for ivy round his dart,
The reformed god now weaves
A finer thyrsus of thy leaves.

Scent to match thy rich perfume
Chemic art did ne'er presume
Through her quaint alembic strain,
None so sovereign to the brain.
Nature, that did in thee excel,
Framed again no second smell.
Roses, violets, but toys
For the smaller sort of boys,
Or for greener damsels meant;
Thou art the only manly scent.

Stinking'st of the stinking kind,
Filth of the mouth and fog of the mind.
Africa, that brags her foison,
Breeds no such prodigious poison,
Henbane, nightshade, both together,
Hemlock, aconite—
    Nay, rather,
Plant divine, of rarest virtue;
Blisters on the tongue would hurt you.
'Twas but in a sort I blamed thee;
None e'er prosper'd who defamed thee;
Irony all, and feigned abuse,
Such as perplex'd lovers use,

A FAREWELL TO TOBACCO

At a need, when, in despair
To paint forth their fairest fair,
Or in part but to express
That exceeding comeliness
Which their fancies doth so strike,
They borrow language of dislike;
And, instead of Dearest Miss,
Jewel, Honey, Sweetheart, Bliss,
And those forms of old admiring,
Call her Cockatrice and Siren,
Basilisk, and all that's evil,
Witch, Hyena, Mermaid, Devil,
Ethiop, Wench, and Blackamoor,
Monkey, Ape, and twenty more;
Friendly Trait'ress, loving Foe,—
Not that she is truly so,
But no other way they know
A contentment to express,
Borders so upon excess,
That they do not rightly wot
Whether it be pain or not.

Or as men, constrain'd to part
With what's nearest to their heart,
While their sorrow's at the height,
Lose discrimination quite,
And their hasty wrath let fall,
To appease their frantic gall,
On the darling thing whatever
Whence they feel it death to sever,
Though it be, as they, perforce,
Guiltless of the sad divorce.

A FAREWELL TO TOBACCO

For I must (nor let it grieve thee,
Friendliest of plants, that I must) leave thee.
For thy sake, Tobacco, I
Would do any thing but die,
And but seek to extend my days
Long enough to sing thy praise.
But as she, who once hath been
A king's consort, is a queen
Ever after, nor will bate
Any tittle of her state,
Though a widow, or divorced,
So I, from thy converse forced,
The old name and style retain,
A right Katherine of Spain;
And a seat, too, 'mongst the joys
Of the blest Tobacco boys;
Where, though I, by sour physician,
Am debarr'd the full fruition
Of thy favours, I may catch
Some collateral sweets, and snatch
Sidelong odours, that give life
Like glances from a neighbour's wife;
And still live in the by-places
And the suburbs of thy graces;
And in thy borders take delight,
An unconquer'd Canaanite.

CHARLES LAMB.

177 *Plays*

ALAS, how soon the hours are over,
    Counted us out to play the lover!
And how much narrower is the stage,
Allotted us to play the sage!

But when we play the fool, how wide
The theatre expands! beside,
How long the audience sits before us!
How many prompters! what a chorus!

W. S. LANDOR.

178   *Ireland never was contented*

IRELAND never was contented.
Say you so? You are demented.
Ireland was contented when
All could use the sword and pen,
And when Tara rose so high
That her turrets split the sky,
And about her courts were seen
Liveried angels robed in green,
Wearing, by St. Patrick's bounty,
Emeralds big as half the county.

W. S. LANDOR.

179   *The last Rose of Summer*

'TIS the last rose of summer left blooming alone,
All her lovely companions are faded and gone.
No flower of her kindred, no rosebud is nigh
To reflect back her blushes or give sigh for sigh.

I'll not leave thee, thou lone one, to pine on the stem;
Since the lovely are sleeping, go sleep thou with them:
Thus kindly I scatter thy leaves o'er the bed
Where thy mates of the garden lie scentless and dead.

331

So soon may I follow when friendships decay,
And from love's shining circle the gems drop away.
When true hearts lie withered and fond ones are flown,
Oh who would inhabit this bleak world alone?

THOMAS MOORE.

180   *To Ladies' Eyes*

TO ladies' eyes around, boy,
   We can't refuse, we can't refuse,
Tho' bright eyes so abound, boy,
   'Tis hard to choose, 'tis hard to choose.
For thick as stars that lighten
   Yon airy bow'rs, yon airy bow'rs,
The countless eyes that brighten
   This earth of ours, this earth of ours.
But fill the cup—where'er, boy,
   Our choice may fall, our choice may fall,
We're sure to find love there, boy,
   So drink them all! so drink them all!

Some looks there are so holy,
   They seem but giv'n, they seem but giv'n
As shining beacons, solely
   To light to heav'n, to light to heav'n.
While some—oh! ne'er believe them—
   With tempting ray, with tempting ray,
Would lead us (God forgive them!)
   The other way, the other way.
But fill the cup—where'er, boy,
   Our choice may fall, our choice may fall,
We're sure to find love there, boy,
   So drink them all! so drink them all!

In some, as in a mirror,
　　Love seems portray'd, love seems portray'd,
But shun the flattering error,
　　'Tis but his shade, 'tis but his shade.
Himself has fix'd his dwelling
　　In eyes we know, in eyes we know,
And lips—but this is telling—
　　So here they go! so here they go!
Fill up, fill up—where'er, boy,
　　Our choice may fall, our choice may fall,
We're sure to find love there, boy,
　　So drink them all! so drink them all!

THOMAS MOORE.

181　　*The Meeting of the Waters*

THERE is not in the wide world a valley so sweet
　As that vale in whose bosom the bright waters meet.
Oh! the last rays of feeling and life must depart,
Ere the bloom of that valley shall fade from my heart.

Yet it was not that Nature had shed o'er the scene
Her purest of crystal and brightest of green;
'Twas not her soft magic of streamlet or hill;
Oh, no—it was something more exquisite still:—

'Twas that friends, the beloved of my bosom, were near,
Who made ev'ry dear scene of enchantment more dear;
And who felt how the best charms of Nature improve
When we see them reflected in looks that we love.

Sweet vale of Avoca! now calm could I rest
In thy bosom of shade with the friends I love best,

333

z

Where the storms that we feel in this cold world should
    cease,
And our hearts, like thy waters, be mingled in peace.

THOMAS MOORE.

182   *Recreation*

WE took our work, and went, you see,
    To take an early cup of tea.
We did so now and then, to pay
The friendly debt, and so did they.
Not that our friendship burnt so bright
That all the world could see the light;
'Twas of the ordinary *genus*,
And little love was lost between us:
We lov'd, I think, about as true
As such near neighbours mostly do.

At first, we all were somewhat dry;
Mamma felt cold, and so did I:
Indeed, that room, sit where you will,
Has draught enough to turn a mill.
'I hope you're warm,' says Mrs. G.
'O, quite so,' says mamma, *says she*;
'I'll take my shawl off by and by.'—
'This room is always warm,' *says I.*

At last the tea came up, and so,
With that, our tongues began to go.
Now, in that house you're sure of knowing
The smallest scrap of news that's going;
We find it *there* the wisest way
To take some care of what we say.

RECREATION

—Says she, 'there's dreadful doings still
In that affair about the *will*;
For now the folks in Brewer's Street
Don't speak to *James's*, when they meet.
Poor Mrs. *Sam* sits all alone,
And frets herself to skin and bone.
For months she manag'd, she declares,
All the old gentleman's affairs;
And always let him have his way,
And never left him night nor day;
Waited and watch'd his every look,
And gave him every drop he took.
Dear Mrs. *Sam*, it was too bad!
He might have left her all he had.'

'Pray, ma'am,' says I, 'has poor Miss A.
Been left as *handsome* as they say?'
'My dear,' says she, ''tis no such thing,
She'd nothing but a mourning ring.
But is it not *uncommon* mean
To wear that rusty bombazeen!'
'She had,' says I, 'the very same.
Three years ago, for—what's his name?'—
'The Duke of *Brunswick*,—very true,
And has not bought a thread of new,
I'm positive,' said Mrs. G.—
So then we laugh'd, and drank our tea.

'So,' says mamma, 'I find it's true
What Captain P. intends to do;
To hire that house, or else to buy—'
'Close to the tan-yard, ma'am,' says I;

335

RECREATION

'Upon my word it's very strange,
I wish they mayn't repent the change!'
'My dear,' says she, ''tis very well
You know, if *they* can bear the smell.'

'Miss F.' says I, 'is said to be
A sweet young woman, is not she?'
'O, excellent! I hear,' she cried;
'O, truly so!' mamma replied.
'How old should you suppose her, pray?
She's older than she looks, they say.'
'Really,' says I, 'she seems to me
Not more than twenty-two or three.'
'O, then you're wrong,' says Mrs. G.
'Their upper servant told our *Jane*,
She'll not see twenty-nine again.'
'Indeed, so old! I wonder why
She does not marry, then,' says I;
'So many thousands to bestow,
And such a beauty, too, you know.'
'A beauty! O, my dear Miss B.
You must be joking now,' says she;
'Her *figure* 's rather pretty,'—'Ah!
That's what *I* say,' replied mamma.

'Miss F.' says I, 'I've understood,
Spends all her time in doing good:
The people say her coming down
Is quite a blessing to the town.'
At that our hostess fetch'd a sigh,
And shook her head; and so, says I,
'It's very kind of her, I'm sure,
To be so generous to the poor.'

RECREATION

'No doubt,' says she, ''tis very true;
Perhaps there may be *reasons* too:—
You know some people like to pass
For *patrons* with the lower class.'

And here I break my story's thread,
Just to remark, that what she said,
Although I took the other part,
Went like a cordial to my heart.

Some innuendos more had pass'd,
Till out the scandal came at last.
'Come then, I'll tell you something more,'
Says she,—'Eliza, shut the door.—
I would not trust a creature here,
For all the world, but you, my dear.
Perhaps it's false—I wish it may,
—But let it go no further, pray!'
'O,' says mamma, 'You need not fear,
We never mention what we hear.'
And so, we draw our chairs the nearer,
And whispering, lest the child should hear her,
She told a tale, at least too *long*
To be repeated in a song;
We, panting every breath between,
With curiosity and spleen.
And how we did enjoy the sport!
And echo every faint report,
And answer every candid doubt,
And turn her motives inside out,
And holes in all her virtues pick,
Till we were sated, almost sick.

—Thus having brought it to a close,
In great good-humour, we arose.
Indeed, 'twas more than time to go,
Our boy had been an hour below,
So, warmly pressing Mrs. G.
To fix a day to come to tea,
We muffled up in cloak and plaid,
And trotted home behind the lad.

JANE TAYLOR.

183   *The Vision of Judgment*

SAINT PETER sat by the celestial gate;
   His keys were rusty, and the lock was dull,
So little trouble had been given of late:
   Not that the place by any means was full,
But since the Gallic era 'eighty-eight',
   The devils had ta'en a longer, stronger pull,
And 'a pull all together', as they say
At sea—which drew most souls another way.

The angels all were singing out of tune,
   And hoarse with having little else to do,
Excepting to wind up the sun and moon,
   Or curb a runaway young star or two,
Or wild colt of a comet, which too soon
   Broke out of bounds o'er the ethereal blue,
Splitting some planet with its playful tail,
As boats are sometimes by a wanton whale.

The guardian seraphs had retired on high,
   Finding their charges past all care below;

THE VISION OF JUDGMENT

Terrestrial business fill'd nought in the sky
  Save the recording angel's black bureau;
Who found, indeed, the facts to multiply
  With such rapidity of vice and woe,
That he had stripp'd off both his wings in quills,
And yet was in arrear of human ills.

His business so augmented of late years,
  That he was forced, against his will no doubt
(Just like those cherubs, earthly ministers),
  For some resource to turn himself about,
And claim the help of his celestial peers,
  To aid him ere he should be quite worn out
By the increased demand for his remarks:
Six angels and twelve saints were named his clerks.

This was a handsome board—at least for heaven;
  And yet they had even then enough to do,
So many conquerors' cars were daily driven,
  So many kingdoms fitted up anew;
Each day, too, slew its thousands six or seven,
  Till at the crowning carnage, Waterloo,
They threw their pens down in divine disgust,
The page was so besmear'd with blood and dust.

This by the way; 'tis not mine to record
  What angels shrink from: even the very devil
On this occasion his own work abhorr'd,
  So surfeited with the infernal revel:
Though he himself had sharpen'd every sword,
  It almost quench'd his innate thirst of evil.
(Here Satan's sole good work deserves insertion—
'Tis, that he has both generals in reversion.)

339

Let's skip a few short years of hollow peace,
    Which peopled earth no better, hell as wont,
And heaven none—they form the tyrant's lease,
    With nothing but new names subscribed upon't:
'Twill one day finish: meantime they increase,
    'With seven heads and ten horns,' and all in front,
Like Saint John's foretold beast; but ours are born
Less formidable in the head than horn.

In the first year of freedom's second dawn
    Died George the Third; although no tyrant, one
Who shielded tyrants, till each sense withdrawn
    Left him nor mental nor external sun:
A better farmer ne'er brush'd dew from lawn,
    A worse king never left a realm undone!
He died—but left his subjects still behind,
One half as mad—and t'other no less blind.

He died! his death made no great stir on earth:
    His burial made some pomp; there was profusion
Of velvet, gilding, brass, and no great dearth
    Of aught but tears—save those shed by collusion.
For these things may be bought at their true worth;
    Of elegy there was the due infusion—
Bought also; and the torches, cloaks, and banners,
Heralds, and relics of old Gothic manners,

Form'd a sepulchral melodrame. Of all
    The fools who flock'd to swell or see the show,
Who cared about the corpse? The funeral
    Made the attraction, and the black the woe.
There throbb'd not there a thought which pierced the
        pall;
    And when the gorgeous coffin was laid low,

THE VISION OF JUDGMENT

It seem'd the mockery of hell to fold
The rottenness of eighty years in gold.

So mix his body with the dust! It might
   Return to what it *must* far sooner, were
The natural compound left alone to fight
   Its way back into earth, and fire, and air;
But the unnatural balsams merely blight
   What nature made him at his birth, as bare
As the mere million's base unmummied clay—
Yet all his spices but prolong decay.

He's dead—and upper earth with him has done;
   He's buried; save the undertaker's bill,
Or lapidary scrawl, the world has gone
   For him, unless he left a German will.
But where's the proctor who will ask his son?
   In whom his qualities are reigning still,
Except that household virtue, most uncommon,
Of constancy to a bad, ugly woman.

'God save the king!' It is a large economy
   In God to save the like; but if He will
Be saving, all the better; for not one am I
   Of those who think damnation better still:
I hardly know, too, if not quite alone am I
   In this small hope of bettering future ill
By circumscribing, with some slight restriction,
The eternity of hell's hot jurisdiction.

I know this is unpopular; I know
   'Tis blasphemous; I know one may be damn'd
For hoping no one else may e'er be so;
   I know my catechism; I know we're cramm'd

With the best doctrines till we quite o'erflow;
  I know that all save England's church have shamm'd
And that the other twice two hundred churches
And synagogues have made a *damn'd* bad purchase.

God help us all! God help me too! I am,
  God knows, as helpless as the devil can wish,
And not a whit more difficult to damn
  Than is to bring to land a late-hook'd fish,
Or to the butcher to purvey the lamb;
  Not that I'm fit for such a noble dish,
As one day will be that immortal fry
Of almost everybody born to die.   LORD BYRON.

184   *Don Juan*

(i)

IF ever I should condescend to prose,
  I'll write poetical commandments, which
Shall supersede beyond all doubt all those
  That went before; in these I shall enrich
My text with many things that no one knows,
  And carry precept to the highest pitch:
I'll call the work 'Longinus o'er a Bottle;
Or, Every Poet his *own* Aristotle'.

Thou shalt believe in Milton, Dryden, Pope;
  Thou shalt not set up Wordsworth, Coleridge, Southey;
Because the first is crazed beyond all hope,
  The second drunk, the third so quaint and mouthey:
With Crabbe it may be difficult to cope,
  And Campbell's Hippocrene is somewhat drouthy:
Thou shalt not steal from Samuel Rogers, nor
Commit—flirtation with the muse of Moore.

DON JUAN

Thou shalt not covet Mr. Sotheby's muse,
  His Pegasus, nor anything that's his;
Thou shalt not bear false witness like 'the Blues'—
  (There's one, at least, is very fond of this);
Thou shalt not write, in short, but what I choose;
  This is true criticism, and you may kiss—
Exactly as you please, or not—the rod;
But if you don't, I'll lay it on, by G—d!

(ii)

Oh, Wellington! (or 'Villainton'—for Fame
  Sounds the heroic syllables both ways:
France could not even conquer your great name,
  But punn'd it down to this facetious phrase—
Beating or beaten, she will laugh the same),
  You have obtain'd great pensions and much praise:
Glory like yours should any dare gainsay,
Humanity would rise, and thunder 'Nay!'

I don't think that you used Kinnaird quite well
  In Marinèt's affair—in fact, 'twas shabby;
And, like some other things, won't do to tell
  Upon your tomb in Westminster's old Abbey.
Upon the rest 'tis not worth while to dwell,
  Such tales being for the tea-hours of some tabby;
But though your years as *man* tend fast to zero,
In fact your Grace is still but a *young hero*.

Though Britain owes (and pays you too) so much,
  Yet Europe doubtless owes you greatly more:
You have repair'd Legitimacy's crutch,
  A prop not quite so certain as before;

343

DON JUAN

The Spanish and the French, as well as Dutch,
    Have seen, and felt, how strongly you *restore*;
And Waterloo has made the world your debtor
(I wish your bards would sing it rather better).

You are 'the best of cut-throats':—do not start:
    The phrase is Shakespeare's, and not misapplied:
War's a brain-spattering, windpipe-slitting art,
    Unless her cause by right be sanctified.
If you have acted *once* a generous part,
    The world, not the world's masters, will decide,
And I shall be delighted to learn who,
Save you and yours, have gain'd by Waterloo?

I am no flatterer—you've supp'd full of flattery:
    They say you like it too—'tis no great wonder.
He whose whole life has been assault and battery,
    At last may get a little tired of thunder;
And, swallowing eulogy much more than satire, he
    May like being praised for every lucky blunder;
Called 'Saviour of the Nations'—not yet saved,
And 'Europe's Liberator'—still enslaved.

I've done. Now go, and dine from off the plate
    Presented by the Prince of the Brazils;
And send the sentinel before your gate
    A slice or two from your luxurious meals:
He fought, but has not fed so well of late.
    Some hunger, too, they say the people feels:—
There is no doubt that you deserve your ration,
But pray give back a little to the nation.

DON JUAN

I don't mean to reflect—a man so great as
  You, my Lord Duke, is far above reflection:
The high Roman fashion, too, of Cincinnatus,
  With modern history has but small connection:
Though as an Irishman you love potatoes,
  You need not take them under your direction;
And half a million for your Sabine farm
Is rather dear!—I'm sure I mean no harm.

Great men have always scorn'd great recompenses:
  Epaminondas saved his Thebes, and died,
Not leaving even his funeral expenses:
  George Washington had thanks, and nought beside,
Except the all-cloudless glory (which few men's is)
  To free his country: Pitt, too, had his pride,
And, as a high-soul'd minister of state, is
Renown'd for ruining Great Britain gratis.

Never had mortal man such opportunity,
  Except Napoleon, or abused it more:
You might have freed fallen Europe from the unity
  Of tyrants, and been blest from shore to shore:
And *now*—what *is* your fame? Shall the Muse tune it ye?
  Now—that the rabble's first vain shouts are o'er?
Go! hear it in your famish'd country's cries!
Behold the world! and curse your victories!

(*iii*)

In the great world—which, being interpreted,
  Meaneth the west or worst end of a city,
And about twice two thousand people, bred
  By no means to be very wise or witty,

But to sit up while others lie in bed,
    And look down on the universe with pity—
Juan, as an inveterate patrician,
Was well received by persons of condition.

He was a bachelor, which is a matter
    Of import both to virgin and to bride,
The former's hymeneal hopes to flatter;
    And (should she not hold fast by love or pride)
'Tis also of some moment to the latter:
    A rib's a thorn in a wed gallant's side,
Requires decorum, and is apt to double
The horrid sin—and, what's still worse, the trouble.

But Juan was a bachelor—of arts,
    And parts, and hearts: he danced and sung and had
An air as sentimental as Mozart's
    Softest of melodies, and could be sad
Or cheerful, without any 'flaws or starts',
    Just at the proper time; and though a lad,
Had seen the world—which is a curious sight,
And very much unlike what people write.

Fair virgins blush'd upon him; wedded dames
    Bloom'd also in less transitory hues;
For both commodities dwell by the Thames,
    The painting and the painted: youth, ceruse,
Against his heart preferr'd their usual claims,
    Such as no gentleman can quite refuse:
Daughters admired his dress, and pious mothers
Inquired his income, and if he had brothers.

DON JUAN

The milliners who furnish 'drapery misses',
  Throughout the season, upon speculation
Of payment ere the honeymoon's last kisses
  Have waned into a crescent's coruscation,
Thought such an opportunity as this is,
  Of a rich foreigner's initiation,
Not to be overlook'd—and gave such credit,
That future bridegrooms swore, and sigh'd, and paid it.

The Blues, that tender tribe, who sigh o'er sonnets,
  And with the pages of the last Review
Line the interior of their heads or bonnets,
  Advanced in all their azure's highest hue;
They talk'd bad French or Spanish, and upon its
  Late authors ask'd him for a hint or two;
And which was softest, Russian or Castilian;
And whether in his travels he saw Ilion?

Juan, who was a little superficial,
  And not in literature a great Drawcansir,
Examined by this learned and especial
  Jury of matrons, scarce knew what to answer,
His duties, warlike, loving, or official,
  His steady application as a dancer,
Had kept him from the brink of Hippocrene,
Which now he found was blue instead of green.

However, he replied at hazard, with
  A modest confidence and calm assurance,
Which lent his learned lucubrations pith,
  And pass'd for arguments of good endurance.

347

DON JUAN

That prodigy, Miss Araminta Smith
    (Who at sixteen translated *Hercules Furens*
Into as furious English), with her best look,
Set down his sayings in her commonplace book.

Juan knew several languages—as well
    He might—and brought them up with skill, in time
To save his fame with each accomplish'd belle,
    Who still regretted that he did not rhyme.
There wanted but this requisite to swell
    His qualities (with them) into sublime;
Lady Fitz-Frisky, and Miss Mævia Mannish,
Both long'd extremely to be sung in Spanish.

However, he did pretty well, and was
    Admitted as an aspirant to all
The coteries, and, as in Banquo's glass,
    At great assemblies or in parties small,
He saw ten thousand living authors pass,
    That being about their average numeral:
Also the mighty 'greatest living poets',
As every paltry magazine can show *its*.

In twice five years the 'greatest living poet',
    Like to the champion in the fisty ring,
Is call'd on to support his claim, or show it,
    Although 'tis an imaginary thing.
Even I—albeit I'm sure I did not know it,
    Nor sought of foolscap subjects to be king—
Was reckon'd a considerable time,
The grand Napoleon of the realms of rhyme.

348

DON JUAN

But Juan was my Moscow, and Faliero
      My Leipsic, and my Mount Saint Jean seems Cain:
La Belle Alliance of dunces down at zero,
      Now that the lion's fall'n, may rise again;
But I will fall at least as fell my hero;
      Nor reign at all, or as a *monarch* reign;
Or to some lonely isle of jailors go,
With turncoat Southey for my turnkey Lowe.

Sir Walter reign'd before me; Moore and Campbell
      Before and after: but now grown more holy,
The muses upon Sion's hill must ramble
      With poets almost clergymen, or wholly;
And Pegasus has a psalmodic amble
      Beneath the very Reverend Rowley Powley,
Who shoes the glorious animals with stilts,
A modern Ancient Pistol—by the hilts!

Still he excels that artificial hard
      Labourer in the same vineyard, though the vine
Yields him but vinegar for his reward—
      That neutralized dull Dorus of the Nine;
That swarthy Sporus, neither man nor bard;
      That ox of verse, who *ploughs* for every line:—
Cambyses' roaring Romans beat at least
The howling Hebrews of Cybele's priest.—

Then there's my gentle Euphues, who, they say,
      Sets up for being a sort of *moral me*:
He'll find it rather difficult some day
      To turn out both, or either, it may be.

AA

DON JUAN

Some persons think that Coleridge hath the sway,
    And Wordsworth hath supporters two or three;
And that deep-mouth'd Bœotian, 'Savage Landor',
Has taken for a swan rogue Southey's gander.

John Keats, who was kill'd off by one critique,
    Just as he really promised something great,
If not intelligible, without Greek,
    Contrived to talk about the gods of late,
Much as they might have been supposed to speak.
    Poor fellow! his was an untoward fate;
'Tis strange the mind, that very fiery particle,
Should let itself be snuff'd out by an article.

The list grows long of live and dead pretenders
    To that which none will gain—or none will know
The conqueror at least; who, ere Time renders
    His last award, will have the long grass grow
Above his burnt-out brain and sapless cinders.
    If I might augur, I should rate but low
Their chances: they are too numerous, like the thirty
Mock tyrants, when Rome's annals wax'd but dirty.

This is the literary *lower* empire,
    Where the prætorian bands take up the matter;—
A 'dreadful trade', like his who 'gathers samphire',
    The insolent soldiery to soothe and flatter,
With the same feelings as you'd coax a vampire.
    Now, were I once at home, and in good satire,
I'd try conclusions with those Janizaries,
And show them *what* an intellectual war is.

DON JUAN

I think I know a trick or two would turn
    Their flanks;—but it is hardly worth my while
With such small gear to give myself concern:
    Indeed, I've not the necessary bile;
My natural temper 's really aught but stern,
    And even my Muse's worst reproof 's a smile;
And then she drops a brief and modern curtsey,
And glides away, assured she never hurts ye.

My Juan, whom I left in deadly peril
    Amongst live poets and blue ladies, past
With some small profit through that field so sterile,
    Being tired in time, and neither least nor last,
Left it before he had been treated very ill;
    And henceforth found himself more gaily class'd
Amongst the higher spirits of the day,
The sun's true son, no vapour, but a ray.

His morns he pass'd in business—which dissected,
    Was like all business, a laborious nothing,
That leads to lassitude, the most infected
    And Centaur Nessus garb of mortal clothing,
And on our sofas makes us lie dejected,
    And talk in tender horrors of our loathing
All kinds of toil, save for our country's good—
Which grows no better, though 'tis time it should.

His afternoons he pass'd in visits, luncheons,
    Lounging, and boxing; and the twilight hour
In riding round those vegetable puncheons
    Call'd 'Parks', where there is neither fruit nor flower,

DON JUAN

Enough to gratify a bee's slight munchings;
　　But, after all, it is the only 'bower'
(In Moore's phrase) where the fashionable fair
Can form a slight acquaintance with fresh air.

Then dress, then dinner, then awakes the world;
　　Then glare the lamps, then whirl the wheels, then roar
Through street and square fast flashing chariots hurl'd
　　Like harness'd meteors; then along the floor
Chalk mimics painting; then festoons are twirl'd;
　　Then roll the brazen thunders of the door,
Which opens to the thousand happy few,
An earthly paradise of 'Or Molu'.

There stands the noble hostess, nor shall sink
　　With the three thousandth curtsey; there the waltz,
The only dance which teaches girls to think,
　　Makes one in love even with its very faults.
Saloon, room, hall, o'erflow beyond their brink,
　　And long the latest of arrivals halts,
'Midst royal dukes, and dames condemn'd to climb,
And gain an inch of staircase at a time.

Thrice happy he who, after a survey
　　Of the good company, can win a corner,
A door that's *in*, or boudoir *out*, of the way,
　　Where he may fix himself like small 'Jack Horner',
And let the Babel round run as it may,
　　And look on as a mourner, or a scorner,
Or an approver, or a mere spectator,
Yawning a little as the night grows later.

But this won't do, save by and by; and he
　　Who, like Don Juan, takes an active share,
Must steer with care through all that glittering sea
　　Of gems, and plumes, and pearls, and silks, to where
He deems it is his proper place to be;
　　Dissolving in the waltz, to some soft air,
Or proudlier prancing, with mercurial skill,
Where Science marshals forth her own quadrille.

Or, if he dance not, but hath higher views
　　Upon an heiress or his neighbour's bride,
Let him take care that that which he pursues
　　Is not at once too palpably descried.
Full many an eager gentleman oft rues
　　His haste: impatience is a blundering guide,
Amongst a people famous for reflection,
Who like to play the fool with circumspection.

But if you can contrive, get next at supper;
　　Or, if forestall'd, get opposite and ogle:—
Oh, ye ambrosial moments! always upper
　　In mind, a sort of sentimental bogle,
Which sits for ever upon memory's crupper,
　　The ghost of vanish'd pleasures once in vogue! Ill
Can tender souls relate the rise and fall
Of hopes and fears which shake a single ball.

But these precautionary hints can touch
　　Only the common run, who must pursue,
And watch and ward; whose plans a word too much
　　Or little overturns; and not the few

Or many (for the number's sometimes such)
　　Whom a good mien, especially if new,
Or fame, or name, for wit, war, sense, or nonsense,
Permits whate'er they please, or *did* not long since.

Our hero, as a hero, young and handsome,
　　Noble, rich, celebrated, and a stranger,
Like other slaves, of course must pay his ransom,
　　Before he can escape from so much danger
As will environ a conspicuous man. Some
　　Talk about poetry, and 'rack and manger',
And ugliness, disease, as toil and trouble;—
I wish they knew the life of a young noble.

They are young, but know not youth—it is anticipated;
　　Handsome but wasted, rich without a sou;
Their vigour in a thousand arms is dissipated;
　　Their cash comes *from*, their wealth goes *to*, a Jew:
Both senates see their nightly votes participated
　　Between the tyrant's and the tribunes' crew;
And having voted, dined, drunk, gamed, and w——d,
The family vault receives another lord.

'Where is the world?' cries Young, at *eighty*. 'Where
　　The world in which a man was born?' Alas,
Where is the world of *eight* years past? *'Twas there*—
　　I look for it—'tis gone, a globe of glass!
Crack'd, shiver'd, vanish'd, scarcely gazed on, ere
　　A silent change dissolves the glittering mass.
Statesmen, chiefs, orators, queens, patriots, kings,
And dandies, all are gone on the wind's wings.

354

DON JUAN

Where is Napoleon the Grand? God knows:
  Where little Castlereagh? The devil can tell:
Where Grattan, Curran, Sheridan, all those
  Who bound the bar or senate in their spell?
Where is the unhappy Queen, with all her woes?
  And where the Daughter, whom the Isles loved well?
Where are those martyr'd saints, the Five per Cents?
And where—oh, where the devil are the Rents?

Where's Brummel? Dish'd. Where's Long Pole Welles-
  ley? Diddled.
  Where's Whitbread? Romilly? Where's George the
  Third?
Where is his will? (That's not so soon unriddled.)
  And where is 'Fum' the Fourth, our 'royal bird'?
Gone down, it seems, to Scotland, to be fiddled
  Unto by Sawney's violin, we have heard:
'Caw me, caw thee'—for six months had been hatching
This scene of royal itch and royal scratching.

Where is Lord This, and where my Lady That?
  The Honourable Mistresses and Misses?
Some laid aside, like an old opera hat,
  Married, unmarried, and remarried: (this is
An evolution oft performed of late:)
  Where are the Dublin shouts—and London hisses?
Where are the Grenvilles? Turn'd, as usual. Where
My friends the Whigs? Exactly where they were.

Where are the Lady Carolines and Franceses?
  Divorced, or doing thereanent. Ye annals
So brilliant, where the lists of routs and dances is—
  Thou *Morning Post*, sole record of the panels

355

Broken in carriages, and all the phantasies
     Of fashion—say what streams now fill those channels ?
Some die, some fly, some languish on the Continent,
     Because the times have hardly left them *one* tenant.

Some, who once set their caps at cautious dukes,
     Have taken up at length with younger brothers:
Some heiresses have bit at sharpers' hooks:
     Some maids have been made wives, some merely
          mothers,
Others have lost their fresh and fairy looks:
     In short, the list of alterations bothers.
There's little strange in this, but something strange is
The unusual quickness of these common changes.

Talk not of seventy years as age: in seven
     I have seen more changes, down from monarchs to
The humblest individual under heaven,
     Than might suffice a modern century through.
I knew that nought was lasting, but now even
     Change grows too changeable, without being new;
Nought's permanent among the human race,
Except the Whigs *not* getting into place.

I have seen Napoleon, who seem'd quite a Jupiter,
     Shrink to a Saturn. I have seen a Duke
(No matter which) turn politician stupider,
     If that can well be, than his wooden look.
But it is time that I should hoist my 'Blue Peter',
     And sail for a new theme:—I have seen, and shook
To see it—the king hiss'd, and then caress'd;
But don't pretend to settle which was best.

DON JUAN

I have seen the Landholders without a rap—
    I have seen Joanna Southcote—I have seen
The House of Commons turn'd to a tax-trap—
    I have seen that sad affair of the late Queen—
I have seen crowns worn instead of a fool's cap—
    I have seen a Congress doing all that's mean—
I have seen some nations, like o'erloaded asses,
Kick off their burthens—meaning the high classes—

I have seen small poets, and great prosers, and
    Interminable—*not eternal*—speakers—
I have seen the funds at war with house and land—
    I have seen the country gentlemen turn squeakers—
I have seen the people ridden o'er, like sand,
    By slaves on horseback—I have seen malt liquors
Exchanged for 'thin potations' by John Bull;
I have seen John half detect himself a fool.—

But *carpe diem*, Juan, *carpe, carpe!*
    To-morrow sees another race as gay
And transient, and devour'd by the same harpy.
    'Life's a poor player'—then 'play out the play,
Ye villains!' and, above all, keep a sharp eye
    Much less on what you do than what you say;
Be hypocritical, be cautious, be
Not what you *seem*, but always what you *see*.

                                        LORD BYRON.

185   *Eheu fugaces*

WHAT HORACE says is—
        Eheu fugaces
Anni labuntur, Postume, Postume!
Years glide away, and are lost to me, lost to me!

Now, when the folks in the dance sport their merry toes,
Taglionis and Ellslers, Duvernays and Ceritos,
Sighing I murmur, '*O mihi praeteritos!*'

R. H. BARHAM.

186   *The Town of Passage*

OH, Passage town is of great renown,
   For we go down in our buggies there
On a Sunday morning, all danger scorning,
   To get a corning at sweet Passage fair.
Oh, 'tis there you'd see the steamboats sporting
   Upon Lough Mahon, all so fair to view;
Bold Captain O'Brien, with his colours flying,
   And he a-vieing with the Waterloo.

There's a patent slipping, and dock for shipping,
   And whale-boats skipping upon the tide;
There ships galore is, and Cove before us,
   With 'Carrigaloe on the other side'.
'Tis there's the hulk that's well stored with convicts,
   Who were never upon decks till they went to sea;
They'll ne'er touch dry land, nor rocky island,
   Till they spy land at sweet Botany Bay.

Here's success to this foreign station,
   Where American ships without horses ride,
And Portugueses from every nation
   Comes in rotation upon the tide.
But not forgetting Haulbowline Island,
   That was constructed by Mrs. Deane:
Herself 's the lady that has stowed the water
   To supply the vessels upon the main.

And these bold sons of Neptune, I mean the boatmen,
   Will ferry you over from Cove to Spike;
And outside the harbour are fishers sporting,
   Watching a nibble from a sprat or pike;
While their wives and daughters, from no danger shrink-
     ing,
All night and morning they rove about
The mud and sand-banks, for the periwinkle,
   The shrimp and cockle, when the tide is out.

ANON.

187   *The bonny Bunch of Roses O*

A County Tyrone Ballad of Napoleon and his Mother

BY the margin of the ocean, one morning in the month
  of June,
The feathered warbling songsters their charming notes
   did sweetly sing,
I there espied a female who seemed to be in grief and woe
Discoursing with young Bonaparte concerning the Bonny
   Bunch of Roses O.

Then up steps young Napoleon and takes his mother by
   the hand,
Saying: 'Mother dear, have patience until I'm able to take
   command;
And I will raise a terrible army, and through termenjous
   dangers go,
And, in spite of all the universe, I will conquer the Bonny
   Bunch of Roses O.'

THE BONNY BUNCH OF ROSES O

'When first you saw great Bonaparte, you fell upon your
    bended knee,
And you asked your father's life of him, which he granted
    most princelee.
And 'twas then he took an army and over the frozen alps
    did go,
And said: "I'll first conquer Moscow, and return to the
    Bonny Bunch of Roses O."

'He took three hundred thousand men with kings likewise
    to bear his train,
He was so well provided for that he could sweep the
    world for gain;
But when he came to Moscow, he was overpowered by the
    Russian snow,
And Moscow was a-blazing when he lost his Bonny Bunch
    of Roses O.'

'Now, son, don't speak so venturesome, for in England
    are the hearts of oak,
There's England, Ireland and Scotland whose unity was
    never broke;
Now, son, think on your father; on the Isle of St Helena
    his body lies low,
And you may follow after him, so beware of the Bonny
    Bunch of Roses O.'

'O mother, adieu for ever, now I am on my dying bed,
If I had lived I would have been clever, but now I droop
    my youthful head;
But whilst our bones lie mouldering, and weeping willows
    o'er us grow,
The deeds of old Napoleon will sing the Bonny Bunch of
    Roses O.'   ANON.

IT was late in the night when the Squire came home
    Enquiring for his lady.
His servant made a sure reply:
She's gone with the gipsum Davy.
        Rattle tum a gipsum gipsum
        Rattle tum a gipsum Davy.

O go catch up my milk-white steed,
The black one's not so speedy,
I'll ride all night till broad daylight,
Or overtake my lady.

He rode and he rode till he came to the town,
He rode till he came to Barley.
The tears came rolling down his cheeks,
And then he spied his lady.

It's come go back, my dearest dear,
Come go back, my honey;
It's come go back, my dearest dear,
And you never shall lack for money.

I won't go back, my dearest dear,
I won't go back, my honey:
For I wouldn't give a kiss from gipsum's lips
For you and all your money.

It's go pull off those snow-white gloves,
A-made of Spanish leather,
And give to me your lily-white hand,
And bid farewell for ever.

It's she pulled off those snow-white gloves,
A-made of Spanish leather,
And gave to him her lily-white hand,
And bade farewell for ever.

She soon ran through her gay clothing,
Her velvet shoes and stockings;
Her gold ring off her finger's gone,
And the gold plate off her bosom.

O once I had a house and land,
Feather-bed and money;
But now I've come to an old straw pad
With the gipsies dancing round me.   ANON.

189   *Nottamun Town*

IN Nottamun Town not a soul would look up,
Not a soul would look up, not a soul would look down,
Not a soul would look up, not a soul would look down,
To tell me the way to Nottamun Town.

I rode a big horse that was called a grey mare,
Grey mane and tail, grey stripes down his back,
Grey mane and tail, grey stripes down his back,
There weren't a hair on him but what was called black.

She stood so still, she threw me to the dirt,
She tore my hide and bruised my shirt;
From stirrup to stirrup I mounted again
And on my ten toes I rode over the plain.

Met the King and the Queen and a company of men
A-walking behind and a-riding before.
A stark naked drummer came walking along
With his hands in his bosom a-beating his drum.

Sat down on a hot and cold frozen stone,
Ten thousand stood round me yet I was alone.
Took my heart in my hand to keep my head warm.
Ten thousand got drowned that never were born. ANON.

190   *Soldier, won't you marry me?*

SOLDIER, soldier, won't you marry me?
   It's O a fife and drum.
How can I marry such a pretty girl as you
When I've got no hat to put on?

Off to the tailor she did go
As hard as she could run,
Brought him back the finest was there.
Now, soldier, put it on.

Soldier, soldier, won't you marry me?
It's O a fife and drum.
How can I marry such a pretty girl as you
When I've got no coat to put on?

Off to the tailor she did go
As hard as she could run,
Brought him back the finest was there.
Now soldier, put it on.

Soldier, soldier, won't you marry me?
It's O a fife and drum.
How can I marry such a pretty girl as you
When I've got no shoes to put on?

Off to the shoe shop she did go
As hard as she could run,
Brought him back the finest was there.
Now, soldier, put them on.

SOLDIER, WON'T YOU MARRY ME?

Soldier, soldier, won't you marry me?
It's O a fife and drum.
How can I marry such a pretty girl as you
And a wife and baby at home?

ANON.

191 *John Peel*

D'YE ken John Peel with his coat so gay?
   D'ye ken John Peel at the break of the day?
D'ye ken John Peel when he's far, far away,
With his hounds and his horn in the morning?
   For the sound of his horn brought me from my bed,
   And the cry of his hounds which he oft-times led,
   Peel's view-halloo would awaken the dead,
   Or the fox from his lair in the morning.

D'ye ken that bitch whose tongue is death?
D'ye ken her sons of peerless faith?
D'ye ken that a fox with his last breath
Cursed them all as he died in the morning?
   For the sound, &c.

Yes, I ken John Peel and Ruby too,
Ranter and Ringwood and Bellman and True;
From a find to a check, from a check to a view,
From a view to a death in the morning.
   For the sound, &c.

And I've followed John Peel both often and far
O'er the rasper-fence and the gate and the bar,
From Low Denton Holme up to Scratchmere Scar,
When we vied for the brush in the morning.
   For the sound, &c.

364

JOHN PEEL

Then here's to John Peel with my heart and my soul,
Let's drink to his health, let's finish the bowl:
We'll follow John Peel through fair and through foul,
If we want a good hunt in the morning.
    For the sound, &c.

D'ye ken John Peel with his coat so gay?
He lived at Troutbeck once on a day;
Now he has gone far, far away;
We shall ne'er hear his voice in the morning.
    For the sound of his horn brought me from my bed,
    And the cry of his hounds which he oft-times led,
    Peel's view-halloo would awaken the dead,
    Or the fox from his lair in the morning.

JOHN WOODCOCK GRAVES.

192   *To Minerva*

(From the Greek)

MY temples throb, my pulses boil,
    I'm sick of Song, and Ode, and Ballad—
So, Thyrsis, take the Midnight Oil,
    And pour it on a lobster salad.

My brain is dull, my sight is foul,
    I cannot write a verse, or read,—
Then, Pallas, take away thine Owl,
    And let us have a lark instead.

THOMAS HOOD.

WHAT different dooms our birthdays bring!
   For instance, one little mannikin thing
     Survives to wear many a wrinkle;
While Death forbids another to wake,
And a son that it took nine moons to make
     Expires without even a twinkle!

Into this world we come like ships,
Launch'd from the docks, and stocks, and slips,
     For fortune fair or fatal;
And one little craft is cast away
In its very first trip in Babbicome Bay,
     While another rides safe at Port Natal.

What different lots our stars accord!
This babe to be hail'd and woo'd as a Lord!
     And that to be shunned like a leper!
One, to the world's wine, honey, and corn,
Another, like Colchester native, born
     To its vinegar, only, and pepper.

One is littered under a roof
Neither wind nor water proof,—
     That's the prose of Love in a Cottage,—
A puny, naked, shivering wretch,
The whole of whose birthright would not fetch,
Though Robins himself drew up the sketch,
     The bid of 'a mess of pottage'.

Born of Fortunatus's kin,
Another comes tenderly usher'd in
     To a prospect all bright and burnish'd:

MISS KILMANSEGG'S BIRTH

No tenant he for life's back slums—
He comes to the world as a gentleman comes
   To a lodging ready furnish'd.

And the other sex—the tender—the fair—
What wide reverses of fate are there!
Whilst Margaret, charm'd by the Bulbul rare,
   In a garden of Gul reposes—
Poor Peggy hawks nosegays from street to street,
Till—think of that, who find life so sweet!—
   She hates the smell of roses!

Not so with the infant Kilmansegg!
She was not born to steal or beg,
   Or gather cresses in ditches;
To plait the straw, or bind the shoe,
Or sit all day to hem and sew,
As females must, and not a few—
   To fill their insides with stitches!

She was not doom'd, for bread to eat,
To be put to her hands as well as her feet—
   To carry home linen from mangles—
Or heavy-hearted, and weary-limb'd,
To dance on a rope in a jacket trimm'd
   With as many blows as spangles.

She was one of those who by Fortune's boon
Are born, as they say, with a silver spoon
   In her mouth, not a wooden ladle:
To speak according to poet's wont,
Plutus as sponsor stood at her font,
   And Midas rock'd the cradle.

MISS KILMANSEGG'S BIRTH

At her first *début* she found her head
On a pillow of down, in a downy bed,
   With a damask canopy over.
For although by the vulgar popular saw,
All mothers are said to be 'in the straw',
   Some children are born in clover.

Her very first draught of vital air
It was not the common chameleon fare
   Of plebeian lungs and noses,—
     No—her earliest sniff
     Of this world was a whiff
   Of the genuine Otto of Roses!

When she saw the light—it was no mere ray
Of that light so common—so everyday—
   That the sun each morning launches—
But six wax tapers dazzled her eyes,
From a thing—a gooseberry bush for size—
   With a golden stem and branches.

She was born exactly at half-past two,
As witness'd a timepiece in or-molu
   That stood on a marble table—
Showing at once the time of day,
And a team of gildings running away
   As fast as they were able,
With a golden god with a golden star,
And a golden spear, in a golden car,
   According to Grecian fable.

Like other babes, at her birth she cried;
Which made a sensation far and wide,
   Ay, for twenty miles around her;

MISS KILMANSEGG'S BIRTH

For though to the ear 'twas nothing more
Than an infant's squall, it was really the roar
   Of a Fifty-thousand Pounder!
     It shook the next heir
     In his library chair,
   And made him cry, 'Confound her!'

Of signs and omens there was no dearth,
Any more than at Owen Glendower's birth,
   Or the advent of other great people:
     Two bullocks dropp'd dead,
     As if knock'd on the head,
     And barrels of stout
     And ale ran about,
     And the village-bells such a peal rang out,
   That they crack'd the village steeple.

In no time at all, like mushroom spawn,
Tables sprang up all over the lawn;
Not furnish'd scantly or shabbily,
   But on scale as vast
   As that huge repast,
   With its loads and cargoes
   Of drinks and botargoes,
At the Birth of the Babe in Rabelais.

Hundreds of men were turn'd into beasts,
Like the guests of Circe's horrible feasts,
   By the magic of ale and cider:
And each country lass, and each country lad,
Began to caper and dance like mad,
And even some old ones appear'd to have had
   A bite from the Naples Spider.

Then as night came on,
    It had scared King John,
Who considered such signs not risible,
    To have seen the maroons,
    And the whirling moons,
    And the serpents of flame,
    And wheels of the same,
That according to some were 'whizzable'.

Oh, happy Hope of the Kilmanseggs!
Thrice happy in head, and body, and legs
    That her parents had such full pockets!
For had she been born of Want and Thrift,
For care and nursing all adrift,
It's ten to one she had had to make shift
    With rickets instead of rockets!

                              THOMAS HOOD.

194   *Shooting of his Dear*

COME all you young people who handle the gun,
    Be aware of those shooting between moon and sun.
I've a story to tell you that's happened of late
Concerning Molly Bander whose beauties were great.

Molly Bander were a-walking and a shower came on.
She stopped under a beech-tree the shower to shun.
Jimmy Randal were a-hunting, he were a-hunting in the
    dark;
He shot his own true love, and he missed not her heart.

And then he run to her and he found her quite dead,
And in her own bosom finding tears he had shed.
He took his gun in his hand, to his uncle did run,
Saying: Uncle, dear uncle, I've killed Molly Ban;

I shot her and killed her. She was the joy of my life.
I always intended for to make her my wife.

Up stepped his old father with his head all so grey,
Saying: Randal, Jimmy Randal, don't run away.
Stay in your own country till your trial comes on;
You shall not be hanged; I'll spend my whole farm.

On the day of his trial her ghost did appear,
Saying: Randal, Jimmy Randal, Jimmy Randal, go clear.
He spied my apron pinned around me, he killed me for a
    swan.
He shot me and killed me. My name's Molly Ban.
                                                ANON.

195   *Young Hunting*

SHE sharpened her knife both sharp and keen,
    She hung it by her side,
As she rode up to the bar-room hall
And passed it by and by.

Her true love a-being standing there,
He looked well and pleased;
As she stepped on up by his side,
She pierced it through his heart.

All of my friends come to me now
And see me what I've done.
Now don't you see my own heart's blood
Come sprinkling down my knee?

YOUNG HUNTING

Must I ride East, or must I ride West,
Or must I ride under the shining sun,
To find that doctor for to come here
And cure those wounded wounds?

You needn't ride East, you needn't ride West,
You needn't ride under the shining sun;
There ain't a doctor but God alone
Can cure those wounded wounds.

This young lady walked out on the street
For to hear the small birds sing.
Go home, go home, you mourny little girl,
And weep and mourn for me.

Come to me, my pretty little bird,
Come and go along with me.
I've got a cage beside the willow tree
For you to sit in and sing.

I won't come there, and I won't go there,
For I'll tell you the reason why.
You've just now killed your own true love,
Just what might happen to me.

I wish I had my bowing little spain,
And it was bow-end on the string,
Then surely I'd shoot that pretty little bird
That sits on the briers and sings.

I wish you had your bowing little spain,
And it was bow-end on the string,
Then surely I would fly from brier to brier,
And I'd sing on as I fly.

ANON.

WHEN I was bound apprentice, in famous Lincoln-
shire,
Full well I served my master for more than seven year,
Till I took up to poaching, as you shall quickly hear:
Oh, 'tis my delight on a shining night, in the season of the
year.

As me and my companions were setting of a snare,
'Twas then we spied the game-keeper, for him we did not
care.
For we can wrestle and fight, my boys, and jump out any
where;
Oh, 'tis my delight on a shining night, in the season of the year.

As me and my companions were setting four or five,
And, taking on 'em up again, we caught a hare alive.
We took the hare alive, my boys, and through the wood
did steer:
Oh, 'tis my delight on a shining night, in the season of
the year.

I threw him on my shoulder, and then we trudgèd home,
We took him to a neighbour's house and sold him for a
crown,
We sold him for a crown, my boys, but I did not tell you
where:
Oh, 'tis my delight on a shining night, in the season of the
year.

Success to every gentleman that lives in Lincolnshire,
Success to every poacher that wants to sell a hare,
Bad luck to every game-keeper that will not sell his deer:
Oh, 'tis my delight on a shining night, in the season of the
year.   ANON.

THE streams of lovely Nancy
  Divide in three parts,
Where young men and maidens
Do a-choose their sweethearts;
For a-drinking sweet liquors
Makes their hearts for to sing,
And the noise in the valley
Makes the rocks for to ring.

On yonder high mountain
A castle does stand;
It's a-builded of ivory
On yonder black strand,
It's a-builded of ivory
And diamonds so bright,
It's a pilot for sailors
On a dark wintry night.

On yonder high mountain
Where wild fowls they fly,
There is one fowl among them
That flies very high.
If I had my true love
Near the diamond's black land,
How soon I would tame her
By the sleight of my hand.

We marchèd from Chester
To Liverpool Town,
And there we spied lasses,
Some fair and some brown;

374

But of all the fine lasses
I ever did see,
The voice of my angel
Is the darling for me.   ANON.

198   *The Turtle-Dove*

'OH! don't you see the turtle-dove
    Sitting under yonder tree
Lamenting for her own true love?
    And I will mourn for thee, my dear,
    And I will mourn for thee.'

'If you must suffer grief and pain,
    'Tis but for a little while;
For, though I go away, I'll return again,
    If I row ten thousand mile, my dear,
    If I row ten thousand mile!'

'Ten thousand mile is very far
    For me to bide alone
With a heavy, heavy sigh, and a bitter, bitter cry;
    No one to hear my moan, my dear,
    No one to hear my moan.'

'I may not stay your grievous moan,
    Your pain I may not ease;
Yet I will love but thee alone;
    Till the streams run from the seas, my dear,
    Till the streams run from the seas!'

'The tides shall cease to beat the shore,
    The stars fall from the sky;
Yet I will love thee more and more
    Until the day I die, my dear,
    Until the day I die.'

'Then let the seas run dry, sweetheart,
   The rocks melt in the sun,
Yet here I will stay, nor ever from thee part,
   Till all my days are done, my dear,
   Till all my days are done!'   ANON.

199   *Green Grass*

A DIS, a dis, a green grass,
   A dis, a dis, a dis;
Come all you pretty fair maids
   And dance along with us.

For we are going roving,
   A roving in this land;
We take this pretty fair maid,
   We take her by the hand.

She shall get a duke, my dear,
   As duck do get a drake;
And she shall have a young prince,
   For her own fair sake.

And if this young prince chance to die,
   She shall get another;
The bells will ring, and the birds will sing,
   And we clap hands together.   ANON.

200   *Lowlands*

I DREAMT a dream the other night
   Lowlands, Lowlands, hurrah, my John.
I dreamt a dream the other night
   My Lowlands a-ray.

LOWLANDS

I dreamt I saw my own true love,
  Lowlands, Lowlands, hurrah, my John.
I dreamt I saw my own true love
  My Lowlands a-ray.

He was green and wet with weeds so cold
  Lowlands, Lowlands, hurrah, my John.
He was green and wet with weeds so cold
  My Lowlands a-ray.

'I am drowned in the Lowland seas', he said
  Lowlands, Lowlands, hurrah, my John.
'I am drowned in the Lowland seas', he said
  My Lowlands a-ray.

'I shall never kiss you again', he said
  Lowlands, Lowlands, hurrah, my John.
'I shall never kiss you again', he said
  My Lowlands a-ray.

I will cut my breasts until they bleed
  Lowlands, Lowlands, hurrah, my John.
I will cut my breasts until they bleed
  My Lowlands a-ray.

I will cut away my bonny hair
  Lowlands, Lowlands, hurrah, my John.
I will cut away my bonny hair
  My Lowlands a-ray.

No other man shall think me fair
  Lowlands, Lowlands, hurrah, my John.
No other man shall think me fair
  My Lowlands a-ray.

377

O my love lies drowned in the windy Lowlands
Lowlands, Lowlands, hurrah, my John.
O my love lies drowned in the windy Lowlands
My Lowlands a-ray.   ANON.

201   *The fair Maid of Amsterdam*

IN Amsterdam there dwelt a maid,
  Mark well what I do say;
In Amsterdam there dwelt a maid,
And she was mistress of her trade.
      And I'll go no more a-roving
      With you, fair maid.
      A-roving, a-roving,
      Since roving's been my ru-i-n,
      I'll go no more a-roving
      With you, fair maid.

Her cheeks was red, her eyes was brown,
      Mark well what I do say;
Her cheeks was red, her eyes was brown,
Her hair like glow-worms hanging down,
      And I'll go no more a-roving
      With you, fair maid.
      A-roving, a-roving,
      Since roving's been my ru-i-n,
      I'll go no more a-roving
      With you, fair maid.   ANON.

202   *The Sailor's Return*

AS I walked out one night, it being dark all over,
  The moon did show no light I could discover,
Down by a river side where ships were sailing,
A lonely maid I spied, weeping and bewailing.

378

I boldly stept up to her, and asked her what grieved her,
She made me this reply, 'None could relieve her,
For my love is pressed, she cried, to cross the ocean,
My mind is like the Sea, always in motion.'

He said, 'My pretty fair maid, mark well my story,
For your true love and I fought for England's glory,
By one unlucky shot we both got parted,
And by the wounds he got, I'm broken hearted.

'He told me before he died his heart was broken,
He gave me this gold ring, take it for a token,—
"Take this unto my dear, there is no one fairer,
Tell her to be kind and love the bearer".'

Soon as these words he spoke she ran distracted,
Not knowing what she did, nor how she acted,
She run ashore, her hair showing her anger,
'Young man, you've come too late, for I'll wed no stranger.'

Soon as these words she spoke, her love grew stronger,
He flew into her arms, he could wait no longer,
They both sat down and sung, but she sung clearest,
Like a Nightingale in spring, 'Welcome home, my dearest.'

He sang, 'God bless the wind that blew him over.'
She sang, 'God bless the ship that brought him over.'
They both sat down and sung, but she sung clearest,
Like a Nightingale in spring, Welcome home, my dearest.

ANON.

203   *The two Magicians*

O SHE looked out of the window,
   As white as any milk;
But He looked into the window,
   As black as any silk.

Hulloa, hulloa, hulloa, hulloa, you coal black smith!
  O what is your silly song?
You never shall change my maiden name
  That I have kept so long;
I'd rather die a maid, yes, but then she said,
And be buried all in my grave,
Than I'd have such a nasty, husky, dusky, musty, fusky,
  Coal black smith

              A maiden I will die.

Then She became a duck,
  A duck all on the stream;
And He became a water dog,
  And fetched her back again.
      Hulloa, &c.

Then She became a hare,
  A hare all on the plain;
And He became a greyhound dog,
  And fetched her back again.
      Hulloa, &c.

Then She became a fly
  A fly all in the air;
And He became a spider,
  And fetched her to his lair.
      Hulloa, &c.   ANON.

204 *The Country Clergyman's Trip to Cambridge*
An Election Ballad, 1827

AS I sat down to breakfast in state,
  At my living of Tithing-cum-Boring,
With Betty beside me to wait,
  Came a rap that almost beat the door in.

THE COUNTRY CLERGYMAN'S TRIP

I laid down my basin of tea,
    And Betty ceased spreading the toast,
'As sure as a gun, sir,' said she,
    'That must be the knock of the post.'

A letter—and free—bring it here—
    I have no correspondent who franks.
No! yes! can it be? Why my dear,
    'Tis our glorious, our Protestant Bankes.
'Dear sir, as I know you desire
    That the Church should receive due protection,
I humbly presume to require
    Your aid at the Cambridge election.

'It has lately been brought to my knowledge,
    That the Ministers fully design
To suppress each cathedral and college,
    And eject every learned divine.
To assist this detestable scheme
    Three nuncios from Rome are come over;
They left Calais on Monday by steam,
    And landed to dinner at Dover.

'An army of grim Cordeliers,
    Well furnished with relics and vermin,
Will follow, Lord Westmoreland fears,
    To effect what their chiefs may determine.
Lollards' bower, good authorities say,
    Is again fitting up as a prison;
And a wood-merchant told me to-day
    'Tis a wonder how faggots have risen.

THE COUNTRY CLERGYMAN'S TRIP

'The finance scheme of Canning contains
 A new Easter-offering tax;
And he means to devote all the gains
 To a bounty on thumb-screws and racks.
Your living, so neat and compact—
 Pray, don't let the news give you pain!—
Is promised, I know for a fact,
 To an olive-faced Padre from Spain.'

I read, and I felt my heart bleed,
 Sore wounded with horror and pity;
So I flew, with all possible speed,
 To our Protestant champion's committee.
True gentlemen, kind and well-bred!
 No fleering! no distance! no scorn!
They asked after my wife, who is dead,
 And my children who never were born.

They then, like high-principled Tories,
 Called our Sovereign unjust and unsteady,
And assailed him with scandalous stories,
 Till the coach for the voters was ready.
That coach might be well called a casket
 Of learning and brotherly love:
There were parsons in boot and in basket;
 There were parsons below and above.

There were Sneaker and Griper, a pair
 Who stick to Lord Mulesby like leeches;
A smug chaplain of plausible air,
 Who writes my Lord Goslingham's speeches;

THE COUNTRY CLERGYMAN'S TRIP

Dr. Buzz, who alone is a host,
　Who, with arguments weighty as lead,
Proves six times a week in the Post
　That flesh somehow differs from bread;

Dr. Nimrod, whose orthodox toes
　Are seldom withdrawn from the stirrup;
Dr. Humdrum, whose eloquence flows,
　Like droppings of sweet poppy syrup;
Dr. Rosygill puffing and fanning,
　And wiping away perspiration,
Dr. Humbug, who proved Mr. Canning
　The beast in St. John's Revelation.

A layman can scarce form a notion
　Of our wonderful talk on the road;
Of the learning, the wit, and devotion,
　Which almost each syllable showed:
Why divided allegiance agrees
　So ill with our free constitution;
How Catholics swear as they please,
　In hope of the priest's absolution;

How the Bishop of Norwich had bartered
　His faith for a legate's commission;
How Lyndhurst, afraid to be martyred,
　Had stooped to a base coalition;
How Papists are cased from compassion
　By bigotry, stronger than steel;
How burning would soon come in fashion,
　And how very bad it must feel.

THE COUNTRY CLERGYMAN'S TRIP

We were all so much touched and excited
   By a subject so direly sublime,
That the rules of politeness were slighted,
   And we all of us talked at a time;
And in tones, which each moment grew louder,
   Told how we should dress for the show,
And where we should fasten the powder,
   And if we should bellow or no.

Thus from subject to subject we ran,
   And the journey passed pleasantly o'er,
Till at last Dr. Humdrum began;
   From that time I remember no more.
At Ware he commenced his prelection,
   In the dullest of clerical drones:
And when next I regained recollection
   We were rumbling o'er Trumpington stones.
LORD MACAULAY.

205   *A Letter of Advice*

*From Miss Medora Trevilian, at Padua, to Miss
Araminta Vavasour, in London*

Enfin, monsieur, un homme aimable;
Voilà pourquoi je ne saurais l'aimer.—*Scribe.*

YOU tell me you're promised a lover,
   My own Araminta, next week;
Why cannot my fancy discover
   The hue of his coat and his cheek?
Alas! if he look like another,
   A vicar, a banker, a beau,
Be deaf to your father and mother,
   My own Araminta, say 'No!'

A LETTER OF ADVICE

Miss Lane, at her Temple of Fashion,
    Taught us both how to sing and to speak,
And we loved one another with passion,
    Before we had been there a week:
You gave me a ring for a token;
    I wear it wherever I go;
I gave you a chain,—is it broken?
    My own Araminta, say 'No!'

O think of our favourite cottage,
    And think of our dear Lalla Rookh!
How we shared with the milkmaids their pottage,
    And drank of the stream from the brook:
How fondly our loving lips faltered
    'What further can grandeur bestow?'
My heart is the same;—is yours altered?
    My own Araminta, say 'No!'

Remember the thrilling romances
    We read on the bank in the glen;
Remember the suitors our fancies
    Would picture for both of us then.
They wore the red cross on their shoulder,
    They had vanquished and pardoned their foe—
Sweet friend, are you wiser or colder?
    My own Araminta, say 'No!'

You know, when Lord Rigmarole's carriage
    Drove off with your cousin Justine,
You wept, dearest girl, at the marriage,
    And whispered 'How base she has been!'

A LETTER OF ADVICE

You said you were sure it would kill you,
  If ever your husband looked so;
And you will not apostatize,—will you?
  My own Araminta, say 'No!'

When I heard I was going abroad, love,
  I thought I was going to die;
We walked arm in arm to the road, love,
  We looked arm in arm to the sky;
And I said 'When a foreign postilion
  Has hurried me off to the Po,
Forget not Medora Trevilian:
  My own Araminta, say "No!"'

We parted! but sympathy's fetters
  Reach far over valley and hill;
I muse o'er your exquisite letters,
  And feel that your heart is mine still;
And he who would share it with me, love,—
  The richest of treasures below—
If he's not what Orlando should be, love,
  My own Araminta, say 'No!'

If he wears a top-boot in his wooing,
  If he comes to you riding a cob,
If he talks of his baking or brewing,
  If he puts up his feet on the hob,
If he ever drinks port after dinner,
  If his brow or his breeding is low,
If he calls himself 'Thompson' or 'Skinner',
  My own Araminta, say 'No!'

386

A LETTER OF ADVICE

If he studies the news in the papers
  While you are preparing the tea,
If he talks of the damps or the vapours
  While moonlight lies soft on the sea,
If he's sleepy while you are capricious,
  If he has not a musical 'Oh!'
If he does not call Werther delicious,—
  My own Araminta, say 'No!'

If he ever sets foot in the City
  Among the stockbrockers and Jews,
If he has not a heart full of pity,
  If he don't stand six feet in his shoes,
If his lips are not redder than roses,
  If his hands are not whiter than snow,
If he has not the model of noses,—
  My own Araminta, say 'No!'

If he speaks of a tax or a duty,
  If he does not look grand on his knees,
If he's blind to a landscape of beauty,
  Hills, valleys, rocks, waters, and trees,
If he dotes not on desolate towers,
  If he likes not to hear the blast blow,
If he knows not the language of flowers,—
  My own Araminta, say 'No!'

He must walk—like a god of old story
  Come down from the home of his rest;
He must smile—like the sun in his glory
  On the buds he loves ever the best;

387

And oh! from its ivory portal
    Like music his soft speech must flow!—
If he speak, smile, or walk like a mortal,
    My own Araminta, say 'No!'

Don't listen to tales of his bounty,
    Don't hear what they say of his birth,
Don't look at his seat in the county,
    Don't calculate what he is worth;
But give him a theme to write verse on,
    And see if he turns out his toe;
If he's only an excellent person,—
    My own Araminta, say 'No!'

                WINTHROP MACKWORTH PRAED.

206   *Good-night to the Season*

      So runs the world away.—*Hamlet.*

GOOD-NIGHT to the Season! 'Tis over!
    Gay dwellings no longer are gay;
The courtier, the gambler, the lover,
    Are scattered like swallows away:
There's nobody left to invite one
    Except my good uncle and spouse;
My mistress is bathing at Brighton,
    My patron is sailing at Cowes:
For want of a better enjoyment,
    Till Ponto and Don can get out,
I'll cultivate rural enjoyment,
    And angle immensely for trout.

Good-night to the Season! the lobbies,
    Their changes, and rumours of change,

388

GOOD-NIGHT TO THE SEASON

Which startled the rustic Sir Bobbies,
   And made all the Bishops look strange;
The breaches, and battles, and blunders,
   Performed by the Commons and Peers;
The Marquis's eloquent blunders,
   The Baronet's eloquent ears;
Denouncings of Papists and treasons,
   Of foreign dominion and oats;
Misrepresentations of reasons,
   And misunderstandings of notes.

Good-night to the Season!—the buildings
   Enough to make Inigo sick;
The paintings, and plasterings, and gildings
   Of stucco, and marble, and brick;
The orders deliciously blended,
   From love of effect, into one;
The club-houses only intended,
   The palaces only begun;
The hell, where the fiend in his glory
   Sits staring at putty and stones,
And scrambles from story to story,
   To rattle at midnight his bones.

Good-night to the Season!—the dances,
   The fillings of hot little rooms,
The glancings of rapturous glances,
   The fancyings of fancy costumes;
The pleasures which fashion makes duties,
   The praisings of fiddles and flutes,
The luxury of looking at Beauties,
   The tedium of talking to mutes;

GOOD-NIGHT TO THE SEASON

The female diplomatists, planners
  Of matches for Laura and Jane;
The ice of her Ladyship's manners,
  The ice of his Lordship's champagne.

Good-night to the Season!—the rages
  Led off by the chiefs of the throng,
The Lady Matilda's new pages,
  The Lady Eliza's new song;
Miss Fennel's macaw, which at Boodle's
  Was held to have something to say;
Miss Splenetic's musical poodles,
  Which bark '*Batti Batti*' all day;
The pony Sir Araby sported,
  As hot and as black as a coal,
And the Lion his mother imported,
  In bearskins and grease from the Pole.

Good-night to the Season!—the Toso,
  So very majestic and tall;
Miss Ayton, whose singing was so-so,
  And Pasta, divinest of all;
The labour in vain of the ballet,
  So sadly deficient in stars;
The foreigners thronging the Alley,
  Exhaling the breath of cigars;
The *loge* where some heiress (how killing!)
  Environed with exquisites sits,
The lovely one out of her drilling,
  The silly ones out of their wits.

Good-night to the Season!—the splendour
  That beamed in the Spanish Bazaar;

GOOD-NIGHT TO THE SEASON

Where I purchased—my heart was so tender—
   A card-case, a pasteboard guitar,
A bottle of perfume, a girdle,
   A lithographed Riego, full-grown,
Whom bigotry drew on a hurdle
   That artists might draw him on stone;
A small panorama of Seville,
   A trap for demolishing flies,
A caricature of the Devil,
   And a look from Miss Sheridan's eyes.

Good-night to the Season!—the flowers
   Of the grand horticultural fête,
When boudoirs were quitted for bowers,
   And the fashion was—not to be late;
When all who had money and leisure
   Grew rural o'er ices and wines,
All pleasantly toiling for pleasure,
   All hungrily pining for pines,
And making of beautiful speeches,
   And marring of beautiful shows,
And feeding on delicate peaches,
   And treading on delicate toes.

Good-night to the Season!—Another
   Will come, with its trifles and toys,
And hurry away, like its brother,
   In sunshine, and odour, and noise.
Will it come with a rose or a briar?
   Will it come with a blessing or curse?
Will its bonnets be lower or higher?
   Will its morals be better or worse?

Will it find me grown thinner or fatter,
  Or fonder of wrong or of right,
Or married—or buried?—no matter:
  Good-night to the Season—good-night!

WINTHROP MACKWORTH PRAED.

207   *Gypsies in the Wood*

MY mother said that I never should
  Play with the gypsies in the wood,
The wood was dark; the grass was green;
In came Sally with a tambourine,
I went to the sea—no ship to get across;
I paid ten shillings for a blind white horse;
I up on his back and was off in a crack,
Sally, tell my Mother I shall never come back.

ANON.

208   *Three Young Rats*

Three young rats with black felt hats,
  Three young ducks with white straw flats,
    Three young dogs with curling tails,
      Three young cats with demi-veils,
        Went out to walk with two young pigs
          In satin vests and sorrel wigs;
            But suddenly it chanced to rain,
              And so they all went home again.

ANON.

O WHERE are you going, says Milder to Malder,
O, I cannot tell, says Festel to Fose,
We're going to the woods, says John the Red Nose,
We're going to the woods, says John the Red Nose.

O, what will you do there, says Milder to Malder,
O, I cannot tell, says Festel to Fose,
We'll shoot the Cutty Wren, says John the Red Nose,
We'll shoot the Cutty Wren, says John the Red Nose,

O, how will you shoot her, says Milder to Malder,
O, I cannot tell, says Festel to Fose,
With arrows and bows, says John the Red Nose,
With arrows and bows, says John the Red Nose.

O, that will not do, says Milder to Malder,
O, what will do then, says Festel to Fose,
Big guns and cannons, says John the Red Nose,
Big guns and cannons, says John the Red Nose.

O, how will you bring her home, says Milder to Malder,
O, I cannot tell, says Festel to Fose,
On four strong men's shoulders, says John the Red Nose,
On four strong men's shoulders, says John the Red Nose.

O, that will not do, says Milder to Malder,
O, what will do then, says Festel to Fose,
Big carts and waggons, says John the Red Nose,
Big carts and waggons, says John the Red Nose.

O, what will you cut her up with, says Milder to Malder,
O, I cannot tell, says Festel to Fose,
With knives and with forks, says John the Red Nose,
With knives and with forks, says John the Red Nose.

O, that will not do, says Milder to Malder,
O, what will do then, says Festel to Fose,
Hatchets and cleavers, says John the Red Nose,
Hatchets and cleavers, says John the Red Nose.

O, how will you boil her, says Milder to Malder,
O, I cannot tell, says Festel to Fose,
In pots and in kettles, says John the Red Nose,
In pots and in kettles, says John the Red Nose.

O, that will not do, says Milder to Malder,
O, what will do then, says Festel to Fose,
Brass pans and cauldrons, says John the Red Nose,
Brass pans and cauldrons, says John the Red Nose.

O, who'll have the spare ribs, says Milder to Malder,
O, I cannot tell, says Festel to Fose,
We'll give them to the poor, says John the Red Nose,
We'll give them to the poor, says John the Red Nose.

ANON.

210   *Kiss in the Ring*

THERE stands a lady on a mountain,
    Who she is I do not know,
All she wants is gold and silver,
    All she wants is a nice young man.

Now you're married I wish you joy—
    First a girl and then a boy;
Seven years after a son and daughter,
    Kiss your bride and come out of the ring.

ANON.

394

211

All, all a-lonely

THREE little children sitting on the sand,
    All, all a-lonely,
Three little children sitting on the sand,
All, all a-lonely,
Down in the green wood shady—
There came an old woman, said Come on with me,
All, all a-lonely,
There came an old woman, said Come on with me,
All, all a-lonely,
Down in the green wood shady—
She stuck her pen-knife through their heart,
All, all a-lonely,
She stuck her pen-knife through their heart,
All, all a-lonely,
Down in the green wood shady.

ANON.

Eaper Weaper

EAPER WEAPER, chimbley-sweeper,
    Had a wife but couldn't keep her,
Had anovver, didn't love her,
Up the chimbley he did shove her.

ANON.

Old Roger

OLD ROGER is dead and gone to his grave,
    He, Hi, gone to his grave.
They planted an apple-tree over his head,
He, Hi, over his head.·

The apples grew ripe and ready to drop,
He, Hi, ready to drop.
There came an old woman of Hipertihop,
He, Hi, Hipertihop,
She began a picking them up,
He, Hi, picking them up,
Old Roger got up and gave her a knock,
He, Hi, gave her a knock,
Which made the old woman go Hipertihop,
He, Hi, Hipertihop.   ANON.

214   *I had a Black Man*

I HAD a black man, he was double-jointed,
I kissed him, and made him disappointed,
All right, Hilda, I'll tell your mother
Kissing the black man round the corner.
How many kisses did he give you?
One, two, three, &c.   ANON.

215   *Up in the North*

UP in the North, a long way off,
The donkey's got the whooping-cough.
                                        ANON.

216   *The Three Huntsmen*

THERE were three jovial Welshmen,
    As I have heard them say,
And they would go a-hunting, boys,
    Upon St. David's Day.
All the day they hunted,
    And nothing could they find,

THE THREE HUNTSMEN

But a ship a-sailing,
  A-sailing with the wind.
    And a-hunting they did go.

One said it was a ship,
  The other he said, Nay;
The third said it was a house
  With the chimney blown away.
And all the night they hunted,
  And nothing could they find,
But the moon a-gliding,
  A-gliding with the wind.
    And a-hunting they did go.

One said it was the moon,
  The other he said, Nay;
The third said it was a cheese
  And half o't cut away.
And all the day they hunted,
  And nothing could they find,
But a hedgehog in a bramble bush,
  And that they left behind.
    And a-hunting they did go.

The first said it was a hedgehog,
  The second he said, Nay;
The third, it was a pincushion,
  The pins stuck in wrong way.
And all the night they hunted,
  And nothing could they find,
But a hare in a turnip field,
  And that they left behind.
    And a-hunting they did go.

The first said it was a hare,
   The second he said, Nay;
The third, he said it was a calf,
   And the cow had run away.
And all the day they hunted,
   And nothing could they find,
But an owl in a holly-tree
   And that they left behind.
     And a-hunting they did go.

One said it was an owl,
   The second he said, Nay;
The third said 'twas an old man
   And his beard growing grey.
Then all three jovial Welshmen
   Came riding home at last,
'For three days we have nothing killed,
   And never broke our fast!'
     And a-hunting they did go.

ANON.

217   *Flowers in the Valley*

O THERE was a woman, and she was a widow,
   Fair are the flowers in the valley.
With a daughter as fair as a fresh sunny meadow,
   The Red, the Green, and the Yellow,
The Harp, the Lute, the Pipe, the Flute, the Cymbal,
   Sweet goes the treble Violin.
The maid so rare and the flowers so fair
   Together they grew in the valley.

There came a Knight all clothed in red,
    Fair are the flowers in the valley.
'I would thou wert my bride,' he said,
    The Red, the Green, and the Yellow.
The Harp, the Lute, the Pipe, the Flute, the Cymbal,
    Sweet goes the treble Violin.
'I would,' she sighed, 'ne'er wins a bride!'
    Fair are the flowers in the valley.

There came a Knight all clothed in green,
    Fair are the flowers in the valley.
'This maid so sweet might be my queen.'
    The Red, the Green, and the Yellow.
The Harp, the Lute, the Pipe, the Flute, the Cymbal,
    Sweet goes the treble Violin.
'Might be,' sighed she, 'will ne'er win me!'
    Fair are the flowers in the valley.

There came a Knight, in yellow was he,
    Fair are the flowers in the valley,
'My bride, my queen, thou must with me!'
    The Red, the Green, and the Yellow.
The Harp, the Lute, the Pipe, the Flute, the Cymbal,
    Sweet goes the treble Violin.
With blushes red, 'I come,' she said;
    'Farewell to the flowers in the valley.'   ANON.

218   *Broom, Green Broom*

THERE was an old man and he lived in a wood,
   And his trade it was making of broom, of broom,
And he had a naughty boy, Jack, to his son,
    And he lay in bed till 'twas noon, 'twas noon,
      And he lay in bed till 'twas noon.

BROOM, GREEN BROOM

The father was vext and sorely perplext,
　　With passion he enters the room, the room,
'Come, sirrah,' he cried, 'I'll leather your hide,
　　If you will not go gather green broom, green broom,
　　　　If you will not go gather green broom.'

Master Jack being sly, he got up by and bye,
　　And went into the town to cry, 'Broom, green broom.'
So loud did he call, and so loudly did bawl,
　　'Pretty maids, do you want any broom, green broom?
　　　　Pretty maids, do you want any broom?'

A lady looked out of her lattice so high,
　　And spied Jack a-selling of broom, green broom,
Says she, 'You young blade, won't you give up your trade,
　　And marry a maid in full bloom, full bloom?
　　　　And marry a maid in full bloom?'

So they sent for the parson without more delay,
　　And married they were in the room, the room,
There was eating and drink, and says Jack, with a wink,
　　'This is better than cutting of broom, green broom,
　　　　This is better than cutting of broom.'

ANON.

219　　　　　*Old Joe*

OLD Joe is dead, and gone to hell,
　　O we say so, and we hope so;
Old Joe is dead, and gone to hell,
　　O poor old Joe.

The ship did sail, the winds did roar,
　　O we say so, and we hope so;
The ship did sail, the winds did roar,
　　O poor old Joe.

OLD JOE

He's as dead as a nail in the lamp-room door,
  O we say so, and we hope so;
He's as dead as a nail in the lamp-room door,
  O poor old Joe.

He won't come hazing us no more,
  O we say so, and we hope so;
He won't come hazing us no more,
  O poor old Joe.

ANON.

220   *The Lover's Arithmetic*

IN love to be sure what disasters we meet,
  what torment what grief and vexation;
I've crosses encountered my hopes to defeat,
  will scarcely admit NUMERATION.
I courted a maid, and I called her divine,
  and begged she would change her condition;
For I thought that her fortune united to mine,
  would make a most handsome ADDITION.
        Heigho, dot and go one,
        Fal lal de ral de ra, &c.

When married, a plaguy SUBTRACTION I found,
  her debts wanted much liquidation;
And we couldn't, so badly our wishes were crowned,
  get forward in MULTIPLICATION.
DIVISION in wedlock is common they say,
  and both being fond of the suction;
I very soon had to exclaim 'Lack-a-day!
  my fortune's got into REDUCTION.'
        Heigho, dot and go one, &c.

The RULES OF PROPORTION Dame Nature forgot
    when my Deary she formed—so the fact is,
And she had a tongue to embitter my lot,
    which she never could keep out of PRACTICE,
One day after breaking my head with a stool,
    said I, 'Ma'am, if these are your actions,
I'm off; for you know I've been so long at school
    I don't want to learn VULGAR FRACTIONS.'
                Heigho, dot and go one, &c.

                        ANON.

221   *The Death of Nelson*

COME all gallant seamen that unite a meeting,
   Attend to these lines that I'm going to relate
And, when that you hear, it will move you with pity
To hear how Lord Nelson, he met with his fate.
For he was a bold and undaunted commander
As ever did sail on the ocean wide
And he made both the French and the Spaniards surrender
By always pouring into them a broadside.

Chorus

    Mourn, England, mourn; mourn and complain,
      For the loss of Lord Nelson, who died on the main.

From aloft to aloft, where he was commanding,
All by a French gun he received a ball
And by the contents, he got mortally wounded
And that was the occasion of Lord Nelson's fall.
Like an undaunted hero, exposed to the fire
As he gave the command, on the quarter-deck stood,
And to hear of his actions, you would much admire,
To see the decks covered all with human blood.

THE DEATH OF NELSON

One hundred engagements he had been into
And never, in his time, was he known to be beat,
For he had lost an arm, likewise his right eye, sir,
No powers on earth could ever him defeat.
His age, at his death, it was forty and seven,
And as long as I live, his great praises I'll sing,
For the whole navigation was given unto him
Because he was loyal and true to his king.

Then up steps the doctor in a very great hurry
And unto Lord Nelson these words he did say,
Indeed then, my Lord, I am very sorry,
To see you lying and bleeding this way.
No matter, no matter whatever about me,
My time it has come, I'm almost at the worst,
And there's my gallant seamen who're fighting so boldly,
Go and discharge your duty to them first.

Then with a loud voice he called out to his captain,
Pray let me know how this battle does go,
I think that our guns continue to rattle,
Though death approaches I very well know.
The antagonist's ship has gone to the bottom,
Eighteen we've captured, and brought them on board,
And here are two of them quite blown out of the ocean,
So that is the news I have brought you, my Lord.

Come all gallant seamen that unite a meeting,
Always let Lord Nelson's memory go round;
For it is your duty when you unite a meeting,
Because he was loyal and true to the Crown;

So now to conclude and to finish these verses,
My time it is come, I am quite at the worst,
May the heavens go with you and ten thousand blessings
May rest in the Fleet with you, Lord Collingwood.

ANON.

222   *Miss Bailey's Ghost*

A CAPTAIN bold, in Halifax, who dwelt in country
quarters,
Seduced a maid, who hang'd herself, one morning, in her
garters,
His wicked conscience smited him, he lost his stomach
daily,
He took to drinking ratafee, and thought upon Miss
Bailey.
    Oh, Miss Bailey! unfortunate Miss Bailey.

One night betimes he went to rest, for he had caught a
fever,
Says he, 'I am a handsome man, but I'm a gay deceiver;'
His candle just at twelve o'clock began to burn quite
palely,
A ghost stepp'd up to his bedside, and said, 'behold Miss
Bailey.'
    Oh, Miss Bailey! unfortunate Miss Bailey.

'Avaunt, Miss Bailey,' then he cried, 'your face looks white
and mealy,'
'Dear Captain Smith,' the ghost replied, 'you've used me
ungenteely;

The Crowner's Quest goes hard with me, because I've
    acted fraily,
And parson Biggs,won't bury me, though I am dead Miss
    Bailey.'
    Oh, Miss Bailey! unfortunate Miss Bailey.

'Dear Corpse,' said he, 'since you and I accounts must once
    for all close,
I've really got a one pound note in my regimental small
    clothes;
'Twill bribe the sexton for your grave.'—The ghost then
    vanish'd gaily,
Crying 'Bless you, wicked Captain Smith, remember poor
    Miss Bailey.'
    Oh, Miss Bailey! unfortunate Miss Bailey.

ANON.

223   *The One Horse Chay*

M RS. BUBB was gay and free, fair, fat and forty-three,
    And blooming as a Peony in buxom May,
The toast she long had been of Farringdon Within,
And she filled the better half of a one horse chay.

Mrs. Bubb said to her lord, 'You can, Bubb, well afford
Whate'er a Common Councilman in prudence may;
We've no brats to plague our lives and the soap concern it
    thrives,
Let us take a trip to Brighton in the one horse chay.

Mr. Bubb said to his wife, 'Now I think upon't, my life,
'Tis three weeks at least to next boiling day;
The dog days are set in and London's growing thin,
So I'll order out old Nobbs and the one horse chay.'

THE ONE HORSE CHAY

Now Nobbs, it must be told, was rather fat and old,
Its colour was white and it had been gray,
He was round as a scot and when roundly whipt would
trot,
Full five miles an hour in a one horse chay.

When at Brighton they were housed and had stuffed and
caroused,
O'er a bowl of arrack Punch Mr. Bubb did say:
'I've ascertained, my dear, the mode of dipping here,
From the ostler who is cleaning up my one horse chay.

You're shut in a box, ill convenient as the stocks,
And eighteen pence each time are obliged to pay;
Court corruption here, says I, makes everything so high
And I wish I had come without my one horse chay.'

'As I hope' says she 'to thrive, 'tis flaying folks alive,
The king and these extortioners are leagued, I say;
'Tis encouraging of such to go and pay so much,
So we'll set them at defiance with our one horse chay.

Old Nobbs I am sure and sartin you may trust with gig or
cart in,
He takes every matter in a very easy way;
He'll stand like a post while we dabble on the coast,
And return back and dress in our one horse chay.'

So out they drove all dressed so gaily in their best,
And finding in their rambles a nice little bay,
They uncased at their leisure, paddled out at their pleasure,
And left everything behind in their one horse chay.

THE ONE HORSE CHAY

But while so snugly sure that all things were secure,
They flounced about like porpoises or whales at play;
Some young unlucky imps who prowled about for shrimps
Stole up to reconnoitre the one horse chay.

Old Nobbs in quiet mood was sleeping as he stood,
(He might possibly be dreaming of his corn or hay):
Not a foot did he wag as they whipt out every rag
And gutted all the contents of the one horse chay.

When our pair were soused enough and returning in their
    buff,
Oh there was the vengeance and Old Nick to pay;
Madame shrieked in consternation, Mr. Bubb he swore
    damnation,
To find the empty state of the one horse chay.

'Come bundle in with me, we must squeeze for once,' says
    he,
'And manage this here business as best we may.
We've no other way to choose, not a moment must we
    lose,
Or the tide will float us off in our one horse chay.'

So noses, sides and knees altogether did they squeeze
And packed in little compass they trotted it away;
As dismal as two dummies, heads and hands stuck out like
    mummies,
From beneath the little apron of the one horse chay.

Mr. Bubb ge-upped in vain and strove to jerk the rein,
Nobbs found he had his option to work or play,
So he wouldn't mend his pace, though they fain would
    have run race
To escape the merry gazers at the one horse chay.

Now good people laugh your fill and fancy if you will,
(For I'm fairly out of breath and have had my say);
The trouble and the rout, to wrap and get them out,
When they drove to their lodgings in their one horse chay.

ANON.

224   *Under the Drooping Willow Tree*

ON a small six-acre farm dwelt John Grist the miller,
  Near a pond not far beyond grew a drooping willow,
Underneath its spreading leaves sat Jane, his only daughter.
Meditating suicide in the muddy water,
Element Aqua Pura, Aqua Impura.
She sat by a duck pond of dark water,
Under the drooping willow tree.

She'd been jilted by a youth who had joined the Rifles,
A young man not worth a rap, who never stuck at trifles.
Though he promised to keep true, act like a faithful lover,
When his rifle suit he got, then leg bail he gave her,
Hooked it, stepped it, toddled, mizzled.
She sat by a duck pond of dark water,
Under the drooping willow tree.

'All alone I'm left,' says she, 'my poor heart is bursting;
Dearly did I love my Joe, though he wore plain fustian.
But my nose is out of joint, and don't it make me nettled.
In this pond I'll drown myself, then I shall be settled.
Bottled, finished, done for, flummoxed.'
She sat by a duck pond of dark water,
Under the drooping willow tree.

She'd no wish to spoil her clothes, so undressed that
    minute;
But the water felt so cold when her toes were in it.

UNDER THE DROOPING WILLOW TREE

'If it weren't so cold,' said she, 'I'd jump in like winking.'
Then she wiped her nose, and sat upon the edge thinking,
Pondering, puzzling, considering, ruminating.
She sat by a duck pond of dark water,
Under the drooping willow tree.

Like a Venus she sat in her nude state staying;
Presently she was frightened by a donkey braying.
Like a frog she gave a leap, but worse luck she stumbled,
Lost her equilibrium, and in the water tumbled,
Fell in, pitched in, dropped in, popped in.
She fell in the duck pond of dark water,
Under the drooping willow tree.

When she found she'd fallen in, she then took to swooning;
Very long it would not have been, before she took to
    drowning.
But her Joseph was close by, saw her in the water,
With his crooked walking stick by the wool he caught her,
Nabbed her, grabbed her, seized her, collared her
From out of the duck pond of dark water,
Under the drooping willow tree.

He beheld her coming to with great acclamation,
And the tree bore witness to their reconciliation.
There it stands in all its pride, and will stand, moreover,
Unless the spot should be required by the London, Chat-
    ham and Dover
Railway, Company, Limited, Good Dividends.
They'll sit by the duck pond of dark water,
Under the drooping willow tree.

ANON.

GOOD people draw near as you pass along
And listen awhile to my alphabetical song.
A is Prince Albert once buxom and keen
Who from Germany came and got spliced to the Queen.

Chorus.

    For they're all a spinning, their cause in triumph
      springing,
    And the poor man he is singing since the Corn bill is
      repailed.

B stands for Smith O'Brien: he an Irishman so true
He hammered at Coercion till he beat them black and blue.
When he got out of prison that bill he did oppose,
With the fright he gave old Wellington, he fell and broke
    his nose.

C is brave Cobden one night it is said
Threw a quarter Loaf at old Buckingham's head.
Concerning the Corn laws he laid it down strong
And he spun out yarn seventeen hour long.

D for the Duncombe who helpt the plan
To give full and plenty to each true in the land.
E stands for Evans who would starve us again
Because he beats 40 thousand old women in Spain.

F stands for Ferrand a protectioner's Tool,
He spoke seven hours and roared like a fool;
G stands for Graham who is early and late,
Breaking seals at the post office a repealer for to take.

SONG ON THE CORN LAW BILL

H is old Hume he is clever do you see,
He subtracted 2 from 1 and got the corn duty free;
I is Bob Inglis aginst free trade blew a blast,
He was seven hours in the stericks when the corn bill did
    pass.

J stands for Jerry who spoke till he was hoarse,
In the middle of the fight his fair daughter he lost;
She followed a soldier and off she went slap,
With gun and a knap-sack slung over her back.

K is for Kelly, he kept up the jaw
Till he got the corn free and brought into law;
L stands for Lyndhurst with his Brushes, Paints, and Pots,
Guess how he was born or how that he was got.

M is Lord Morpeth who nobly fought
Each night in succession for the corn law;
N is old Nosey who opposes him it's true,
For to lose 15 thousand he is quite in the blues.

O is O'Connell to them told the Law
And is still biding time for old Erin Gobraugh.
P stands for Peel who is acting upright,
As between you and me he has got a long sight.

Q is the question of Coercion they say,
So they're stuck in the trap Bob cut away;
R is Lord Russell who's making all haste
To run down to Windsor to fill Bobby's place.

To ride in Peel's saddle he'll find it a job,
For he shakes on his legs like a staggering Bob.
S is Lord Stanley who's shaking with fear,
For his tenants payed him their rent with a bullet this year.

SONG ON THE CORN LAW BILL

And swore if they catch him he'll never elope
Till they well oil his body with flails of good oak;
T is the teasel that combs them all down,
U is for Uxbridge who wonders have done.

V stands for Villiers whom the farmers detest,
For to slaughter the corn law he did do his best;
For free trade he struggled by day and by night,
He is next in command to Cobden and Bright.

W stands for Wakley a doctor so bold,
Who swore on the corn bill an Inquest he'd hold;
When the jury he charged he let them all see,
A verdict was returned for the corn to be free.

X is a letter which puts me in mind
Of a ship load of landlords that sailed against wind;
Now over the ocean they must all away
To spend their last days in Botany Bay.

Y stands for York the archbishop so big
Who loves for to dine on a little tithe pig;
Free trade on last Sunday did so him perplex
That he sang rule Brittania and thought it the text.

Z is for Zetland an old English peer
Who swore he'd have bread and potatoes so dear.
The corn bill is pàst, the landlords are very bad,
They must be muzzled in the dog days for fear they might
    go mad.

A<small>NON</small>.

'HOW pleasant to know Mr. Lear!'
    Who has written such volumes of stuff!
Some think him ill-tempered and queer,
    But a few think him pleasant enough.

His mind is concrete and fastidious,
    His nose is remarkably big;
His visage is more or less hideous,
    His beard it resembles a wig.

He has ears, and two eyes, and ten fingers,
    Leastways if you reckon two thumbs;
Long ago he was one of the singers,
    But now he is one of the dumbs.

He sits in a beautiful parlour,
    With hundreds of books on the wall;
He drinks a great deal of Marsala,
    But never gets tipsy at all.

He has many friends, laymen and clerical,
    Old Foss is the name of his cat:
His body is perfectly spherical,
    He weareth a runcible hat.

When he walks in a waterproof white,
    The children run after him so!
Calling out, 'He's come out in his night-
    gown, that crazy old Englishman, oh!'

He weeps by the side of the ocean,
    He weeps on the top of the hill;
He purchases pancakes and lotion,
    And chocolate shrimps from the mill.

413

He reads but he cannot speak Spanish,
　　He cannot abide ginger-beer:
Ere the days of his pilgrimage vanish,
　　How pleasant to know Mr. Lear!

EDWARD LEAR.

227　　　　*The Jumblies*

I

THEY went to sea in a Sieve, they did,
　　In a Sieve they went to sea:
In spite of all their friends could say,
On a winter's morn, on a stormy day,
　　In a Sieve they went to sea!
And when the Sieve turned round and round,
And every one cried, 'You'll all be drowned!'
They called aloud, 'Our Sieve ain't big,
But we don't care a button! we don't care a fig!
　　In a Sieve we'll go to sea!'
　　　　Far and few, far and few,
　　　　　　Are the lands where the Jumblies live;
　　　　　Their heads are green, and their hands are blue,
　　　　　And they went to sea in a Sieve.

II

They sailed away in a Sieve, they did,
　　In a Sieve they sailed so fast,
With only a beautiful pea-green veil
Tied with a riband by way of a sail,
　　To a small tobacco-pipe mast;
And every one said, who saw them go,
'O won't they be soon upset, you know!

THE JUMBLIES

For the sky is dark, and the voyage is long,
And happen what may, it's extremely wrong
 In a Sieve to sail so fast!'
  Far and few, far and few,
   Are the lands where the Jumblies live;
   Their heads are green, and their hands are blue,
   And they went to sea in a Sieve.

III

The water it soon came in, it did,
 The water it soon came in;
So to keep them dry, they wrapped their feet
In a pinky paper all folded neat,
 And they fastened it down with a pin.
And they passed the night in a crockery-jar,
And each of them said, 'How wise we are!
Though the sky be dark, and the voyage be long,
Yet we never can think we were rash or wrong,
 While round in our Sieve we spin!'
  Far and few, far and few,
   Are the lands where the Jumblies live;
   Their heads are green, and their hands are blue,
   And they went to sea in a Sieve.

IV

And all night long they sailed away;
 And when the sun went down,
They whistled and warbled a moony song
To the echoing sound of a coppery gong,
 In the shade of the mountains brown.
'O Timballoo! How happy we are,
When we live in a Sieve and a crockery-jar,

THE JUMBLIES

And all night long in the moonlight pale,
We sail away with a pea-green sail,
  In the shade of the mountains brown!'
    Far and few, far and few,
     Are the lands where the Jumblies live;
     Their heads are green, and their hands are blue,
     And they went to sea in a Sieve.

v

They sailed to the Western Sea, they did,
  To a land all covered with trees,
And they bought an Owl, and a useful Cart,
And a pound of Rice, and a Cranberry Tart,
  And a hive of silvery Bees.
And they bought a Pig, and some green Jack-daws,
And a lovely Monkey with lollipop paws,
And forty bottles of Ring-Bo-Ree,
  And no end of Stilton Cheese.
    Far and few, far and few,
     Are the lands where the Jumblies live;
     Their heads are green, and their hands are blue,
     And they went to sea in a Sieve.

vi

And in twenty years they all came back,
  In twenty years or more,
And every one said, 'How tall they've grown!
For they've been to the Lakes, and the Torrible Zone,
  And the hills of the Chankly Bore';
And they drank their health, and gave them a feast
Of dumplings made of beautiful yeast;

And every one said, 'If we only live,
We too will go to sea in a Sieve,—
    To the hills of the Chankly Bore!'
     Far and few, far and few,
      Are the lands where the Jumblies live;
      Their heads are green, and their hands are blue,
      And they went to sea in a Sieve.
                 EDWARD LEAR.

228   *The Owl and The Pussy Cat*

THE Owl and the Pussy-Cat went to sea
  In a beautiful pea-green boat.
They took some honey, and plenty of money
  Wrapped up in a five-pound note.
The Owl looked up to the stars above,
  And sang to a small guitar,
'O lovely Pussy! O Pussy, my love,
What a beautiful Pussy you are,
      You are,
      You are!
What a beautiful Pussy you are!'

Pussy said to the Owl, 'You elegant fowl!
  How charmingly sweet you sing!
O let us be married! too long we have tarried:
  But what shall we do for a ring?'
They sailed away, for a year and a day,
  To the land where the Bong-Tree grows,
And there in a wood a Piggy-wig stood,
With a ring at the end of his nose,
      His nose,
      His nose!
With a ring at the end of his nose.

'Dear Pig, are you willing to sell for one shilling
    Your ring?' Said the Piggy, 'I will.'
So they took it away, and were married next day
    By the Turkey who lives on the hill.
They dinèd on mince, and slices of quince,
    Which they ate with a runcible spoon;
And hand in hand, on the edge of the sand
    They danced by the light of the moon,
            The moon,
            The moon,
    They danced by the light of the moon.

                                EDWARD LEAR.

229 *Incidents in the Life of My Uncle Arly*

I

O MY aged Uncle Arly!
    Sitting on a heap of Barley
Thro' the silent hours of night,—
Close beside a leafy thicket:—
On his nose there was a Cricket,—
In his hat a Railway-Ticket
(But his shoes were far too tight).

II

Long ago, in youth, he squander'd
All his goods away, and wander'd
To the Tiniskoop-hills afar.
There on golden sunsets blazing,
Every evening found him gazing,—
Singing,—'Orb! you're quite amazing!
How I wonder what you are!'

MY UNCLE ARLY

III

Like the ancient Medes and Persians,
Always by his own exertions
He subsisted on those hills;—
Whiles,—by teaching children spelling,—
Or at times by merely yelling,—
Or at intervals by selling
'Propter's Nicodemus Pills'.

IV

Later, in his morning rambles
He perceived the moving brambles—
Something square and white disclose;—
'Twas a First-class Railway-Ticket;
But, on stooping down to pick it
Off the ground,—a pea-green Cricket
Settled on my uncle's Nose.

V

Never—Never more,—oh! never,
Did that Cricket leave him ever,—
Dawn or evening, day or night;—
Clinging as a constant treasure,—
Chirping with a cheerious measure,–
Wholly to my uncle's pleasure
(Though his shoes were far too tight).

VI

So for three and forty winters,
Till his shoes were worn to splinters,
All those hills he wanders o'er,—

Sometimes silent;—sometimes yelling;—
Till he came to Borley-Melling,
Near his old ancestral dwelling
(But his shoes were far too tight).

VII

On a little heap of Barley
Died my aged Uncle Arly,
And they buried him one night;—
Close beside the leafy thicket;—
There,—his hat and Railway-Ticket;—
There,—his ever-faithful Cricket
(But his shoes were far too tight).

EDWARD LEAR.

230   *Limericks*

I

THERE was a Young Lady of Ryde,
  Whose shoe-strings were seldom untied;
    She purchased some clogs
    And some small spotty dogs,
And frequently walked about Ryde.

II

THERE was a young person of Smyrna,
Whose Grandmother threatened to burn her;
    But she seized on the cat,
    And said, 'Granny, burn that!
You incongruous Old Woman of Smyrna.'

III

THERE was a Young Lady of Portugal,
Whose ideas were excessively nautical;
   She climbed up a tree
   To examine the sea,
But declared she would never leave Portugal.

IV

THERE was an Old Man who said, 'Hush!
I perceive a young bird in this bush!'
   When they said, 'Is it small?'
   He replied, 'Not at all!
It is four times as big as the bush.'

EDWARD LEAR.

231   *Annette Myers, or, A Murder in St. James's Park*

ANOTHER dreadful tale of woe as I will here unfold
   Has taken place, and seldom such before was ever
   told.
Female named Annette Myers—how horrible and true—
On Friday night in St. James's Park a soldier there she slew.
Chorus:
   Annette Myers in a frenzy went—how awful to im-
     part—
   And shot a soldier dead in St. James's Park.

A servant girl the female was as we can understand,
Henry Ducker was a soldier and aged twenty-one,
Belonging to the Coldstream Guards, of good character we
   find;
He loved this maid though jealousy had poisoned his mind.

She and her soldier loving words did to each other talk,
As they were walking arm-in-arm along the Birdcage Walk;
When sudden she the weapon placed unto her lover's head,
And the trigger drew and the soldier slew who on the
    ground fell dead.

When she the pistol fired she prepared to go away,
But the officer detained her and thus to her did say:
'Did you the pistol fire?' 'I did' she said 'Indeed
And am quite satisfied' as we may plainly read.

Great consternation it has caused as we can understand,
This soldier one-and twenty was, a sprightly gay young
    man;
Henry Ducker was his name, of the Coldstream Guards
    we see.
What dreadful tidings to convey unto his family.   ANON.

232   *Billy in the Darbies*

GOOD of the Chaplain to enter Lone Bay
    And down on his marrow-bones here and pray
For the likes just o' me, Billy Budd.—But look:
Through the port comes the moon-shine astray!
It tips the guard's cutlass and silvers this nook;
But 'twill die in the dawning of Billy's last day.
A jewel-block they'll make of me to-morrow,
Pendant pearl from the yard-arm-end
Like the ear-drop I gave to Bristol-Molly—
Oh, 'tis me, not the sentence, they'll suspend.
Ay, Ay, all is up; and I must up too
Early in the morning, aloft from alow.
On an empty stomach, now, never it would do.
They'll give me a nibble—bit o' biscuit ere I go.

BILLY IN THE DARBIES

Sure, a messmate will reach me the last parting cup;
But turning heads away from the hoist and the belay,
Heaven knows who will have the running of me up!
No pipe to those halyards—But aren't it all sham?
A blur's in my eyes; it is dreaming that I am.
A hatchet to my panzer? all adrift to go?
The drum roll to grog, and Billy never know?
But Donald he has promised to stand by the plank;
So I'll shake a friendly hand ere I sink.
But—no! It is dead then I'll be, come to think.
I remember Taff the Welshman when he sank.
And his cheek it was like the budding pink.
But me, they'll lash me in hammock, drop me deep
Fathoms down, fathoms down, how I'll dream fast asleep.
I feel it stealing now. Sentry, are you there?
Just ease these darbies at the wrist,
And roll me over fair.
I am sleepy, and the oozy weeds about me twist.

HERMAN MELVILLE.

233   *Death of My Aunt*

MY aunt she died a month ago,
    And left me all her riches,
A feather-bed and a wooden leg,
    And a pair of calico breeches;
A coffee pot without a spout,
    A mug without a handle,
A baccy box without a lid,
    And half a farthing candle.

ANON.

I

As I sat at the Café I said to myself,
  They may talk as they please about what they call
    pelf,
They may sneer as they like about eating and drinking,
But help it I cannot, I cannot help thinking
  How pleasant it is to have money, heigh-ho!
  How pleasant it is to have money.

I sit at my table *en grand seigneur*,
And when I have done, throw a crust to the poor;
Not only the pleasure itself of good living,
But also the pleasure of now and then giving:
  So pleasant it is to have money, heigh-ho!
  So pleasant it is to have money.

They may talk as they please about what they call pelf,
And how one ought never to think of one's self,
How pleasures of thought surpass eating and drinking,—
My pleasure of thought is the pleasure of thinking
  How pleasant it is to have money, heigh-ho!
  How pleasant it is to have money.

II

Le Diner

Come along, 'tis the time, ten or more minutes past,
And he who came first had to wait for the last;
The oysters ere this had been in and been out;
Whilst I have been sitting and thinking about
  How pleasant it is to have money, heigh-ho!
  How pleasant it is to have money.

SPECTATOR AB EXTRA

A clear soup with eggs; *voilà tout*; of the fish
The *filets de sole* are a moderate dish
A la Orly, but you're for red mullet, you say:
By the gods of good fare, who can question to-day
  How pleasant it is to have money, heigh-ho!
  How pleasant it is to have money.

After oysters, sauterne; then sherry; champagne,
Ere one bottle goes, comes another again;
Fly up, thou bold cork, to the ceiling above,
And tell to our ears in the sound that they love
  How pleasant it is to have money, heigh-ho!
  How pleasant it is to have money.

I've the simplest of palates; absurd it may be,
But I almost could dine on a *poulet-au-riz*,
Fish and soup and omelette and that—but the deuce—
There were to be woodcocks, and not *Charlotte Russe!*
  So pleasant it is to have money, heigh-ho!
  So pleasant it is to have money.

Your chablis is acid, away with the hock,
Give me the pure juice of the purple médoc:
St. Peray is exquisite; but, if you please,
Some burgundy just before tasting the cheese.
  So pleasant it is to have money, heigh-ho!
  So pleasant it is to have money.

As for that, pass the bottle, and d—n the expense,
I've seen it observed by a writer of sense,
That the labouring classes could scarce live a day,
If people like us didn't eat, drink, and pay.
  So useful it is to have money, heigh-ho!
  So useful it is to have money.

One ought to be grateful, I quite apprehend,
Having dinner and supper and plenty to spend,
And so suppose now, while the things go away,
By way of a grace we all stand up and say
　　How pleasant it is to have money, heigh-ho!
　　How pleasant it is to have money.

III

Parvenant

I cannot but ask, in the park and the streets
When I look at the number of persons one meets,
What e'er in the world the poor devils can do
Whose fathers and mothers can't give them a *sou*.
　　So needful it is to have money, heigh-ho!
　　So needful it is to have money.

I ride, and I drive, and I care not a d—n,
The people look up and they ask who I am;
And if I should chance to run over a cad,
I can pay for the damage, if ever so bad.
　　So useful it is to have money, heigh-ho!
　　So useful it is to have money.

It was but this winter I came up to town,
And already I'm gaining a sort of renown;
Find my way to good houses without much ado,
Am beginning to see the nobility too.
　　So useful it is to have money, heigh-ho!
　　So useful it is to have money.

SPECTATOR AB EXTRA

O dear what a pity they ever should lose it,
Since they are the people that know how to use it;
So easy, so stately, such manners, such dinners,
And yet, after all, it is we are the winners.
    So needful it is to have money, heigh-ho!
    So needful it is to have money.

It's all very well to be handsome and tall,
Which certainly makes you look well at a ball;
It's all very well to be clever and witty,
But if you are poor, why it's only a pity.
    So needful it is to have money, heigh-ho!
    So needful it is to have money.

There's something undoubtedly in a fine air,
To know how to smile and be able to stare.
High breeding is something, but well-bred or not,
In the end the one question is, what have you got.
    So needful it is to have money, heigh-ho!
    So needful it is to have money.

And the angels in pink and the angels in blue,
In muslins and moirés so lovely and new,
What is it they want, and so wish you to guess,
But if you have money, the answer is Yes.
    So needful, they tell you, is money, heigh-ho!
    So needful it is to have money.

ARTHUR HUGH CLOUGH.

OH, don't you remember sweet Betsey from Pike,
    Who crossed the big mountains with her lover Ike,
With two yoke of cattle, a large yellow dog,
A tall shanghai rooster, and one spotted hog.

> *Chorus:* Tooral lal looral lal looral lal la,
>   Tooral lal looral, &c.

One evening quite early they camped on the Platte,
'Twas near by the road on a green shady flat,
Where Betsey, sore-footed, lay down to repose—
With wonder Ike gazed on that Pike County Rose.

> *Chorus:* Tooral lal looral, &c.

Their wagons broke down with a terrible crash,
And out on the prairie rolled all kinds of trash;
A few little baby clothes done up with care—
'Twas rather suspicious, though all on the *square*.

> *Chorus:* Tooral lal looral, &c.

The shanghai ran off, and their cattle all died;
That morning the last piece of bacon was fried;
Poor Ike was discouraged, and Betsey got mad,
The dog drooped his tail and looked wondrously sad.

> *Chorus:* Tooral lal looral, &c.

They stopped at Salt Lake to inquire the way,
When Brigham declared that sweet Betsey should stay;
But Betsey got frightened and ran like a deer,
While Brigham stood pawing the ground like a steer.

> *Chorus:* Tooral lal looral, &c.

SWEET BETSEY FROM PIKE

They soon reached the desert, where Betsey gave out,
And down in the sand she lay rolling about;
While Ike, half distracted, looked on with surprise,
Saying, 'Betsey, get up, you'll get sand in your eyes.'

    Chorus: Tooral lal looral, &c.

Sweet Betsey got up in a great deal of pain,
Declared she'd go back to Pike County again;
But Ike gave a sigh and they fondly embraced,
And they travelled along with his arm round her waist.

    Chorus: Tooral lal looral, &c.

They suddenly stopped on a very high hill,
With wonder looked down upon old Placerville;
Ike sighed when he said, as he cast his eyes down,
'Sweet Betsey, my darling, we've got to Hangtown.'

    Chorus: Tooral lal looral, &c.

Long Ike and sweet Betsey attended a dance;
Ike wore a pair of his Pike County pants;
Sweet Betsey was covered with ribbons and rings;
Says Ike, 'You're an angel, but where are your wings?'

    Chorus: Tooral lal looral, &c.

A miner said, 'Betsey, will you dance with me?'
'I will that, old hoss, if you don't make too free;
But don't dance me hard; do you want to know why?
Dog on you! I'm chock full of strong alkali.'

    Chorus: Tooral lal looral, &c.

FF

This Pike County couple got married of course,
And Ike became jealous—obtained a divorce;
Sweet Betsey, well satisfied, said with a shout,
'Good-by, you big lummux, I'm glad you've backed out!'

   Chorus: Tooral lal looral, &c.   ANON.

236   *Polly Perkins*

I AM a broken-hearted milkman, in grief I'm arrayed,
  Through keeping of the company of a young servant
    maid,
Who lived on board and wages the house to keep clean
In a gentleman's family near Paddington Green.

   Chorus:

         She was as beautiful as a butterfly
         And as proud as a Queen
       Was pretty little Polly Perkins of
       Paddington Green.

She'd an ankle like an antelope and a step like a deer,
A voice like a blackbird, so mellow and clear,
Her hair hung in ringlets so beautiful and long,
I thought that she loved me but I found I was wrong.

When I'd rattle in a morning and cry 'milk below',
At the sound of my milk-cans her face she would show
With a smile upon her countenance and a laugh in her eye,
If I thought she'd have loved me, I'd have laid down to die.

When I asked her to marry me she said 'Oh! what stuff',
And told me to 'drop it, for she had quite enough
Of my nonsense'—at the same time I'd been very kind,
But to marry a milkman she didn't feel inclined.

'Oh, the man that has me must have silver and gold,
A chariot to ride in and be handsome and bold,
His hair must be curly as any watch spring,
And his whiskers as big as a brush for clothing.'

The words that she uttered went straight through my
    heart,
I sobbed, I sighed, and straight did depart;
With a tear on my eyelid as big as a bean,
Bidding good-bye to Polly and Paddington Green.

In six months she married,—this hard-hearted girl,—
But it was not a Wi-count, and it was not a Nearl,
It was not a 'Baronite', but a shade or two wuss,
It was a bow-legged conductor of a twopenny bus.

                                ANON.

237   *The Ratcatcher's Daughter*

IN Westminster not long ago,
   There lived a Ratcatcher's Daughter,
She was not born at Westminster
    But on the t'other side of the water.
Her father killed rats and she sold sprats,
    All round and over the water,
And the gentlefolks they all bought sprats
    Of the pretty Ratcatcher's Daughter.

She wore no hat upon her head,
    No cap nor dandy bonnet,
The hair of her head it hung down her neck
    Like a bunch of carrots upon it.

THE RATCATCHER'S DAUGHTER

When she cried sprats in Westminster,
    She had such a sweet loud voice, Sir,
You could hear her all down Parliament Street
    As far as Charing Cross, Sir.

The rich and poor, both far and near,
    In matrimony sought her;
But at friends and foes she cocked her nose,
    Did this pretty little Ratcatcher's Daughter.
For there was a man cried 'Lily white Sand',
    Who in Cupid's net had caught her,
And over head and ears in love
    Was the pretty little Ratcatcher's Daughter.

Now 'Lily white Sand' so ran in her head,
    When coming down the Strand oh,
She forgot that she'd got sprats on her head
    And cried: 'buy my lily white Sand oh!'
The folks amazed all thought her crazed,
    All along the Strand oh,
To hear a girl with sprats on her head
    Cry, 'buy my lily white Sand, oh!'

Now Ratcatcher's Daughter so ran in his head,
    He didn't know what he was arter,
Instead of crying 'Lily white Sand',
    He cried: 'Do you want any Ratcatcher's Daughter?'
His donkey cocked his ears and brayed,
    Folks couldn't tell what he was arter,
To hear a lily white sand man cry,
    'Do you want any Ratcatcher's Daughter?'

Now they both agreed to married be
  Upon next Easter Sunday,
But the Ratcatcher's Daughter had a dream
  That she shouldn't be alive next Monday.
To buy some sprats once more she went
  And tumbled into the water,
Went down to the bottom all covered with mud,
  Did the pretty little Ratcatcher's Daughter.

When Lily white Sand he heard the news,
  His eyes ran down with water,
Says he, 'In love I'll constant prove
  And blow me if I live long arter.'
So he cut his throat with a piece of glass
  And he stabbed his donkey arter,
So there was an end of Lily white Sand,
  His ass and the Ratcatcher's Daughter.   ANON.

238   *Execution of Alice Holt*

A DREADFUL case of murder,
    Such as we seldom hear,
Committed was at Stockport,
  In the County of Cheshire.
Where a mother, named Mary Bailey,
  They did so cruelly slaughter,
By poison administered all in her beer,
  By her own daughter.

The daughter insured the life of the mother
  For twenty-six pounds at her death,
Then she and the man that she lived with
  Determined to take away her breath.

EXECUTION OF ALICE HOLT

And when Betty Wood represented the mother
    She didn't act with propriety,
For the poor mother lost her life,
    And they all swindled the Society.

'Now that the old gal's life's insured,'
    Holt to the daughter did say,
'Better in the grave she were immured,
    And the money will make us gay.'
'Now that you have got me in the family way,
    And from me my virtue you've wrung,
You'll never be happy a day
    Till on the gallows I'm hung.'

She laid a plan to murder her,
    As we now see so clear,
To put a quantity of arsenic
    Into her poor mother's beer.
To see her lay in agony,
    Upon that dreadful night,
With a dreadful dose of arsenic,
    Oh, it was a dreadful sight.

She lived but just six hours,
    Then the poor woman did die,
And this base murdering wretch
    The dreadful deed did deny.
On the man Holt she laid the blame,
    Vowed he did her mother slay,
Holt on her did the same,
    Saying she took the mother's life away.

But there's no doubt the base wretch
    Did her poor mother slay,
For which on Chester's scaffold
    Her life did forfeit pay.
So all young women a warning take
    By this poor wretch you see,
A-hanging for the mother's sake
    On Chester's fatal tree.

ANON.

239   *All the Pretty Little Horses*

HUSHABY,
    Don't you cry,
Go to sleepy, little baby,
When you wake,
You shall have,
All the pretty little horses—
Blacks and bays,
Dapples and grays,
Coach and six-a little horses.
Hushaby,
Don't you cry,
Go to sleepy, little baby.

Hushaby,
Don't you cry,
Go to sleepy, little baby,
Way down yonder
In de medder
There's a po' lil lambie,
De bees an' de butterflies
Peckin' out its eyes,

De po' lil thing cried, 'Mammy!'
Hushaby,
Don't you cry,
Go to sleepy, little baby. ANON.

240 *The Rebel Soldier*

ONE morning, one morning, one morning in May,
I heard a poor soldier lamenting and say,
I heard a poor soldier lamenting and mourn:
I am a rebel soldier and far from my home.

It's grape-shot and musket and the cannons lumber loud.
There's a many a mangled body, a blanket for their
shroud,
There's a many a mangled body left on the field alone.
I am a rebel soldier and far from my home.

I'll eat when I'm hungry and drink when I am dry.
If the Yankees don't kill me I'll live until I die,
If the Yankees don't kill me and cause me to mourn.
I am a rebel soldier and far from my home.

I'll build me a castle on some green mountain high,
Where the wild geese can see me as they do pass me by,
Where the wild geese can see me and hear my sad mourn:
I am a rebel soldier and far from my home. ANON.

241 *The Rebel*

OH, I'm a good old rebel, that's what I am,
And for this land of freedom, I don't give a damn;
I'm glad I fought agin her, I only wish we'd won,
And I ain't axed any pardon for anything I've done.

THE REBEL

I fought with old Bob Lee for three years about,
Got wounded in four places and starved at Point Lookout.
I caught the rheumatism a-campin' in the snow,
And I killed a chance of Yankees and I wish I'd killed
      some mo'!

Three hundred thousand Yankees is dead in Southern dust,
We got three hundred thousand before they conquered us;
They died of Southern fever, of Southern steel and shot—
I wish they was three million instead of what we got.

I hate the Constitution, this great republic, too;
I hate the nasty eagle, and the uniform so blue;
I hate their glorious banner, and all their flags and fuss.
Those lying, thieving Yankees, I hate 'em wuss and wuss.

I hate the Yankee nation and everything they do;
I hate the Declaration of Independence, too;
I hate the glorious Union, 'tis dripping with our blood;
I hate the striped banner, I fought it all I could.

I won't be reconstructed! I'm better now than them;
And for a carpetbagger, I don't give a damn;
So I'm off for the frontier, soon as I can go,
I'll prepare me a weapon and start for Mexico.

I can't take up my musket and fight them now no mo',
But I'm not goin' to love 'em, and that is certain sho';
And I don't want no pardon for what I was or am,
I won't be reconstructed and I don't give a damn.

INNES RANDOLPH.

IN the town of Athy one Jeremy Lanigan
 Battered away till he hadn't a pound,
His father he died and made him a man again,
 Left him a farm and ten acres of ground!
He gave a grand party to friends and relations
 Who hadn't forgot him when sent to the wall;
And if you'll just listen, I'll make your eyes glisten
 With the rows and the ructions of Lanigan's ball.

Myself, of course, got free invitations
 For all the nice boys and girls I'd ask,
And in less than a minute the friends and relations
 Were dancing away like bees round a cask.
Miss O'Hara, the nice little milliner,
 Tipped me the wink to give her a call,
And soon I arrived with Timothy Glenniher
 Just in time for Lanigan's ball.

There was lashins of punch and wine for the ladies,
 Potatoes and cakes and bacon and tay,
The Nolans and Doolans and all the O'Gradys
 Were courtin' the girls and dancin' away.
Songs there were as plenty as water,
 From 'The Harp that once thro' Tara's ould Hall',
To 'Sweet Nelly Gray' and 'The Ratcatcher's Daughter',
 All singing together at Lanigan's ball.

They were startin' all sorts of nonsensical dances,
 Turning around in a nate whirligig;
But Julia and I soon scattered their fancies,
 And tipped them the twist of a rale Irish jig.

438

LANIGAN'S BALL

Och Mavrone! 'twas she that was glad o' me:
    We danced till we thought the ceilin' would fall
(For I spent three weeks in Burke's Academy
    Learning a step for Lanigan's ball).

The boys were all merry, the girls were all hearty,
    Dancin' away in couples and groups,
When an accident happened—young Terence McCarty
    He put his right foot through Miss Halloran's hoops.
The creature she fainted, and cried 'Millia murther!'
    She called all her friends and gathered them all.
Ned Carmody swore he'd not stir a step further,
    But have satisfaction at Lanigan's ball.

In the midst of the row Miss Kerrigan fainted—
    Her cheeks all the while were as red as the rose—
Some of the ladies declared she was painted,
    She took a small drop of potheen, I suppose.
Her lover, Ned Morgan, so pow'rful and able,
    When he saw his dear colleen stretched out by the wall,
He tore the left leg from under the table,
    And smashed all the china at Lanigan's ball.

Oh, boys, there was the ructions—
    Myself got a lick from big Phelim McHugh,
But I soon replied to his kind introductions,
    And kicked up a terrible hullabaloo.
Old Shamus the piper had like to be strangled,
    They squeezed up his pipes, bellows, chanters, and all;
The girls in their ribbons they all got entangled,
    And that put an end to Lanigan's ball.

ANON.

OFTEN, when o'er tree and turret,
　Eve a dying radiance flings,
By that ancient pile I linger
　Known familiarly as 'King's'.
And the ghosts of days departed
　Rise, and in my burning breast
All the undergraduate wakens,
　And my spirit is at rest.

What, but a revolting fiction,
　Seems the actual result
Of the Census's enquiries
　Made upon the 15th ult.?
Still my soul is in its boyhood;
　Nor of year or changes recks,
Though my scalp is almost hairless,
　And my figure grows convex.

Backward moves the kindly dial;
　And I'm numbered once again
With those noblest of their species
　Called emphatically 'Men':
Loaf, as I have loafed aforetime,
　Through the streets, with tranquil mind,
And a long-backed fancy-mongrel
　Trailing casually behind:

Past the Senate-house I saunter,
　Whistling with an easy grace;
Past the cabbage-stalks that carpet
　Still the beefy market-place;

'HIC VIR, HIC EST'

Poising evermore the eye-glass
   In the light sarcastic eye,
Lest, by chance, some breezy nursemaid
   Pass, without a tribute, by.

Once, an unassuming Freshman,
   Through these wilds I wandered on,
Seeing in each house a College,
   Under every cap a Don:
Each perambulating infant
   Had a magic in its squall,
For my eager eye detected
   Senior Wranglers in them all.

By degrees my education
   Grew, and I became as others;
Learned to blunt my moral feelings
   By the aid of Bacon Brothers;
Bought me tiny boots of Mortlock,
   And colossal prints of Roe;
And ignored the proposition
   That both time and money go.

Learned to work the wary dogcart
   Artfully thro' King's Parade;
Dress, and steer a boat, and sport with
   Amaryllis in the shade:
Struck, at Brown's, the dashing hazard;
   Or (more curious sport than that)
Dropped, at Callaby's, the terrier
   Down upon the prisoned rat.

441

'HIC VIR, HIC EST'

I have stood serene on Fenner's
    Ground, indifferent to blisters,
While the Buttress of the period
    Bowled me his peculiar twisters:
Sung 'We won't go home till morning';
    Striven to part my backhair straight;
Drunk (not lavishly) of Miller's
    Old dry wines at 78/-:—

When within my veins the blood ran,
    And the curls were on my brow,
I did, oh ye undergraduates,
    Much as ye are doing now.
Wherefore bless ye, O beloved ones:—
    Now unto mine inn must I,
Your 'poor moralist', betake me,
    In my 'solitary fly'.

C. S. CALVERLEY.

244   *John Henry*

JOHN HENRY was a lil baby,
    Sittin' on his mama's knee,
Said: 'De Big Bend Tunnel on de C. & O. road
Gonna cause de death of me,
Lawd, lawd, gonna cause de death of me.'

Cap'n says to John Henry,
'Gonna bring me a steam drill 'round,
Gonna take dat steam drill out on de job,
Gonna whop dat steel on down,
Lawd, Lawd, gonna whop dat steel on down.

JOHN HENRY

John Henry tol' his cap'n,
Lightnin' was in his eye:
'Cap'n, bet yo' las' red cent on me,
Fo' I'll beat it to de bottom or I'll die,
Lawd, Lawd, I'll beat it to de bottom or I'll die.'

Sun shine hot an' burnin',
Wer'n't no breeze a-tall,
Sweat ran down like water down a hill,
Dat day John Henry let his hammer fall,
Lawd, Lawd, dat day John Henry let his hammer fall.

John Henry went to de tunnel,
An' dey put him in de lead to drive,
De rock so tall an' John Henry so small,
Dat he lied down his hammer an' he cried,
Lawd, Lawd, dat he lied down his hammer an' he cried.

John Henry started on de right hand,
De steam drill started on de lef'—
'Before I'd let dis steam drill beat me down,
I'd hammer my fool self to death,
Lawd, Lawd, I'd hammer my fool self to death.'

White man tol' John Henry,
'Nigger, damn yo' soul,
You might beat dis steam an' drill of mine,
When de rocks in dis mountain turn to gol',
Lawd, Lawd, when de rocks in dis mountain turn to gol'.'

John Henry said to his shaker,
'Nigger, why don' you sing?
I'm throwin' twelve poun's from my hips on down,
Jes' listen to de col' steel ring,
Lawd, Lawd, jes' listen to de col' steel ring.'

443

JOHN HENRY

Oh, de captain said to John Henry,
'I b'lieve this mountain's sinkin' in.'
John Henry said to his captain, oh my!
'Ain' nothin' but my hammer suckin' win',
Lawd, Lawd, ain' nothin' but my hammer suckin' win'.'

John Henry tol' his shaker,
'Shaker, you better pray,
For, if I miss dis six-foot steel,
Tomorrow'll be yo' buryin' day,
Lawd, Lawd, tomorrow'll be yo' buryin' day.'

John Henry tol' his captain,
'Look yonder what I see—
Yo' drill's done broke an' yo' hole's done choke,
An' you cain' drive steel like me,
Lawd, Lawd, an' you cain' drive steel like me.'

De man dat invented de steam drill,
Thought he was mighty fine.
John Henry drove his fifteen feet,
An' de steam drill only made nine,
Lawd, Lawd, an' de steam drill only made nine.

De hammer dat John Henry swung,
It weighed over nine pound;
He broke a rib in his lef'-han' side,
An' his intrels fell on de groun',
Lawd, Lawd, an' his intrels fell on de groun'.

All de womens in de Wes',
When dey heared of John Henry's death,
Stood in de rain, flagged de eas'-boun' train,
Goin' where John Henry fell dead,
Lawd, Lawd, goin' where John Henry fell dead.

John Henry's lil mother,
She was all dressed in red,
She jumped in bed, covered up her head,
Said she didn' know her son was dead,
Lawd, Lawd, didn' know her son was dead.

Dey took John Henry to de graveyard,
An' dey buried him in de san',
An' every locomotive come roarin' by,
Says, 'Dere lays a steel-drivin' man,
Lawd, Lawd, dere lays a steel-drivin' man.'

ANON.

245 *Stagolee*

STAGOLEE, he was a bad man, an' ev'body know,
He toted a stack-barreled blow gun an' a blue steel 44.

Way down in New Orlean', called de Lyon club,
Ev'y step you walkin', you walkin' in Billy Lyon blood.

It was early one mornin' when I heard my little dog bark,
Stagolee and Billy Lyon was arg'in in de dark.

Stagolee and Billy Lyon was gamblin' one night late,
Stagolee fell seven, Billy Lyon, he fell cotch eight.

Slowly Stack walked from de table, he said, 'I can't let you
go wid dat.
You will win all of my money an' my milk-white Stetson
hat.'

Stagolee, he went walkin' right down dat I.C. track,
'I ain' gonna hurt you now, Billy, bet' not be here when
I get back!'

445

GG

Next day Stack went runnin' in de red-hot broilin' sun,
'Look in my chiffro drawer, Alberta, han' me my smoke-
less 41.'

Alberta looked at Stack, said, 'Babe, you all out of breath,
You look like you gonna be de cause of somebody's death.'

Stack took out his Elgin, looked direc'ly at de time,
'I got an argument to settle wid dat bad man, Billy Lyon.'

'Kiss me, good woman, you may not see me when I come
back.'
And Stack went runnin' up dat Great Northern track.

Well, he got outside in front of de barroom, an' he eased
up to de door,
Billy Lyon had his 44 special, pacin' up an' down de floor.

Billy Lyon began to scream, 'Stack, don't take my life,
I've got five lil helpless chilluns an' one po' pitiful wife.'

He shot him three times in the forehead an' two times in de
side,
Said, 'I'm goin' keep on shootin' till Billy Lyon died.'

Billy Lyon got glassy, an' he gapped an' hung his head,
Stack say, 'I know by expression on his face dat Billy Lyon
dead.'

Mrs. Billy she went runnin' an' screamin': 'Stack, I don'
b'lieve it's so.
You an' my lil Billy been frien's since many long years
ago.'

Stagolee tol' Mrs. Billy, 'Ef you don't b'lieve yo' man is
dead,
Come to de barroom, see de hole I shot in his head.'

STAGOLEE

Mrs. Lyon fell to her knees, an' she said to her oldes' son,
'When you git lil bit bigger, gonna buy you a 41.'

'Mama, mama, oh, mama, you sho ain't talkin' to me,
He killed po' papa, now you gonna let him kill me.'

It was early one mornin', Stagolee looked at de clouds an'
   say,
'Baby, it look mighty cloudy, it mus' be my jedgment day.'

Chief Maloney tol' his deputies: 'Git yo' rifles an' come
   wid' me,
We got to arres' dat bad nigger, Stagolee.'

Oh, de deputies took dey shiny badges, an' dey laid em' on
   de shelf,
'Ef you wants dat nigger, go git him by yo' own damn self.'

Slowly Chief Maloney, he walked to de barroom door,
Po' Stagolee was drunk an' layin' on de barroom floor.

Chief Maloney said to de bartender, 'Who kin dat drunk
   man be?'
'Speak softly,' said de bartender. 'It's dat bad nigger
   Stagolee.'

Chief Maloney touch Stack on de shoulder, say, 'Stack,
   why don' you run?'
'I don't run, white folks, when I got my 41.'

Stagolee, he tried to get up, staggered, pulled his pistol,
   could not get it out;
Chief Maloney pulled his pistol, shot de po' boy in de
   mouth.

447

STAGOLEE

Stagolee he went runnin' an' stagg'in' down Dumaine
    Street,
Boy, don' you know de blood was runnin' from his head
    down to his feet.

De jedge, he found Stack guilty, de clerk he wrote it down,
Nex' col' winter mornin' Stack was Angola bound.

It was early one mornin', one bright summer day,
Chief Maloney 'ceived a wireless—Stack had runned
    away.

Chief Maloney got his men, an' he put dem roun' de town,
'Nex' time you see Stagolee, be sho' to shoot him down.'

   .   .   .   .

De hangman put de mask on, tied his han's behin' his back,
Sprung de trap on Stagolee, but his neck refused to crack.

Hangman, he got frightened, he said: 'Chief, you see how
    it be,
I cain' hang this man, you better let him go free.'

Chief Maloney said to de hangman, 'Befo' I'd let him go
    alive—'
He up wid his police special an' shot him six times in de
    side.

Al de mans dey shouted, but de womens put on black an'
    mourned
Dat de good man Stagolee has laid down, died, an' gone.

Dey come a-slippin' an' a-slidin' up an' down de street,
In deir big mother hubbards an' deir stockin' feet.

He had a three-hundred-dollar funeral and a thousand-
    dollar hearse,
Satisfaction undertaker put him six feet under earth.

448

When de devil wife see Stack comin' she got up in a
    quirl,—
'Here come dat bad nigger an' he's jus' from de udder
    worl'.'

All de devil' little chillun went sc'amblin' up de wall,
Say, 'Catch him, pappa, befo' he kill us all.'

Stack he tol' de devil, 'Come on, le's have a lil fun,
You stick me wid yo' pitchfork an' I'll shoot you wid my
    41.'

Stagolee say, 'Now, now, Mister Devil, ef me an' you
    gonna have some fun,
You play de cornet, Black Betty beat de drum.'

Stagolee took de pitchfork an' he laid it on de shelf—
'Stand back, Tom Devil, I'm gonna rule Hell by myself.'

ANON.

246   *Frankie and Johnny*

FRANKIE and Johnny were lovers.
    O my Gawd how they did love!
They swore to be true to each other,
As true as the stars above.
He was her man but he done her wrong.

Frankie and Johnny went walking,
Johnny in a brand new suit.
Frankie went walking with Johnny,
Said: 'O Gawd don't my Johnny look cute.'
He was her man but he done her wrong.

FRANKIE AND JOHNNY

Frankie went down to Memphis,
Went on the morning train,
Paid a hundred dollars,
Bought Johnny a watch and chain.
He was her man but he done her wrong.

Frankie lived in a crib-house,
Crib-house with only two doors,
Gave her money to Johnny,
He spent it on those parlour whores.
He was her man but he done her wrong.

Frankie went down to the hock-shop,
Went for a bucket of beer,
Said: 'O Mr. Bartender
Has my loving Johnny been here?
He is my man but he's doing me wrong.'

'I don't want to make you no trouble,
I don't want to tell you no lie,
But I saw Johnny an hour ago
With a girl name Nelly Bly.
He is your man but he's doing you wrong.'

Frankie went down to the hotel.
She didn't go there for fun,
'Cause underneath her kimona
She toted a 44 gun.
He was her man but he done her wrong.

Frankie went down to the hotel.
She rang the front-door bell,
Said: 'Stand back all you chippies
Or I'll blow you all to hell.
I want my man for he's doing me wrong.'

FRANKIE AND JOHNNY

Frankie looked in through the key-hole
And there before her eye
She saw her Johnny on the sofa
A-loving up Nelly Bly.
He was her man; he was doing her wrong.

Frankie threw back her kimona,
Took out a big 44,
Root-a-toot-toot, three times she shoot
Right through that hard-ware door.
He was her man but was doing her wrong.

Johnny grabbed up his Stetson,
Said; 'O my Gawd Frankie don't shoot.'
But Frankie pulled hard on the trigger
And the gun went root-a-toot-toot.
She shot her man who was doing her wrong.

'Roll me over easy,
Roll me over slow,
Roll me over on my right side
'Cause my left side hurts me so.
I was her man but I done her wrong.'

Johnny he was a gambler,
He gambled for the gain;
The very last words he ever said
Were—'High-low Jack and the game.'
He was her man but he done her wrong.

'Bring out your rubber-tired buggy,
Bring out your rubber-tired hack;
I'll take my Johnny to the graveyard
But I won't bring him back.
He was my man but he done me wrong.

FRANKIE AND JOHNNY

Lock me in that dungeon,
Lock me in that cell,
Lock me where the north-east wind
Blows from the corner of Hell.
I shot my man 'cause he done me wrong.'

Frankie went down to the Madame,
She went down on her knees.
'Forgive me Mrs. Halcombe,
Forgive me if you please
For shooting my man 'cause he done me wrong.'

'Forgive you Frankie darling,
Forgive you I never can,
Forgive you Frankie darling
For shooting your only man,
For he was your man though he done you wrong.'

It was not murder in the first degree,
It was not murder in the third.
A woman simply shot her man
As a hunter drops a bird.
She shot her man 'cause he done her wrong.

Frankie said to the Sheriff
'What do you think they'll do?'
The Sheriff said to Frankie
'It's the electric chair for you.
You shot your man 'cause he done you wrong.'

Frankie sat in the jail-house,
Had no electric fan,
Told her little sister:
'Don't you marry no sporting man.
I had a man but he done me wrong.'

FRANKIE AND JOHNNY

Frankie heard a rumbling,
Away down in the ground;
Maybe it was little Johnny
Where she had shot him down.
He was her man, but he done her wrong.

Once more I saw Frankie,
She was sitting in the chair
Waiting for to go and meet her God
With the sweat dripping out of her hair.
He was her man, but he done her wrong.

This story has no moral,
This story has no end,
This story only goes to show
That there ain't no good in men.
He was her man but he done her wrong.

ANON.

247   *Casey Jones*

COME all you rounders if you want to hear
    The story of a brave engineer;
Casey Jones was the hogger's name,
On a big eight-wheeler, boys, he won his fame.
Caller called Casey at half-past four,
He kissed his wife at the station door,
Mounted to the cabin with orders in his hand,
And took his farewell trip to the promised land.

    Casey Jones, he mounted to the cabin,
    Casey Jones, with his orders in his hand!
    Casey Jones, he mounted to the cabin,
    Took his farewell trip into the promised land.

CASEY JONES

Put in your water and shovel in your coal,
Put your head out the window, watch the drivers roll,
I'll run her till she leaves the rail,
'Cause we're eight hours late with the Western Mail!
He looked at his watch and his watch was slow,
Looked at the water and the water was low,
Turned to his fireboy and said,
'We'll get to 'Frisco, but we'll all be dead!'

(*Refrain*)

Casey pulled up Reno Hill,
Tooted for the crossing with an awful shrill,
Snakes all knew by the engine's moans
That the hogger at the throttle was Casey Jones.
He pulled up short two miles from the place,
Number Four stared him right in the face,
Turned to his fireboy, said 'You'd better jump,
'Cause there's two locomotives going to bump!'

(*Refrain*)

Casey said, just before he died,
'There's two more roads I'd like to ride.'
Fireboy said, 'What can they be?'
'The Rio Grande and the Old S.P.'
Mrs. Jones sat on her bed a-sighing,
Got a pink that Casey was dying,
Said, 'Go to bed, children; hush your crying,
'Cause you'll get another papa on the Salt Lake line.'

Casey Jones! Got another papa!
Casey Jones, on the Salt Lake Line!
Casey Jones! Got another papa!
Got another papa on the Salt Lake Line!

ANON.

WHEN I was a bachelor, I lived by myself
    And I worked at the weaver's trade;
The only, only thing that I ever did wrong
Was to woo a fair young maid.
I wooed her in the winter time,
And in the summer too;
And the only, only thing that I ever did wrong
Was to keep her from the foggy, foggy dew.

One night she came to my bedside
Where I lay fast asleep;
She laid her head upon my bed,
And then began to weep.
She sighed, she cried, she damn near died,
She said—'What shall I do?'—
So I hauled her into bed and I covered up her head,
Just to save her from the foggy, foggy dew.

Oh, I am a bachelor, I live with my son,
And we work at the weaver's trade;
And every, every time that I look into his eyes,
He reminds me of that maid.
He reminds me of the winter time,
And of the summer too;
And the many, many times that I held her in my arms,
Just to keep her from the foggy, foggy dew.

ANON.

I N winter, when the fields are white,
 I sing this song for your delight—

   *   *   *

In spring, when woods are getting green,
I'll try and tell you what I mean.

   *   *   *

In summer, when the days are long,
Perhaps you'll understand the song:

In autumn, when the leaves are brown,
Take pen and ink, and write it down.

   *   *   *

I sent a message to the fish:
I told them 'This is what I wish.'

The little fishes of the sea
They sent an answer back to me.

The little fishes' answer was
'We cannot do it, Sir, because——'

   *   *   *

I sent to them again to say
'It will be better to obey.'

The fishes answered with a grin
'Why, what a temper you are in!'

I told them once, I told them twice:
They would not listen to advice.

I took a kettle large and new,
Fit for the deed I had to do.

My heart went hop, my heart went thump;
I filled the kettle at the pump.

Then some one came to me and said
'The little fishes are in bed.'

I said to him, I said it plain,
'Then you must wake them up again'.

I said it very loud and clear;
I went and shouted in his ear.

     *   *   *

But he was very stiff and proud;
He said 'You needn't shout so loud!'

And he was very proud and stiff;
He said 'I'd go and wake them, if——'

I took a corkscrew from the shelf:
I went to wake them up myself.

And when I found the door was locked,
I pulled and pushed and kicked and knocked.

And when I found the door was shut
I tried to turn the handle, but——

CHARLES LUTWIDGE DODGSON (LEWIS CARROLL).

250   *Evidence Read at the Trial of the*
Knave of Hearts

THEY told me you had been to her,
   And mentioned me to him:
She gave me a good character,
   But said I could not swim.

He sent them word I had not gone,
    (We know it to be true:)
If she should push the matter on,
    What would become of you?

I gave her one, they gave him two,
    You gave us three or more;
They all returned from him to you,
    Though they were mine before.

If I or she should chance to be
    Involved in this affair,
He trusts to you to set them free,
    Exactly as we were.

My notion was that you had been
    (Before she had this fit)
An obstacle that came between
    Him, and ourselves, and it.

Don't let him know she liked them best,
    For this must ever be
A secret, kept from all the rest,
    Between yourself and me.

CHARLES LUTWIDGE DODGSON (LEWIS CARROLL).

251   *Little Birds are playing*

LITTLE Birds are playing
    Bagpipes on the shore,
      Where the tourists snore:
'Thanks!' they cry. ' 'Tis thrilling!
Take, oh, take, this shilling!
      Let us have no more!'

LITTLE BIRDS ARE PLAYING

Little Birds are bathing
    Crocodiles in cream,
    Like a happy dream:
Like, but not so lasting—
Crocodiles, when fasting,
    Are not all they seem!

Little Birds are choking
    Baronets with bun,
    Taught to fire a gun:
Taught, I say, to splinter
Salmon in the winter—
    Merely for the fun.

Little Birds are hiding
    Crimes in carpet-bags,
    Blessed by happy stags:
Blessed, I say, though beaten—
Since our friends are eaten
    When the memory flags.

Little Birds are tasting
    Gratitude and gold,
    Pale with sudden cold;
Pale, I say, and wrinkled—
When the bells have tinkled,
    And the Tale is told.

CHARLES LUTWIDGE DODGSON (LEWIS CARROLL).

252   *This Train*

THIS train is bound for glory, this train,
  This train is bound for glory, this train,
This train is bound for glory,
If you ride in it, you must be holy, this train.

THIS TRAIN

This train don' pull no extras, this train,
Don' pull nothin' but de Midnight Special.

This train don' pull no sleepers, this train,
Don' pull nothin' but the righteous people, this train.

This train don' pull no jokers, this train,
Neither don' pull no cigar smokers, this train.

This train is bound for glory, this train.
If you ride in it, you mus' be holy, this train.   ANON.

253   *Hell and Heaven*

Chorus

I been 'buked an' I been scorned,
Childrens, I been 'buked an' I been scorned,
Childrens, I been 'buked an' I been scorned,
I been talked 'bout sure as you're born.

I met ol' Satan on the way,
I met ol' Satan on the way,
I met ol' Satan on the way,
He says, 'Young man, you're too young to pray.'

Ef you want to see ol' Satan run,
Jes' fire off dat gospel gun.

Ol' Satan wears a mighty big shoe,
Ef you don' watch, gwine slip it on you.

Ol' Satan's like a snake in de grass,
Always in some Christian's pass.

What's ol' Satan grumblin' about?
He's in hell and he cain't get out.

Ol' Satan's mad, an' I am glad,
He missed de soul he thought he had.

460

HELL AND HEAVEN

Ol' Satan's like an ol' greyhoun',
Runnin' dem sinners roun' an' roun'.

Ol' Satan's a-settin' on a red-hot seat,
A-coolin' of his head an' a-warmin' of his feet.

I'd rather pray myself away,
Dan live an' burn in hell one day.

Oh, hell is deep an' hell is wide,
Oh, hell ain' got no bottom or side.

.   .   .   .

Two milk-white hosses, side by side,
Me an' Jesus gwinter take a ride.

King Jesus give me a little broom,
Jes' fer to sweep my heart clean.

What kin' o' shoes does de angels wear?
Don' wear none, case dey walks on de air.

One o' dese mornin's bright an' fair,
Gwinter hitch my wings an' try de air.

When I gits to heaven, got nothin' to do
But fly aroun' an' sing hallelu.

Away up in heaven where I'm gwinter shout,
Nobody dere to put me out.

I haven' been to heaven, but I've been tol',
De streets in heaven are paved in gol'.

I want to go to heaven at my own expense,
Ef I cain' git through the gate, I'll jump de fence.

When I go to heaven, I want to go right,
I want to go to heaven all dressed in white.

When I git to heaven, gwinter take my stan',
Gwinter wrastle wid my Lawd like a nachul man.

When I git to heaven, gwinter sit an' tell,
Tell dem angels ring dem bells.

When I git to heaven, gwinter be at ease,
Me an' my God's gwinter do as we please! ANON.

254 *Dese Bones Gwine to Rise Again*

DE Lord he thought he'd make a man—
   Dese bones gwine to rise again;
Made him out-a dirt an' a little bit o' sand—
Dese bones gwine to rise again.

Refrain
   I know it, 'deed I know it,
   Dese bones gwine to rise again.

Adam was de fust he made—
He put him on de bank and lay him in de shade—

Thought He'd make a 'ooman, too—
Didn't know 'xactly what to do—

Took a rib from Adam's side—
Made Miss Eve for to be his bride—

Put 'em in a gyarden, rich and fair—
Tol' 'em dey might eat whatever wuz dere—

But to one tree dey mus' not go—
Mus' leave de apples dere to grow—

Ol' Miss Eve come walkin' round—
Spied a tree all loaded down—

DESE BONES GWINE TO RISE AGAIN

Sarpint quoiled around a chunk—
At Miss Eve his eye he wunk—

Firs' she took a little pull—
Den she fill her apron full—

Den Adam took a little slice—
Smack his lips an' say 'twas nice—

De Lord he come a-wanderin' roun'—
Spied dem peelin's on de groun'—

De Lord he speaks wid a monstrus voice—
Shuck dis ol' worl' to its ve'y joists—

'Adam, Adam, where art thou?'
'Heah, Marse Lord, Ise a-comin' now.'

'Stole my apples, I believe?'
'No, Marse Lord, but I spec' it wuz Eve.'

De Lord he riz up in his wrath—
Told 'em, 'Yo' beat it down de path.'

'Out o' dis gyarden you mus' git.
'Earn yo' living by yo' sweat.'

He put an angel at de do'—
Tol' 'em not to never come dere no mo'—

Ob dis tale dere ain' no mo'—
Dese bones gwine to rise again.
Eve eat de apple, gib Adam de co'—
Dese bones gwine to rise again.

Refrain

    I know it, 'deed I know it,
    Dese bones gwine to rise again.   ANON.

EF I had wings like Noah's dove,
I'd fly up the river to the man I love.
Fare thee well, O Honey, fare thee well.

Ise got a man, an' he's long and tall,
Moves his body like a cannon ball.
Fare thee well, O Honey, fare thee well.

One o' dese days, an' it won't be long,
Call my name an' I'll be gone.
Fare thee well, O Honey, fare thee well.

'Member one night, a-drizzlin' rain,
Roun' my heart I felt a pain.
Fare thee well, O Honey, fare thee well.

When I wo' my ap'ons low,
Couldn't keep you from my do'.
Fare thee well, O Honey, fare thee well.

Now I wears my ap'ons high,
Sca'cely ever see you passin' by.
Fare thee well, O Honey, fare thee well.

Now my ap'on 's up to my chin,
You pass my do' an' you won' come in.
Fare thee well, O Honey, fare thee well.

Ef I had listened to whut my mama said,
I'd be at home in my mama's bed.
Fare thee well, O Honey, fare thee well.

ANON.

OF all the pleasant ways
    To pass an afternoon,
Is in a pony chaise
One sultry day in June.
To drive between the trees
In Hyde Park round and round,
It brings a pleasant sense of ease
In spinning o'er the ground.
The men raise hats to me,
I mean, the men I know,
They smile, kiss hands, then laugh to see
The flying pony go.
And then I come in sight
Of one against the rails
Whose handsome face lights up so bright
As he my presence hails.

Driving in the Park,
Driving in the Park;
Love may haunt the drive,
And no one ever mark.
Glances meet with joy,
Alighting with love's spark.
Sweet one. Naughty boy.
Driving in the Park.

And very nice it seems
Among the beats I know,
When early sunlight gleams,
To gallop round the Row.

At ten some breezy morn
All care away I fling,
Luxurious days of rest I scorn,
The gallop is the thing.
I challenge all my friends
To run a race with me,
And when the madcap scamper ends,
The blood flows fresh and free.
And nicer yet to walk
The horse while some one near
Engages me with tender talk,
So very sweet to hear.

Riding in the Park,
Riding in the Park;
Love may haunt the Row
And no one ever mark.
Love may bend his bow,
Make two hearts his mark,
No one ever know—
Riding in the Park.

ANON.

257 *Tarpauling Jacket*

I AM a young jolly brisk sailor,
  Delights in all manner of sport,
When I'm in liquor I'm mellow,
  The girls I then merrily court.
But love is surrounded with trouble,
  And puts such strange thoughts in my head,
Is it not a terrible story,
  That love it should strike me stone dead?

Here's a health to my friends and acquaintance,
    When death for me it doth come,
And let them behave in their station
    And send me a cask of good rum,
Let it be good royal stingo,
    With three barrels of beer,
To make my friends the more welcome
    When they meet me at derry down fair.

Let there be six sailors to carry me,
    Let them be damnable drunk,
And as they are going to bury me,
    Let them fall down with my trunk.
Let there be no sighing and sobbing,
    But one single favour I crave,
Take me up in a tarpauling jacket,
    And fiddle and dance to my grave.

ANON.

258 *The Dream*

LAST night I supped on lobster; it nearly drove me mad
For when at last I got to sleep a funny dream I had.

I dreamed the famous Albert Hall was turned into a pub,
And there was held a sort of Philharmonic club.
With poets, painters, politicians, famous statesmen too,
With actors, authors, clergymen, and ladies not a few.

Chorus
    For everyone of them had to sing; if anyone said: 'I've
    a cold,'
    'Sing or settle for drinks all round', they very soon were
    told.

THE DREAM

The Prince of Wales was chairman, and of course he
    opened the Ball
And sang the chorus of every song at the concert in
    Albert Hall.

When Princess Beatrice rose to sing, with cheers the
        building rang;
'I'll never never marry if he's got no cash,' she sang.
Then Henry, Prince of Battenberg, got up and made a
    bow
And sang in sweet harmonic tones: 'I'm living with
    mother now.'

Chorus

For everyone of them had to sing; if anyone said: 'I've
    a cold,'
'Sing or settle for drinks all round,' they very soon were
    told.
The Prince of Wales was chairman, and of course he
    opened the Ball
And sang the chorus of every song at the concert in
    Albert Hall.

Then Dizzy sang God save the Queen, but Parnell hissed
        him down,
And Mr. Gladstone tried to sing The Harp without a
    Crown.
But Chamberlain soon shut him up, for he sang: 'Not for
    Joe;'
While Henry Churchill warbled: 'Is it likely? O dear
    no.'

468

THE DREAM

Chorus

    For everyone of them had to sing; if anyone said: 'I've
      a cold,'

    'Sing or settle for drinks all round,' they very soon were
      told.

    The Prince of Wales was chairman, and of course he
      opened the Ball

    And sang the chorus of every song at the concert in
      Albert Hall.

ANON.

259   *Nursery Rhymes*

I

IF you don't like my apples,
  Then don't shake my tree;
I'm not after your boy friend,
He's after me.

II

Judge, judge, tell the judge
Mamma has a baby.
It's a boy, full of joy,
Papa's going crazy.
Wrap it up in tissue paper,
Send it down the elevator.
How many pounds did it weigh?
One, two, three, &c.

III

I asked my mother for fifty cents
To see the elephant jump the fence;

He jumped so high
He reached the sky,
And never came back till the Fourth of July.

IV

Yellow-belly, yellow-belly, come and take a swim;
Yes, by golly, when the tide comes in.

ANON.

260   *Darky Sunday School*

JONAH was an immigrant, so runs the Bible tale,
  He took a steerage passage in a transatlantic whale;
Now, Jonah in the belly of the whale was quite compressed,
  So Jonah pressed the button, and the whale he did the
    rest.

Chorus

Young folks, old folks, everybody come,
Join our darky Sunday School, and make yourself to
  hum.
There's a place to check your chewing gum and razors
  at the door,
And hear such Bible stories as you never heard before.

Adam was the first man that ever was invented.
  He lived all his life and he never was contented;
He was made out of mud in the days gone by
  And hung on the fence in the sun to get him dry.

The good book says Cain killed his brother Abel,
  He hit him on the head with a leg of a table.
Then along came Jonah in the belly of the whale,
  The first submarine boat that ever did sail.

470

DARKY SUNDAY SCHOOL

Esau was a cowboy of the wild and woolly make,
  Half the farm belonged to him and half to Brother
  Jake;
Now, Esau thought his title to the farm was none too clear,
  So he sold it to his brother for a sandwich and a beer.

Noah was a mariner who sailed around the sea,
  With half a dozen wives and a big menagerie;
He failed the first season when it rained for forty days,
  For in that sort of weather no circus ever pays.

Elijah was a prophet who attended country fairs,
  He advertised his business with a pair of dancing bears;
He held a sale of prophecies most every afternoon,
  And went up in the evening in a painted fire balloon.

Then down came Peter, the Keeper of the Gates,
  He came down cheap on excursion rates.
Then along came Noah a-stumblin' in the dark,
  He found a hatchet and some nails and built himself an
  ark.

David was a shepherd and a scrappy little cuss,
  Along came Goliath, just a-spoilin' for a muss;
Now, David didn't want to fight, but thought he must or
  bust,
  So he cotched up a cobblestone and busted in his crust.

Ahab had a wife, and her name was Jezebel;
  She went out in the vineyard to hang the clothes and fell.
She's gone to the dogs, the people told the king,
  Ahab said he'd never heard of such an awful thing.

Samson was a strong man of the John L. Sullivan school,
  He slew ten thousand Philistines with the jawbone of a
    mule.
But Delilah captured him and filled him full of gin,
  Slashed off his hair and the coppers run him in.

Samson was a husky guy as every one should know,
  He used to lift five hundred pounds as strong man in his
    show.
One week the bill was rotten, all the actors had a souse,
  But the strong-man act of Samson's, it just brought
    down the house.

Salome was a chorus girl who had a winning way,
  She was the star attraction in King Herod's Cabaret.
Although you can hardly say discretion was her rule,
  She's the favourite Bible figure in the Gertrude Hoff-
    man school.

There are plenty of these Bible tales. I'll tell you one to-
    morrow
  How Lot, his wife and family fled from Sodom and
    Gomorrah;
But his wife she turned to rubber and got stuck upon the
    spot,
  And became a salty monument and missed a happy Lot.

Now Joey was unhappy in the bowels of the soil,
  He lost his pretty rainbow coat because he wouldn't
    toil.
He hollered, howled, and bellowed until far into the night,
  But of course you couldn't see him, for he was out of
    sight.

It happened that a caravan was passing by the place,
　　Laden down with frankincense and imitation lace.
They heard the Sheeney yelling and pulled him from the
　　well,
　　If this ain't a proper ending, then you can go to Hell.
ANON.

261　　　　　　　*I wish I were*

I WISH I were a
　Elephantiaphus
And could pick off the coconuts with my nose
But, oh! I am not,
(Alas! I cannot be)
An Elephanti-
Elephantiaphus.
But I'm a cockroach
And I'm a water-bug,
I can crawl around and hide behind the sink.

I wish I were a
Rhinoscerèeacus
And could wear an ivory toothpick in my nose.
But, oh! I am not,
(Alas! I cannot be)
A Rhinoscōri-
Rhinoscerèeacus.
But I'm a beetle
And I'm a pumpkin-bug,
I can buzz and bang my head against the wall.

I wish I were a
Hippopōpotamus
And could swim the Tigris and the broad Gangès.

473

But, oh! I am not,
(Alas! I cannot be)
A hippopōpo-
Hippopōpotamus.
But I'm a grasshopper
And I'm a katydid,
I can play the fiddle with my left hind-leg.

I wish I were a
Levileviathan
And had seven hundred knuckles in my spine.
But, oh! I am not,
(Alas! I cannot be)
A Levi-ikey-
A Levi-ikey-mo.
But I'm a firefly
And I'm a lightning-bug,
I can light cheroots and gaspers with my tail.   Anon.

262   *O God! O Montreal!*

STOWED away in a Montreal lumber room
The Discobolus standeth and turneth his face to the
    wall;
Dusty, cobweb-covered, maimed and set at naught,
Beauty lieth in an attic and no man regardeth:
                O God! O Montreal!

Beautiful by night and day, beautiful in summer and
    winter,
Whole or maimed, always and alike beautiful—
He preacheth gospel of grace to the skins of owls
And to one who seasoneth the skins of Canadian owls;
                O God! O Montreal!

O GOD! O MONTREAL!

When I saw him I was wroth and I said, 'O Discobolus!
Beautiful Discobolus, a Prince both among Gods and men,
What doest thou here, how camest thou hither, Discobolus,
Preaching gospel in vain to the skins of owls?'
                              O God! O Montreal!

And I turned to the man of skins and said unto him, 'O
        thou man of skins,
Wherefore hast thou done thus to shame the beauty of the
        Discobolus?'
But the Lord had hardened the heart of the man of skins,
And he answered, 'My brother-in-law is haberdasher to
        Mr. Spurgeon.'
                              O God! O Montreal!

'The Discobolus is put here because he is vulgar,
He has neither vest nor pants with which to cover his limbs;
I, Sir, am a person of most respectable connections—
My brother-in-law is haberdasher to Mr. Spurgeon.'
                              O God! O Montreal!

Then I said, 'O brother-in-law to Mr. Spurgeon's haber-
        dasher,
Who seasonest also the skins of Canadian owls,
Thou callest trousers "pants", whereas I call them
        "trousers",
Therefore, thou art in hell-fire and may the Lord pity
        thee!'
                              O God! O Montreal!

'Preferrest thou the gospel of Montreal to the gospel of
        Hellas,
The gospel of thy connection with Mr. Spurgeon's haber-
        dashery to the gospel of the Discobolus?'

                                                    475

O GOD! O MONTREAL!

Yet none the less blasphemed he beauty saying, 'The Disco-
     bolus hath no gospel,
But my brother-in-law is haberdasher to Mr. Spurgeon.
               O God! O Montreal!

SAMUEL BUTLER.

263   *Poor but Honest*

SHE was poor, but she was honest,
     Victim of the squire's whim:
First he loved her, then he left her,
     And she lost her honest name.

Then she ran away to London,
     For to hide her grief and shame;
There she met another squire,
     And she lost her name again.

See her riding in her carriage,
     In the Park and all so gay:
All the nibs and nobby persons
     Come to pass the time of day.

See the little old-world village
     Where her aged parents live,
Drinking the champagne she sends them;
     But they never can forgive.

In the rich man's arms she flutters,
     Like a bird with broken wing:
First he loved her, then he left her,
     And she hasn't got a ring.

See him in the splendid mansion,
     Entertaining with the best,
While the girl that he has ruined,
     Entertains a sordid guest.

See him in the House of Commons,
    Making laws to put down crime,
While the victim of his passions
    Trails her way through mud and slime.

Standing on the bridge at midnight,
    She says : 'Farewell, blighted Love.'
There 's a scream, a splash—Good Heavens !
    What is she a-doing of ?

Then they drag her from the river,
    Water from her clothes they wrang,
For they thought that she was drownded ;
    But the corpse got up and sang :

'It 's the same the whole world over ;
    It 's the poor that gets the blame,
It 's the rich that get the pleasure.
    Isn't it a blooming shame ?'   ANON.

264 *Penal Servitude for Mrs. Maybrick*

SHE WILL NOT HAVE TO CLIMB GOLDEN STAIRS

THE Maybrick trial is over now, there 's been a lot of
    jaw,
Of doctors' contradiction, and expounding of the law ;
She had Sir Charles Russell to defend her as we know,
    But tho' he tried his very best it all turned out no go.

Chorus
    But Mrs. Maybrick will not have to climb the golden
        stairs ;
    Tho' the Jury 's found her guilty and she nearly said
        her prayers ;

477

II

PENAL SERVITUDE FOR MRS. MAYBRICK

She's at another kind of mashing and at it she must stop,
  Old Berry he's took down a peg with his big long
    drop.

Now at the trial the doctors had a very gay old time,
  They all told different stories about this cruel crime;
Some said that Mr. Maybrick to death had dosed himself,
  While others said it was his wife that put him on the shelf.

Then came the servants' story how the flypapers were
    found,
  In fact it seems the missis had arsenic all around,
In food and drink of every kind, in cupboard and in box,
  In handkerchiefs, and even in the pockets of her frocks.

Next came the waiter's story about her trip to town,
  Which proved that from the virtue of a wife she had fell
    down,
And when a woman like her from her husband goes astray,
  It plainly shows she wishes that he was out of the way.

Then came the fatal letter that fairly cooked her goose,
  It seemed to say to Brierly that she soon meant to be
    loose;
And tho' she made a statement to explain it all away,
  The Jury wouldn't have it, you are guilty they did say.

Then to each gay and flighty wife may this a warning be,
  Don't write to any other man or sit upon his knee;
When once you start like Mrs. Maybrick perhaps you
    couldn't stop,
  So stick close to your husband and keep clear of Berry's
    drop.

ANON.

IT doesn't always do to let a mug know everything.
   Can't you rumble? I can.
   Look at Charlie Piecan.
He's a bloke as happy as the birds upon the wing.
   Charlie don't believe in
   Worrying and grieving.
He gave me half a quid a day or two ago, to back a horse.
   The gee-gee came in last of course.
He doesn't grumble but takes his beating like a don.
He little thinks that I forgot to put the money on.

Chorus

   I haven't told him, not up to now,
   And if I did, most likely it would only cause a row.
   He doesn't know.   I don't see any reason why he
     should.
   He wouldn't be any the happier if he did, so what's the
     good?

I used to think my sister would be left upon the shelf.
   So just as a finale,
   I hitched her on to Charlie.
I told him to look after her and keep her for himself.
   Nothing could be nicer;
   Charlie's going to splice her.
She's been and told him that she's only twenty-three. As
     I'm alive,
   She's getting on for forty-five.
And though he's always taking Liza for a walk,
He hasn't found that one of her legs is only made of cork.

> I haven't told him, not up to now,
> And if I did, most likely it would only cause a row.
> He doesn't know. I don't see any reason why he should.
> He wouldn't be any the happier if he did, so what 's the
>   good?   F. Murray and F. Leigh.

266   *Nightmare*

WHEN you're lying awake with a dismal headache,
    and repose is taboo'd by anxiety,
I conceive you may use any language you choose to indulge
    in, without impropriety;
For your brain is on fire—the bedclothes conspire of usual
    slumber to plunder you:
First your counterpane goes, and uncovers your toes, and
    your sheet slips demurely from under you;
Then the blanketing tickles—you feel like mixed pickles—
    so terribly sharp is the pricking,
And you're hot, and you're cross, and you tumble and toss
    till there 's nothing 'twixt you and the ticking.
Then the bedclothes all creep to the ground in a heap, and
    you pick 'em all up in a tangle;
Next your pillow resigns and politely declines to remain at
    its usual angle!
Well, you get some repose in the form of a doze, with hot
    eye-balls and head ever aching,
But your slumbering teems with such horrible dreams that
    you'd very much better be waking;
For you dream you are crossing the Channel, and tossing
    about in a steamer from Harwich—
Which is something between a large bathing machine and
    a very small second-class carriage—

NIGHTMARE

And you're giving a treat (penny ice and cold meat) to a
      party of friends and relations—
They're a ravenous horde—and they all came on board at
      Sloane Square and South Kensington Stations.
And bound on that journey you find your attorney (who
      started that morning from Devon);
He's a bit undersized, and you don't feel surprised when
      he tells you he's only eleven.
Well, you're driving like mad with this singular lad (by-
      the-bye the ship's now a four-wheeler),
And you're playing round games, and he calls you bad
      names when you tell him that 'ties pay the dealer';
But this you can't stand, so you throw up your hand, and
      you find you're as cold as an icicle,
In your shirt and your socks (the black silk with gold
      clocks), crossing Salisbury Plain on a bicycle:
And he and the crew are on bicycles too—which they've
      somehow or other invested in—
And he's telling the tars, all the particu*lars* of a company
      he's interested in—
It's a scheme of devices, to get at low prices, all goods from
      cough mixtures to cables
(Which tickled the sailors) by treating retailers, as though
      they were all vege*t*ables—
You get a good spadesman to plant a small tradesman, (first
      take off his boots with a boot-tree),
And his legs will take root, and his fingers will shoot, and
      they'll blossom and bud like a fruit-tree—
From the greengrocer tree you get grapes and green pea,
      cauliflower, pineapple, and cranberries,
While the pastrycook plant, cherry brandy will grant,
      apple puffs, and three-corners, and banberries—

The shares are a penny, and ever so many are taken by
    Rothschild and Baring,
And just as a few are allotted to you, you awake with a
    shudder despairing—
You're a regular wreck, with a crick in your neck, and no
    wonder you snore, for your head's on the floor, and
    you've needles and pins from your soles to your shins,
    and your flesh is a-creep for your left leg's asleep, and
    you've cramp in your toes, and a fly on your nose, and
    some fluff in your lung, and a feverish tongue, and a
    thirst that's intense, and a general sense that you
    haven't been sleeping in clover;
But the darkness has passed, and it's daylight at last, and
    the night has been long—ditto ditto my song—and
    thank goodness they're both of them over!

                          WILLIAM SCHWENCK GILBERT.

267   *Waiting both*

    A STAR looks down at me,
        And says: 'Here I and you
    Stand each in our degree:
    What do you mean to do,—
        Mean to do?'

    I say: 'For all I know,
    Wait, and let Time go by,
    Till my change come.'—'Just so,'
    The star says: 'So mean I:—
        So mean I.'

                          THOMAS HARDY.

ON THE COMPLETION OF THEIR LEXICON

(*Written after the death of Liddell in 1898. Scott had
died some ten years earlier*)

'WELL, though it seems
　　　Beyond our dreams,'
Said Liddell to Scott,
'We've really got
To the very end,
All inked and penned
Blotless and fair
Without turning a hair,
This sultry summer day, A.D.
Eighteen hundred and forty-three.

'I've often, I own,
　Belched many a moan
　　At undertaking it,
　　And dreamt forsaking it.
　　—Yes, on to Pi,
　　When the end loomed nigh,
And friends said: "You've as good as done,"
I almost wished we'd not begun.
Even now, if people only knew
My sinkings, as we slowly drew
Along through Kappa, Lambda, Mu,
They'd be concerned at my misgiving,
And how I mused on a College living
　　Right down to Sigma,
　　But feared a stigma

483

If I succumbed, and left old Donnegan
For weary freshmen's eyes to con again:
And how I often, often wondered
What could have led me to have blundered
So far away from sound theology
To dialects and etymology;
Words, accents not to be breathed by men
Of any country ever again!'

  'My heart most failed,
  Indeed, quite quailed,'
  Said Scott to Liddell,
  'Long ere the middle! . . .
  'Twas one wet dawn
  When, slippers on,
  And a cold in the head anew,
  Gazing at Delta
  I turned and felt a
  Wish for bed anew,
  And to let supersedings
  Of Passow's readings
  In dialects go.
  "That German has read
  More than we!" I said;
Yea, several times did I feel so! . . .

'O that first morning, smiling bland,
With sheets of foolscap, quills in hand,
To write ἀάατος and ἀαγής,
Followed by fifteen hundred pages,
  What nerve was ours
  So to back our powers,

Assured that we should reach ὠώδης
While there was breath left in our bodies!'

Liddell replied: 'Well, that's past now;
The job's done, thank God, anyhow.'

'And yet it 's not,'
Considered Scott,
'For we've to get
Subscribers yet
We must remember;
Yes; by September.'

'O Lord; dismiss that. We'll succeed.
Dinner is my immediate need.
I feel as hollow as a fiddle,
Working so many hours,' said Liddell.

THOMAS HARDY.

269   *Poor Poll*

I SAW it all, Polly, how when you had call'd for sop
    and your good friend the cook came & fill'd up your pan
you yerk'd it out deftly by beakfuls scattering it
away far as you might upon the sunny lawn
then summon'd with loud cry the little garden birds
to take their feast. Quickly came they flustering around
Ruddock & Merle & Finch squabbling among themselves
nor gave you thanks nor heed while you sat silently
watching, and I beside you in perplexity
lost in the maze of all mystery and all knowledge
felt how deep lieth the fount of man's benevolence
if a bird can share it & take pleasure in it.

485

POOR POLL

If you, my bird, I thought, had a philosophy
it might be a sounder scheme than what our moralists
propound: because thou, Poll, livest ín the darkness
which human Reason searching from outside would pierce,
but, being of so feeble a candle-power, can only
show up to view the cloud that it illuminates.
Thus reason'd I: then marvell'd how you can adapt
your wild bird-mood to endure your tame environment
the domesticities of English household life
and your small brass-wire cabin, who sh^{dst} live on wing
harrying the tropical branch-flowering wilderness:
Yet Nature gave you a gift of easy mimicry
whereby you have come to win uncanny sympathies
and morsell'd utterance of our Germanic talk
as schoolmasters in Greek will flaunt their hackney'd tags
φωνᾶντα συνετοῖσιν and κτῆμα ἐς ἀεὶ
ἡ γλῶσσ᾽ ὀμώμοχ᾽, ἡ δὲ φρὴν ἀνώμοτος
tho' you with a better ear copy ús more perfectly
nor without connotation as when you call'd for sop
all with that stumpy wooden tongue & vicious beak
that dry whistling shrieking tearing cutting pincer
now eagerly subservient to your cautious claws
exploring all varieties of attitude
in irrepressible blind groping for escape
—a very figure & image of man's soul on earth
the almighty cosmic Will fidgeting in a trap—
in your quenchless unknown desire for the unknown life
of which some homely British sailor robb'd you, alas!
'Tis all that doth your silly thoughts so busy keep
the while you sit moping like Patience on a perch
—*Wie viele Tag᾽ und Nächte bist du geblieben!*
La possa delle gambe posta in tregue—

POOR POLL

the impeccable spruceness of your grey-feather'd poll
a model in hairdressing for the dandiest old Duke
enough to qualify you for the House of Lords
or the Athenaeum Club, to poke among the nobs
great intellectual nobs and literary nobs
scientific nobs and Bishops *ex officio*:
nor lack you simulation of profoundest wisdom
such as men's features oft acquire in very old age
by mere cooling of passion & decay of muscle
by faint renunciation even of untold regrets;
who seeing themselves a picture of that wh: man should-be
learn almost what it were to be what they are-not.
But you can never have cherish'd a determined hope
consciously to renounce or lose it, you will live
your threescore years & ten idle and puzzle-headed
as any mumping monk in his unfurnish'd cell
in peace that, poor Polly, passeth Understanding—
merely because you lack what we men understand
by Understanding. Well! well! that's the difference
C'est la seule différence, mais c'est important.
Ah! your pale sedentary life! but would you change?
exchange it for one crowded hour of glorious life,
one blind furious tussle with a madden'd monkey
who would throttle you and throw your crude fragments
     away
shreds unintelligible of an unmeaning act
dans la profonde horreur de l'éternelle nuit?
Why ask? You cannot know. 'Twas by no choice of yours
that you mischanged for monkeys' man's society,
'twas that British sailor drove you from Paradise—
Εἴθ᾽ ὤφελ᾽ Ἀργοῦς μὴ διαπτάσθαι σκάφος!
I'd hold embargoes on such ghastly traffic.

POOR POLL

I am writing verses to you & grieve that you sh^d be
absolument incapable de les comprendre,
Tu, Polle, nescis ista nec potes scire:—
Alas! Iambic, scazon and alexandrine,
spondee or choriamb, all is alike to you—
my well-continued fanciful experiment
wherein so many strange verses amalgamate
on the secure bedrock of Milton's prosody:
not but that when I speak you will incline an ear
in critical attention lest by chánce I míght
póssibly say sómething that was worth repeating:
I am adding (do you think?) pages to literature
that gouty excrement of human intellect
accumulating slowly & everlastingly
depositing, like guano on the Peruvian shore,
to be perhaps exhumed in some remotest age
(*pits secunda, vate me, detur fuga*)
to fertilize the scanty dwarf'd intelligence
of a new race of beings the unhallow'd offspring
of them who shall have quite dismember'd & destroy'd
our temple of Christian faith & fair Hellenic art
just as that monkey would, poor Polly, have done for you.

ROBERT BRIDGES.

270   *Limericks*

I

THERE once was a man who said: 'Damn!
   It is borne in upon me I am
     An engine that moves
     In predestinate grooves,
I'm not even a 'bus I'm a tram.'

MAURICE EVAN HARE.

II

There was an Archdeacon who said:
'May I take off my gaiters in bed?'
    But the Bishop said: 'No,
    Wherever you go
You must wear them until you are dead.'

III

There was a young poet of Thusis
Who took twilight walks with the Muses.
    But these nymphs of the air
    Are not quite what they were,
And the practice has led to abuses.

IV

There was an old man of Khartoum
Who kept two black sheep in his room.
    'They remind me', he said,
    'Of two friends who are dead',
But he never would tell us of whom.

V

There was a young man of Bengal
Who went to a fancy-dress ball.
    He went just for fun
    Dressed up as a bun,
And a dog ate him up in the hall.   ANON.

271   *Infant Innocence*

THE Grizzly Bear is huge and wild;
    He has devoured the infant child.
The infant child is not aware
He has been eaten by the bear.

ALFRED EDWARD HOUSMAN.

The Laws of God

THE laws of God, the laws of man,
He may keep that will and can;
Not I: let God and man decree
Laws for themselves and not for me;
And if my ways are not as theirs
Let them mind their own affairs.
Their deeds I judge and much condemn,
Yet when did I make laws for them?
Please yourselves, say I, and they
Need only look the other way.
But no, they will not; they must still
Wrest their neighbour to their will,
And make me dance as they desire
With jail and gallows and hell-fire.
And how am I to face the odds
Of man's bedevilment and God's?
I, a stranger and afraid
In a world I never made.
They will be master, right or wrong;
Though both are foolish, both are strong.
And since, my soul, we cannot fly
To Saturn nor to Mercury,
Keep we must, if keep we can,
These foreign laws of God and man.

ALFRED EDWARD HOUSMAN.

273   *The Stars have not dealt*

THE stars have not dealt me the worst they could do:
My pleasures are plenty, my troubles are two.
But oh, my two troubles they reave me of rest,
The brains in my head and the heart in my breast.

O grant me the ease that is granted so free,
The birthright of multitudes, give it to me,
That relish their victuals and rest on their bed
With flint in the bosom and guts in the head.

                    ALFRED EDWARD HOUSMAN.

274   *Danny Deever*

'WHAT are the bugles blowin' for?' said Files-on-
        Parade.
'To turn you out, to turn you out,' the Colour-Sergeant
    said.
'What makes you look so white, so white?' said Files-on-
    Parade.
'I'm dreadin' what I've got to watch,' the Colour-Sergeant
    said.
    For they're hangin' Danny Deever, you can hear the
        Dead March play,
    The regiment 's in 'ollow square—they're hangin' him
        to-day;
    They've taken of his buttons off an' cut his stripes
        away,
    An' they're hangin' Danny Deever in the mornin'.

'What makes the rear-rank breathe so 'ard?' said Files-on-
    Parade.
'It 's bitter cold, it 's bitter cold,' the Colour-Sergeant said.
'What makes that front-rank man fall down?' says Files-
    on-Parade.
'A touch o' sun, a touch o' sun,' the Colour-Sergeant said.
    They are hangin' Danny Deever, they are marchin' of
        'im round,

                                        491

DANNY DEEVER

They 'ave 'alted Danny Deever by 'is coffin on the
    ground;
An' 'e'll swing in 'arf a minute for a sneakin' shootin'
    hound—
O they're hangin' Danny Deever in the mornin'.

''Is cot was right-'and cot to mine,' said Files-on-Parade.
''E 's sleepin' out and far to-night,' the Colour-Sergeant
    said.
'I've drunk 'is beer a score o' times,' said Files-on-Parade.
''E 's drinkin' bitter beer alone,' the Colour-Sergeant said.
    They are hangin' Danny Deever, you must mark 'im to
      'is place,
    For 'e shot a comrade sleepin'—you must look 'im in
      the face;
    Nine 'undred of 'is county an' the regiment's disgrace,
    While they're hangin' Danny Deever in the mornin'.

'What 's that so black agin the sun?' said Files-on-Parade.
'It 's Danny fightin' 'ard for life,' the Colour-Sergeant said.
'What 's that that whimpers over'ead?' said Files-on-
    Parade.
'It 's Danny's soul that 's passin' now,' the Colour-Sergeant
    said.
    For they're done with Danny Deever, you can 'ear the
      quickstep play,
    The regiment 's in column, an' they're marchin' us
      away;
    Ho! the young recruits are shakin' an' they'll want their
      beer to-day
    After hangin' Danny Deever in the mornin'.

RUDYARD KIPLING.

275 *Boston*

I COME from the city of Boston,
  The home of the bean and the cod,
Where Cabots speak only to Lowells,
And Lowells speak only to God.

SAMUEL C. BUSHNELL.

276 *Rye Whisky*

I'LL eat when I'm hungry,
  I'll drink when I'm dry;
If the hard times don't kill me,
  I'll lay down and die.

Chorus

  Rye whisky, rye whisky,
    Rye whisky, I cry,
  If you don't give me rye whisky,
    I surely will die.

I'll tune up my fiddle,
  And I'll rosin my bow,
I'll make myself welcome,
  Wherever I go.

Beefsteak when I'm hungry,
  Red liquor when I'm dry,
Greenbacks when I'm hard up,
  And religion when I die.

They say I drink whisky,
  My money's my own,
All them that don't like me,
  Can leave me alone.

KK

RYE WHISKY

Sometimes I drink whisky,
   Sometimes I drink rum,
Sometimes I drink brandy,
   At other times none.

But if I get boozy,
   My whisky's my own,
And them that don't like me,
   Can leave me alone.

Jack o' diamonds, jack o' diamonds,
   I know you of old,
You've robbed my poor pockets,
   Of silver and gold.

Oh, whisky, you villain,
   You've been my downfall,
You've kicked me, you've cuffed me—
   But I love you for all.

If the ocean was whisky,
   And I was a duck,
I'd dive to the bottom,
   To get one sweet suck.

But the ocean ain't whisky
   And I ain't a duck,
So we'll round up the cattle
   And then we'll get drunk.

My foot's in my stirrup,
   My bridle's in my hand,
I'm leaving sweet Lillie,
   The fairest in the land.

RYE WHISKY

Her parents don't like me,
   They say I'm too poor;
They say I'm unworthy
   To enter her door.

Sweet milk when I'm hungry,
   Rye whisky when I'm dry,
If a tree don't fall on me,
   I'll live till I die.

I'll buy my own whisky,
   I'll make my own stew;
If I get drunk, madam,
   It's nothing to you.

I'll drink my own whisky,
   I'll drink my own wine;
Some ten thousand bottles
   I've killed in my time.

I've no wife to quarrel,
   No babies to bawl;
The best way of living
   Is no wife at all.

Way up on Clinch Mountain
   I wander alone;
I'm as drunk as the devil,
   Oh, let me alone.

You may boast of your knowledge
   En' brag of your sense,
'Twill all be forgotten
   A hundred years hence.

ANON.

OH, the girl that I loved she was handsome,
   I tried all I knew her to please.
But I couldn't please her a quarter as well
As the man on the flying trapeze.

Chorus

   Oh, he flies through the air with the greatest of ease,
   This daring young man on the flying trapeze.
   His figure is handsome, all girls he can please,
   And my love he purloined her away.

Last night as usual I went to her home.
There sat her old father and mother alone.
I asked for my love and they soon made it known
That she-e had flown away.

She packed up her box and eloped in the night,
To go-o with him at his ease.
He lowered her down from a four-story flight,
By means of his flying trapeze.

He took her to town and he dressed her in tights,
That he-e might live at his ease.
He ordered her up to the tent's awful height,
To appear on the flying trapeze.

Now she flies through the air with the greatest of ease,
This daring young girl on the flying trapeze.
Her figure is handsome, all men she can please,
And my love is purloinèd away.

Once I was happy, but now I'm forlorn,
Like an old coat that is tattered and torn,
Left to this wide world to fret and to mourn,
Betrayed by a maid in her teens.   ANON.

278

When I am dead

WHEN I am dead I want you to dress me
In a black silk coat and a Stetson hat;
Put a twenty-dollar goldpiece on my watchchain
That the boys may know that I died standing pat.

And sixteen coal-black horses
To carry me when I'm gone.
And flowers, I want flowers on my coffin
While my burial is carried on.

ANON.

Honey, Take a Whiff on Me

OH, whiffaree an' a-whiffo-rye,
Gonna keep a-whiffin', boys, till I die.
Ho, ho, honey, take a whiff on me.

Chorus
Take a whiff on me, take a whiff on me,
Hi, hi, baby, take a whiff on me,
Ho, ho, honey, take a whiff on me.

I went down to Mister Apperson's place,
Says to Mister Apperson, right to his face—
Ho, ho, honey, take a whiff on me—

'I ain' gonna buy coke here no mo','
An' Mister Apperson slam de do'.
Ho, ho, honey, take a whiff on me.

Went to Mister Lehman's on a lope,
Sign in de window said, 'No mo' coke.'
Ho, ho, honey, take a whiff on me.

HONEY, TAKE A WHIFF ON ME

Well, I wake up in de mornin' by de city clock bell,
An' de niggers up town givin' cocaine hell,
Ho, ho, honey, take a whiff on me.

Goin' up State Street, comin' down Main,
Lookin' for a woman dat use cocaine,
Ho, ho, honey, take a whiff on me.

De blacker de berry, de sweeter de juice,
Takes a brown-skin woman for my pertickeler use.
Ho, ho, honey, take a whiff on me.

I'se got a nickel, you's got a dime,
You buy de coke an' I'll buy de wine.
Ho, ho, honey, take a whiff on me.

I chew my terbacker, I spit my juice,
I love my baby, till it ain' no use,
Ho, ho, honey, take a whiff on me.

Well, de cocaine habit is mighty bad,
It kill ev'body I know it to have had.
Ho, ho, honey, take a whiff on me.

Cocaine's for hosses an' not for men,
De doctors say it'll kill you, but dey don' say when.
Ho, ho, honey, take a whiff on me.

Chorus
  Take a whiff on me, take a whiff on me,
  Hi, hi, baby, take a whiff on me,
  Ho, ho, honey, take a whiff on me.

ANON.

D ID you ever hear about Cocaine Lil?
    She lived in Cocaine town on Cocaine hill,
She had a cocaine dog and a cocaine cat,
They fought all night with a cocaine rat.

She had cocaine hair on her cocaine head.
She had a cocaine dress that was poppy red:
She wore a snowbird hat and sleigh-riding clothes,
On her coat she wore a crimson, cocaine rose.

Big gold chariots on the Milky Way,
Snakes and elephants silver and gray.
Oh the cocaine blues they make me sad,
Oh the cocaine blues make me feel bad.

Lil went to a snow party one cold night,
And the way she sniffed was sure a fright.
There was Hophead Mag with Dopey Slim,
Kankakee Liz and Yen Shee Jim.

There was Morphine Sue and the Poppy Face Kid,
Climbed up snow ladders and down they skid;
There was the Stepladder Kit, a good six feet,
And the Sleigh-riding Sister who were hard to beat.

Along in the morning about half past three
They were all lit up like a Christmas tree;
Lil got home and started for bed,
Took another sniff and it knocked her dead.

They laid her out in her cocaine clothes:
She wore a snowbird hat with a crimson rose;
On her headstone you'll find this refrain:
'She died as she lived, sniffing cocaine.'

ANON.

A^S I came over Windy Gap
   They threw a halfpenny into my cap,
For I am running to Paradise;
And all that I need do is to wish
And somebody puts his hand in the dish
To throw me a bit of salted fish:
And there the king *is* but as the beggar.

My brother Mourteen is worn out
With skelping his big brawling lout,
And I am running to Paradise;
A poor life do what he can,
And though he keep a dog and a gun,
A serving maid and a serving man:
And there the king *is* but as the beggar.

Poor men have grown to be rich men,
And rich men grown to be poor again,
And I am running to Paradise;
And many a darling wit's grown dull
That tossed a bare heel when at school,
Now it has filled an old sock full:
And there the king *is* but as the beggar.

The wind is old and still at play
While I must hurry upon my way,
For I am running to Paradise;
Yet never have I lit on a friend
To take my fancy like the wind
That nobody can buy or bind:
And there the king *is* but as the beggar.

WILLIAM BUTLER YEATS

JUSTIFY all those renowned generations;
  They left their bodies to fatten the wolves,
They left their homesteads to fatten the foxes,
Fled to far countries, or sheltered themselves
In cavern, crevice, hole,
Defending Ireland's soul.

'*Drown all the dogs,*' *said the fierce young woman,*
'*They killed my goose and a cat.*
Drown, drown in the water-butt,
Drown all the dogs,' *said the fierce young woman.*

Justify all those renowned generations,
Justify all that have sunk in their blood,
Justify all that have died on the scaffold,
Justify all that have fled, that have stood,
Stood or have marched the night long
Singing, singing a song.

'*Drown all the dogs,*' *said the fierce young woman,*
'*They killed my goose and a cat.*
Drown, drown in the water-butt,
Drown all the dogs,' *said the fierce young woman.*

Fail, and that history turns into rubbish,
All that great past to a trouble of fools;
Those that come after shall mock at O'Don-
    nell,
Mock at the memory of both O'Neills,
Mock Emmet, mock Parnell:
All the renown that fell.

'Drown all the dogs,' said the fierce young woman,
'They killed my goose and a cat.
Drown, drown in the water-butt,
Drown all the dogs,' said the fierce young woman.

WILLIAM BUTLER YEATS.

283   *Lord Lundy*

LORD LUNDY from his earliest years
   Was far too freely moved to Tears.
For instance, if his Mother said,
'Lundy! It's time to go to Bed!'
He bellowed like a Little Turk.
Or if his father, Lord Dunquerque,
Said, 'Hi!' in a Commanding Tone,
'Hi, Lundy! Leave the Cat alone!'
Lord Lundy, letting go its tail,
Would raise so terrible a wail
As moved His Grandpapa the Duke
To utter the severe rebuke:
'When I, Sir! was a little Boy,
An Animal was not a Toy!'
His father's Elder Sister, who
Was married to a Parvenoo,
Confided to Her Husband, 'Drat!
The Miserable, Peevish Brat!
Why don't they drown the Little Beast?'
Suggestions which, to say the least,
Are not what we expect to hear
From Daughters of an English Peer.
His grandmamma, His Mother's Mother,
Who had some dignity or other,

LORD LUNDY

The Garter, or no matter what,
I can't remember all the Lot!
Said, 'Oh! that I were Brisk and Spry
To give him that for which to cry!'
(An empty wish, alas! for she
Was Blind and nearly ninety-three.)
The Dear Old Butler thought—but there!
I really neither know nor care
For what the Dear Old Butler thought!
In my opinion, Butlers ought
To know their place, and not to play
The Old Retainer night and day.
I'm getting tired and so are you,
Let's cut the Poem into two!

Second Canto

It happened to Lord Lundy then,
As happens to so many men:
Towards the age of twenty-six,
They shoved him into politics;
In which profession he commanded
The income that his rank demanded
In turn as Secretary for
India, the Colonies, and War.
But very soon his friends began
To doubt if he were quite the man:
Thus, if a member rose to say
(As members do from day to day),
'Arising out of that reply . . .!'
Lord Lundy would begin to cry.
A Hint at harmless little jobs

LORD LUNDY

Would shake him with convulsive sobs.
While as for Revelations, these
Would simply bring him to his knees,
And leave him whimpering like a child.
It drove his Colleagues raving wild!
They let him sink from Post to Post,
From fifteen hundred at the most
To eight, and barely six—and then
To be Curator of Big Ben! . . .
And finally there came a Threat
To oust him from the Cabinet!

The Duke—his aged grandsire—bore
The shame till he could bear no more.
He rallied his declining powers,
Summoned the youth to Brackley Towers,
And bitterly addressed him thus—
'Sir! you have disappointed us!
We had intended you to be
The next Prime Minister but three:
The stocks were sold; the Press was squared;
The Middle Class was quite prepared.
But as it is! . . . My language fails!
Go out and govern New South Wales!'
* * * * * *
The Aged Patriot groaned and died:
And gracious! how Lord Lundy cried!

Hilaire Belloc.

Lord Heygate

LORD HEYGATE had a troubled face,
His furniture was commonplace—
The sort of Peer who well might pass
For someone of the middle class.
I do not think you want to hear
About this unimportant Peer.

HILAIRE BELLOC.

285   *Lord Finchley*

LORD FINCHLEY tried to mend the Electric Light
Himself.   It struck him dead: And serve him right!
It is the business of the wealthy man
To give employment to the artisan.

HILAIRE BELLOC.

286   *On his Books*

WHEN I am dead, I hope it may be said:
'His sins were scarlet, but his books were read.'

HILAIRE BELLOC.

287   *On a great Election*

THE accursed power which stands on Privilege
(And goes with Women, and Champagne and
Bridge)
Broke—and Democracy resumed her reign:
(Which goes with Bridge, and Women and Champagne).

HILAIRE BELLOC.

HEAVEN shall forgive you Bridge at dawn,
  The Clothes you wear—or do not wear—
And Ladies' Leap-frog on the lawn
And dyes and drugs and *petits verres*.
Your vicious things shall melt in air . . .
. . . But for the Virtuous Things you do,
The Righteous Work, the Public Care,
It shall not be forgiven you.

Because you could not even yawn
When your Committees would prepare
To have the teeth of paupers drawn,
Or strip the slums of Human Hair;
Because a Doctor Otto Maehr
Spoke of 'a segregated few'—
And you sat smiling in your chair—
It shall not be forgiven you.

Though your sins cried to—Father Vaughan,
These desperate you could not spare
Who steal, with nothing left to pawn;
You caged a man up like a bear
For ever in a jailer's care
Because his sins were more than two . . .
. . . I know a house in Hoxton where
It shall not be forgiven you.

ENVOI

Princess, you trapped a guileless Mayor
To meet some people that you knew . . .
When the last trumpet rends the air
It shall not be forgiven you.

                    GILBERT KEITH CHESTERTON.

Form 8889512, Sub-section Q

HOW slowly learns the child at school
The names of all the nobs that rule
From Ponsonby to Pennant;
Ere his bewildered mind find rest
Knowing his host can be a Guest,
His landlord is a Tennant.

He knew not, at the age of three,
What Lord St. Leger next will be,
Or what he was before;
A Primrose in the social swim
A Mr. Primrose is to him,
And he is nothing more.

But soon, about the age of ten,
He finds he is a Citizen,
And knows his way about;
Can pause within, or just beyond,
The line 'twixt Mond and Demi-Mond,
'Twixt getting On—or Out.

The Citizen will take his share
(In every sense) as bull and bear;
Nor need this oral ditty
Invoke the philologic pen
To show you that a Citizen
Means something in the City.

Thus gains he, with the virile gown,
The fasces and the civic crown,

The forum of the free;
Not more to Rome's high law allied
Is Devonport in all his pride
Or Lipton's self than he.

For he will learn, if he will try,
The deep interior truths whereby
We rule the Commonwealth;
What is the Food-Controller's fee
And whether the Health Ministry
Are in it for their health.

GILBERT KEITH CHESTERTON.

290 *J. S. Mill*

JOHN STUART MILL,
By a mighty effort of will,
Overcame his natural bonhomie
And wrote 'Principles of Political Economy'.

EDMUND CLERIHEW BENTLEY.

291 *Lord Clive*

WHAT I like about Clive
Is that he is no longer alive.
There is a great deal to be said
For being dead.

EDMUND CLERIHEW BENTLEY.

292 *George III*

GEORGE the Third
Ought never to have occurred.
One can only wonder
At so grotesque a blunder.

EDMUND CLERIHEW BENTLEY.

293   *Savonarola*

SAVONAROLA
Declined to wear a bowler,
Expressing the view that it was gammon
To talk of serving God and Mammon.

EDMUND CLERIHEW BENTLEY.

294   *Epitaph on a Dentist*

STRANGER, approach this spot with gravity;
John Brown is filling his last cavity.

ANON.

295   *Rhymes*

A CLERGYMAN, in want
Of a second-hand movable font,
    Would dispose, for the same,
    Of a portrait (in frame)
Of the Bishop, elect, of Vermont.

There once was a man who said: 'God
Must think it exceedingly odd
    That the sycamore tree
    Continues to be
When there's no one about in the quad.'

RONALD ARBUTHNOTT KNOX.

There was a young man of Montrose
Who had pockets in none of his clothes.
    When asked by his lass
    Where he carried his brass,
He said: 'Darling, I pay through the nose.'

ARNOLD BENNETT.

There was an old party of Lyme
Who married three wives at one time.
  When asked: 'Why the third?'
  He replied: 'One's absurd,
And bigamy, sir, is a crime.'

There was a young lady called Bright
Who would travel faster than light.
  She started one day
  In the relative way
And returned on the previous night.

There was an old man of Boulogne
Who sang a most topical song.
  It wasn't the words
  Which frightened the birds,
But the horrible double-entendre.

ANON.

296 *Bryan, Bryan, Bryan, Bryan*

THE CAMPAIGN OF EIGHTEEN NINETY-SIX, AS VIEWED AT
THE TIME BY A SIXTEEN-YEAR-OLD, ETC.

I

IN a nation of one hundred fine, mob-hearted, lynching,
 relenting, repenting millions,
There are plenty of sweeping, swinging, stinging, gorgeous
 things to shout about,
And knock your old blue devils out.

I brag and chant of Bryan, Bryan, Bryan,
Candidate for president who sketched a silver Zion,

BRYAN, BRYAN, BRYAN, BRYAN

The one American Poet who could sing outdoors,
He brought in tides of wonder, of unprecedented splendor
Wild roses from the plains, that made hearts tender,
All the funny circus silks
Of politics unfurled,
Bartlett pears of romance that were honey at the cores,
And torchlights down the street, to the end of the world.

There were truths eternal in the gab and tittle-tattle.
There were real heads broken in the fustian and the rattle.
There were real lines drawn:
Not the silver and the gold,
But Nebraska's cry went eastward against the dour and old,
The mean and cold.

It was eighteen ninety-six, and I was just sixteen
And Altgeld ruled in Springfield, Illinois,
When there came from the sunset Nebraska's shout of joy:
In a coat like a deacon, in a black Stetson hat
He scourged the elephant plutocrats
With barbed wire from the Platte.
The scales dropped from their mighty eyes.
They saw that summer's noon
A tribe of wonders coming
To a marching tune.

Oh, the longhorns from Texas,
The jay hawks from Kansas,
The plop-eyed bungaroo and giant giassicus,
The varmint, chipmunk, bugaboo,
The horned-toad, prairie-dog and ballyhoo,
From all the newborn states arow,

Bidding the eagles of the west fly on,
Bidding the eagles of the west fly on.
The fawn, prodactyl and thing-a-ma-jig,
The rakaboor, the hellangone,
The whangdoodle, batfowl and pig,
The coyote, wild-cat and grizzly in a glow,
In a miracle of health and speed, the whole breed abreast,
They leaped the Mississippi, blue border of the West,
From the Gulf to Canada, two thousand miles long:—
Against the towns of Tubal Cain,
Ah,—sharp was their song.
Against the ways of Tubal Cain, too cunning for the
  young,
The longhorn calf, the buffalo and wampus gave tongue.

These creatures were defending things Mark Hanna never
  dreamed:
The moods of airy childhood that in desert dews gleamed,
The gossamers and whimsies,
The monkeyshines and didoes
Rank and strange
Of the canyons and the range,
The ultimate fantastics
Of the far western slope,
And of prairie schooner children
Born beneath the stars,
Beneath falling snows,
Of the babies born at midnight
In the sod huts of lost hope,
With no physician there,
Except a Kansas prayer,
With the Indian raid a howling through the air.

BRYAN, BRYAN, BRYAN, BRYAN

And all these in their helpless days
By the dour East oppressed,
Mean paternalism
Making their mistakes for them,
Crucifying half the West,
Till the whole Atlantic coast
Seemed a giant spider's nest.

And these children and their sons
At last rode through the cactus,
A cliff of mighty cowboys
On the lope,
With gun and rope.
And all the way to frightened Maine the old East heard
    them call,
And saw our Bryan by a mile lead the wall
Of men and whirling flowers and beasts,
The bard and the prophet of them all.
Prairie avenger, mountain lion,
Bryan, Bryan, Bryan, Bryan,
Gigantic troubadour, speaking like a siege gun,
Smashing Plymouth Rock with his boulders from the
    West,
And just a hundred miles behind, tornadoes piled across
    the sky,
Blotting out sun and moon,
A sign on high.

Headlong, dazed and blinking in the weird green light,
The scalawags made moan,
Afraid to fight.

II

When Bryan came to Springfield, and Altgeld gave him
 greeting,
Rochester was deserted, Divernon was deserted,
Mechanicsburg, Riverton, Chickenbristle, Cotton Hill,
Empty: for all Sangamon drove to the meeting—
In silver-decked racing cart,
Buggy, buckboard, carryall,
Carriage, phaeton, whatever would haul,
And silver-decked farm-wagons gritted, banged and rolled,
With the new tale of Bryan by the iron tires told.

The State House loomed afar,
A speck, a hive, a football,
A captive balloon!
And the town was all one spreading wing of bunting,
 plumes, and sunshine,
Every rag and flag, and Bryan picture sold,
When the rigs in many a dusty line
Jammed our streets at noon,
And joined the wild parade against the power of gold.

We roamed, we boys from High School,
With mankind,
While Springfield gleamed,
Silk-lined.
Oh, Tom Dines, and Art Fitzgerald,
And the gangs that they could get!
I can hear them yelling yet.
Helping the incantation,
Defying aristocracy,
With every bridle gone,

BRYAN, BRYAN, BRYAN, BRYAN

Ridding the world of the low down mean,
Bidding the eagles of the West fly on,
Bidding the eagles of the West fly on,
We were bully, wild and woolly,
Never yet curried below the knees.
We saw flowers in the air,
Fair as the Pleiades, bright as Orion,
—Hopes of all mankind,
Made rare, resistless, thrice refined.
Oh, we bucks from every Springfield ward!
Colts of democracy—
Yet time-winds out of Chaos from the star-fields of the
    Lord.

The long parade rolled on. I stood by my best girl.
She was a cool young citizen, with wise and laughing
    eyes.
With my necktie by my ear, I was stepping on my dear,
But she kept like a pattern, without a shaken curl.

She wore in her hair a brave prairie rose.
Her gold chums cut her, for that was not the pose.
No Gibson Girl would wear it in that fresh way.
But we were fairy Democrats, and this was our day.

The earth rocked like the ocean, the sidewalk was a deck.
The houses for the moment were lost in the wide wreck.
And the bands played strange and stranger music as they
    trailed along.
Against the ways of Tubal Cain,
Ah, sharp was their song!
The demons in the bricks, the demons in the grass,
The demons in the bank-vaults peered out to see us pass,

And the angels in the trees, the angels in the grass,
The angels in the flags, peered out to see us pass.
And the sidewalk was our chariot, and the flowers bloomed
    higher,
And the street turned to silver and the grass turned to fire,
And then it was but grass, and the town was there again,
A place for women and men.

III

Then we stood where we could see
Every band,
And the speaker's stand.
And Bryan took the platform.
And he was introduced.
And he lifted his hand
And cast a new spell.
Progressive silence fell
In Springfield,
In Illinois,
Around the world.
Then we heard these glacial boulders across the prairie
    rolled:
'The people have a right to make their own mistakes. . . .
You shall not crucify mankind
Upon a cross of gold.'

And everybody heard him—
In the streets and State House yard.
And everybody heard him
In Springfield,
In Illinois,
Around and around and around the world,

That danced upon its axis
And like a darling broncho whirled.

IV

July, August, suspense.
Wall Street lost to sense.
August, September, October,
More suspense,
And the whole East down like a wind-smashed fence.

Then Hanna to the rescue,
Hanna of Ohio,
Rallying the roller-tops,
Rallying the bucket-shops.
Threatening drouth and death,
Promising manna,
Rallying the trusts against the bawling flannelmouth;
Invading misers' cellars,
Tin-cans, socks,
Melting down the rocks,
Pouring out the long green to a million workers,
Spondulix by the mountain-load, to stop each new tornado,
And beat the cheapskate, blatherskite,
Populistic, anarchistic,
Deacon—desperado.

V

Election night at midnight:
Boy Bryan's defeat.
Defeat of western silver.
Defeat of the wheat.

Victory of letterfiles
And plutocrats in miles
With dollar signs upon their coats,
Diamond watchchains on their vests
And spats on their feet.
Victory of custodians,
Plymouth Rock,
And all that inbred landlord stock.
Victory of the neat.
Defeat of the aspen groves of Colorado valleys,
The blue bells of the Rockies,
And blue bonnets of old Texas,
By the Pittsburg alleys.
Defeat of alfalfa and the Mariposa lily.
Defeat of the Pacific and the long Mississippi.
Defeat of the young by the old and silly.
Defeat of tornadoes by the poison vats supreme.
Defeat of my boyhood, defeat of my dream.

VI

Where is McKinley, that respectable McKinley,
The man without an angle or a tangle,
Who soothed down the city man and soothed down the
    farmer,
The German, the Irish, the Southerner, the Northerner,
Who climbed every greasy pole, and slipped through every
    crack;
Who soothed down the gambling hall, the bar-room, the
    church,
The devil vote, the angel vote, the neutral vote,
The desperately wicked, and their victims on the rack,

BRYAN, BRYAN, BRYAN, BRYAN

The gold vote, the silver vote, the brass vote, the lead vote,
Every vote? . . .

Where is McKinley, Mark Hanna's McKinley,
His slave, his echo, his suit of clothes?
Gone to join the shadows, with the pomps of that time,
And the flame of that summer's prairie rose.

Where is Cleveland whom the Democratic platform
Read from the party in a glorious hour,
Gone to join the shadows with pitchfork Tillman,
And sledge-hammer Altgeld who wrecked his power.

Where is Hanna, bulldog Hanna.
Low-browed Hanna, who said: 'Stand pat'?
Gone to his place with old Pierpont Morgan.
Gone somewhere . . . with lean rat Platt.

Where is Roosevelt, the young dude cowboy,
Who hated Bryan, then aped his way?
Gone to join the shadows with mighty Cromwell
And tall King Saul, till the Judgment day.

Where is Altgeld, brave as the truth,
Whose name the few still say with tears?
Gone to join the ironies with Old John Brown,
Whose fame rings loud for a thousand years.

Where is that boy, that Heaven-born Bryan,
That Homer Bryan, who sang from the West?
Gone to join the shadows with Altgeld the Eagle,
Where the kings and the slaves and the troubadours rest.

Vachel Lindsay.

297

The Death of King Edward VII

THE will of God we must obey
  Dreadful—our King taken away
Greatest friend of the nation
Mighty monarch and protector.

Heavenly Father, help in sorrow
Queen-Mother, and them to follow,
How to do without him who is gone
Pray help, help, and do lead us on.

Greatest sorrow England ever had
When death took away our dear Dad;
A king he was from head to sole,
Beloved by his people one and all.

His mighty work for the nation
Strengthening peace and securing union,
Always at it since on the throne
Has saved the country more than one billion.

ANON.

298

The Hearse Song

THE old Grey Hearse goes rolling by,
  You don't know whether to laugh or cry;
For you know some day it'll get you too,
And the hearse's next load may consist of you.

They'll take you out, and they'll lower you down,
While men with shovels stand all around;
They'll throw in dirt, and they'll throw in rocks,
And they won't give a damn if they break the box..

And your eyes drop out and your teeth fall in,
And the worms crawl over your mouth and chin;
They invite their friends and their friends' friends too,
And you look like hell when they're through with you.

ANON.

299 *The dying Airman*

A HANDSOME young airman lay dying,
     And as on the aerodrome he lay,
To the mechanics who round him came sighing,
These last dying words he did say:

'Take the cylinders out of my kidneys,
The connecting-rod out of my brain,
Take the cam-shaft from out of my backbone,
And assemble the engine again.'   ANON.

300 *Don'ts*

FIGHT your little fight, my boy,
     fight and be a man.
Don't be a good little, good little boy
being as good as you can
and agreeing with all the mealy-mouthed, mealy-mouthed
truths that the sly trot out
to protect themselves and their greedy-mouthed, greedy-
          mouthed
cowardice, every old lout.

Don't live up to the dear little girl who costs
you your manhood, and makes you pay.
Nor the dear old mater who so proudly boasts
that you'll make your way.

DON'TS

Don't earn golden opinions, opinions golden,
or at least worth Treasury notes,
from all sorts of men; don't be beholden
to the herd inside the pen.

Don't long to have dear little, dear little boys
whom you'll have to educate
to earn their living; nor yet girls, sweet joys
who will find it so hard to mate.

Nor a dear little home, with its cost, its cost
that you have to pay,
earning your living while your life is lost
and dull death comes in a day.

Don't be sucked in by the su-superior,
don't swallow the culture bait,
don't drink, don't drink and get beerier and beerier,
do learn to discriminate.

Do hold yourself together, and fight
with a hit-hit here and a hit-hit there,
and a comfortable feeling at night
that you've let in a little air.

A little fresh air in the money sty,
knocked a little hole in the holy prison,
done your own little bit, made your own little try
that the risen Christ should be risen.

DAVID HERBERT LAWRENCE.

IT is strange to think of the Annas, the Vronskys, the
Pierres, all the Tolstoyan lot
wiped out.

And the Alyoshas and Dmitris and Myshkins and Stavro-
gins, the Dostoevsky lot
all wiped out.

And the Tchekov wimbly-wambly wet-legs all wiped out.

Gone! Dead, or wandering in exile with their feathers
plucked,
anyhow, gone from what they were, entirely.

Will the Proustian lot go next?
And then our English imitation intelligentsia?
Is it the *Quos vult perdere Deus* business?

Anyhow the Tolstoyan lot simply asked for extinction:
Eat me up, dear peasant!—So the peasant ate him.
And the Dostoevsky lot wallowed in the thought:
Let me sin my way to Jesus!—So they sinned themselves
off the face of the earth.
And the Tchekov lot: I'm too weak and lovable to live!—
So they went.
Now the Proustian lot: Dear darling death, let me wriggle
my way towards you
like the worm I am!—So he wriggled and got there.
Finally our little lot: I don't want to die, but by Jingo if I
do!—
—Well, it won't matter so very much, either.

DAVID HERBERT LAWRENCE.

The General

'GOOD morning; good morning!' the General said
　　　When we met him last week on our way to the line.
Now the soldiers he smiled at are most of 'em dead,
And we're cursing his staff for incompetent swine.
'He's a cheery old card,' grunted Harry to Jack
As they slogged up to Arras with rifle and pack.
　　.　　　.　　　.　　　.　　　.　　　.
But he did for them both by his plan of attack.

　　　　　　　　　　　　　　SIEGFRIED SASSOON.

　　　　Westgate-on-Sea

HARK, I hear the bells of Westgate,
　　　I will tell you what they sigh,
Where those minarets and steeples
　　　Prick the open Thanet sky.

Happy bells of eighteen-ninety,
　　　Bursting from your freestone tower!
Recalling laurel, shrubs and privet,
　　　Red geraniums in flower.

Feet that scamper on the asphalt,
　　　Through the Borough Council grass,
Till they hide inside the shelter
　　　Bright with ironwork and glass,

Striving chains of ordered children
　　　Purple by the sea-breeze made,
Striving on to prunes and suet
　　　Past the shops on the Parade,

WESTGATE-ON-SEA

Some with wire around their glasses,
   Some with wire across their teeth,
Writhing frames for running noses
   And the drooping lips beneath.

Church of England bells of Westgate!
   On this balcony I stand,
White the woodwork wriggles round me,
   Clock towers rise on either hand.

For me in my timber arbour
   You have one more message yet,
'Plimsolls, plimsolls in the summer,
   Oh goloshes in the wet!'

JOHN BETJEMAN.

304   *'New King arrives in his capital
       by air . . .'*—DAILY NEWSPAPER

SPIRITS of well-shot woodcock, partridge, snipe
   Flutter and bear him up the Norfolk sky:
In that red house in a red mahogany book-case
The stamp collection waits with mounts long dry.
The big blue eyes are shut which saw wrong clothing
And favourite fields and coverts from a horse;
Old men in country houses hear the clocks ticking
Over thick carpets with a deadened force;
Old men who never cheated, never doubted,
Communicated monthly, sit and stare
At a red suburb ruled by Lady Liner
Where a young man lands hatless from the air.

JOHN BETJEMAN.

INDEX OF AUTHORS

The references are to the numbers of the poems. Anonymous pieces are not listed here, but their titles will be found in the Index on pages 530–44.

INDEX OF AUTHORS

INDEX OF AUTHORS

INDEX OF TITLES

See p. xxii. References are to pages.

INDEX OF TITLES

INDEX OF TITLES

INDEX OF TITLES

INDEX OF TITLES

INDEX OF TITLES

INDEX OF TITLES

INDEX OF TITLES

INDEX OF TITLES

INDEX OF TITLES

INDEX OF TITLES

NN

INDEX OF TITLES

INDEX OF TITLES

543

INDEX OF TITLES

INDEX OF FIRST LINES

References are to pages.

INDEX OF FIRST LINES

INDEX OF FIRST LINES

INDEX OF FIRST LINES

INDEX OF FIRST LINES

549

INDEX OF FIRST LINES

INDEX OF FIRST LINES

INDEX OF FIRST LINES